For Mary, Martin and Melanie

SIR ARTHUR LAWLEY
ELOQUENT KNIGHT ERRANT

**The Life and Times of Sir Arthur Lawley,
The Sixth and Last Lord Wenlock.**

By David J. Hogg.

ISBN 978-0-9554457-1-2

Printed and bound by CPI Antony Rowe, Eastbourne

First published in 2007 by David J. Hogg.

Foreword by Lord Wraxall

The Right Honourable the Lord Wraxall, KCVO, CMG.

My grandfather died in 1932 when I was only three years old and although he no doubt saw me from time to time as a toddler, I have no recollection of him at all. After my grandmother came to live at Tyntesfield during the war, I then heard a great deal about him, and my mother often spoke about her father in terms which made clear her strong affection and admiration for him. Of course neither my grandmother nor my mother ever gave a continuous account of my grandfather's life; their references to him were as it were episodic. They were however enough to convince me that he had indeed been a remarkable man, who lived a life of exceptional interest.

I know that both of them would have been delighted that at last a biography of him had been written, which shows just how exceptional his life had been. Moreover owing to David Hogg's indefatigable research work much more information has come to light, of which even my grandparents were unaware. For example my mother always maintained that the origins of the Cunard family were lost in the mists of time. Now we know precisely where they came from in Germany and when they emigrated to America.

For all his painstaking research and the valuable information it has produced, but above all for his undertaking to write a life of my grandfather, I owe David Hogg a major debt of gratitude. I believe this biography makes an important addition to knowledge of the British Empire in its heyday and enables us better to understand the actions and motives of those entrusted with its administration.

Wraxall -

THE 3RD BARON WRAXALL, of Clyst St George

SIR ARTHUR LAWLEY
ELOQUENT KNIGHT ERRANT

Figure 1: Sir Arthur Lawley by Philip de Laszlo, 1914.

The Life and Times of Sir Arthur Lawley,
The Sixth and Last Lord Wenlock.
By David J. Hogg

Contents

Acknowledgements

I would like to thank in particular Eustace, the current Lord Wraxall, who has given me invaluable help and advice, and permitted me to use his family portraits and photograph albums, which have helped to put this story into context. He has been patient, hospitable and kind and not only I, but also the National Trust at Tyntesfield, owe him an immense debt of gratitude.

I should also like to thank the staff at Tyntesfield; Adam Teasdale, Jo Hopkins, Paul McManus and Vicky Washington of the Empire and Commonwealth Museum's Photo Archive; Mrs Penny Hatfield, the Archivist of Eton College; the Royal Military Academy Sandhurst; Colin Harris of the Bodleian Library's John Johnson Collection of Modern Papers and Lucy McCann of the Bodleian Library of Commonwealth and African Studies at Rhodes Mandela House, Oxford; Pamela Atkinson for researching Captain Lawley's diary; Lorraine Haines of Lady Lawley Cottage and the staff of the Battye Library in Western Australia; the South African National Archives; the staff of the British Library's Oriental and Indian Collection and of the Library's Newspaper Collection; the National Archives at Kew; Robert Kent of the New York Public Library; the National Library of Canada; Robert Bell for his advice on the Geoffrey Dawson diaries; Sam Taylor for his research at Escrick; Elizabeth Pickersgill for her help with research at the University Library in Cambridge; the staff of the Royal Collection at Windsor; my son, Martin, for his advice on word processing, and my wife and family for their tolerance, patience and understanding.

1. The majority of the photographs are from Lord Wraxall's albums, some kept by him, but most are on loan to the Empire and Commonwealth Museum. "Images of Empire". (http://www.imagesofempire.com).
2. The map of the Boer War and additional photographs relating to that war are from the Museum of the Anglo Boer War in South Africa.
3. The photographs in Figure 4 and of the Delhi Durbar are courtesy of the Royal Collection. © 2006 Her Majesty Queen Elizabeth II. The quotations from Queen Mary's diaries and correspondence are with the permission of Her Majesty Queen Elizabeth II.
4. The photographs of the Red Cross in Mesopotamia are from Captain Weaver's albums held by Dr Gerry Bulger. (gerard@careprovider.com).
5. Various cartoons, lithographs and prints are taken from the Newspaper Collection of the British Library.
6. Historic Maps of Mafeking and the Madras Presidency are from The Times History of the Boer War and the 19th century Atlas of India respectively.
7. The photo, Figure 82, of Sir Arthur Lawley as Governor of Western Australia is by courtesy of the Battye Library, Perth.
8. The Photo in Figure 83 is by courtesy of Lady Lawley Cottage Hospital, Cottesloe, Western Australia.
9. The photo of the De Dion car in Figure 148 is by courtesy of Father Denzil of Saint Aloysius College, Mangalore, India.
10. The photos in Figures 183, 252, 253 and 256 were taken by the author with the permission of the National Trust at Tyntesfield.
11. Figure 259, Sir Humphrey Gibbs, the last Governor of Southern Rhodesia, 1965, is from a picture published by the Government of Southern Rhodesia.

Preface

In June 2002, the National Trust purchased Tyntesfield, the Victorian Country House of the late Lord Wraxall, following his sad death in July 2001. The house was bought with most of its contents making this an almost unique acquisition. Upstairs in a tin trunk the Inventory Team discovered the Court Dress of Lady Wraxall's father, Sir Arthur Lawley, when he was the Governor of Madras in India. Inside the trunk was a signed photograph of Sir Arthur wearing the Court Dress of the Governor of the Madras Presidency.

The Third Lord Wraxall loaned the Lawley Photo Albums from Tyntesfield to the Empire and Commonwealth Museum. As a research volunteer at the Museum, I had the task of captioning the hundreds and hundreds of photographs, which the many large albums contained. As an historical research volunteer at Tyntesfield, I began to gather information on the life of Sir Arthur Lawley. This set me on a trail which took me to libraries and archives all over the country and via the Internet all over the world. After two and a half years searching in every conceivable place, I believe I am now able to present the first biography of this extraordinary man. In Edwardian and First World War Britain, everyone had heard of Sir Arthur Lawley. But his story was never told and it took the Lawley Photo Albums and the Court Dress at Tyntesfield to launch me on my quest.

The story I unravelled is of one of the most fascinating lives of the late Victorian and Edwardian Empire, which led to War Service with the Red Cross and impressive post-war charitable work. It is more than the story of one man. It is the story of an era which saw the swan song of the British Empire, the cataclysm of the First World War and the inevitable decline of Britain's power and position in the world. It is also the story of a family and its numerous links with Tyntesfield. Sir Arthur and Lady Lawley's daughter, Ursula, married George Abraham Gibbs, became Lady Wraxall, and was mistress of Tyntesfield for over fifty years.

There are portraits of Lady Lawley (Lady Wenlock after 1931) by Sir Oswald Birley (Figure 256) and of her son, Richard, by W.E. Miller (Figure 183) in the Oratory at Tyntesfield. There were also many things in the house which belonged to Lady Wenlock, who came to live at Tyntesfield at the beginning of the Second World War, and died there in 1944. The portrait of Sir Arthur Lawley by Philip de Laszlo (Figure 1) used to hang above the mantelpiece in Mrs Gibbs' sitting room, while that of his wife by Sir James Jebusa Shannon (Figure 7) was hung to the left of the fireplace.

The story which follows shows how the extraordinary life of Sir Arthur and Lady Lawley shaped the character of their children and led Lady Wraxall to become the redoubtable lady who saved Tyntesfield for her family and future generations. It gives us an insight into an age when courage, high ideals, dedication and a spirit of adventure enabled Britain's aristocracy to make a contribution to improving the world in which they lived.

David J. Hogg - November 2006.

Introduction by the Governor of Western Australia

His Excellency Lieutenant-General John Sanderson, AC., Governor of Western Australia

Effective leadership can be defined by strong ethical principles, bolstered by courage, determination and imagination - all the traits displayed by Captain Sir Arthur Lawley in his illustrious career and life.

Sir Arthur came to Western Australia when he was appointed Governor of the State on the cusp of federation of the Australian nation. The State was just newly formed, and faced great challenges to carve out a solid place in the new united nation.

On his arrival, to take up his appointment in 1901, Sir Arthur presented his credentials in Perth then immediately set sail to Melbourne to represent Western Australia at the opening of the Federal Parliament in Melboume in May by the Duke of York, later King George V.

Sir Arthur's governorship was not a long one. He quit the position on the Declaration of Peace in 1902 to take up the important post of Lieutenant-Govemor of the Transvaal. History records that though his time was brief, he carried out his duties as the Crown's representative with great ability, handling several political crises during his time.

He laid the foundation stones for two of the State's most important institutions - the Parliament of Western Australia and the Supreme Court of Westem Australia.

His sense of justice and compassion was reflected in his support for the Australian forces sent to relieve Mateking during the Boer War and his expressed sympathy for the injured and dead soldiers.

He was also reputed to have led the State's social life with aplomb, supported admirably by his wife, Lady Annie Lawley, who identified herself with community welfare issues and organisations. Lady Lawley was the instigator of the Lady Lawley Cottage for children in Cottesloe, which today still bears her name. Her husband, too, felt bound by moral considerations to support society's underprivileged and later in life became Chairman of the Child Emigration Society in Britain (from 1921 until his death in 1932), a position he used to give strong assistance to the Fairbridge Farm School in Western Australia. He was able to get support from the Royal family with the then Prince of Wales giving the scheme his enthusiastic backing. Later the Duke and Duchess of York visited Fairbridge in 1927.

Sir Arthur also persuaded his friend from his days in South Africa, Sir Herbert E. Baker, to accept the commission as architect of the chapel at Fairbridge. Sir Arthur and Lady Lawley last visited Western Australia in 1927 and made a particular point of going to Fairbridge and to Lady Lawley Cottage.

Western Australians are very familiar with the name Lawley. Mount Lawley is a flourishing inner suburb of the State's City of Perth, named after Sir Arthur. His wife agreed to a suggestion that it be named after her husband - but only on her strict instruction that no licensed hotels would be built in the suburb!

This book gives us all a better appreciation of the man and his achievements as a leader and contributor to society on a broad worldly scale. It will be a particularly useful reference for those Western Australians keen to examine the State's history in more detail, especially so because it includes rare photographs of Western Australia and of the opening of the Federal Parliament from Sir Arthur's personal albums that were unearthed after laying hidden for many years at Tyntesfield, the home of the late Lord Richard Wraxall, near Bristol.

GOVERNOR

Chapter 1
The Playing Fields of Eton

Lying to the south of the city of York, set in beautiful countryside, is the village of Escrick. It was here that Arthur Lawley was born on November 12th 1860. He was the fifth son of the second Baron Wenlock. His mother was Elizabeth Grosvenor, the sister of the first Duke of Westminster, one of England's richest aristocrats. Arthur spent his early years at Escrick Park, the 22,000 acre family estate. In 1834, his grandfather – the first Baron Wenlock – had built a model village there for his estate workers. This act of considerate generosity was admired by his grandsons. Arthur had five brothers – Beilby, Francis, Richard, Algernon and Robert, and four sisters Caroline, Alethea, Constance and Katherine.[A] Sadly, Francis died on the day he was born.[1] The family was very close and the brothers, in particular, enjoyed the open air life of the Yorkshire countryside.

Figure 2: The House at Escrick Park in 1831.

Escrick Park was a wonderful place for a child to grow up. Originally an Elizabethan mansion, many subsequent additions had been made to the house. There was a fine library. Among the pictures were paintings by Rembrandt, Van Dyke, Gainsborough and Hoppner. There was a billiard room with hunting trophies on the walls and a winter garden with delightfully coloured stained glass. The park, which enclosed about 450 acres, was well wooded and stocked with deer. Holly Carr Woods close by were planted with rhododendrons which in the early summer, when laden

---

[A] The following dates of birth and death have been verified – Caroline (1848-1934), Beilby (1849-1912), Francis (died on the day he was born 21st April 1852), Constance (1854-1951), Richard (1856-1918), Algernon (1857-1931), Alethea (1859-1929), Robert (1863 to September 18th 1924).

with blossom, were a stunning sight. The gardens around the hall were beautifully laid out; especially the Italian garden on the south, which in the summer and autumn months was a perfect blaze of colour. This was captured in a water colour painted by Constance Lady Wenlock.[2]

Figure 3: Holly Carr Woods painted by Constance Lady Wenlock.

School boy

Arthur Lawley was educated at Eton where he was one of the more able pupils.[3] He was there from September 1873 to July 1879, initially in William Wayte's House and after Mr. Wayte's retirement in Charles Caldecott James' House. He enjoyed sports and played racquets, fives, cricket and the Field Game, an Eton version of football. He played these sports for Mr. C. C. James' House. His best sports were racquets and football for which he was chosen by the Keepers for the list of best players – the Racquet Choices and the Football Choices for 1878 to 1879. He was Number Five on the Football list. He was selected for the Twenty Two versus the First Eleven in the cricket match of May 1879. He scored 9 in the first innings and 4 in the second. In the Sports Day of March 14th and 15th 1879, he came second in the Couples Race accompanied by Pothill Turner.

Arthur Lawley was a member of the Literary Society. In July 1876, he was elected as a member of Pop (the Eton Society). This was a society of senior boys with a restricted membership. The Eton Society held regular debates. In October 1876, in his first contribution to the debates on the issue of "Admiration for France or Germany" – he said, "I entirely agree with the opener in thinking the Germans more worthy of our admiration than the French," and he then continued to explain the reasons for this statement. Other topics for debate were:

- "Riches or learning, which gives a man greater influence?" (Nov. 26th 1876),

- "Whether the submarine tunnel (between England and France) is likely to prove a success", (Nov. 28th 1878),

- "Liberty of the Press should be restrained", (Feb. 10th 1879),

- "Is the use of tobacco beneficial?" (Feb. 17th 1879),

- "Trades Unions are beneficial to the working classes", (Mar. 8th 1879), and "Does the Government deserve censure with regard to the Zulu War?" (April 1879).

Arthur Lawley spoke occasionally in debates. On February 19th 1877, on the topic of "Painting or Sculpture which is the finest art?" he said:

"I think that painting has so may advantages over sculpture in the way of light and colour. The accessories to painting give much more vividness than can be given in sculpture. In spite of the durability of marble, painting is the finest art."

On May 14th 1877, on the topic of "Are we justified in regarding with equanimity the advances of Russia on our Indian frontier?" he said:

"In my opinion we need have no fear with regard to the Russians advancing on India. For if they ever get to the frontier, which as has been pointed out is a matter of great difficulty, they would not yet have got possession of India. They would find it easier said than done to wrest India from the British Government."

On Monday 1st October 1877 there was a debate on "Is a lawyer morally justified in defending his client knowing him to be guilty?" Arthur Lawley in part of his submission stated,

"I consider that a man who defends his client knowing him to be guilty makes himself an accessory to the crime after the fact; and if a counsel is certain either in his own mind or by the confession of the prisoner of his client's guilt, it is a duty which he owes to his country, to society and to himself to refuse to participate in the crimes of the wicked. Rather than do so he should throw up the brief."

On Monday March 11th 1878, the Eton Society discussed the question, "Is the character of the Athenians or the Spartans more to be admired?" Arthur Lawley opened the discussion with a well informed and carefully crafted speech disparaging the militarism of Sparta and eulogising the art, drama, literature, philosophy, poetry, politics and civilisation of Athens. He concluded his speech by saying,

"What statesmen can Sparta boast to equal Pericles? What general greater than Miltiades? Had they to endure a life of hardship to make them what they were? Did they not rather spend a life more worthy of admiration, a life more polished and refined than that of the Lacedaemonian boors? At Sparta the young men were taught to despise what they considered the effeminate weaknesses of literature and art, which were practised with such success at Athens, which make her with all her other noble qualities far more worthy of our admiration."

In July 1878, Arthur Lawley was elected President of the Eton Society. He was also chosen to be Editor of the Eton Chronicle from 1878 to 1879.[4] As Editor, he was responsible for the writing of the leading articles. On Thursday October 31st 1878, the theme was "The Decay of Intellect at Eton." On Thursday 14th November, the leading article was on "Charity". This leader ended by saying, "It is not right, nay more it is downright wrong, that in a place like Eton...there should be any lack of that kindly feeling towards others which is called charity, and which is a better testimony to high character than either popularity or success."[5]

Figure 4: Arthur Lawley as a young officer in the Tenth Hussars.

Lawley's contemporaries at Eton included George Nathaniel Curzon (Viceroy of India from 1899 to 1905) who was a frequent contributor to Pop debates, the Earl of Hopetoun (Governor of Victoria from 1889 to 1895 and then the First Governor General of Australia from 1900 to 1902), John Frederick Rawlinson (responsible for the Enquiry into the Jameson Raid into the Transvaal), and Geoffrey Carr Glyn (later Sir Arthur Lawley's A.D.C.). Other contemporaries - Lord Arthur Grosvenor (a cousin), Arthur Gosling and Gordon Cunard – were or would become members of the family.[6]

Soldier

In October 1879, Arthur Lawley went on to Trinity College, Cambridge. Although academically able, the prospect of adventure on the far-flung frontiers of the Empire appealed to him more than academia. So, like many other aristocratic young men of his generation, he left university to join the army. Arthur Lawley entered the Royal Military College Sandhurst as a gentleman cadet on September 1st 1880, aged 19 years 10 months. He was examined in the following subjects: Mathematics; Fortification; Military Survey; Tactics; Military Law; Military Administration; Riding; Gymnastics; and Drill. As reported in the Times of August 5th 1881, he passed out as 19th out of 136 gentlemen cadets with 2306 marks. His conduct was described as 'exemplary'.

The Sandhurst course at that time lasted for one year, and Lawley's colleagues were commissioned in October 1881. At this stage the register normally gives the date of commission and the regiment entered, but in the case of Lawley it does not. A check in the Army lists shows that Arthur Lawley was not commissioned until August 9th 1882.[7] The most likely explanation for this would be illness. Lieutenant Lawley then joined the Tenth Hussars, the Prince of Wales' Own Royal Regiment.[8]

In December he sailed to India to join his regiment which was stationed at Lucknow. There he encountered the life of the British Raj and all the exotic colour of a land of Moguls and Maharajahs. In January 1883, he was ordered to leave Lucknow and go out for a period of duty on reconnaissance. He also had to undertake outpost duties with the Hussars, which gave him the opportunity to see the real India away from the colonial world of a garrison town. In India there were great sporting facilities for the British regiments. Arthur Lawley was a very accomplished horseman and the officers played polo and enjoyed hunting. Riding and cricket were other popular pastimes. There were also garrison and ceremonial duties to perform and occasionally these involved a royal visitor. On December 12th 1883, their Royal Highnesses the Duke and Duchess of Connaught visited Lucknow. They were accompanied by the Viceroy of India, Viscount Downe and Lady Downe, Sir Maurice Fitzgerald and Dr F.B. Scott. On the last stage of their journey to the General's house, the party was accompanied by an escort of the Tenth Hussars commanded by Lieutenant the Honourable Arthur Lawley. On December 14th, the Duke reviewed all the troops in the garrison and on the following day he inspected the Cavalry Lines and saw a squadron of the Tenth Hussars ride over the Steeple Chase Course. Then the Duke of Connaught held a Levée to meet all the officers while the Duchess received the ladies. With his easy manner and his aristocratic connections, Arthur felt quite at home in such company. Afterwards their Royal Highnesses watched a game of polo and in the evening they dined with the officers in their Mess before leaving by train for Meerut.[9]

In December 1883, the Tenth Hussars were due to leave India. On December 4th, the order was received to proceed by rail to Bombay as soon as the 17th Lancers had arrived to relieve them. They were to prepare for embarkation on H.M.S. Jumna at the beginning of February 1884. On December 23rd, a Farewell Ball was given for the Hussars by the citizens of Lucknow. The British residents were very grateful to have the soldiers stationed in their town. Less than thirty years had passed since Lucknow had been the scene of a prolonged siege during the Indian Mutiny. In the New Year, the Hussars sold their horses and mules to be ready for departure. On January 28th, the regiment set out on the three day train journey to Bombay passing through Allahabad, Jabalpur, Khandwa and Deolali. Luckily it was the dry and cool season, sunny and warm by day, but without the sweltering heat of the Monsoon. In Bombay on February 6th, they embarked on board the troopship H.M.S. Jumna commanded by Captain Uvedale Singleton and prepared to sail home to England.

The regiment was expecting a pleasant cruise home through the Suez Canal and the Mediterranean with perhaps the chance to visit Cairo and see the Pyramids. They reckoned without the Sudan, where the Mahdi, an Islamic religious fanatic, was leading a widespread rebellion against Egyptian rule. The rebels were advancing on General Charles Gordon in Khartoum. Gordon had been sent to Khartoum by the British Prime Minister, Gladstone, with orders to evacuate the Anglo Egyptian forces and the foreign nationals from the Sudan. He disobeyed these orders and chose to stay in Khartoum and confront the Mahdi.

Figure 5: Captain Arthur Lawley of the Tenth Hussars.

At Aden on February 14th, the Hussars received orders to take on board camp equipment and to disembark at the Red Sea port of Suakin on the coast of the Sudan. When they arrived at Suakin, they went straight to the market place to purchase whatever horses and mules were available. On February 20th, they paraded for the first time on their new mounts for inspection by their commander, Lieutenant Colonel R. S. Liddell. The H.M.S. Jumna was ordered to stay at Suakin and act as regimental headquarters and as a hospital ship for the wounded.

In the Sudan an Egyptian army led by Colonel Hicks Pasha and British officers had been massacred on November 3rd and 4th 1883 by an Arab army commanded by Osman Digma under the fanatical leadership of the Mahdi, who was otherwise known as Mohammed Ahmed. Now the Mahdi's forces had taken most of the inland forts behind the Red Sea coast and were besieging the garrisons of Sinkat 30 miles inland and Tokar 50 miles south of Suakin on the shores of the Red Sea. General Baker Pasha had arrived with an Egyptian force of 3500 men to attempt to relieve the two garrison towns, but his square of soldiers had been broken by the Arab army on February 4th with heavy casualties. He had led the remnants of his soldiery back to the port of Suakin. 2500 of his men had been slaughtered in the battle. The British sought revenge.

On March 2nd, their newly arrived army under the command of General Graham advanced on the Arab forces that were assembled at El Teb.[10] The Infantry moved forward in a square under the command of Brigadier General Redvers Buller. The Cavalry Brigade followed commanded by Sir Herbert Stewart. The Tenth Hussars were in the very first line under the command of Colonel Wood. Lieutenant Lawley was about to experience his very first cavalry charge. Colonel Wood gave the order to charge. Time after time Arthur Lawley and his comrades charged headlong at the Arab hordes. Eventually under the heavy fire of the British guns, the relentless advance of the infantry and the repeated charges of the cavalry, the Arab forces broke and fled. The Arabs left 2500 dead on the battle field and many more wounded. The British casualties were relatively light – 28 killed, 142 wounded and two soldiers missing. Four Krupp guns, two brass howitzers, a Gatling gun and a large quantity of ammunition were captured. There was celebration in the town of Tokar as the Arab insurgents abandoned their siege. The town was relieved and then the whole force moved down to the nearby coastal town of Trinkitat. That evening there was cause to celebrate. The officers of the Tenth Hussars gave a dinner on board H.M.S. Jumna for General Graham and his staff and for Captain Singleton RN and his naval officers. After the dinner, there was an open air concert attended by the naval and military commanders and most of the soldiers in the camp.[11]

The British Command now decided to advance once more and attack the tribesmen who had withdrawn to their stronghold of Tamaii. On March 12th, the cavalry moved out to where General Baker Pasha had previously had his zareba or fortified camp. They arrived there at 10.00 am. A few hours later, the whole force under General Graham advanced six miles further to the foot of the hills. The force was accompanied by a battery of artillery under Major Holley armed with six pound guns drawn by mules. The infantry moved forward and the artillery opened fire. Under the withering gun fire the enemy withdrew.

At 5.00 am on March 13th, the cavalry brigade moved forward again to join the infantry. They arrived at 7.00 am, shortly after sunrise, at the advanced zareba. With the early morning sun behind them, the whole force was ordered to advance on the enemy, who were estimated to number about ten thousand men. Located in a steep valley or nullah, they had difficulty seeing the British army silhouetted against the rising sun. The British suffered their worst casualties when a gap opened in their line through which some enemy soldiers penetrated to attack from the rear. To counter this, a cavalry charge was ordered. This was more dangerous than it seemed. Lieutenant Arthur Lawley was grateful for his skill as a horseman because suddenly the cavalry had to rein in their horses right on the edge of a sheer precipice. They did so just in time. Then the cavalry dismounted and began to open fire at the same time as Major Holley's gunners opened withering and destructive artillery fire on the enemy. The Second Brigade rallied while the First Brigade descended behind the fleeing Arabs into the nullah, crossed the ridge and swept into Osman Digma's camp and the villages of Tamaii. Bags of money, Korans, talismans, orders and Osman Digma's standard were captured. Large numbers of Remington rifles and much ammunition were found and destroyed with loud explosions. The British losses on the day were 70 killed and 100 wounded. The 42nd, the 65th and the Naval Brigades suffered the highest casualties.

In the days which followed, the British reconnoitred but found little evidence of the enemy other than small pockets of resistance, and on March 28th orders were received to prepare for evacuation. So on March the 29th, H.M.S. Jumna steamed out of Suakin harbour on her way to the Suez Canal. After sailing through the canal and the Mediterranean, the ship was delayed by bad weather in the Bay of Biscay and did not arrive in Portsmouth until April 21st. The following Sunday, the whole regiment was taken to Canterbury Cathedral for a Service of Thanksgiving.

Suakin was secured, but General Charles Gordon remained trapped in Khartoum to await the fall of the city and a tragic death, speared through the heart, on the steps of the Governor's Palace. Lieutenant Lawley received the campaign medal with clasp. The newspapers in Britain were ecstatic at the victories. Punch Magazine published the poem below in praise of Arthur Lawley's regiment. The man on the old white horse was Valentine Baker Pasha, who had been defeated by Osman Digma. He was the brother of the illustrious explorer of the Nile, Sir Samuel Baker.

When the sand and the lonely desert have covered the plain in strife

Where the English fought for the rescue, and the Arab stood for his life,

When the crush of the battle is over, and healed are our wounds and our scars

There will live in our island story a tale of the Tenth Hussars.

They had charged in the grand old fashion with furious shout and swoop,

With a "follow me lads!" from the Colonel and an answering roar from the troop;

On the Staff as the troopers passed it, in glory and pride and pluck,

They heard and they never forgot it, one following shout, "Good luck!"

Wounded and worn he sat there, in silence of pride and pain,

The man who had led them often, but was never to lead them again!

Think of the secret anguish - think of the dull remorse

To see the Hussars sweep past him, unled by the old white horse.

An alien not a stranger, with heart of a comrade still

He had borne his sorrow bravely, as a soldier must and will;

And when the battle was over, in deepening gloom and shade,

He followed the Staff in silence and rode to the grand parade;

For the Tenth had another hero all ripe for the General's praise,

Who was called to the front that evening, by the name of Trooper Hayes.

He had slashed his way to fortune, when scattered, unhorsed, alone,

And saving the life of a comrade he managed to guard his own.

The General spoke out bravely, as ever a soldier can,

"The army's proud of your valour, the regiment proud of its man."

Then across the lonely desert, at the close of the General's praise,

Came a cheer, then a quick short tremble on the lips of Trooper Hayes.

"Speak out," said the kindly Colonel, "if you've anything lad to say,

Your Queen and your dear old country shall hear what you've done today."

But the trooper gnawed his chin strap, then sheepishly hung his head.

"Speak out old chap," said his comrades. With an effort at last he said:

"I came to the front with my pals here, the boys and the brave old tars;

I've fought for my Queen and my country, and rode with the Tenth Hussars;

I'm proud of the fine old regiment –"Then the Colonel shook his hand.

"So I'll ask for one single favour from my Queen and my native land.

There sits by your side in the Staff, sir, a man we are proud to own,

He was struck down first in the battle, but never was heard to groan;

If I've done aught to deserve it" – then the General smiled, "Of course."

"Give back to the Tenth their Colonel, the man on the old white horse."

Private Hayes later received the Distinguished Service Medal from the Queen at Windsor Castle. On July 3rd 1884, the whole regiment assembled at Aldershot. On September 21st, Major the Earl of Airlie, Lieutenant the Hon. Arthur Lawley and thirty five non-commissioned officers and men received orders to proceed to Kensington Barracks to take up orderly duties in London. Here they were able to enjoy the vibrant life of the capital city of the Empire. Young cavalry officers, especially from the Prince of Wales Own Royal Tenth Hussars, were much in demand on the London social scene. During the winter of 1884 to 1885, the officers kept a pack of drag hounds and enjoyed many gallops across the Vale of Ashford. They also set to work to re-establish their reputation on the Polo Field. Horsemanship was a way of life for a cavalry officer.

Figure 6: Princess May of Teck, later Queen Mary.

On June 7th 1885, Prince Albert Victor of Wales, the eldest son of the heir to the throne, joined the Tenth Hussars. He was given the rank of Lieutenant and soon afterwards became the Duke of Clarence. He was known to the family as Prince Eddy. His father, Prince Edward of Wales (later King Edward VII), was the Colonel of the Tenth Hussars. In 1891, Prince Eddy became engaged to Princess May of Teck, who later became Queen Mary. Queen Victoria was the match maker. She thought May would make an excellent queen. Lieutenant Lawley already knew Princess May. His military duties in Kensington and his social life in London brought him into occasional contact with the Princess. She was very taken with the young cavalry officer. Shy and unsure of herself, she was given confidence by the very sociable and understanding Arthur Lawley. When Prince Eddy, the Duke of Clarence died in January 1892, Arthur was sympathetic and supportive. Thus began a life long friendship between Arthur Lawley and Queen Mary. The photograph of Lieutenant

Arthur Lawley as a young hussar comes from one of Queen Mary's albums - for the year 1886 - at Windsor Castle. May of Teck was then 18 years old. Her oldest and favourite brother, Prince Adolphus Charles of Teck, married Arthur Lawley's first cousin, Lady Margaret Grosvenor, at Eaton Hall on December 12th 1894. [12] Princess May; now Duchess of York, attended the wedding with her husband George.

Figure 7: Annie Lawley (née Cunard) by Sir James Jebusa Shannon.

Arthur Lawley meanwhile had met another more self assured young woman. She was Annie Cunard, the grand daughter of Sir Samuel Cunard, who founded the Cunard shipping line. They probably met through Annie's brother Gordon Cunard, who was a contemporary of Arthur Lawley at Eton.[13]   She was a beautiful and head-strong young lady, artistic, talkative and full of life. In a letter to her sister Mamie, her grandmother described her as being very independent. [14]

Figure 8: Annie Cunard at the Vanderbilt Ball.

Annie was born on 21st June 1863 in the city of New York.[15] She had three sisters – Mary, Jeannette and Caroline, and three brothers – Bache, Edward and Gordon.[B] The deaths of their mother, Mary Lady Cunard, on May 26th 1866 [16] and of their father, Sir Edward Cunard, on April 6th 1869 left the children orphans.[17] The

---

[B] Mary (known as Mamie, born 4th November 1852), Jeannette (born 20th July 1859), and Caroline Margaret (born 25th May 1866), and Bache (born 15th May 1851), Edward (born 2nd January 1855), and Gordon (born 22nd May 1857). Thomas Addis Emmet: "The Emmet Family: With Some Incidents Relating to Irish History." 1898. New York.

children's grandmother, Jane Erin McEvers, took the young family under her wing. The family went to live near Market Harborough in Leicestershire at first as tenants at Hallaton Hall, and then, in 1876, Edward Cunard bought Nevill Holt Hall. On August 31st 1877, Edward, who was a subaltern in the 10th Hussars, died in an accident playing polo at Shorncliffe, and Sir Bache Cunard succeeded him as the owner of the Hall at Nevill Holt.[18] It was there that Annie spent her teenage years.

Figure 9: Sir Samuel Cunard painted by J. J. Napier (formerly at Tyntesfield).

Annie Cunard spent the Christmas of 1882 and the New Year of 1883 in New York.[19] On December 19th, she was at a wedding at the Calvary Protestant Episcopal Church. On January 2nd, she attended the New Year Ball of the Family Circle

Dancing Club at Delmonico's. In the spring of 1883, she was again in New York and was invited to the Fancy Dress Ball given by the Vanderbilts at their newly built home at 640, Fifth Avenue on March 26th. The Ball featured guests dressed as courtiers, witches, royalty, goddesses, and opera and nursery rhyme characters. Quadrilles were performed by guests dressed according to particular themes. At the time, the ball was considered to be one of the most lavish in New York City's history. [20]

Figure 10: Jane Erin McEvers.

Jane Erin McEvers was a remarkable lady. Her father was the Irish patriot Thomas Addis Emmet who with his brother Robert had been a leader of the United Irishmen's rebellion in 1798. Robert Emmet was executed by the British in 1803 and became a martyr for the cause of Ireland. Thomas was imprisoned and then banished. He emigrated to the United States and took up residence in New York, where he became an eminent lawyer and Chief Justice of New York State. Jane Erin was musical, artistic, romantic and full of vitality with a sense of humour and love of good company that came straight from the Emerald Isle. Her husband, Bache McEvers, died in Paris on Bastille Day 1851 shortly after visiting the Great Exhibition in London's Hyde Park. When her daughter and son-in-law died, she took over as mother to the seven orphans as to the manner born. Indefatigable she brought up the seven children and lived on to the ripe old age of 88 years.

Figure 11: Nevill Holt Hall.

Annie's maternal grandfather, Bache McEvers, was a New York millionaire, Chairman of the New York Insurance Company and of his own Mercantile House. His mother, Mary Bache, had an uncle, Richard Bache, who married Benjamin Franklin's only legitimate child, Sarah "Sally" Franklin.[21] Benjamin Franklin visited Richard's mother in Preston in 1771, when he was serving as Agent for Pennsylvania in England.[C] Bache McEvers was an incurable romantic who wrote poetry, collected good puns, epigrams and charades, and loved the company of children.[22]

Between 1881 and 1884, Annie was learning to paint in Paris. It was a wonderful time for a young artist to be in Paris. Renoir, Manet, Monet, Pissarro, Toulouse-Lautrec and their fellow artists were launching impressionism. Annie certainly met John Singer Sargent, who was a friend of her cousin, Jane Erin Emmet. She travelled far and wide. A portfolio of her water colours was found at Tyntesfield with paintings from Brittany, dated 1881, Canada, Kentucky and Alabama, dated 1883, Frankfurt, Homburg, Heidelberg and the Black Forest, dated 1884, the West Country, Arran and Ireland.[23] She combined the Cunard's enterprise with the McEvers imagination, artistic talents, musicality and sense of fun. Arthur found this irresistible. He asked Annie to be his wife and they became engaged to be married.

Marriage

The New York Times' column, "World of Society" stated on July 5th 1885, "Sir Bache Cunard arrived in New York on the "Etruria" on Monday. He is son of the late

---

[C] Annie Cunard's parents, their first baby who died, Samuel, her maternal grand father, Bache McEvers, and great grand father, Charles McEvers, were all buried in Trinity Churchyard, Manhatten, right next to Ground Zero in New York.

Sir Edward Cunard, Chairman of the Cunard Line of Atlantic steamers. His sister, Miss Annie Cunard, a handsome girl, who was out here a few years ago visiting relatives and was a great success in society, will soon be married to the Hon. Arthur Lawley, who is the third brother of Lord Wenlock. He is about 25 years of age, and a Lieutenant in the Tenth Hussars."[24]

Figure 12: Annie Cunard and Arthur Lawley, 1885.

On October 15th 1885, Lieutenant Arthur Lawley married Annie Allen Cunard. The wedding took place at Nevill Holt Church in Leicestershire. Arthur's brother, the Honourable Reverend Algernon Lawley and the Rector, the Reverend C. Eastburn, officiated at the ceremony. Because Annie's parents were both deceased, her eldest brother, Sir Bache Cunard, gave the bride away. The groom's brother, the Honourable Richard Thompson Lawley was the best man.[25] The bride wore a white satin dress with a train trimmed with Honiton lace. Mrs Jane Erin McEvers, Annie's grandmother, gave her a brooch with a large emerald surrounded by diamonds. The couple left after the reception for a honeymoon in Paris.[26]

Annie Cunard was 22 years old when she married Arthur Lawley. For the first few years of their marriage Arthur continued his army career. On May 8th 1887, their first child was born, a boy christened Richard Edward whom the family called Ned. On June 8th 1888, their first daughter was born, Ursula Mary, an adorable baby and the apple of her mother's eye. A year later, on June 15th 1889, their second daughter, Margaret Cecilia was born.[27] She was a pretty and lively child and was always called Cecilia.

Queen Victoria had her Golden Jubilee in 1887. On the 9th and 10th July, the Tenth Hussars took part in the Golden Jubilee Review before Her Majesty the Queen in the Long Valley at Windsor. Two years later on August 10th 1889, Arthur Lawley was promoted to the rank of Captain and on October 20th 1890 he became Adjutant to the

Prince of Wales, the Colonel of the Tenth Hussars.[28] When he was on leave, Captain Lawley took his wife and family on holidays to Norway, to Florence and Tuscany, and to Bavaria and Austria where they visited Berchtesgaden, Bad Ischl and Vienna.[29]

Arthur was a very keen horseman and enjoyed hunting and playing polo. The Regimental History praises his performance in a Polo Match at Hurlingham in 1885. He also played in the Tenth Hussars cricket team and is recorded as having scored 33 runs in a match in 1886 and 43 runs in a match against Hovingham in 1890. The cricket season of 1888 was particularly successful with the Hussars playing twelve matches and winning them all. Arthur Lawley was described in the official history of the Tenth Hussars as being an excellent cricketer. One regimental cricket match was played at his family home, Escrick Park, where cricket is still played today.

Figure 13: Ursula and Ned at Neville Holt.

Arthur Lawley also enjoyed amateur dramatics. He appeared at "Snaresborough Town Hall", really Knaresborough, on October 4th and 5th 1888, in two plays: "Which is which?" with Viscount Lewisham and Miss C. Lascelles, and "Uncle" with his sister Alethea Lawley and Mr. B. Lascelles. At Eaton Hall, on December 29th and 30th 1892, Captain Lawley starred in two plays: "Turn him out," with the Duke of Westminster and the Duchess of Sutherland, and "Cool as a cucumber".[30]

Mrs Annie Lawley was meanwhile coming out on the social scene. She befriended Princess May and through her husband's family connections was invited to functions at Buckingham Palace. On Saturday March 5th 1891, she attended a Reception in Queen Victoria's Drawing Room. Then on Saturday 11th July that year she was invited to a State Ball at Buckingham Palace. On May 19th 1892, she was once again a guest at Queen Victoria's Drawing Room Reception and on July 14th 1896 she attended the Queen's Garden Party.

Private Secretary

Meanwhile Captain Arthur Lawley was tiring of the military way of life and so he decided to seek employment elsewhere. On March 21st 1892, he resigned his commission in the 10th Hussars and relinquished his military career for a life in politics. He became private secretary to his uncle, the Duke of Westminster. The family moved into a cottage on the Duke's estate at Eaton Hall. Arthur's uncle was known as the Anglo-Armenian duke because he championed the Armenian cause against Ottoman Turkey. Arthur accompanied his uncle on his many official engagements and therefore had the opportunity to mix with the highest echelons of society.[31]

Figure 14: Eaton Hall, Cheshire.

The Duke, Hugh Lupus Grosvenor, was the richest man in England, the owner of vast landed estates as well as much of Mayfair and Belgravia in London. From 1847 until 1869, he was the Liberal Member of Parliament for Chester. In the years after his succession to the family title in 1869, he spent £600,000 building his Victorian Gothic mansion at Eaton Hall designed by the architect Alfred Waterhouse.[32] It was in 1874 that the Prime Minister, W.E. Gladstone, recommended that the then Marquis of Westminster be raised to the title of Duke of Westminster. The Duke had a passion for the turf and was the owner of a large stud of famous race horses including five Derby winners. He was an enthusiastic huntsman too. He was also a most generous supporter of numerous charities and of the Church.[33]

On March 11th 1896, Captain Arthur Lawley accompanied the Duke of Westminster to Crewe, where he spoke in support of the Duke in the Town Hall in connection with the opening of the Crewe Liberal Unionist Club.[34] Here he demonstrated his strong adherence to the cause of the British Empire. Concluding his speech he said:

"Following the Jameson Raid,[D] a telegram was sent to President Kruger by the present Emperor of Germany... It is impossible to ignore the fact that the situation in South Africa is full of grave import... We awoke from our dream and found ourselves quite alone. But at the very moment that our isolation seemed almost complete, over the dark waves of the Atlantic (from Canada) and up from Australia's distant shores came to us a sound as of a great cry, 'Englishmen once, we're Englishmen ever'.

Figure 15: The Lawley family, in 1894, at Eaton Hall.

"I venture to stake my faith in the British Empire. It is an Empire of great communities scattered far and wide, but their interests, their hearts are one. I venture to believe that the day is not far distant when they shall unite in one great system of national defence, one splendid Imperial Federation, and that the strength of that mighty union shall rest secure. Then these dark war clouds will seem but phantoms, shadows huger than the fears that cause them, which, in the golden dawn of Greater Britain's golden glory, shall like the Arabs, in silence fold their tents, and shall in silence steal away." [35]

[D] The Jameson Raid was an attempted military coup to take over the Transvaal and its Rand Goldfield in which Cecil Rhodes was implicated. The Boer leader, Paul Kruger, informed of the raid by careless telegrams was able to foil this attempted coup.

Figure 16: The Duke of Westminster.

In March 1896 Arthur Lawley accepted the post of Secretary to Earl Grey. Albert Henry George Grey had been requested by the Colonial Secretary, Joseph Chamberlain, to go out to Rhodesia and ensure that the country was administered in the interests of the United Kingdom. Earl Grey was to be the Administrator of Mashonaland and Matabeleland. This was in consequence of the débacle of the Jameson Raid, which had ruined the reputation of Cecil Rhodes and forced him to resign from the Premiership of the Cape of Good Hope. Arthur Lawley found himself launched on a course of action, which would in due course lead him into the service of Cecil Rhodes and the British South Africa Company.[36]

Figure 17: Arthur Lawley (left) and Earl Grey at Groote Schuur, Cecil Rhodes' home.

On March 21st, Captain Lawley embarked with Earl Grey on the Union Castle liner, Dunottar Castle, to sail to Cape Town.[37] The British High Commissioner, Sir Hercules Robinson, was very anxious about events in Rhodesia, where a full scale rebellion was under weigh. The Matabele and Mashona had risen up against the white settlers and the British South Africa Company. Cecil Rhodes had been surrounded by Matabele warriors in the small township of Gwelo.[38] British forces had been despatched to the region and the settlers themselves had formed a pioneer force to fight back. [39]

The crisis was unfolding as they sailed southwards towards the Cape. To Earl Grey's original purpose of taking over the administration of Rhodesia was added the far more daunting task of quelling a full scale uprising by the indigenous people and restoring peace in the country.

[1] "The Peerage.com." Daryl Lundy, Wellington, New Zealand. 2004.
   Family Search International Genealogical Index. 2004
   Family Who's Who. Geoffrey Leake. 2002
   Updated Family Who's Who. Geoffrey Leake. April 2004
   The Times. Estates. November 4th 1924. Robert Lawley died in Cheltenham on September 18th aged 61, son of the Second Baron Wenlock. He left an estate of gross value of £20,388.
[2] Lady of the Souls. Constance Lady Wenlock. Jane Sellars. Harewood House Trust. 2001
   Washington Post. April 28th 1913, page 6.
   Escrick. A Village History. J.P.G. Taylor. Oblong. York. 2002. ISBN 0 9536574 0
[3] Eustace Lord Wraxall in conversation – Tuesday 12th July 2005. As reported by Ursula Lady Wraxall.
[4] Eton College Archives.
[5] Eton Chronicle for October 31st and November 14th 1878.
[6] Eton College Archives.
[7] London Gazette. 8th August 1882.
[8] Royal Military College Sandhurst Archives.
[9] The Memoirs of the Tenth Royal Hussars (Prince of Wales Own) historical and social. Lieutenant Colonel Robert Spencer Liddell. Longmans. 1891. Pages 426 and 427.
[10] The Times. Monday March 3rd 1884. Page 5. Column A.
[11] The Memoirs of the Tenth Royal Hussars (Prince of Wales Own) historical and social. Lieutenant Colonel Robert Spencer Liddell. Longmans. 1891. Pages 434 to 446.
[12] www. thepeerage.com
[13] Eton School Register. Gordon Cunard is recorded as being at Eton from 1871 to 1876.
[14] Letter to Mamie Cunard at the Hotel Liverpool, Rue Castiglione in Paris. April 24th 1882.
[15] UK Census 1881.
   Lord Wraxall in conversation – February 23rd 2006.
   Geoffrey Dawson Diary. 21st June 1924. Bodleian Library, Oxford.
   Reference 17 – "The Emmet Family".
[16] The Patriot. Prince Edward Island. June 2nd 1866.
[17] Thomas Addis Emmet: "The Emmet Family: With Some Incidents Relating to Irish History." (New York privately printed in 1898).
[18] Washington Post. April 28th 1913, page 6
   Eustace Lord Wraxall in conversation, September 10th 2004.
   Medbourne. A History of the County of Leicestershire: Volume V, J.M. Lee, R.A. McKinley (1964). 2003. University of London & History of Parliament Trust.
   The Times. Wednesday 4th November 1925. Page 16. Column E.
   www.Roots Web's World Connect Project Emmet Family 2.htm
[19] New York Times. December 20th 1882 and January 3rd 1883.
[20] New York Historical Society - Guide to the Costume Ball Photograph Collection, 1875-1932.
[21] The New York City Directory, 1836-37 editions. The entry for Bache McEvers reads: "merchant 35, Broad Street."
   The New York City Directory ,1848-49 edition. Bache McEvers' entry reads: "President New York Insurance Co., 50, Wall Street and commercial merchant of 44, Broad Street, Home - Manhattanville."
   Thomas Addis Emmet: "The Emmet Family: With Some Incidents Relating to Irish History." (New York privately printed in 1898).
[22] Two morocco bound note books of hand written poems, charades, enigmas and epigrams by Bache McEvers dated 1815 (Hamburg) and 1819 (New Orleans). These are kept by the National Trust at Tyntesfield.

[23] Annie Cunard's portfolio of art for 1881 to 1884. Tyntesfield.

[24] New York Times   July 5th 1885, page 4.

[25] The Times. Saturday 17th October 1885.

[26] The Market Harborough Advertiser. October 19th 1885.

[27] From Robert Bell of Langcliffe, her grandson.

[28] Royal Military College Sandhurst Archives.

[29] The Lawley album for 1885 to 1895. Tyntesfield.

[30] The Lawley album for 1885 to 1895. Tyntesfield.

[31] Eustace Lord Wraxall in conversation on Tuesday 20th September 2005.

[32] The Victorian Country House. Mark Girouard. Yale University Press. 1979.

[33] The Times. Obituary of the Duke of Westminster. Saturday 23rd December 1899.

[34] The Courant. Wednesday March 11th 1896.

[35] "Rhodes, the Race for Africa" by Anthony Thomas. BBC Books. London.1996.

[36] Times Obituary for Lord Wenlock, Wednesday June 15th 1932.

[37] The Times. Friday March 20th 1896. Page 10. Column B.
The Times. Monday March 23rd 1896. Page 9. Column F.

[38] "Rhodes, the Race for Africa" by Anthony Thomas. Chapter 20. BBC Books. London.1996.

[39] Eustace Lord Wraxall's Lawley albums. The Empire and Commonwealth Museum. Bristol. U.K.

Chapter 2
Rhodesia in Crisis

Earl Grey and Captain Lawley felt a sense of urgency as they sailed across the Equator and into the Southern Hemisphere. Events in Rhodesia seemed to be unfolding in quite unexpected ways. As the Union Castle liner, Dunottar Castle, approached the Cape of Good Hope, the Cape rollers which had rocked the ship further north gave way to calmer waters.[1] Table Bay was covered in autumnal fog and through the misty haze the silhouettes of the Devil's Peak, Table Mountain and the Lion's Head appeared above Cape Town. A cascade of misty cloud was descending from the edge of Table Mountain – christened the table cloth by the local inhabitants. The tug boats came out to meet the ship and manoeuvred her into the harbour. Earl Grey and Captain Lawley were met at the quayside by the High Commissioner's staff and taken to see Sir Hercules Robinson. They were told the news of the rebellion by the Matabele and Mashona tribes in Rhodesia, and discussed what measures needed to be taken. They stayed for a few days in Cape Town and visited Cecil Rhodes' home at Groote Schuur to get the latest information on the situation in Rhodesia

Cecil John Rhodes was the dominant Imperial figure in Southern Africa towards the end of the nineteenth century. He was an Empire builder par excellence. One of his ambitions was to create a new country called Rhodesia on the high plateaux to the north of the River Limpopo. In 1890, a pioneer column backed by Cecil Rhodes' British South Africa Company crossed the Limpopo and marched across the middle and high veldt to Mount Hampden. There beneath a rocky outcrop known as a kopje they founded the city of Salisbury (now Harare). To the west, the Matabele under their King Lobengula had just signed an agreement with Rhodes and white settlers had moved in to develop mining in Matabeleland. "As far as the Cape Colony was concerned, of which Rhodes became Prime Minister in 1890, northward expansion would make the territory the main gateway into the Interior and the predominant state in Southern Central Africa. British expansion north of the Limpopo would in turn form the stepping stone of a new magnificent Empire, stretching from the Cape to Cairo."[2] These plans were threatened in 1893 by a native uprising across Rhodesia and the British South Africa Company moved in to crush the rebellion. The Matabele armies, trained to charge in close formation, and poor shots were unable to withstand the mobility and fire-power of the small settler force, numbering only 670 men, which was mobilized in Mashonaland. The Matabele were crushed with surprising swiftness, Bulawayo was occupied and Lobengula perished fleeing from his enemies.

Then, in 1895, Dr Starr Jameson led an abortive raid into the Transvaal to attempt a coup to overthrow Paul Kruger, the Boer leader. Gold had been discovered in the Witwatersrand in 1886 and in the ensuing Gold Rush many foreign prospectors, called Uitlanders in Afrikaans, moved into the Transvaal. They soon outnumbered the Dutch. Cecil Rhodes's company, Gold Fields, had major mining interests there. He had given tacit support to the raid. Rhodes wanted the British to take control of the Transvaal and of the Witwatersrand Gold Field. Dr Starr Jameson had been the first Administrator of Mashonaland in Rhodesia from 1890 to 1895. Hence his involvement had implications for Rhodesia too. Before dawn on December 30th 1895, Jameson led a force of 700 mounted men into the Transvaal moving towards

Johannesburg. Telegrams were sent. In the first, addressed to Abe Bailey, he chose to call himself "Godolphin", a curious nom de guerre. The telegram stated:

> *"The veterinary surgeon has left for Johannesburg with some good horseflesh and backs himself for seven hundred."*

Any doubt this slightly cryptic message may have left in the minds of the recipients was dispelled by a second telegram sent to the railway engineer, Mr A.L. Lawley:[E] [3]

> *"The contractor has started on the earthworks with 700 boys; hopes to reach terminus on Wednesday."* [4]

The Boers, having read the telegrams, were fully prepared to meet the invading force. Dr. Jameson capitulated to a much larger commando led by Cronje at Doornkop. Jameson and his men had been promised their lives by the victorious Commandant Cronje. In the fighting the raiders had had 16 men killed and 56 wounded. Some 35 men were missing and may have slipped away. By nightfall the unwounded prisoners, who numbered about 400, were lodged in Pretoria gaol.

Dr Starr Jameson and his fellow conspirators were brought home to England and put on trial. Jameson was sentenced to 15 months in prison but without hard labour. Joseph Chamberlain, the Secretary of State for the Colonies, requested Albert Henry George, the fourth Earl Grey, to become a director of the Chartered Company and to go out to Rhodesia to keep a watch on Rhodes in the interests of the Empire. Grey chose Arthur Lawley to be his Secretary. Earl Grey was to serve as the administrator of Rhodesia from 2nd May 1896 until 24th July 1897.

Figure 18: Salisbury in Mashonaland was the capital of the new Rhodesia. View taken in 1897 from the Kopje looking down on Pioneer Street.

"In 1896, the Matabele and also many of the Mashona tribes rose to exterminate the Europeans. They believed that the Chartered Company had been fatally weakened by the defeat of its forces in the abortive 'Jameson Raid', which had failed to overthrow President Kruger's government. The 'Raid' left the country north of the Limpopo virtually undefended and now, for the first time in their history, a large proportion of the tribes managed to co-operate militarily. The rising was thus altogether a much more serious affair than the Matabele War. The Matabele military organization had not been fully smashed and the Matabele were further strengthened

---

[E] A.L. Lawley supervised the construction of the railways from Mafeking to Bulawayo and from Beira on the coast of Mozambique to Umtali in Rhodesia.

by numerous deserters from the Native Police with their European training and their rifles."

The rising was triggered off by the action of the Administration in slaughtering Matabele cattle in order to control an outbreak of rinderpest. The revolt began with the murder of a policeman on March 10th 1896, followed by the murder of Mr Bentley, a government official, and other Europeans on March 24th. Then the whole Matabele population rose up against the white settlers. On March 26th, the town of Bulawayo with 1547 inhabitants was surrounded, separated by 600 miles of hostile country from the railway terminus at Mafeking. By March 30th, 140 white men, women and children on outlying farms had been killed. "Whole families were hacked and bludgeoned to death and their bodies horribly mutilated." [5] A telegram was sent to Lord Rosemead and the news was relayed to London.

On the evening of April 9th, Earl Grey and Captain Lawley left Cape Town by rail. Their train journey took them through the mauve tinted Cape Ranges, past the vineyards of Paarl and Worcester, through the Langeberg Mountains, across the Little Karoo, through the Swartberg Mountains and across the wide, arid plains of the Great Karoo. Then they climbed up over the Nuweveld Mountains and on to the High Veldt. The train continued north to the diamond mining town of Kimberley,[6] where they assembled men and supplies ready to depart on April 13th by rail for Mafeking.[7] Here they completed their arrangements for the transport of the relief force and supplies to Bulawayo.[8] On Sunday April 19th, they left Mafeking and travelled along the partly completed railway towards Tati in Bechuanaland.[9] Thence they journeyed on northwards by wagon train and on horseback across Matabeleland. On April 29th, Earl Grey and Captain Arthur Lawley and their relief force reached Bulawayo with welcome stocks of food and ammunition.[10]

Colonel Plumers was en route with 700 armed volunteers from the settler population, and his force remained in the region around Bulawayo until October, defeating the Matabele in two major encounters.[11] The British government sent 300 men of the Seventh Hussars and 150 Mounted Infantry from Natal to relieve Bulawayo. With the Seventh Hussars was Arthur Lawley's brother, Major Richard Lawley. Sir Frederick Carrington was appointed as commander. His chief of staff was Colonel Robert Baden-Powell.

On June 1st, Cecil Rhodes arrived in Bulawayo shortly after Carrington, having travelled down from Gwelo with the relief force from Salisbury. The men and women cheered themselves hoarse at Rhodes' arrival. "Now that Rhodes is here everything will be alright," was heard on every side. Cecil Rhodes had a meeting with Earl Grey and Captain Arthur Lawley. Rhodes was very keen to cultivate their friendship. As a result of the encounter, Alfred Earl Grey fell under Rhodes' spell and forwarded his interests not Chamberlain's.[12] Captain Lawley was appointed Secretary to the administration of Rhodesia in May 1896, and lived for a while in Salisbury. In November of that year Captain Lawley was promoted to be the Deputy Administrator for Matabeleland.

The war in Matabeleland went on intermittently until August, when Cecil Rhodes conceived the daring idea of going into the rebel camp in the Matopos Hills unarmed, accompanied only by Colenbrander, Grootboom and Sauer, with James Makunga as interpreter, to try the effect of friendly persuasion. The negotiations or indabas, in the Matabele tongue, with chiefs Somabulan and Sekombo were entirely successful. After three meetings for indabas the Matabele decided to make peace.[13]   Earl Grey and Captain Lawley attended the third and final meeting, which was a very grand affair.

Figure 19: The Bulawayo laager in 1896.

Figure 20: The Matabele Chiefs at the Third Indaba with Cecil Rhodes in the Matopos, photographed by Captain Arthur Lawley.

At the end of July 1896, there was a Census of the White Settler Population of Matabeleland. The Census showed that Bulawayo had a population of 1,823 of whom 257 were female, Gwelo 355 of whom 49 were female and the total white population for the whole of Matabeleland was 3,725.[14] The town of Bulawayo was already developing fast. There was a rectilinear pattern of streets and avenues with sufficient width to turn an ox wagon. The Administration was in Government House. There were three churches – Roman Catholic, Wesleyan, and Saint John the Baptist

Anglican churches, a High Court, three hotels – Goldfields' Hotel, Tattersall's Hotel and the Palace Hotel, a Hospital, a Sanitary Board, and a Fire Brigade with its fire engines and twenty volunteer fire-men. A large Market Square and a Stock Exchange were focal points for commerce. There were banks like the Standard Bank and the Rhodesian Building Society and Savings Bank. There were stores like Kerr and Company and Dawson's and a photographer – Barnett Photos. For recreation there were sports clubs such as the Queen's Club for cricket, tennis, soccer and rugby,[15] the Rifle Club, the Turf Club for horse racing, Gymkhanas, and the New Club completed in August 1896. The Bulawayo Chronicle stated, "A walk over to the New Club will be rather a surprise. It could scarcely be expected that such a superb building would be erected in these times."[16]

The army were still hunting down the Matabele warriors. On August 9th it was reported that "Colonel Plumer's orders were for a midnight start. Just before that hour the men were awakened and proceeded to fall in, in absolute silence. Colonel Baden-Powell was responsible for our route." [17] He was developing the tracking and pursuit skills which would later be taught to Boy Scouts. Eventually on the 6th October, Baden-Powell reported "the capture of Wedza's stronghold after two days and nights work. The position consisted of six granite heights on which were eight large kraals."[18]

Figure 21: Cecil John Rhodes.

In the early autumn of 1896, Earl Grey, as the Administrator of Mashonaland, arrived one afternoon in Bulawayo to consult with Rhodes on various points. The next morning at day break they set off for a ride into the hills. At ten o'clock they came back and Rhodes was in great spirits. He said, "Grey and I have made a wonderful discovery; we've found a hill from the top of which a marvellous view is to be seen…You must ride there this evening and we will show it to you." At 3.00 pm. they went back. Rhodes walked to and fro along the crest and all at once burst forth,

"I shall be buried here, Grey", he said, "I call this one of the world's views." All agreed to that, and so "World's View" in the Matopo Hills was in due course to become the site of the grave of Cecil John Rhodes. Captain Arthur Lawley accompanied Rhodes and Grey, and took photographs of the excursion. On Friday October 16th 1896, Earl Grey wrote from Bulawayo, "Mr Rhodes left for Salisbury on Wednesday, the day after the indaba in the Matopos Hills. He has gone to pacify the discontent which exists at Salisbury owing to the slow progress of the railway from Beira. I hope to be able to follow Mr Rhodes either today or tomorrow, but that depends on the replies we receive from the telegrams to the High Commissioner. Captain Lawley, who has given me invaluable assistance and is proving more useful every day, will represent me here during my absence." [19]

Figure 22: Captain Arthur Lawley, known to family and friends as Joe, with Cecil Rhodes and colleagues in the Matopo Hills ready to meet the Matabele chiefs.

In November 1896, Captain the Honourable Arthur Lawley took up his post as Deputy Administrator in Matabeleland. The Administrator of Rhodesia was Earl Grey in Salisbury. On November 14th, the Chronicle reported that "it had been decided to erect a statue of Mr Rhodes at Bulawayo in recognition of his services to the British Empire, to South Africa and to Rhodesia in particular. On Monday 30th November, Arthur Lawley presided at a St Andrew's Day Banquet at Tattersall's Hotel. His cousin, Gordon Forbes Thompson and Prince Alexander of Teck[F] were among the guests. Arthur Lawley was received with three cheers when he gave the after dinner speech thanking Sir Richard Martin and the assembled gentlemen in the name of the Administration of Rhodesia for their loyalty and patriotism in resisting the rebellion.[20]

[F] Prince Alexander of Teck was the brother of May of Teck, later Queen Mary.

Just before Christmas, the news came through that, on the night of December 15th, Cecil Rhodes' home at Groote Schuur in Cape Town had burned down. Rhodes had the house rebuilt the following year and no expense was spared. In Bulawayo the Chief Native Commissioner, Mr H. J. Taylor, returned in time to celebrate Christmas after a tour of more than two weeks around South East Matabeleland. He was ascertaining that all was now quiet after the uprising. Arthur Lawley spent the festive season in Government House, a fine Dutch Colonial residence built where Chief Lobengula had once located his Royal Kraal. A Union Jack flew from the flagstaff beside the house. A fine garden was being laid out with paths, lawns, fruit trees, shrubs and an abundance of flowers.

Figure 23: Government House. The covered wagon is beside the tree beneath which Chief Lobengula used to sit to review his Matabele warriors.

During the first week of January 1897, all 85 of the Matabele Chiefs or Indunas gathered together in the Stock Exchange Hall to meet with the Administration. The entrance of Captain the Honourable Arthur Lawley, the Acting Administrator, Mr H. J. Taylor, the Chief Native Commissioner, and Mr J. Collebrander was the signal for loud and simultaneous greetings of "Inkosi". Captain Lawley, in the name of Earl Grey, explained the general principles under which the country would be governed in future. Matabeleland would be divided into twelve districts instead of the five that had existed under Lobengula. Each of these districts would be under a Chief paid by the Government, who would be responsible for the good conduct of the people in his district. In each district a Native Commissioner would be stationed with an assistant. Over all there would be a Chief Native Commissioner in Bulawayo.[21] Taking the population of Matabeleland as 150,000, this meant that each chief would have about 12,500 people under his control.

In order to increase their numbers new Native Commissioners and Head Indunas were appointed. These were:

1. Mr H.J.G. Jackson and Chief Sekombo for Umzingwani District.
2. Mr Staples and Chief Umlugulu for Gwanda District.
3. Mr D.H. Moodie with Assistant Commissioner Mr. E. Armstrong and Chief Dhiliso for Matopo District.
4. Mr C.T. Stuart and Chief Faku for Malema District.

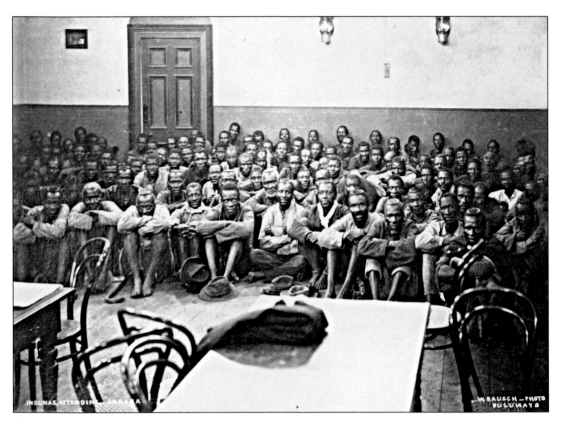

Figure 24: The Indunas attending the Indaba in the Stock Exchange Hall.

The Indunas were to be paid an annual salary of between £3 and £5. Captain Lawley then spoke to the assembled chiefs. He said,

"I wish to speak to you about your cattle. The government recently thought fit to put certain restrictions upon the sale of your cattle in order to buy them from you through our officials. The reason for this action was that certain unscrupulous men were taking advantage of the condition of your people to extort from them by intimidation and threats cattle at prices far below their proper value...."

"Indunas. You will be held responsible for the good conduct of your people and in return for the salary you receive you will be loyal servants of the Government. The Government makes you responsible for the behaviour of your people to exercise control over them and punish those that are guilty, and I will uphold your authority in doing so by every power under the law."

There followed a detailed discourse on the problems facing the African population and the relationship between the Administration and the indigenous people. "The chiefs listened with respectful attention to Captain Lawley's happy and tactful address and as far as one can gather from their expressive countenances accorded it their entire approval." [22]

Figure 25: Captain Arthur Lawley in Bulawayo with his Native Commissioners.

Figure 26: Captain Lawley and Family en route for Bulawayo.

Figure 27: First Class passengers on the S.S. Norman sailing to South Africa in 1897. Annie Lawley is to the right of the Captain. Lady Hely Hutchinson is to his left.

Figure 28: Arthur and Annie camping en route to Bulawayo.

In March 1897, when peace was restored, Annie Lawley and the children sailed out to join Arthur on the Union Castle liner, the S.S. Norman. [23]

Figure 29: Ursula and Cecilia with Captain Holdsworth in Rhodesia.

The Diamond Jubilee of Queen Victoria

In June 1897, Britain and the Empire celebrated the Diamond Jubilee of Queen Victoria. The prospect of the Diamond Jubilee awakened interest in music in Bulawayo. There were three concerts reported in the Bulawayo Chronicle on May 1st 1897. There was an enthusiastically supported local band which, on June 5th, performed at a Promenade Concert.

On Wednesday June 16th, the Jubilee celebrations began with an "At Home" at Government House. The Bulawayo Chronicle of June 19th reported,

> *"The Old Dutch residence on the site of Lobengula's Palace presented an*
> *animated appearance on Wednesday afternoon when Captain the Honourable*
> *Arthur Lawley and Mrs Lawley were "At Home" to a large number of the*
> *inhabitants of Bulawayo. It was a surprise to see so many of the fair sex in*
> *Bulawayo and it is an instance that the confidence in the country has returned*
> *when such a large proportion of ladies grace a gathering..... The band was*
> *listened to with pleasure, while the famous tree under which Lobengula sat in state*
> *to review his warriors was an object of interest."*

On Sunday 20th June there was a Thanksgiving Service in the Market Hall. On the Monday morning, Captain Lawley planted a commemorative tree and then laid the foundation stone of the New Jubilee Memorial Wing of the Hospital. In the afternoon,

Arthur Lawley laid a further foundation stone for the new Jewish synagogue in Bulawayo. The Jewish community was joined by most of its Christian neighbours including Bishop Gaul of the Anglican Church.[24] Mrs Lawley and her brother-in-law, Mr Athole Hay, attended the ceremony. At 8.00 pm that evening there was a Promenade Concert at the Queen's Club. On Tuesday 22nd, there was a General Parade in the Market Square at 9.30 am followed at 10.30 am by a Gymkhana and a Race Meeting.

The following day, all the chiefs assembled for a meeting of the Indunas at the Court House. Cecil Rhodes arrived to take part. Mr Rhodes and Captain Lawley sat at the Clerk of the Court's table facing the indunas. Arthur Lawley greeted the chiefs.

> *"Indunas, you have been invited to Bulawayo today on the occasion of the 60th year of the reign of Queen Victoria, the Great White Queen…. During the time she has been Queen the country has grown and grown and this, the country of Matabeleland, is the latest addition to her realm…. We have therefore celebrated the occasion with various rejoicings, and the Government of the country invited you as Indunas to come and take a part.*

> *"Since I last saw you we have been living at peace with one another. As I told you at that time, Mr Rhodes, the Great White Chief, who had gone to England, would return and he is with us today….*

> *"It was the Government's intention that the Hut Tax should have been enforced this year. But as you know due to the drought and the locusts your crops have not been as good as in ordinary years. You have had rinderpest among your cattle and much sickness among your people. Therefore the Government is willing to relax the Hut Tax."*

Cecil Rhodes said that for the tax to be paid it was necessary that the young men go out to work. They would not be forced to do so, but this was the best way forward. Arthur Lawley confirmed this and encouraged the Indunas to send their young men to work for the white settlers in the farms, mines and towns of the new Rhodesia. There followed a lengthy discussion after which the chiefs were served with food and refreshed with African beer. This was the conclusion of the Jubilee celebrations.[25]

Earl Grey departs

In July 1897, Earl Grey came through Bulawayo from the capital of Rhodesia, Salisbury, and said farewell to Cecil Rhodes and Arthur Lawley before departing on the journey home to England. Rhodes said of Albert Grey,

> *"During the one and a half years he has been in the country, he has done wonderful work and never spared himself in its interests."*

As the railway track was still under construction, there was only one train a week, and Grey had to leave by it that evening. Rhodes was very upset at his departure and despite bad weather drove with him to the rail head. When he had gone, he said,

> *"He's a fine fellow, Grey, a fine character. When I found myself with my back to the wall after the Transvaal trouble, he gave up all his great interests at home and came to Rhodesia to stand by me and help to make the country. He has done wonderful work and endeared himself to everyone, and not until he has seen that all is going well has he ever thought of leaving. A lovable character. Take heed of*

him all of you, for in him you see one of the finest products of England – an
English gentleman."[26]

Earl Grey sailed from Cape Town on Wednesday 28th July.[27] After leaving Africa
he was appointed Vice President of the Chartered Company otherwise known as the
British South Africa Company, a post which he held until 1904. His interest in
Rhodesia thus continued. He was eventually to become the Governor General of
Canada from 1904 to 1911.

The Arrival of the Railway

Rhodes's Chartered Company's major economic contribution was the creation of a
system of railway communications designed to exploit Rhodesia's mining wealth
rather than its agricultural possibilities. In November 1897, the railway reached
Bulawayo from the south, linking Matabeleland with the South African railway
system, which was now joined to its Rhodesian economic hinterland. The railway
gave access to Mafeking, Kimberley and Cape Town. It had a military and an
economic significance which would become very apparent in the forthcoming Boer
War.

**Figure 30: Captain Arthur Lawley spoke at the ceremony celebrating the opening of the rail link
on behalf of Cecil Rhodes and the British South Africa Company.**

Sir Alfred Milner, later Lord Milner, as Britain's High Commissioner in South
Africa and the Governor of the Cape of Good Hope, opened the new rail link on
November 4th 1897. Cecil Rhodes had been taken sick and to his great disappointment
he was not yet strong enough to go down to the opening ceremony. Captain Arthur
Lawley, who had rapidly acquired a reputation as an administrator and as a public
orator, stood in for Mr. Rhodes.[28] He gave the speech opening the new rail link from
the Cape to Bulawayo and his oration was long remembered by those present.[29] First

of all he read a cable from Earl Grey, who was staying at Balmoral Castle,[30] which said:

"The Queen desires me to convey to the people of Bulawayo her heart felt congratulations on the arrival of the railway and her good wishes for their future prosperity."

Figure 31: The Lawley – one of the earliest trains used on the Bulawayo line in Rhodesia.

Then Captain Lawley read the address to His Excellency Sir Alfred Milner, the High Commissioner for South Africa and Governor of the Cape of Good Hope.

"We as representatives of the inhabitants of the town of Bulawayo beg very respectfully to extend a most hearty and cordial welcome to Your Excellency not only in your capacity as Her Most Gracious Majesty's representative, but to yourself personally.

"We trust that the occasion that has brought you among us will be the signal for the awakening of a new era of great prosperity to the whole country of Rhodesia as well as to every part of South Africa…. To you, Sir, during your time of office as High Commissioner – which we trust may be a long one – we shall always turn in the hour of necessity fully believing that you will firmly uphold the honour of our Queen and Country and the interests of her loyal subjects, and that under your guidance all racial feelings, which unfortunately have existed in the past, may entirely disappear and be forgotten in the future; and that happiness, peace and prosperity may extend to all.

"This year, this of Her Majesty's Diamond Jubilee, in which Matabeleland has first been honoured by a visit from the High Commissioner, is one which will live long in the memory of man and we trust that this may be the first of many

*occasions on which we shall be honoured by your presence and we beg to extend
to Your Excellency a welcome to this province, hailing with acclamation the fact
that you should have come amongst us to assist us in the realization of an
enterprise from which such great benefits will be derived by the inhabitants of
Rhodesia."*

Figure 32: The opening of the Railway to Bulawayo by Sir Alfred Milner in 1897.

Sir Alfred Milner then cut the ribbon and declared the railway open. There
followed the arrival of the specially decorated train with all the guests on board
including the great explorer Henry Morton Stanley, Mr Jack Pease, whose family
financed the Stockton and Darlington Railway, Sir Walter Hely Hutchinson, Governor
of Natal and his wife, and Members of Parliament from the Cape of Good Hope and
Natal.[31]   Other events included a children's picnic in mule-drawn coaches at the
Khami River and a visit to the Matopos where the visitors met Lomalonga, one of
King Lobengula's wives, and his daughter Secuneleza.   At the grand Indaba at
Government House which more than one hundred Ndebele Indunas attended, Rhodes'
sister Edith gave presents to Lobengula's son, Nyanda, and to the Chiefs Gambo and
Sekombo.

*"Nothing in the description of the railway festivities was more striking than the
part played by the native indunas. They were taken for a trip on the railway, and
when the train first moved many of them were so much astonished that they were
with difficulty persuaded to keep their places, but after a very short experience they
showed the utmost delight, and at the end of the journey were eager for more
locomotion. Captain Lawley improved the occasion by explaining to them that the
railway would in future be at the service of natives as well as whites, but that its*

services could only be secured by paying for them, and that for this purpose money, which could be earned by working, became a necessity. They received the statement with cheers. The suggestion that the railway would be used to bring cattle again into Matabeleland was received with wild bursts of applause." [32]

Last of all there was a great gathering on William Napier's farm at Matsheumhlope when about a thousand Ndebele came along to perform their traditional dances. The visitors were absolutely enthralled, and were busy snapping away with their Kodak cameras. [33]

On November 5th 1897, Sir Alfred Milner laid the Foundation Stone of the Eighth Avenue Library Building in Bulawayo. The building was opened five months later.

"On the evening of March 31st 1898, a large and fashionable gathering assembled at the new Public Library to inaugurate the occupation of the new building. Nearly the whole of Bulawayo was present. The building looked splendid, brightly lit by electricity. The large Hall was filled with people. Captain Arthur Lawley, the Deputy Administrator, declared the new Library Building open. In his speech he congratulated everybody involved in the project. He mentioned the New Club – and said that the Library had gone one better because it was a double storey building – and he hoped that there would be room for a Museum as well. He congratulated Mr. Hughes, the architect, and the builders, and said that in future no doubt the building would form one of the chief architectural beauties of the town". [34]

On the evening of 7th November 1897, there was a banquet at the Palace Hotel in Bulawayo. [35] Captain Arthur Lawley proposed the toast of the High Commissioner of South Africa. He said:

"The people of Bulawayo regard it as a very great honour that upon the occasion of the opening of their railway, which is to them an event of great moment, they should find themselves supported by leading representatives from the arenas of politics, religion and science, and of commerce, not only in South Africa but in England itself. The opening of the railway will be the means of rapid communication between Rhodesia and the neighbouring states and the Mother Country. It is the channel by which we will have easy access to all the commodities of civilized existence. It is the artery through which the hot life blood of the country will dance into the veins of a young and, I hope, a prosperous state. But apart from the material advantages which will accrue to us with the arrival of the railway, I congratulate Bulawayo upon having so representative a gathering, for I read in the presence of the visitors a deeper significance than mere friendly interest in the successful issue of a great engineering enterprise and I consider your presence here to denote a deep sympathy in the work which we in Rhodesia have in hand, which is first and foremost the development and expansion of the British Empire.

I take it as the expression of determination to weld more closely the links of a chain that should bind together the whole of the white community of South Africa and therefore from the bottom of my heart I bid the visitors welcome. Sir Alfred Milner comes amongst us as the representative of Her Most Gracious Majesty the Queen. On that account alone especially in this year of her Diamond Jubilee, we shall accord him a welcome that will assure him of our loyalty to the Crown. Moreover we hail him as an exponent of a consistent Imperial policy. I lay some stress upon the word "consistent" for if I might venture to criticise the policy of past English Governments regarding South Africa, I think that many of the problems of the past and the present, I will not say the future, are traceable to the consistent inconsistency that has marked the actions of successive ministries at Home. No matter which party has been in power, the actions of successive statesmen in carrying the work of colonisation forward – and I regret to say too often backwards – seem to have been prompted partly by a desire to shuffle out of existing obligations and partly by the fear of incurring fresh responsibilities. I dare however to hope that those days are dead and gone. England has declared, with no uncertain voice, that she has resolved to justify her position as the Paramount Nation in South Africa, while she extends to all her subjects the same rights and privileges of citizenship, and therein I believe lies the salvation of South Africa.

There exists in some parts of this continent, though I am happy to say not in Matabeleland, a racial rivalry, and I am sorry to say that there is an inclination on the part of some of those who guide the tendency of political thought to foster that rivalry, to water that upas tree.[G] I am however sanguine enough to believe that the day will dawn when Dutchmen and Englishmen alike will realise that they have common interests which far outweigh any differences that might now keep them asunder when together they will carry forward the standard of civilisation in that strength which union and union alone can give. The High Commissioner's influence will help to solve this problem and I am confident in the qualifications of the present holder of that difficult office. Sir Alfred Milner has come amongst us with the evident intention of making himself thoroughly acquainted with our country and its resources. We appreciate this, for it inspires us with the assurance that in these delicate and complicated questions of policy and administration, which must necessarily arise between the Imperial Government and ourselves, we may rely on his judgement not only as a sagacious statesman but as a sympathetic friend. This is the first visit His Excellency has paid to Rhodesia. I use no empty phrase when I say that I sincerely hope that it may by no means be the last."

The toast was drunk to Sir Alfred Milner, who replied at length with a speech indicating the imperial intentions of the British in Southern Africa. During this oration he said,

"Assuming as I think we must that South Africa is a country where both races, white men and natives, must live side by side, it is obviously the duty of the Government to ensure that the supremacy of the white man must be maintained and that the native must be governed and not left to govern himself."[36]

On November 1st, the Chairman of the Chamber of Mines had announced that the Executive intended to approach Cecil Rhodes with a view to obtaining the construction of a railway to the Zambesi. At the dinner for Sir Alfred Milner, the Commissioner of Mines and Works reiterated this desire to extend the railway to the River Zambesi.

On November 8th 1897, Sir Alfred Milner wrote to Arthur Lawley to express his thanks. He said:

[G] A fabulous Javanese tree that poisoned everything for miles around.

Dear Captain Lawley

I cannot leave Bulawayo without offering my warmest congratulations to you and the other members of the Reception Committee on the splendid success of the festivities connected with the opening of the Railway to Bulawayo.

As your guest I have enjoyed and admired along with others hospitality which would have been striking anywhere but which, in view of all the difficulties of entertaining so large a company in what only a few years ago was a wilderness, is really an extraordinary feat of organisation as well as a remarkable proof alike of the great resources and great liberality of your young community....

Speaking as High Commissioner, I feel that the unmistakable signs of vitality, of enterprise and of progress which have met us on every side are full of promise for the future of Rhodesia and that the same spirit and capacity which have made the proceedings of the last few days such an unparalleled success are destined at no distant future to raise this country to a high place among the great self governing communities which owe allegiance to the British Crown.

Believe me with my warm personal thanks to yourself for your kindly and thoughtful hospitality yours very truly,

Alfred Milner.

Figure 33: Sir Alfred Milner (centre) and the other guests with Arthur and Annie Lawley.

The cultural life of Bulawayo was now flourishing. In July 1897, a Literary and Debating Society was formed and on Monday 30th January 1898, a packed house greeted the New Variety Company.[37] With the growing population there was concern about water supplies and at the beginning of 1898, the construction of new dams for the Municipal Waterworks and the laying of pipes for new water mains began.

Figure 34: Indaba of Ndbele Indunas at Government House, November 1897.

Visit to the King of Barotseland

Cecil Rhodes wanted to extend the railway northwards. At the end of 1897 prospectors and traders moved north towards the Zambesi. They had discovered a coalfield but no gold deposits. In the spirit of Cecil Rhodes' dictum, "Go north, young man, go north", Captain Arthur Lawley decided to visit the King of Barotseland, a territory which lay beyond the Zambesi. His capital was at Lialui on the Zambesi about 44 miles up from the Victoria Falls. Here Major Coryndon, supported by a small detachment of British South Africa Police, acted as Her Majesty's representative and the agent of the British South Africa Company. The company had negotiated rights under the Lochner Concession.

Arthur Lawley invited King Lewanika and Major Coryndon to meet him at the Victoria Falls on June 1st 1898. He wanted to review and clearly define the company's rights and settle any problems that were causing difficulties for Lewanika and his people. He also wanted to meet other chiefs like Wankie and to establish a Government Representative in the North West of Matabeleland in the Sebungu District.[38]

At the end of 1896, Mr. F. Lewis had marked out a road towards the Falls part of which had been cut by Mr. Frost in 1897. Captain Arthur Lawley decided to reconnoitre this new road. About the middle of March 1898, he sent off in hired wagons everything that he would require at the Falls and the supplies for his return journey. On April 18th, Captain Jesser Coope left Bulawayo with two wagons, five mounted police and thirty natives to cut the road through the thick bush and clear and deepen the water holes. On April 25th a second party with twelve policemen and one wagon set out under Sergeant Major Norris of the British South Africa Police. On May 3rd, Arthur Lawley's party took its leave of Bulawayo. It consisted of Captain Lawley, his brother, Major Richard Lawley of the Seventh Hussars, Mr Vladimir Gielgud (later a Native Commissioner), Mr R. Blanckenberg (Secretary to the Administration), Dr Ellis and Mr. S. Rodger (Arthur Lawley's man servant). Two wagons and twenty horses, a Cape Cart and six mules, and twelve pack donkeys formed the transport train.

Figure 35: Alan Wilson and the Shangaani Patrol, December 4th 1893.

Only five years previously Major Alan Wilson and his patrol of 17 troops, who were pursuing King Lobengula, had been surrounded in the Shangaani valley and all killed. Their orders had been to find the king and report back before nightfall. Wilson disobeyed these orders and with an advanced reconnaissance patrol endeavoured to capture the king and win lasting fame. He did achieve the latter but posthumously. This journey was still not without its hazards.

At Nyamandhlovu, 30 miles from Bulawayo, the party had problems with their transport and were given help by two pioneers, Messrs C. and L. Green, who ran the store there. The wagons and Cape Cart had been delayed and did not arrive until Friday May 6th, having covered only 24 miles in two and a half days. It was decided to lighten the loads. They borrowed a light wagon and four good oxen and redistributed the load. Captain Lawley resolved to continue on to Esibombom's kraal where he hoped to get in some shooting and inspect the timber in the forests on the Gwaai River. The night of May 6th was spent at Nkoni's kraal.

Arthur Lawley wrote:

"It was a lovely night. The outlines of the trees, so hard and vivid in the fierce sunlight, were softened under the caressing touch of the moonlight to a monotone of ideal beauty. There was not a breath of wind to stir the branches of the trees or sway the straggling branches of spear-grass. The silence was almost oppressive, and only broken from time to time by the mocking laugh of a hyena or the plaintiff note of a bush-owl. Truly a South African night has a fascination all its own..... We slept every night on a bed of dry grass, curled up in a roll of blankets or a big kaross rug, our toes to a huge log fire and above us the everlasting stars."

Leaving at daybreak on May 7th, they trekked for 12 miles through a dense belt of forest until they reached the Insezi River which they followed until its junction with the Gwaai. They lived by hunting guinea fowl and other birds and carried only six pounds of tinned beef to last them from Bulawayo to the Victoria Falls.

On the morning of May 9th, they crossed the River Gwaai at its confluence with the Insezi. They proceeded down the west bank of the Gwaai, but six miles further on one of the wheels of the Cape Cart broke. They improvised a sleigh from the forked trunk of a tree on which they packed the contents of the cart. At their camp that night, they were met by two Zambesi African messengers on their way to Bulawayo, who were carrying the Barotse mail. There was a letter from Coryndon saying that he intended to meet Arthur Lawley and his party at either Deka or Thama Setchie and advising him not to take the Lewis Road, advice which came too late now that they were 90 miles from Bulawayo and only three miles from Esibombom's kraal. Coryndon also said that he thought the King of Barotseland, who was an old man, would not leave his capital to journey as far as the Victoria Falls.

At Esibombom's kraal they camped and spent two days hunting without much success. While there, they got news of Captain Jesser Coope and Sergeant Major Norris, the latter having reached Huilili Hill just ahead of them. On the second day the donkeys came in with supplies from the wagons and the following morning they left with their pack train to go to Huilili, where they arrived in the late afternoon. Norris had just left so they followed after him and travelled together until they were too tired to continue. Then they camped for the night. By preparing the wagons during the latter part of the night, they were ready to leave at daybreak. They pushed on to Inganjana Pan, where there was a good supply of permanent water. Here Dick Lawley and Gielgud, accompanied by Arthur Lawley, followed a herd of wildebeest, shot and wounded two bucks and continued to track them until they slowed down, when they were both dispatched with a second bullet. That night there was a feast in the camp. From the skins the African bearers made themselves sandals.

The next day they continued to Makololo Pan where they were obliged to wait for the wagons. Captain Lawley went hunting and killed another blue wildebeest, a particularly fine bull, which provided more meat for their food supply.

On May 17th, a message arrived from Captain Jesser Coope at Chekwankie, which he had reached after a hard journey due to the thickness of the bush and the lack of water. Over the next 73 miles there was only one source of water which might not last more than five days. Arthur Lawley reduced his number of wagons from four to two and sent six of the police back to Bulawayo. The weaker horses and sickly bullocks went with them. The wagons were reduced to less than 3000 lbs and carried only the barest necessities. Arthur Lawley decided to press on with his train of pack animals to the Falls and send back supplies from there, anticipating a dry sandy stretch between Thama Setchie and Deka.

They trekked on to the Kumbulabaswil tributary of the Linquazi River, which they reached at 10 p.m. Heavy rain had fallen there and the men were very tired. Leaving at dawn on the 20th, they reached Ingwershia at about 10 a.m., where they found a deserted wagon belonging to two prospectors whose donkeys had been taken by lions the previous year. Nearby they found a starving bushwoman whose husband had been killed by lions some days before. They gave her meat which she ate ravenously. The Bushmen round Chekwankie lived off wild roots and berries, but some of the men had guns which enabled them to hunt for meat. Leaving Ingwershia at 3 pm., they slowly trekked twelve miles in seven hours to their next camp. The bearers were very tired.

Figure 36: Two wagons at an overnight camp en route to Victoria Falls.

Thus they continued their march towards the Falls, leaving each day at sunrise, stopping at midday to cook and eat the guinea fowls or pheasants they had shot en route, and departing again at 3 to 4 pm. to trek as a rule well into the night. Each camp was surrounded by fires tended by groups of men to keep the lions and wolves at bay.

At Thama Setchie the water supply was quite limited. Twenty miles north at Henry's Vlei, they found a small supply of muddy water. There were several local tribesmen there taking water and Arthur Lawley sent two Matabele to follow them. They came back with the headman or induna and several other tribesmen, all Makalaka Bushmen. The induna was smothered in beads. The Matabele said they had killed a sable and an eland the day before – royal game which belonged to the king. The induna denied hunting. Arthur Lawley and his men went to his kraal where they found the meat of the sable antelope and the eland hung out to dry to make biltong. Arthur confiscated two of his guns and some meat for his bearers. He told the induna that the next time he was caught hunting royal game he would not get off so lightly. Now that Lobengula was dead, the Chartered Company had taken the place of the king and owned the royal game.

They continued towards Deka across dreary, flat terrain covered with deep sands, scattered bush and very few good trees. Guinea fowl were numerous with occasional pheasants. These supplied their food. There were sporadically located Bushmen's kraals. At Deka the landscape changed to broken terrain with rocky kopjes, steep hills with rounded summits covered with low scrub. The Deka River was full of fresh water and from there to the junction with the Zambesi the valley was well watered and fertile.

Before the arrival of rinderpest the area was wonderfully rich with eland, kudu, sable, water buck and buffalo. Invasion by the Basuto had brought the tsetse fly and sleeping sickness. The local people, who had survived the invasion and the raids by the Barotse and Matabele, had left the area with their remaining animals. With the departure of the livestock and extermination of the game by rinderpest, the tsetse numbers had declined.

Next morning they reached Pandamatenka which was well watered and fertile. There had been a Jesuit Mission Station there and a small white colony. Only one settler remained, Nicholas Villiers, from whom Arthur Lawley learned that Coryndon had met Coope there, and that they had both gone on to the Falls.

They left Pandamatenka and two mornings later came to the top of a hill from where they could see the Matesi River running through wooded hills to the north east. On the horizon was a small white cloud – the spray from the Victoria Falls. About five miles on they stopped for breakfast. They climbed a little kopje and from the summit they could hear the dull thunder of the cascading waters. At six o'clock that evening they reached Coryndon's camp on the Zambesi. They had arrived at Coryndon's camp on June 1st, the day they had promised three months before. The animals and men were exhausted and supplies were low – a few handfuls of flour and a little tea. One of Coope's wagons was sent back to take provisions for the police and the drivers in the party following behind. These men had been obliged to leave their wagons behind and six of their oxen had died of thirst within reach of water. Their supply of flour was exhausted and the relief wagon was most welcome.

When the rear party arrived, Arthur Lawley's orderly, Bland, was lying on the wagon. He had gone out to find a stray horse taking with him two horses, one as a pack-horse. Almost as soon as he left, the stray horse returned, but Bland was unaware of this and continued out into the bush. Camping out on the second night, he kept a good fire going and slept behind a ring of thorn-bushes called a scherm. There were two lions prowling outside, and Bland made the mistake of venturing beyond the scherm and firing his gun at one of the lions, who attacked him, bit and scratched him about the arm and thigh. The lions then went for one of the horses who was badly mauled. The other horse broke his tether and was chased by the lions out into the bush. Bland set off with the injured horse to retrace his steps back to camp. During the coming night he ran out of firewood and the lions penetrated the scherm protecting him and attacked again. Bland managed to climb into a tree, but the other horse was taken. At dawn he set off with a full water bag. He walked for three more days and spent the two intervening nights up trees. On the evening of the third day, he was met by Dr. Ellis and the relief party from the wagon, who carried him back in a state of complete exhaustion and delirium to the camp which they reached at 5 a.m. Thanks to the doctor's unremitting care and attention, within six weeks he had made a full recovery.

At Coryndon's camp Arthur Lawley met Mr F. Lewis who had pioneered the route he had just taken. He had just returned from a tour of Bakota and Mashukumbwe country and said that King Lewanika was at Shesheke. Arthur Lawley decided to leave his main party behind and go 70 miles north up the Zambesi where he would cross the river to a location on the Nequezi tributary where Mr. Lewis had recently camped and where there was plenty of game for the larder. Because of the tsetse fly they would have to travel without horses. He sent a messenger ahead to tell the King that it was his intention to leave on June 16th. After a medical parade of the African bearers, the party set off for the Victoria Falls and spent the rest of the day admiring the stunning sight.

Figure 37: Lion encountered by Arthur Lawley near the Victoria Falls.

In his report of the expedition, Arthur Lawley wrote:

"The spray, in which the greater part of the falls is always enveloped, is so thick that a great deal of their form and beauty has to be left to the imagination. Here and there I could see a great volume of water hurling itself into the abyss – in itself a beautiful cascade, but only a tiny portion of the mighty mass, which for a mile in width, is for ever rolling over a wall of rock and falling to a depth of 400 feet into the seething chasm below.

"From the chasm itself a dense cloud of spray perpetually rises and hangs like a white curtain above the great cleft of rock into which the waters fall; around and about the curtain the sunlight is reflected in a thousand flashes of brilliant prismatic colours, and rainbow chases rainbow through the shifting sheets of mist. The roar from the falling waters is deafening, and the whole effect is very grand and very weird. It is like a wet 'Walpurgisnacht'. But one longs for a mighty

broom to sweep away the thick curtain of spray, and catch, if only for a moment, a sight of the river from bank to bank rolling its slumberous sheet of foam below."

Figure 38: The Eastern Cataract of the Victoria Falls, 1898.

The following morning Arthur Lawley crossed the river to see the camp that was being built for the King on the northern bank. They rowed from forested island to palm covered island across the river, which was nearly two miles wide at this point. Returning at 2.30 pm., they found the two Zambesi African messengers they had met earlier returned from Bulawayo with their English mail from home.

Captain Lawley's party walked up the river bank to Sekute's ferry, where they had to cross in detachments using the one available canoe. Arthur Lawley wrote:

"I cannot describe the beauty of the river at the moment that we crossed. At this point the river runs east and west, and as we glided over the water we had on our left the golden glory of the sunset and on our right the silver splendour of the moon. The perfect stillness was only broken by the regular splash of the paddles, and from time to time the distant bellow of a hippo bull."

Figure 39: Captain Arthur Lawley's Camp at the Victoria Falls.

The next morning they departed at the crack of dawn and formed a line of march up the river. The route passed through thick bush with scattered kraals of the Batoka people who had been reduced to squalid conditions by the raids of the Barotse and Matabele slaving parties. Their fields were extensively cultivated and they had just reaped abundant crops of mabele corn, mealies, canary seed, sweet potatoes, monkey-nuts and tobacco. The soil in this area was very fertile. The slave raids had reduced the Batoka to poverty. The women and children were taken, and the men who did not escape were speared through by assegais. At one spot Arthur Lawley found the ground littered with the skulls of men, women and children. One of his Matabele bearers, who had been with one of Lobengula's impis on a slave raid in this area, explained that small pox had broken out among the Batoka children and that the Matabele had decided to kill all their prisoners. When strangers arrived, the Batoka always fled, and had confidence only in the white man. Many years ago, David Livingstone had visited the area. Arthur Lawley and his party travelled for four days through a landscape of undulating hills covered with trees and divided by open glades and streams of water. On the fourth evening they reached Lewis's camp on the Nqesi

River in which were traces of fine gold, but only in small quantities. The following day, Major Richard Lawley shot two fine eland and two Lichtenstein hartebeest with his 0.256 Mannlicher.

After two days Arthur and Dick Lawley moved on with Lewis to Sipatinyana's kraal on the edge of the Batoka Plateau, a vast rolling plain of grass with hardly a tree on it. The plateau is broken by a series of little valleys whose streams provide an abundance of water. They camped about a mile from Sipatinyana's kraal beneath a fig tree in the middle of a field of mabele corn with lofty stalks just ready for harvest. The country in this area was full of game, but after two days they had to retrace their steps and after four days of hard trekking reached Coryndon's camp. On the way back outside Sekute's kraal, Arthur Lawley found three desperately hungry and very sick white men, part of a group of six who had left Bulawayo with the idea of trading in Barotseland. After three months they had reached the river but had no food and were stricken with fever. Arthur Lawley sent his canoe back to pick up these men and bring them to his camp where they gradually recovered, although one died on the wagon journey back to Bulawayo.

Arthur Lawley's party had plenty of meat. In four days of hunting they had killed nineteen head of big game including eland, Lichtenstein hartebeest, roan antelope, zebra, reedbuck and wild pig. The following day the King was due at the camp. King Lewanika had been met at Kazungula by Coryndon, who arranged to escort him back to camp.

The next day King Lewanika arrived at the Camp. Arthur Lawley wrote:

"There was a general outburst of shouts and songs, and a beating of drums and tom-toms which was kept up until midnight. The King brought with him his little son Letia, who had adopted the Christian faith and his chief councillors. His retinue included a band, in which the drums played a most conspicuous part, choristers, dancers and about a thousand followers. The female element was entirely omitted. His having undertaken a journey of 400 miles at my bidding was regarded by the whole nation as an event of the greatest importance. The younger councillors were very averse to it, as they regarded it as an act of homage to the white man, whose growing ascendancy with the King they looked on with disfavour."

"The etiquette and formality maintained by the King and his court are quite remarkable amongst South African chiefs. The attitude of every one of his subjects, including Letia, is positively servile. No one is allowed to approach his majesty except on bended knees, and even Letia on approaching his father kneels and salutes profoundly."

Arthur Lawley's wagons arrived on June 18th and he received the King on June 20th. The thirty Matabele bearers, having spent the morning cleaning the camp, were drawn up as a guard of honour facing the entrance to the camp. The camp had a neat row of huts built with poles and grass laced with palm leaves. Around the camp was a nine feet high reed fence in which were neatly made doorways. With a small number of canoes at his disposal, the King brought only a small part of his retinue.

The councillors awaited the King at the landing stage near Coryndon's camp, where there was a Guard of Honour of 14 British South Africa Police. The King received the salute and proceeded with Major Coryndon 300 yards to Arthur Lawley's camp. Here Arthur Lawley greeted him and shook his hand before taking him to his own quarters. Arthur Lawley wrote:

"The King's costume was rather remarkable. On his head he wore a black-brimmed felt hat over a scarlet night-cap. A long bright blue dressing gown much embroidered with scarlet braid in Manchester style, a flannel shirt, tweed waistcoat, trousers and aggressively new yellow boots completed his costume. This was evidently his holiday attire, for on other days his scarlet night cap was replaced by a blue tam-o-Chanter and the dressing gown by a shoddy ulster."

The King and Lawley sat opposite the door looking out on the river. They talked about their journeys and about hunting, and were entertained by the King's choristers accompanied by tinkling on a piano which had been brought by wagon from Bulawayo. They then went down to inspect the big boat which Lawley had brought with him, which was in the course of construction by his carpenters. The King and his son admired the carpenter's tools. Letia had learned carpentry from French protestant missionaries at Kazungula. The party were photographed.

Figure 40: King Lewanika, Paramount Chief of the Barotse (B.S.A.C. Photo).

Arthur Lawley made a return visit to the King, which involved a great reception by the King and his people. They crossed the Zambesi in several canoes and were met by Letia and some of the chief councillors. Wide paths led to the King's council chamber or klotha, and on either side were lined up various detachments of Barotse, who as they walked past greeted Letia and his visitors with prolonged shouts of "Yosho", a royal greeting, accompanied by hand clapping and prostration on the ground as they passed by. The King's camp consisted of groups of long huts surrounded by a high reed fence. The whole of the camp was floored with a smooth surface of sun dried clay kept conspicuously clean with regular sweeping and garnishing. Arthur Lawley and his aides were met by the King at the entrance to the lotha, which was outside the main camp. Here they discussed the doings of the day before adjourning to the King's private audience chamber. Most of Lawley's party went off to view the Victoria Falls from the south bank, while Arthur Lawley, Coryndon, Blanckenberg and Worthington remained to discuss the new concession with the King and his councillors. After a discussion of several hours the visitors left and rode to the Falls which they reached at 4.00 pm. They had a late luncheon, but afterwards, as the sun was sinking fast, they had to hurry in order to get back up the river and across to the other side before dark. The views of the river as they returned were exquisitely beautiful.

The following day they went back for detailed discussion of the new Concession with the King and his councillors. Returning at about two o'clock, they left on horse back for some islands about ten miles up river to try and shoot a hippo. The canoes travelled with them up the river. They only got five miles before they had to camp for the night. This meant that they did not get to the islands until ten o'clock by which time the hippos were off the land and desporting themselves in the middle of the river. They were unable to get a successful shot despite some manoeuvring to do so.

The next day they returned for talks with the King and despite discussions lasting all morning failed to reach a conclusion. At three thirty the King came to lunch at Arthur Lawley's camp but the gymkhana in his honour had to be postponed until the next day. The following morning all the points at issue were settled. The whole of the new Concession had been read and interpreted clause by clause. The King and his people expressed themselves perfectly satisfied with its terms.

The postponed gymkhana then took place. Arthur Lawley writes:

"That afternoon we held the first meeting of the Victoria Falls Turf Club under the patronage of the Royal Family of Barotseland. Coryndon and Coope had laid out a small course and organised an excellent programme. The royal stand consisted of a bush wagon covered with chairs on which sat the King, Letia, the Gambella and other members of his court. Nothing could have been more successful, and the King was hugely delighted with the fun. A bending race, steeple chase, V.C. race, postillion race, and several foot races formed the various events. The foot race for the natives was most amusing. There were nearly a hundred competitors all in the wildest state of excitement. The Barotse, I regret to say, completely defeated the Matabele; but Sikobokobo, my induna, gravely informed me that this was only because I had fed the Matabeles so much better than the King fed the Barotse that they were far too fat to run.

"After the meeting I escorted the King to the water's edge, and there he wished me goodbye. At parting the King handed me a very handsome kaross of his own making and two "royal mats", which he asked me to give my wife as a present from himself. Letia also presented me with a beautiful rug of evenly matched leopard-skins. In addition to these presents the King had also sent me over seven oxen for slaughter purposes and his son gave me a cow. The Zambesi cows are very diminutive in size, but good milkers....

"The King was much pleased at being presented with a double barrelled rifle and two salted horses, and we parted the best of friends.

"In the evening all the police came to my camp for a 'sing-song' round a huge wood fire and it was nearly midnight when the National Anthem rang out over the waters of the Upper Zambesi."

Figure 41: Captain Arthur Lawley in the Rhodesian bush.

For the return journey Arthur Lawley sent the wagons back by the normal transport road through Pandamatenka, while he made his way with a small party and a pack train to Wankie's Kraal, which is 110 miles below the Victoria Falls near Devil's Gorge at the confluence of the Zambesi and the Gwaai Rivers. After two days they had assembled sufficient porters to carry their goods as far as Wankie's. They set off on June 29th with fifty three Zambesi carriers, thirty Matabele servants and a pack train of six mules and twelve donkeys. Arthur Lawley was accompanied by his brother, Dick, by Gielgud, Coope, Dr. Ellis, Blanckenberg and Rodger.

The record of Arthur Lawley's trek home across the veldt towards Bulawayo is in his diary covering the period from June 26th to July 17th 1898, which is now in the National Archive of Zimbabwe. He wrote:

Monday June 27th: "Aitkens arrived and reported that the road to Wankie's is very rough and mountainous and at least seven days from camp. I decided to start as soon as we could get carriers, leaving the rest to follow with the pack mules. The carriers turned up next morning and we got off at 12 o'clock exactly four weeks after arriving at the Falls."

Figure 42: Samannga Pool.

Chief Wankie had coal seams on his land. Indeed the Wankie Coalfield was developed there in due course. Lawley was looking for coal to fire the locomotives for the extension of the railway north over the Zambesi. He was also looking for a suitable location for a railway bridge. The diary continued:

"Our party consisted of 53 carriers and 20 Matabele boys. I handed my grey horse 'Trumpeter' over to Coryndon and selected one of the Natal ponies to ride back. Our course lay for twenty miles along the Pandamatenka Road. Coryndon was to have accompanied us but he did not turn up that night. The next day (June 29th) after going about ten miles, we left the road and turned eastward to September's Kraal on the Johetshigumbo River. Just as we were starting Coryndon turned up to wish us good bye."

Coryndon was one of Cecil Rhodes' most trusted henchmen. That evening the party were entertained to African music. Sir Arthur wrote:

"Last night we had some Barobe music and I sent for musicians whose instruments were made from a calabash with a sounding board across the mouth on which were fastened pieces of curved iron. These instruments were played with the thumb. At a distance the sound is rather pleasant, but when played close it is rather jangling. The musicians, who appeared very nervous on being asked to play in public, treated us to a very painful ditty which seemed to consist of a single word sung over and over again in a minor key."

Arthur Lawley had mixed success at hunting, missing a duyker and failing to effectively stalk a waterbuck. Some of the African lads were set to work clearing the road through. The country was rough and rugged with dense bush. Then a successful shoot brought down three guinea fowl and ended two days of eating bully beef. On the evening of July 1st, some young Africans arrived with the mail. The following day after a difficult ten mile trek on foot, Arthur's men reached a vantage point with a splendid view below which laid the Dikka River.

The diary continues:

"Next morning we started late and through a very hot morning, but the road was not nearly so rough as it had been up to this point. For the first time we came across signs of coal and we passed a beacon which I imagine is one of those marking out what is known as Wankie's Coal Area.... I got a shot at an impala, but missed. Camped close to one of Wankie's kraals."

They were visited by one of the chief's men who brought a gift of six eggs. That evening they saw an eclipse of the moon. Led by a guide they made their way to Wankie's main kraal. En route Arthur wrote:

"At 9.30 we stopped and had a delightful bathe in a river and then breakfasted.... After an easy march we reached Wankie's about 3.00 pm."

Arthur was evidently not fully aware of the hazards of the bilharzia fluke, which is found in most river water in tropical Africa and carries schistosomiasis, a slowly debilitating condition which if untreated is eventually fatal.

As soon as Captain Lawley arrived at his kraal, Chief Wankie came over to pay his respects. Arthur had been planning to go to Senaries, but when the chief informed him that it was ten days march in the opposite direction from Bulawayo, he decided to change his plans and return by the Shangaani River south towards Bulawayo. He had one of the oxen killed to feed his bearers and young African helpers.

On July 5th he met with Chief Wankie. The diary continues:

"Spent the morning reading and interviewing Wankie and his people. I told him of my intention to establish Gielgud over the river and to send a representative of the Government as Native Commissioner in Wankie's district. I also gave him instructions to prepare his people for the payment of hut tax and instructed him to send in as much grain as possible for me to purchase as I find we may be short."

Vladimir Gielgud was later employed by the Matabeleland Administration as Native Commissioner of the Sebengu District. Sir Arthur then wrote:

"In the evening I went out and shot half a dozen pheasants. Wankie presented me with two fine leopard skins and I have returned the compliment with blankets, knives etc."

Figure 43: Arthur Lawley's camp in Wankie's Country.

On July 6th, Arthur Lawley's brother, Richard Thompson Lawley, arrived in camp with his girl friend to spend a month or so hunting. The girl friend may have been Rhoda Edith Knox Little, whom he married in 1909. The diary continues:

"Wankie brought in two sheep for which I paid him and having traded another two hundred pounds of meal, I am able to ration our parties fairly well. This morning I sent off Burka and two Matabeles with presents and trading goods for Gielgud's use when he takes up his quarters in the Sebungwe…. Among our surplus goods was a large supply of hats so I have presented one to each of the Matabeles which apparently gave great satisfaction as they gathered round me while Burka shouted a panegyric in my honour.

"This afternoon a German prospector turned up with a few donkeys and gave a very alarming description of the horrors of the country between the Gwaai and the Shangaani. However I am determined to push on and get through."

On July 7th the going was indeed rough and a good deal of chopping and clearing had to be done to get a path through. Arthur Lawley left 30 tins of corned beef with Chief Wankie to be given to the post runners in case of emergency.

The next morning they started up the side of a stony kopje and were half way up when two of the donkeys rolled back down again with their packs and one of the boys. Luckily no harm was done and by 10 o'clock they reached the water of a stream. Here Dick (Richard Lawley) shot some guinea fowl for breakfast. At sundown, at the end of the day's trek, they camped in an open glade, but the night was very cold especially for the African members of the party.

On July 9th, they made an early start with the carriers going ahead at sun rise. Arthur and the others followed on horse back and found the African bearers had made fires in the veldt to keep warm. By noon they reached Lugoba's kraal.

Figure 44: Dick (Richard Thompson Lawley) and Joe (Arthur Lawley) on horseback.

Leaving early the following morning, they reached the River Gwaai. They had driven their way through thick bush and up and down steep and broken hills. The diary continues:

> *"The few kraals in the district were very wide apart and the number of inhabitants very small. It will be desirable to try and collect these natives and locate them so that some control can be exercised over them. At present they are very shy and very averse to render any assistance to travellers.... Having crossed the Gwaai, we camped under some big mapane trees and immediately after breakfast, Gielgud started off with four boys to make his way to the Shangaani, from whence he was to send back word to us as to the path...."*

> *"The following morning (July 11th) I went up the right bank of the Gwaai and saw a troop of impala but could not get a shot, missed a duyker and came back to breakfast cross and tired. About 11.30 I got a note from Gielgud to the effect that he had reached the Shangaani about ten miles from the Gwaai and as soon as we could pack we started on his tracks but only trekked for about 5 miles before camping for the night.*

"We left at 6.30 that morning of the 12th and reached Gielgud's camp at 8.00 a.m. where we off-saddled and breakfasted. We found he had killed an impala and a bush pig..., but his report of the country – thick bush with dense belts of essimanja and impenetrable thorn scrub – does not induce me to wish to remain here. At this point the Shangaani is a wide stream full of water and crocodiles and there are swarms of guinea fowl and pheasants on either bank."

They left at midday and followed the Shangaani south east through mapane bush country, encountering a troop of impala and some waterbuck at which they shot unsuccessfully. The diary continues:

"Dark was coming in when we made our camp on the bank of the river in a thick feverish jungle where we would not have stayed had we time to pick a better spot. At night we had a long discussion. Gielgud was in favour of retracing our steps ... to the junction of the Gwaai with the Bembezi and up this river to the Queen's Kraals. I was determined to push on to either the Lupani or Lucampi Rivers. The following morning (July 13th) the whole party pushed on to the junction of the Kana and the Shangaani Rivers. We made a short trek and off-saddled early in a delightful grove of tall mapane where we had an excellent breakfast, changed our clothes, baked and eventually got under weigh about 12 o'clock, when we separated into three parties and started for a hill which was supposed to mark the junction of the two rivers....

"Gielgud and I...walked together to the hill and climbed about half way up it, from there we got a fine view of the surrounding country and could plainly see the line of the Kana on our right and its junction with the Shangaani about three miles off.... We found that Dick and Coope had come up, and moved on with them to a point about ½ mile further up the river and built a capital camp..... We slaughtered our remaining bullock and the natives had a great feast."

"The following morning we wished Dick and Gielgud good bye, leaving them to hunt along the Kana and make their way into Bulawayo by about the middle of August. We did not get under weigh until after breakfast and we trekked about twelve miles camping as usual on the river.

"Monday 15th. We made an early start getting well under weigh by 6.30. Before we had gone a couple of miles I saw a small troop of waterbuck which Coope went after but they were very wild and he never got a shot. A little further on we came across another troop of six and among them a fine bull. I got a galloping shot but misjudged the distance and my bullet struck at his heels. We trekked till 10 o'clock and off-saddled for breakfast.... Trekked again at 2.00 pm. camping as usual at sun-down on the river bank. The night was bitterly cold and in the morning there was ice ½ inch thick on the water in the buckets."

On the veldt plateau the clear skies lead to great heat loss at night and as July is winter over the southern hemisphere, freezing temperatures are indeed possible. Arthur Lawley's trek was now reaching higher altitudes and this further reduced the temperatures.

The diary continues:

"On the 16th the camp was astir at 5.30 and an hour later we were on the move. The Zambesi carriers are ill equipped for the cold weather and though they lie packed together as close as herrings in a tub in such old sacks as we have been able to give them with fires all around them, there are many of them suffering from

colds and coughs. In the early morning they are very poor things and it is difficult to get them along, but we have to consider the grazing of our horses and mules as we are without grain and it is absolutely necessary to make a long trek in the morning starting as early as possible.[39]

"About 10 o'clock on the morning of the 16th, Coope shot a young waterbuck which came in handy as meat for the boys. We fried the liver and kidney for breakfast, hoping that the meat of so young a buck would not be very rank. This was the first and I hope that last time that I have ever tasted waterbuck. The afternoon was uneventful and the night again bitterly cold. We kept an enormous fire going all night. We were up again at 5.30 and off at 6.30.

"17th July. We shot a few pheasants and some guinea fowl before breakfast and after breakfast we left the Shangaani River at its junction with the Nkabela River and proceeded up the latter for about 3 miles. We camped at 3 o'clock at the point beyond which there was no water...in the stream.

"We are proceeding by a path to the Lupani River instead of going as we originally intended further east to the King's Road.... I have sent two boys from here to Inyati with instructions to Carbutt to meet me at the Queen's Kraal on the 23rd."

At this point the diary ends, but Arthur Lawley did write a concluding paragraph summarizing the latter part of the trek.

"I have been pleasantly surprised in the sate of the country from the Gwaai River to this point. I have met with no difficulties whatever and there are no insuperable difficulties to wagons between here and the junction of the Shangaani and Gwaai. The road runs close to the river throughout and it is principally through the mapane belts, and there are many small dongas but these can easily be avoided, and only a small amount of chopping would be necessary to make a road. If a good road can be found from Lugoba's Kraal through Wankies it would be far the best road to the Falls as water is plentiful everywhere."

Arthur Lawley's Report finishes the story:

"At times we found the country wrapped in a dense mist which the native people call magasi. In the morning we passed through grass in Indian file which was seven or eight feet high and dripping wet. A cold wind drove the mist onto our faces, cutting our cheeks like sleet before a north easter and it was not until nine o'clock that the sun in his strength mercifully rolled away the clouds and we were warm and dry once more. Just here too was a miracle of luck for actually we came across another party of boys making their way to the north with our English mail.

"I rested a day or two on the Gwampa, for the boys were quite knocked up. From here we made a long trek through thick bush to the Bembezi River. The day was grilling hot and we travelled slowly – in fact some of the carriers did not reach camp until the following morning. At the river I met Captain Carden who had come out to meet me with fresh horses and a light wagon of supplies. A bottle of foaming lager beer at the end of a long hot ride was very delicious. On our arrival Queen Laseki came to pay her respects. She is a very tall handsome woman of very ample proportions. She was one of Lobengula's favourite wives in spite of the constant trouble at court caused by her jealousy and love of intrigue. It was mainly due to her influence that Lobengula condemned to death his favourite sister. A young woman still, her ambition and love of power are a thorn in the side

of the Government Induna of the district, for she is perpetually finding ways of belittling him in the eyes of his people. Four more of Lobengula's queens live with her, but they are all indifferent personages by the side of Laseki, whose quick intelligence and ready wit make her remarkable among Matabele women.

Figure 45: Four of Lobengula's Queens – Lomalonuve, Sitshwapa, Myoiyana and Mfungu.

"I knew that with a fresh horse I could easily cover in one day the 60 miles that lay between the Bambezi and Bulawayo. Our nags were stale and leg-weary, and it was a refreshing experience to be on a quick, active little horse that I picked from Carden's lot. I off-saddled for a couple of hours at Shiloh Police Fort, and it was nearly 10 p.m. when I rode down the main road of Bulawayo on July 23rd after an absence of nearly three months. The brilliant electric lamps reflected in the plate glass windows reminded me that I was back once more in civilized regions. I realised the fact with a sigh, for I knew that I should often long for the freedom and unconventionality which, with the constant variety of incident and the possibility of excitement and occasionally danger, give a peculiar charm to life on the African veldt."[40]

Cecil Rhodes had the ambition to build a railway linking Cape Town to Cairo. The plan was to cross the Zambesi at the Victoria Falls and continue the railway line northwards towards what became the Copper Belt of Northern Rhodesia. This was very much to the forefront in Rhodes' projected scheme. Arthur Lawley was looking at a possible route for road and rail links between Bulawayo and the Falls. This was not an aimless safari.

The paternalistic attitude towards the African porters and the use of the word "boy" for a full grown man were patronising and later would be regarded as offensive.

However, during late Victorian and Edwardian times such language was the accepted norm and widely used. The imposition of a hut tax on the indigenous population and the appointment of Native Commissioners to collect this tax showed that imperial power was in earnest in Matabeleland.

Figure 46: Punch cartoon of Cecil Rhodes as the Colossus of Africa.

On the 24th August 1898, Rhodes wrote in a telegram:

"Captain Lawley has obtained a very good concession from Lewanika, King of Barotseland, which I hope the Board of Directors will do their utmost to get ratified by the Foreign Office. In my opinion the territory north of the Zambesi should be left to the Foreign Office. Coryndon can get the same powers as Codrington. When the Railway gets north of the Zambesi the territory will practically become part of Southern Rhodesia. Matabeleland and the country under Coryndon's jurisdiction can be administered by the Administrator for Matabeleland, and Mashonaland and Mpseni's country can be administered by the Administrator for Mashonaland."

Figure 47: Captain Arthur Lawley and Annie Allen Lawley with Cecil Rhodes and friends.

Rhodes's mind was on the grand design, the creation of a single network of communications across the continent. The railway and the telegraph, spreading from end to end of Africa, not only north to south but east to west also, were his major pre-occupations between the Jameson Raid and the Boer War. As he had written to the Company Secretary, in support of Captain Lawley's new concession, he believed that the extension of the railway north of the Zambesi would make the union of Northern and Southern Rhodesia practically inevitable. With Kitchener advancing southwards into the Sudan, the old dream of uniting Africa in a network of communications became what Rhodes called "a practical question", and he burned with competitive ardour to reach Uganda first.

The Administration of Matabeleland

On his return from the Victoria Falls, Arthur Lawley was very keen to do something to protect the wild life of Matabeleland. On September 28th 1898, he published the Game Preservation Regulations. These stated that "it shall not be lawful to kill, pursue, hunt or shoot at any kind of game in several districts of Southern Rhodesia".[41] The economic conditions at the end of 1898 were unfavourable in Matabeleland. At the Caledonian Dinner on December 2nd, Captain Arthur Lawley endeavoured to look on the bright side. This prompted one diner to say,

"The Chartered Company is fortunate in having so eloquent a representative in Matabeleland as the Deputy Administrator and the earnest, thoughtful manner of Captain Lawley goes far to rehabilitate the Company in the minds of the people. He is sincere and his silver toned oratory convinces one almost against one's will." [42]

Figure 48: The Railway Celebrations Committee – Captain Arthur Lawley seated at centre.

Friday December 24th was the end of the school term and St George's Public School had a Sports Day. That evening, the Administrator and Mrs Lawley attended the Prize Giving at St John's Public School.[43] Captain Lawley distributed the prizes. There was also an English Church Grammar School for Boys and Girls in Abercorn Street. Bulawayo with three schools was beginning to acquire all the attributes of an established town.

In 1898, Cecil Rhodes went to England to negotiate with the Government about the development and extension of Rhodesian railways. Rhodesia was in the throes of its first election for members of the newly constituted Legislative Council, which had been formed by the Order in Council promulgated in October 1898, by which it was ordered that two members from Matabeleland and two from Mashonaland were to be elected to represent the settlers in the country on the new Council, with five members of the British South Africa Company. The result of this election showed that Dr Hans Sauer and Mr Hutchinson had been elected for Matabeleland, and Colonel Grey and Mr Grimmer for Mashonaland. The nominees of the Chartered Company were Sir Thomas Scanlan, K.C.M.G., Mr Justice Vintcent, and Messrs Castens, Griffin, and Orpen, while the Administrator of Mashonaland (Mr William H. Milton), the Administrator of Matabeleland (Captain the Hon. Arthur Lawley), and the Resident Commissioner (Lieutenant-Colonel Sir M. J. Clarke, K.C.M.G.) were members ex officio. The first meeting of this Council took place on May 15, 1899, in Salisbury, Mr Milton, as senior Administrator, presiding.[44]

In December 1898, Captain Arthur Lawley became the Administrator of Matabeleland and in July 1899, Acting Administrator of Mashonaland during the absence of the Administrator, William Milton. Rhodes was faithful to his earlier method of indicating his personal choice of the right man for the job, and leaving the rest to the man on the spot. Men such as Coillard, the French Protestant missionary, Coryndon in Barotseland, Codrington, whom he sent as Milton's deputy to Mashonaland, and Captain Arthur Lawley were Rhodes's men, some of them known as the "Apostles".[45]

Figure 49: June 1899. The First Train from Beira arrives in Salisbury.

Cecil Rhodes was a frequent visitor to Bulawayo and usually stayed with the Lawleys. He liked to travel by rail. On 19th June 1899, the Beira-Salisbury Railway was completed and Southern Rhodesia acquired an outlet through Mozambique to the east coast. Three years later, the two systems were connected and the hitherto isolated provinces of Matabeleland and Mashonaland were effectively united.[46]

The building of a railway system was a most impressive achievement. Apart from making the country more secure strategically against another rising, it made mining on a larger scale profitable for the first time. Machinery could now be imported much more cheaply than before; bulky ores and agricultural produce could be exported with some hope of profit and the country ceased to rely on the muscles of the carriers. Coal, a new source of fuel in a country that had previously relied on wood, could now be delivered directly to the gold mines from the newly developing Wankie coalfield. The reckless buying up of gold claims and the flotation of fraudulent companies diminished, and more productive work was performed. At the same time, the British South Africa Company introduced important changes in its mining policy. Originally, its legislation had been designed to encourage large companies to come into the country, possessing enough capital to develop the "New Rand", which Rhodes and his associates believed to exist somewhere in the "Far North". But no second Johannesburg arose on the veldt of Rhodesia. Instead it became clear that the country's geological structure with its scattered gold deposits, was more favourable to the "small worker", able to carry on with only a little capital.

As the man in charge of the Administration of Matabeleland, Arthur Lawley had to deal with all the problems of a new colonial territory. At the beginning of May 1898, he wrote to Cecil Rhodes to say that he was moving the Government Store to a location alongside the new railway, constructing new stables and building a new kitchen and offices at Government House. He stated that he would like this work to be done in time to install his family. Annie Lawley and the children were on leave when Arthur went to visit King Lewanika. Indeed Mrs Arthur Lawley met Queen Victoria in the Drawing Room of Buckingham Palace on March 12th and attended a reception for the Prince of Wales at York on July 5th 1898.

Figure 50: Ned, Richard Lawley, aged ten with his gun in the African bush by W.E. Miller 1897.

On January 4th 1899, Arthur and Annie Lawley and their children left Bulawayo on horse back, with an accompanying Cape Cart, to visit Native Commissioner H. J. Jackson and to see the Umzingwane district. They met with Chief Sekombo, his witch doctor and some of his indunas. There were splendid tribal dances performed on a day full of festivities which Ned, Ursula and Cecilia Lawley seem to have enjoyed enormously.[47]

Annie Lawley told her grandsons Richard and Eustace Gibbs that when she was travelling by Cape Cart across the bush on one of their treks, the men left the women to go off hunting. A pride of about eight lions arrived and surrounded their cart. She and her maid, Honor, stayed completely still and eventually the lions decided to leave. When the men returned, they did not believe the ladies' story so they went out into the bush to verify the facts for themselves. To their consternation they found the pride of lions and shot and killed those that did not manage to escape.[48]

Figure 51: Native dancers at Umzingwane – Cape Cart and resting horses in the foreground.

Arthur Lawley was particularly concerned with the health of the horses in Matabeleland and Dr. Turner came up from the Cape to assist with establishing Inoculation Centres. Indeed Lawley wished to contract Dr. Turner to the service of Matabeleland for two years in order to stamp out horse sickness.[49] In August 1899, Lawley suggested to Rhodes that cheap freight rates on the railway should be given to breeding cattle to encourage the building up of the herds decimated by rinderpest on the Rhodesian veldt farms.[50]

The landowners were anxious about their property rights and there was much legal wrangling on this issue.[51] Surveyors were in the process of undertaking cadastral surveys to delineate properties. In 1899, the Southern Rhodesian Land Ordinance was enacted to regularise the ownership of land. Farmers had mineral rights over limestone and building materials, but the government retained control of gold, silver, bauxite, copper, coal, chrome, precious stones, and other minerals. There were prospectors with mineral claims who requested permission to erect batteries and sink shafts to mine gold. Mr. J.C. Fleming applied to the Commissioner of Mines, Mr. N.

Macglashan, to work gold on conditions other than those laid down in the Mining and Minerals Ordinance. The Mashonaland Central Gold-mining Company applied to the Mining Commissioner for permission to reserve all the timber on its lands for fuel in its mines. The miners of course wanted timber, and restrictions on cutting timber were laid down with extensive forests being put in reserves under government control. In due course a Government Mining Engineer, Mr. H.A. Piper, was appointed.[52] In September 1899, Arthur Lawley suggested to Cecil Rhodes that a Geological Survey of Southern Rhodesia should be undertaken.[53]

Figure 52: Arthur and Annie Lawley sitting in the garden with Cecil Rhodes.

The purchase of Native Reserves was suggested by Earl Grey in a letter to Rhodes in May 1897. He proposed that Forbes, Arthur Lawley's brother-in-law, buy up farms in the Shangaani and Gwaai valleys to create these reserves. He thought it would cost about £50,000 to purchase the required land. African farmland had to be protected and farm workers on settler farms were given land to cultivate for their own subsistence.[54] Their labour on the farm was regarded as being in lieu of rent.

There were plenty of disputes to settle. A certain C.H. Zeederberg had got into debt during and following the Matabele uprising. Cecil Rhodes and the British South Africa Company agreed to wipe out half his debts, reducing his indebtedness by £8000.[55] In December 1898, a mining assayer, Mr. Garthwaite, arrived to verify the purity of gold and other metals. Although the Standard Bank was already assaying gold, Arthur Lawley suggested setting up a Government Assay Office which would bring in revenue for the territory.[56] So the Standard Bank then decided that they would reduce their charges. This induced Lawley to reconsider his proposed scheme.

There was a problem of shortage of labour. In 1898, the population of Rhodesia was estimated at about 360 thousand, which for a country the size of France was a very low figure. Much of the land was simply empty. The Arab slave traders had been very active in the past and tribal warfare had also decimated the population. A certain Mr. Frank Smitheman had been north to Lake Nyasa in search of a labour supply. Captain Arthur Lawley suggested to Rhodes that this man might be employed to recruit labour for the Rhodesian mining industry.[57] Occasionally refugees from tribal skirmishes, famine or drought would arrive. 446 Venda refugees arrived from the Transvaal at the end of 1898 under Chiefs Mabashe and Musheke with more refugees to follow under Chief Impefu.[58] The British South Africa Company welcomed such people who represented a further source of labour. There were negotiations to import labour both from the Transvaal and from Portuguese East Africa. Arthur Lawley suggested to Cecil Rhodes that the support of the British High Commissioner would be very useful in dealing with this issue. Nevertheless preliminaries were prepared and arrangements made to receive Shangaan immigrant labourers from the Transvaal.[59] The manager of the Globe and Phoenix Mine went further and suggested that labour might be imported from India. Arthur Lawley supported this idea on condition that there were limits on the number of workers and the duration of their stay in Rhodesia.[60]

Figure 53: Captain and Mrs Lawley's Home in Bulawayo.

In 1899, in order to raise revenue, the Southern Rhodesian administration proposed to levy customs duties on liquor and other imported goods. The tax took effect on August 1st and there were the inevitable questions about existing stocks being taxed and the necessary concessions were made. All this was done through the British South Africa Company with Cecil Rhodes approval. Indeed a whole series of telegrams went between Bulawayo and Cape Town on this and other issues where

Rhodes' approval was sought.[61]   One consequence of the impending import duties was that traders imported large quantities of goods to avoid these tariffs. Hence there was a surplus of supplies in both Bulawayo and Mafeking when the Boer War began.

To deal with legal disputes there were law courts. A public prosecutor and an attorney general served the administration. There were legal disputes involving the railway and adjacent farmers, concerning the allocation of water supplies between farmers and miners, and a significant case brought by Sauer's Rhodesia Exploration and Development Co. Ltd. against the British South Africa Company in relation to claims pegged before August 1895. In due course this dispute was settled amicably but Lawley was keen to ensure that Rhodes was properly represented and that the settlement was water-tight.[62]

Figure 54: The new stables at Government House, Bulawayo.

In July 1899, Arthur Lawley became Acting Administrator of Mashonaland as well as Administrator of Matabeleland with residences in Salisbury and Bulawayo. He was therefore effectively the ruler of Rhodesia while William Milton, the Administrator of Mashonaland, was on leave.

To strengthen the military position in Rhodesia, Arthur Lawley began a volunteer scheme for young men to undertake part time military service. £20,000 was allocated to this scheme for the year 1899. On Saturday 14th January, the Bulawayo Chronicle reported that "the volunteer recruit movement appeared to be going admirably and that several of the troops had more than the fifty requisite minimum number." The British South Africa Police had a band and on the Saturday evening of January 21st it performed in the new B.S.A.P. theatre. Martial music encouraged recruits. The concert was attended by Captain and Mrs Lawley and by Colonel Nicholson and his officers in the B.S.A.P.[63]   Aware of approaching hostilities; Captain Lawley spoke at various events to encourage the volunteer recruit movement. On March 17th, there was a St Patrick's Day Banquet at the Imperial Hotel and Arthur Lawley addressed the Irishmen's Association.[64] On May 23rd, he spoke at a Special Luncheon to celebrate the arrival in Salisbury of the railway line from the Port of Beira in Portuguese East Africa.[65] On August 5[th,] as war approached it was reported that most of the volunteer troops were getting under weigh.[66] In September 1899, Lawley proposed to Rhodes that a good drill hall and gymnasium should be constructed in Bulawayo. He thought that these facilities would be excellent for the training and recreation of the young volunteers. There were 400 recruits in Bulawayo and Lawley hoped that a good volunteer force would eventually enable reductions in police numbers to be effected.[67] War however intervened. On September 23rd, the Administration advertised in the Bulawayo Chronicle in preparation for the coming conflict.

The Imperial Light Horse wanted new recruits. Only men who could ride and shoot
*   should apply.*
The Special 'L' Service Squadron announced a full parade for Sunday 24th
*   September.*
The Southern Rhodesia 'E' Troop of Cyclists were to meet on Tuesday 26th
*   September.*

On October 11th 1899, the Boer War began. Five days later, Cecil Rhodes found himself trapped in the siege of Kimberley, which lasted until relief forces arrived under General French and the siege was broken on February 15th 1900. Arthur Lawley meanwhile dedicated himself to the war-time administration of Rhodesia and endeavoured to inform the African chiefs of the outbreak of hostilities and the consequences thereof.

On the outbreak of the war, the first thought of Arthur Lawley and the other leaders in Rhodesia was to save as much of the railway line south as was possible. For this purpose an armoured train with 50 members of 'D' Troop was dispatched on October 14th 1899, [68] only three days after the expiration of the ultimatum, to the point four hundred miles south of Bulawayo, where the frontiers of the Transvaal and of Bechuanaland joined. Colonel Holdsworth commanded the small British force. That same day the last train arrived from Mafeking.

The Boers, a thousand or so in number, had descended upon the railway, and an action followed in which Colonel Holdsworth's train appears to have had better luck than was usual for armoured trains. The Boer commando was driven back and a number were killed. The adventurous armoured train pressed on as far as Lobatsi, where it found the bridges destroyed. So it returned to its original position, having another brush with the Boer commandos, and again, in some marvellous way, escaping its likely fate.

Rhodesia's armed strength on Octobers 27th was stated to be 301 men, 14 officers and 43 horses. A further 17 horses were to be purchased. Captain Lawley wanted to increase this. That week he had inspected a parade of the Bulawayo Volunteers, who for twelve days had been training at the Hussar's Camp. Headed by fifty splendidly mounted members of the British South Africa Police, they paraded in Market Square under Colonel Holdsworth. Arthur Lawley had always supported the volunteer movement and had sent the volunteers to train under the command of two trusted officers – Colonel Nicholson and Colonel Holdsworth. The Administration also requisitioned guns, ammunition and explosives for the war effort. [69]

From Bulawayo further forces were sent southwards to endeavour to relieve the small town of Mafeking on the railway to the Cape. Volunteer forces, intended for the defence of Rhodesia, went south down the railway line. They were pioneers, farmers and miners, many of whom had fought in the recent Matabele Wars.[70] Colonel J.S. Nicholson, Commandant-General of the British South Africa Police, acted as base commander in Bulawayo. He was in charge of the logistics and supplies. From October through into the New Year the railway line was kept open by an admirable system of patrolling to within a hundred miles or so of Mafeking.

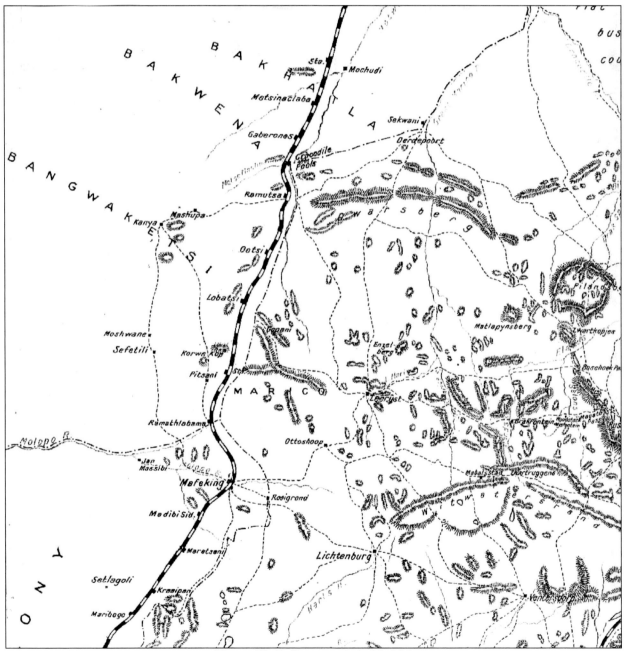

Figure 55: Railway route to Mafeking.

The Rhodesian forces used Fort Tuli north of the Transvaal border as a base from which to harass the Boers along the frontier. Colonel Plumer's columns arrived there within a week of the start of the war.[71]

An aggressive spirit and a power of dashing initiative were shown in the British operations on this side of the front, which was too often absent elsewhere. The African tribes also wished to attack the Boers and on November 10th, Segali, the brother of Chief Linchwe of the Bakhatla, requested permission to attack the Boer laager at Sekwani. This was refused by Captain Arthur Lawley, the Administrator. Instead on November 25th, some limited success was gained by a surprise attack on Sekwani, planned and carried out by Colonel G. L. Holdsworth. To assist him, he was authorized to make use of Linchwe's men as guides and porters. The Boer laager was approached and attacked in the early morning by a force of one hundred and twenty frontiersmen. At the first shots Linchwe's men got out of hand, crossed the Great Marico River and, firing wildly in all directions, got in front of Holdsworth and frustrated his plans. They then attacked the laager, killed some of the enemy and looted the few houses that were scattered along the valley. Thirty Boers were killed or wounded, and the rest scattered.

The British South Africa Company reported, " Thanks to the prompt and capable action of our Acting Administrator, Captain Lawley, the self-reliance and courage of our fellow countrymen in Rhodesia, and the able leadership of Colonel Baden-Powell, Colonel Nicholson, Colonel Plumer and the other Imperial and Volunteer officers to whom command of our frontiers has been given, the efforts of the Boers in the north of the Transvaal have been frustrated. No serious incursion into Rhodesia has been effected."[72]

The Relief of Mafeking

Lieutenant-Colonel Herbert Charles Onslow Plumer had been appointed commander of the newly-raised Rhodesian Regiment formed in August 1899. Like Arthur Lawley he had served in India and had fought in the Suakin campaign in the Sudan in 1885. He had commanded the Bulawayo Field Force relieving the besieged white settlers during the Matabele uprising. He now took command of the small army which was operating from the north along the railway line with Mafeking for its objective.

Plumer was an officer of considerable experience in African warfare, a small, quiet, resolute man, with a knack of gently enforcing discipline upon the very rough material with which he had to deal. With his weak force – which never exceeded a thousand men, and was usually from six to seven hundred – he had to keep the long line behind him open, repair the railway line in front of him and gradually creep forwards in face of a formidable and enterprising enemy. For a long time Gaberones, which is eighty miles north of Mafeking, remained his headquarters, and thence he kept up precarious communications with the besieged garrison. In the middle of March he advanced as far south as Lobatsi, which was less than fifty miles from Mafeking, but the enemy proved to be too strong, and Plumer had to drop back again with some loss to his original position at Gaberones. Sticking doggedly to his task, Plumer again came south, and this time made his way as far as Ramathlabama, within a day's march of Mafeking. He had with him, however, only three hundred and fifty men, and had he pushed through the effect might have been an addition of hungry men to the garrison. In the event, the troops of the relieving force were fiercely attacked by the Boers and driven back on to their camp with a loss of twelve killed, twenty-six wounded, and fourteen missing. Some of the British were dismounted men, and it says much for Plumer's conduct of the fight that he was able to extricate these safely from the midst of an aggressive mounted enemy. Personally he set an admirable example by sending away his own horse and walking with his rearmost soldiers. Captain Crewe Robertson and Lieutenant Milligan, the famous Yorkshire cricketer, were killed, and Rolt, Jarvis, Maclaren, and Plumer himself were wounded. The Rhodesian force withdrew again to near Lobatsi, and gathered for another advance southwards.

Colonel Plumer received reinforcements, consisting of two hundred men of the British South Africa Police with one 2.5 inch gun and fifty men of the Mashonaland squadron of the Rhodesia regiment. Then on the very day of his departure he was joined by C battery of the Royal Canadian Field Artillery commanded by Major Eudon with four 12-pounder guns and two other field guns. These were escorted by a force of dismounted men of the Queensland Mounted Infantry – four officers and 100 other ranks with Major C. W. Kellie commanding. These forces were part of the small army which came with General Carrington through Beira. They had been conveyed across thousands of miles of ocean to Cape Town, transported by ship another two thousand miles or so to Beira, transferred by a narrow-gauge railway to Bamboo Creek and changed to a broader gauge railway line to Marandellas. Their journey had then continued with a 280 mile trip in coaches drawn by mules, horses and bullock teams from Marandellas to Bulawayo. There were as many as 20 men and their equipment in each coach with fresh mules, horses and oxen every 12 miles or so. They had then transferred to trains for another four or five hundred miles to Ootsi, and had finally undertaken a forced march of a hundred miles, which brought them forward to near Jan Masibi's. Their advance, which averaged twenty-five miles a day on foot for four consecutive days over deplorable roads, was one of the finest performances of the war. With these high spirited reinforcements and with his own hardy Rhodesians, Colonel Plumer pushed on to the outskirts of Jan Masibi's.[73] In Bulawayo a telegram arrived from the south dated May 15th 1900. It said, "Our scouts fell in with the advanced guard of the southern column at day break this morning. Shortly afterwards Colonel Plumer joined the main body of the Relief Force which is commanded by Colonel Mahon. With the southern column is Colonel Frank Rhodes D.S.O."

On Tuesday May 15th, the Daily Telegraph's correspondent received the following message from Colonel Mahon's Column at Jan Masibi's twenty miles west of Mafeking:

"This morning at daybreak we arrived at this place after trekking all night until day light this morning nearly thirty miles. So accurately were matters fixed that as our main body arrived at this large native town, the main body of Colonel Plumer's forces was entering the place on the northern side. Colonel Plumer's men, who shared our joy at being reinforced, have also reason to be proud of their achievement. They marched 26 miles in 25 hours and did it on foot and encumbered with a heavy transport train. In addition to the Rhodesians composing this force there were some Canadian Gunners and Queensland Infantry, so that although not all South Africans, the force is entirely colonial…. The animals are being rested here all day and we start on the final journey to Mafeking at daylight tomorrow." [74]

The British southern column had advanced from Kimberley under Colonel B. Mahon with 1100 men and four guns. The two forces joined to advance on Mafeking. The Boer commander, General Snyman, vacillated. However the arrival of General

De la Rey changed the situation. He ordered the Boers with 2000 men and seven guns to form in a semi-circle to oppose the British advance.

The gallant and tenacious Boers would not abandon their prey without a last effort. As Colonel Mahon and Colonel Plumer's columns advanced upon Mafeking, they found, when about halfway, that the enemy had possession of the only water supply and of the hills which surrounded it. For an hour the Boers gallantly held their ground, and their artillery fire was, as usual, most accurate. However the British guns were more numerous and just as well manned so that the Boer position was soon made untenable. In due course their forces were driven back and the British and Imperial troops relieved Mafeking. The Boers retired past Mafeking and took refuge in the trenches on the eastern side of the town. Baden-Powell with his war-hardened garrison sallied out and, supported by the artillery fire of the relieving column, drove the Boers from their trenches. With their usual admirable tactics, the Boer's larger guns had been removed, but one small cannon was secured as a souvenir by the townsfolk together with a number of wagons and a considerable quantity of supplies. A long rolling trail of dust upon the eastern horizon told that the famous siege of Mafeking had at last come to an end. It was Thursday May 17th 1900. The siege had lasted 217 days.[75] The next day when the news arrived, there were wild celebrations in London. "The Queen and her Court were present on Saturday 19th May at a Grand Torchlight Demonstration which took place in the Quadrangle at Windsor Castle in celebration of the raising of the siege of Mafeking."[76]

Figure 56: Colonel Baden-Powell 13th Hussars.

Colonel Robert Baden-Powell was proclaimed a national hero. He received the CB (Commander of the Order of the Bath) and was made a Major-General. At 43, he was the youngest general in the British army. Queen Victoria sent a telegram of congratulations:

> *"I and my whole Empire greatly rejoice at the Relief of Mafeking, after the splendid defence made by you through all these months. I heartily congratulate you and all under you, military and civil, British and Native, for the heroism and devotion you have shown.   V.R. and I (Victoria, Queen and Empress)."*

The Administrator of Matabeleland, Arthur Lawley, had in no small measure helped to ensure this success. In January 1900, he had gone to Salisbury to take all possible measures to improve the route from Beira across Rhodesia to Bulawayo.[77] He had instigated the conversion of the final 60 miles narrow gauge to broad gauge on the railway from Beira to Salisbury.[78] He had ensured that the logistics were in place to move military forces and supplies. When Arthur Lawley's eldest daughter, Ursula, heard the news of the Relief of Mafeking, she rushed outside and hauled the Union Jack up the flagpole of Government House, Bulawayo. The children danced around the flag pole in celebration. The Relief of Mafeking became part of British folklore and was commemorated for many years to come. Half a century later, her sons Richard and Eustace, attended the Fiftieth Anniversary Mafeking Luncheon on May 18th 1950 accompanied by General Alexander Godley, who as a young officer had served under Colonel Baden-Powell at Mafeking.[79]

Figure 57: Mafeking Victory Parade in Bulawayo, May 24th 1900.

In Bulawayo, the administration proclaimed three days of public holiday beginning on May 24th in celebration of the Relief of Mafeking. The town had been short of supplies for months because the railway had been cut and out of action. In the Market Square on Thursday May 24th, in honour of the Queen's birthday, there was a parade of troops, including Australian Bushmen, a contingent of the Chartered Company's Police and the local Volunteer Forces. An open air Thanksgiving Service was then held followed by a public meeting at which Mr. Justice Vintcent presided and Captain Lawley was the principal speaker. Resolutions were passed congratulating Colonel Baden-Powell and the defenders of Mafeking and the whole proceedings were most enthusiastic. In the evening there was a concert followed by a display of fireworks.

On Friday 25th May, the railway line was reopened. Then finally the telegraph lines were reconnected when the 12 miles of telegraph wire and poles, which the Boers had removed between Ramathlabama and Mafeking, were replaced.[80] On Tuesday 29th May 1900, Captain the Honourable Arthur Lawley and party arrived by train in Mafeking.[81] On Tuesday 19th June, there was a celebratory march past of the Australian troops at the Race Course in Bulawayo attended by Mrs Annie Lawley and the Bishop of Mashonaland. [82] Once more Bulawayo was linked to the outside world.

Once the country had got over the disastrous crisis brought about by the Boer War, Southern Rhodesia pushed ahead steadily.[83] The most spectacular development was in the field of mining and during the years that elapsed between the turn of the century and the Great War, the production of gold rose from 54,981 to 3,580,209 ounces. Gold became Southern Rhodesia's chief export, but in addition a beginning was also made in the field of base metal mining, which generally proved more suitable for the large investor and copper, coal, asbestos and chrome began to be mined in varying quantities. The development of mining in turn created new markets for the farmer, and slowly there were improvements in existing methods. Many of the earlier farmers were men with limited capital looking for cheap land, cheap labour, and cheap cattle. Their methods of farming were extensive. Colonists were able to acquire 3000 acre farms for small payments, but only cultivated a small portion of their estates, moving on to work another patch once the land had been exhausted. Such methods were inevitable under conditions where markets were few, capital and skilled labour scarce and only the land was plentiful.

During the second half of 1900, Captain Lawley made a trek with the First Pioneers across the Zambezi at Kazengula above the Victoria Falls, over the veldt to the Gorge on the Kafue and on towards Katanga where Cecil Rhodes wished to extend his Cape to Cairo railroad. He met a group of tribesmen from Katanga bringing ivory downstream to sell at European trading posts.[84] Eventually a railway line was constructed along this route leading to the Copper Belt of Northern Rhodesia (now Zambia).

Arthur Lawley closed his last official report on Matabeleland with these words. "The spirit of the Rhodesians has been one of calm and patient confidence, confidence in the vast potentialities and resources of the land of their adoption, which I believe will be fully justified in the days which are to come."[85] Bulawayo had become a thriving pioneer town by the time that Captain Arthur Lawley and his family left Rhodesia at the beginning of 1901. In 1904, a statue of Cecil Rhodes was unveiled in the centre of the town.

Figure 58: Unveiling the Statue of Cecil John Rhodes in Bulawayo, 1904.

On January 24th 1901, on the departure of Arthur Lawley, William Milton became the sole administrator of Southern Rhodesia. Captain and Mrs Lawley and their young family returned by ocean liner on leave to England. On their way home they visited the island of Madeira.[86] The children were growing up. Richard was now 13, Ursula 12, and Cecilia 11 years old.[H] On his return to Britain, Arthur Lawley was granted a knighthood in recognition of his services and received the news of his appointment as Governor of Western Australia. Lawley Road in Bulawayo still bears the name of Sir Arthur today.

Walter H. Wills in the "Anglo-African Who's Who" of 1907 wrote,

"Arthur Lawley was Administrator of Matabeleland from 1896 to 1901, during which time he earned golden opinions by the happy tact which he exercised between the Chartered Company on the one part and the settlers on the other. The difficult questions of land tenure, native labour and other matters, which were the subject of local agitation, owed much to the attention which he gave them and to the care with which he endeavoured to reconcile conflicting differences of interest. In the early days of the South African War, he went in person to inform the chiefs of the outbreak of hostilities and to explain the situation to them."

[H] Richard was born on the 9th May 1887 and Ursula on the 8th June 1888. Margaret Cecilia was born on the 15th June 1889. She was always called Cecilia. Richard was known to the family as Ned.

[1]   The Times. Monday 20th March. Page 10. Column B

[2]   "Handbook to the Federation of Rhodesia and Nyasaland". Edited by W.V. Brelsford. Salisbury, Southern Rhodesia. 1960. Page 61.

[3]   Volume 31 – Some African Milestones. H. F. Varian. Rhodesiana Reprints. Bulawayo, Rhodesia .1973. ISBN 086920060 7

[4]   "Rhodes" by J.G. Lockhart and the Hon. C.M. Woodhouse. Hodder and Stoughton. London 1963. Page 327

[5]   "Rhodes, the Race for Africa" by Anthony Thomas. Chapter 20. BBC Books. London.1996

[6]   The Times. Friday April 10th 1896. Page 7. Column A.

[7]   The Times. Tuesday April 14th 1896. Page 5. Column A.

[8]   The Times. Wednesday April 15th 1896. Page 5. Column A.

[9]   The Times. Monday April 20th 1896. Page 5. Column A.

[10] The Times. Friday May 1st 1896. Page 5. Column A.

[11] The Real Rhodesia. Ethel Tawse Jollie M.L.A. Rhodesiana Reprints. Volume 19. Bulawayo. Rhodesia. 1973

[12] Joseph Chamberlain, Entrepreneur in Politics by Peter Marsh, page 374. Yale University Press 1994

[13] "Rhodes" by J.G. Lockhart and the Hon. C.M. Woodhouse. Hodder and Stoughton. London 1963. Pages 351 to 355
      "Heroes of Discovery in South Africa." N. Bell. Walter Scott, Ltd. London. 1899. Pages 410 to 411.

[14] Bulawayo Chronicle. Saturday August 8th 1896.

[15] Bulawayo Chronicle. February 28th 1897.

[16] Bulawayo Chronicle. August 15th 1896.

[17] Bulawayo Chronicle. August 22nd 1896.

[18] Bulawayo Chronicle. October 24th 1896.

[19] The Times. Saturday 28th November 1896. Page 9. Column C.

[20] Bulawayo Chronicle. December 5th 1896.

[21] The Times. January 5th 1897.

[22] Bulawayo Chronicle. Saturday 9th January.

[23] Eustace Lord Wraxall's Lawley albums. The Empire and Commonwealth Museum. Bristol. U.K.

[24] Bulawayo Chronicle. June 1897.

[25] Bulawayo Chronicle. June 19th and 26th 1897.

[26] Rhodes, A Life by J.G. McDonald. Rhodesiana Reprints, Volume 16. Bulawayo, Rhodesia. 1974. Page 290

[27] The Times. Friday July 30th 1897. Page 3. Column F.

[28] Rhodes, A Life by J.G. McDonald. Rhodesiana Reprints, Volume 16. Bulawayo, Rhodesia. 1974. Page 279.

[29] The Times Obituary for Lord Wenlock, Wednesday June 15th 1932.

[30] The Times. Saturday November 6th 1897. Page 8. Column C.

[31] Bulawayo Chronicle. November 11th 1997

[32] The Times. December 7th 1897. Page 14. Column B.

[33] Bulawayo Chronicle. November 1897.

[34] Bulawayo Chronicle. April 1st 1898.

[35] Bulawayo Chronicle. November 11th 1897.

[36] Bulawayo Chronicle. November 11th 1897. "Our Railway".

[37] Bulawayo Chronicle. February 4th 1898.

[38] From Bulawayo to the Victoria Falls: A Mission to King Lewanika. Captain the Hon. Arthur Lawley. Rhodes Mandela House, Oxford.

[39] Captain Arthur Lawley's diary June 26th 1898 to July 17th 1898. National Archives of Zimbabwe.

[40] From Bulawayo to the Victoria Falls: A Mission to King Lewanika. Captain the Hon. Arthur Lawley. Rhodes Mandela House, Oxford.

[41] Bulawayo Chronicle. October 8th 1898.

[42] Bulawayo Chronicle. Friday December 3rd 1898.

[43] Bulawayo Chronicle. December 24th 1898.

[44] History of Rhodesia. Chapter 18 by Howard Hensman. William Blackwood and Sons. Edinburgh and London. August 1900

[45] "Rhodes" by J.G. Lockhart and the Hon. C.M. Woodhouse. Hodder and Stoughton. London 1963. Page 397

[46] "Handbook to the Federation of Rhodesia and Nyasaland". Edited by W.V. Brelsford. Salisbury, Southern Rhodesia. 1960. Pages 66 and 67.

[47] Eustace Lord Wraxall's Lawley Albums. Empire and Commonwealth Museum. Bristol. UK

[48] Eustace Lord Wraxall in conversation. 20th September 2005.

[49] Rhodes Papers. Rhodes Mandela House C1/Volume 1 – folios 19 and 20

[50] Rhodes Papers. Rhodes Mandela House C1/Volume 1 – folio 79

[51] Rhodes Papers. Rhodes Mandela House C1/Volume 1 – folios 44a, 45, 65 and 81

[52] Rhodes Papers. Rhodes Mandela House C1/Volume 1 – folio 56

[53] Rhodes Papers. Rhodes Mandela House C1/Volume 1 – folio 86

[54] Rhodes Papers. Rhodes Mandela House C1/Volume 1 – folio 12

[55] Rhodes Papers. Rhodes Mandela House C1/Volume 1 – folio 69

[56] Rhodes Papers. Rhodes Mandela House C1/Volume 1 – folio 75

[57] Rhodes Papers. Rhodes Mandela House C1/Volume 1 – folio 72

[58] Rhodes Papers. Rhodes Mandela House C1/Volume 1 – folio 73

[59] Rhodes Papers. Rhodes Mandela House C1/Volume 1 – folios 59 and 85

[60] Rhodes Papers. Rhodes Mandela House C1/Volume 1 – folios 83 and 84

[61] Rhodes Papers. Rhodes Mandela House C1/Volume 1 – folios 77, 78, 79

[62] Rhodes Papers. Rhodes Mandela House C1/Volume 1 – folios 83 and 88

[63] Bulawayo Chronicle. January 28th 1899.

[64] Bulawayo Chronicle. March 25th 1899.

[65] Bulawayo Chronicle. May 23rd 1899.

[66] Bulawayo Chronicle. August 5th 1899.

[67] Rhodes Papers. Rhodes Mandela House C1/Volume 1 – folio 89

[68] Bulawayo Chronicle. October 20th 1899.

[69] Bulawayo Chronicle. 27th October 1899.

[70] Arthur Conan Doyle, The Great Boer War: A Two-Years' Record, 1899-1901. London, Smith, Elder & Co., 1901

[71] Bulawayo Chronicle. October 20th 1899.

[72] The Times. Friday December 15th 1899. Page 4. Column E.

[73] The History of the War in South Africa by Sir Frederick Maurice and M.H. Grant. Volume III - Chapter VII. "Colonel Plumer's Operations in Rhodesia".

[74] Daily Telegraph. May 18th 1900.

[75] The History of the War in South Africa by Sir Frederick Maurice and M.H. Grant. Volume III - Chapter VI.

[76] The Standard. May 21st 1900.

[77] The Times. Monday January 22nd 1900. Page 5. Column E.

[78] The Times. Thursday May 17th. 1900. Page 5. Column B.

[79] Eustace Lord Wraxall in conversation – March 4th 2005.
The Times. Thursday May 18th 1950. Page 3. Column C.

[80] The Times. May 26th 1900.

[81] Bulawayo Chronicle. Saturday June 2nd 1900.

[82] Bulawayo Chronicle. Saturday June 23rd 1900.

[83] "Handbook to the Federation of Rhodesia and Nyasaland". Edited by W.V. Brelsford. Salisbury, Southern Rhodesia. 1960.

[84] Eustace Lord Wraxall's Lawley Albums. Empire and Commonwealth Museum. Bristol. UK.

[85] The Times. Wednesday November 13th 1901. Page 12b.

[86] Eustace Lord Wraxall's Lawley Albums. Empire and Commonwealth Museum. Bristol. UK.

Chapter 3
Creating a New Country - Australia

Western Australia

Western Australia was not a long established colony. On 2 May 1829 Captain Charles Fremantle claimed what was then the Swan River Colony for Britain. A month later a party of free settlers arrived under the leadership of Captain Sterling. The plan was to establish a colony without convict labour near the mouth of the Swan River. By 1831 the population of the colony had reached 1,500 but the difficulties of clearing the land and growing crops were so great that by 1850 the population had only increased to just 5,886. This population settled around the south western coastline at Bunbury, Augusta and Albany and slowly moved inland looking for pastures for their flocks of sheep, while cutting hardwoods and sandalwood for export to Asia.

In spite of its relative success, the colony could not resist the temptation of convict labour and in June 1850, the first boatload of convicts arrived. Western Australia was becoming a convict state at the same time that the eastern states, largely due to the gold rushes, were abandoning convict labour. Between 1850 and 1868, when transportation stopped, a total of 9,718 convicts arrived. Their effect on the colony's economy was considerable and by 1869 the population had increased to 22,915. The harshness of the climate and the marginal nature of the land ensured that Western Australia would never be densely populated. Even Perth, which was to grow into a particularly beautiful modern city, struggled with its population. In 1849, only 1,148 people were living in Perth and by 1891 this had grown to a population of just 8,447. By the 1901 census it had become a small country town with a population of 27,471. The other important towns were Fremantle with a 1901 population of 14,623, the gold mining centres of Kalgoorlie (3,989) and Coolgardie (2,389), and the port of Albany (3,610).[1] The total population of Western Australia in 1901 was 182,553. The Trans-Australian Railway did not arrive until 1917.[2] Western Australia was the last of the self governing colonies to decide whether to join the Australian Federation. The vote took place in July 1900, and the result was decisive. There were 48,400 Yes votes against 19,691 No votes.[3]

Following the death of Queen Victoria in January 1901, King Edward VII and his new Queen Alexandra were unable to travel any great distance from England because of the preparations necessary for their Coronation in 1902. An extended Royal Tour of the Empire was thought to be desirable after the death of the Queen and all the bad press which had been caused by the Boer War. An Official Tour by senior members of the Royal Family to meet the peoples of the British colonies, who were most affected by the war, was regarded as being the best way forward. The new King, Edward VII, also wanted Princess Mary (May) out of the way because she was quarrelling with Queen Alexandra over the extensive jewellery collection left by Queen Victoria. Hence Prince George and Princess Mary, the Duke and Duchess of York and Cornwall, undertook a Royal Tour.

The 7000 ton Orient Line steamship Ophir was specially commissioned by the Royal Navy and completely refitted with every luxury for an 8 months tour of the British Colonies from March 16th 1901. There were very spacious and luxurious saloons, lounges and dining rooms on board. The Duke and Duchess had separate cabins and sitting rooms. The State Rooms were lavishly furnished with thick carpets and the walls and chairs were upholstered in pale blue brocade. The wash stands were of alabaster and onyx – worth two hundred pounds each.[4]

In January 1901, Captain Lawley and his family returned to England via Madeira for a short period of leave. In London on Wednesday January 30th, the King approved Arthur Lawley's appointment as Governor of Western Australia[5] and on February 14th, he dubbed him as Knight Commander of the Order of St. Michael and St. George. Then with the help of his elder brother, Lord Wenlock, he managed to secure a passage to Australia with the Royal Household on board the RMS Ophir. Lady Lawley and the children travelled separately. Accompanied by Mr. Jose, they sailed to Australia with the Orient Line, arriving in Perth one week before Sir Arthur. Hence Annie Lawley was there to greet her husband upon his arrival at Albany in Western Australia on Tuesday 30th April.[6]

The passengers on board the R.M.S. Ophir included:

1. Prince George, the Duke of York and Cornwall – aged 36, the second son of Edward VII and Queen Alexandra. This tour was his very first as heir to the throne of Great Britain.
2. Princess Mary, (May) Duchess of York and Cornwall – aged 34. She had left her four children (aged five, four, two and one) at home with nannies in England to be with her husband.
3. Lord Wenlock (Sir Arthur Lawley's elder brother Beilby Lawley) was the Head of Household.
4. Prince Alexander of Teck (Algernon), the future Earl of Athlone. He was the younger brother of Princess May and also the brother of Aldophus, who had married Lady Margaret Grosvenor, daughter of the Duke of Westminster in 1894. Prince Alexander had fought in the Matabele Wars and was with Arthur Lawley in Rhodesia.

Figure 59: Cecila, Ned and Ursula Lawley with Mr Jose riding donkeys at Port Said.

Figure 60: The Royal Party on the deck of the RMS Ophir with Prince Alexander, Sir Arthur Lawley and Beilby Lord Wenlock to the right of Prince George.

Figure 61: R.M.S. Ophir berthed on the quayside at Fremantle. July 1901.

Officially the trip to Australia was to open the First Commonwealth Parliament at the Exhibition Buildings in Melbourne, but it also gave the British Royal Family a good opportunity to "fly the flag" for the British Empire. Britain needed to thank her colonies for their support in the Boer War campaigns. Ports of call included Gibraltar, Suez, Aden, Colombo and Singapore, with extended stops in Australia and New Zealand. The return journey was to be via Mauritius to Durban and Cape Town in South Africa, where the Boer War had not yet ended. Thence they were to sail to the

Caribbean and Canada before the tour came to a conclusion in Portsmouth on November 1st. There the Duke and Duchess were to be met by King Edward VII and Queen Alexandra.[7]

In a letter of 2nd April 1901 written from the Red Sea to her brother, Prince Adolphus, Mary wrote, "We are both delighted with Lord Wenlock and "Joe" Lawley is too charming and a great addition to our party." Sir Arthur was known as "Joe" to his friends and family. Prince Algernon, who was with the Royal Party as ADC, wrote to Prince Adolphus at the end of April, describing a concert party in which "Joe recited, taking off Irving and Ellen Terry wonderfully well in the 'Merchant of Venice'. As he remarked in clear tones 'Enter Shylock!' in stepped May's Malay cat, presented at Singapore, quite unabashed amid a roar of laughter! Joe, having flicked the beast off the stage, proceeded quite at ease with his recitation. He is extremely cool!" Sir Arthur disembarked at Albany so that he could be sworn in as Governor of Western Australia, while the rest of the royal party went on to Melbourne.[8]

Figure 62: Sir Arthur Lawley being sworn in as Governor of Western Australia.

Sir Arthur Lawley was taken off the R.M.S. Ophir by the Harbour Master's launch at Albany in Western Australia at ten o'clock on the evening of April 30th. Three hearty cheers were given for the new Governor as he walked from the harbour to the railway station to board the special train for Perth. He was accompanied by Lady Lawley, Bishop Riley and Premier George Throssell with members of his ministry. In Perth the next morning, Sir Arthur was introduced to the Chief Justice, the Mayors of Perth and Fremantle, and other dignitaries. Sir Arthur and Lady Lawley were then given three cheers and after an inspection of the guard of honour they were both driven to the Town Hall escorted by the Chief Justice and Government Ministers. A large and surging crowd filled Wellington and Barrack Streets.

At the Town Hall, the Acting Chief Secretary to the Executive Council read the Commission appointing Sir Arthur Lawley as Governor of Western Australia. Sir Arthur took the Oath of Office and then the Chief Justice said, "I declare that His

Excellency Sir Arthur Lawley has duly taken the Oath of Office and assumed the Governorship of this State". The assembled audience all cheered. The Mayor of Perth, Councillor Quinlan, and the Premier of Western Australia wished Sir Arthur and Lady Lawley a hearty welcome to Western Australia. Sir Arthur replied:

"Mr Mayor, Ladies and Gentlemen, I confess I feel rather at a loss for words to express the appreciation of the cordiality with which you have welcomed me to your shores, but I can assure you that I am deeply sensible of your kindness not only to myself as soon as I arrived in this state last night, but also to my wife when she reached these shores last week. I beg that you will believe me when I say that I thank you from the bottom of my heart.

"I have at this moment only one cause for regret and it is this – that this, my first visit to Perth, should be of such short duration…. To represent you as your Governor the Ceremony of today had to be completed…. Ladies and Gentlemen, I feel proud and honoured that His Majesty should have selected me to be the representative of this state at the Opening of the First Federal Parliament in Melbourne next week, which will be the crowning act which will mark high endeavour and lofty aspirations on the part of the Australian Nation."

Sir Arthur and Lady Lawley and their children then he set sail for Melbourne in the State of Victoria, where Sir Arthur was to represent Western Australia at the opening of the Federal Parliament by the Duke and Duchess of York on the 9th May 1901.

The First Federal Parliament

Beilby Lord Wenlock in his letter of May 7[th]1901 to his wife Constance from Government House Melbourne, wrote, "Here we are at last on Australian ground. We got through our State Entry in the most splendid manner. I never saw such an amount of enthusiasm – at it was one roar of cheering from start to finish – nearly seven miles in length. Huge crowds and most demonstrative…. We had a most excellent journey across the Great Australian Bight where we were expecting very bad weather, and yesterday we had the most brilliant sunshine for our State Entry. It is cool here – but not cold – and a clear bright air. We expect Joe and Annie[1] to turn up today – and I hear that young Ivo Vesey is here – so we shall be a sort of family party out in the Antipodes."[9]

On May 9th, the official opening of the Federal Parliament of Australia took place. The Duke of York and Cornwall made the speech opening the parliament. His Royal Highness advanced to the edge of the dais, and placing his hat on his head, read as follows: -

"Gentlemen of the Senate and Gentlemen of the House of Representatives, my beloved and deeply-lamented grandmother, Queen Victoria, had desired to mark the importance of the opening of this, the first Parliament of the Commonwealth of Australia, and to manifest her special interest in all that concerns the welfare of her loyal subjects in Australia, by granting to me a commission to open the first session. The commission had been duly signed before the sad event which has plunged the whole Empire into mourning, and the King, my dear father, fully sharing her late Majesty's wishes, decided to give effect to them, although his Majesty stated on the occasion of his opening his first Parliament that a

---

[1] Sir Arthur and Lady Lawley.

separation from his son at such a time could not be otherwise than deeply painful to him.

"His Majesty has been pleased to consent to this separation, moved by his sense of the loyalty and devotion which prompted all the colonies in the South African war, both in its earlier and more recent stages, and of the splendid bravery of the colonial troops. It is also his Majesty's wish to acknowledge the readiness with which the ships of the special Australian Squadron were placed at his disposal for service in China, and the valuable assistance rendered there by the naval contingents of the several colonies. His Majesty further desired in this way to testify his heartfelt gratitude for the warm sympathy extended by every part of his dominions to himself and his family in the irreparable loss they have sustained by the death of his beloved mother.

Figure 63: The opening of the Federal Parliament by the Duke and Duchess of Cornwall and York on the 9th May 1901 in the Exhibition Building, Melbourne, Victoria.

A	Prince George and Princess Mary, Duke and Duchess of York and Cornwall
B	Lord John Hopetoun, Governor General
C	Sir Arthur Lawley, Governor of Western Australia, and Lady Lawley
D	Lord and Lady Tennyson, South Australia
E	Lord and Lady Lamington, Queensland

"His Majesty has watched with the deepest interest the social and material progress made by his people in Australia, and has seen with thankfulness and heartfelt satisfaction the completion of that political union of which this Parliament is the embodiment.

"The King is satisfied that the wisdom and patriotism which have characterised the exercise of the wide powers of self-government hitherto enjoyed by the colonies will continue to be displayed in the exercise of the still wider powers with which the United Commonwealth has been endowed.

"His Majesty feels assured that the enjoyment of these powers will, if possible, enhance that loyalty and devotion to his Throne and Empire of which the people of Australia have already given such signal proofs.

"It is his Majesty's earnest prayer that this union so happily achieved may under God's blessing prove an instrument for still further promoting the welfare and advancement of his subjects in Australia, and for the strengthening and consolidation of his Empire.

"Gentlemen of the Senate and Gentlemen of the House of Representatives, it affords me much pleasure to convey to you this message from his Majesty. I now, in his name and on his behalf, declare this Parliament open."

At the conclusion of his address, his Royal Highness removed his hat, and stepped back beside the Duchess of York. At the same time there was a flourish of trumpets, and the Field Artillery outside the Exhibition Building fired a royal salute.

As there was an overland and submarine cable linking Britain and Australia, direct telegram contact with the United Kingdom was possible. A message was sent from London by the cables of the Eastern Telegraph Company and the British-Australian Telegraph Company. The cable ran through the Mediterranean, along the Suez Canal, beneath the Red Sea and Indian Ocean to India and Java, and thence to Darwin in the Northern Territory of Australia where a land line completed the link to Sydney and Melbourne. The cable connection was completed in 1872.[10] The Suakin Campaign in the Sudan in 1885 had been to secure the passage through the Red Sea for shipping and to safeguard this cable connection.[J] The Duke read out the message from King Edward VII which said:

"My thoughts are with you on today's important ceremony. Most fervently do I wish Australia prosperity and happiness." Edward R. I.

The Duke sent the following cable in reply back to London:

"I have just delivered your message, and in your name declared open the first Parliament of the Commonwealth of Australia. I also read your kind telegram of good wishes, which is deeply appreciated by your loving Australian subjects, and was received with great enthusiasm. Splendid and impressive ceremony with over 12,000 people in the Exhibition Building." [11]

In Melbourne there were decorations and illuminations in the streets. On the morning of May 10th, there was a Levée at Government House followed by a Stockmen's Procession. In the afternoon the Duke and Duchess visited the warships in the harbour and distributed medals to the soldiers who had fought in the Boer War. Five hundred soldiers were so honoured. Later there was an Evening Parade to the

---

[J] Major Horatio Kitchener was given command at Suakin after the defeat of the Mahdi's forces

Carlton Gardens for the King's Message to Australia to be read to the crowds by the Duke of York in the Melbourne International Exhibition Hall. This was followed by a concert with choir and orchestra. [12]

On May 14th, Lord Wenlock wrote to his wife, "I am wonderfully well and, on the whole, am enjoying myself... We have had the most magnificent reception here and such a crowd of functions that is impossible for me to attempt to describe them all. I have ordered all sorts of papers to be sent to you and the elderly gentleman in uniform in the Royal Carriage is myself. Lord Hopetoun made the most excellent arrangements all through and the ceremony on Thursday was a masterpiece of organization. Young Ivo Vesey looks so well in his guard's uniform and Joe will make him work hard as his A.D.C. Annie looked worn and tired. She will not be sorry when she bids her Royal guests farewell on July 25th."

On May 16th, the Royal Party set sail from Melbourne to Brisbane. Their itinerary then took them to Sydney, to Auckland and Wellington in New Zealand, to Hobart in Tasmania and to Adelaide in South Australia. The Duke and Duchess were to visit Perth from the 21st to the 25th of July. Sir Arthur and Lady Lawley returned to Perth by sea and en route visited Lord and Lady Tennyson in Adelaide. [13]

Figure 64: Sir Arthur and Lady Lawley with Lord and Lady Tennyson in Adelaide in May 1901. Ivo Vesey, Lord Richard Neville and Captain Wolfe Murray standing.

Later, in May 1901, Sir Arthur Lawley received the resignation of Premier Throssell of Western Australia, the first of a series of political crises to occur during his time in office. At the end of May 1901, George Leake was elected as the new Premier of Western Australia. Sir Arthur asked him to form a new administration. The priorities of the new Leake Government were formally outlined before

Parliament in an official speech by the new Governor, His Excellency the Honourable Sir Arthur Lawley. They included the following:

1. The rearrangement of Departments as a result of the Federal Government taking control over several functions.
2. Dealing with restrictions on the taxing power of the State due to Federation.
3. Amending the Electoral Act to establish a system of electors' rights, to abolish plural voting and to redistribute seats: and
4. Giving earnest and close consideration to the finances of the State.[14]

On Wednesday June 5th there was an Official Welcome at Queen's Hall in Perth for Sir Arthur and Lady Lawley. The Mayor of Perth said, "I need scarcely tell Your Excellency and Lady Lawley that the people of Western Australia welcome you gladly and will do all in their power to make your stay in this state one of the most pleasing."[15]

In mid June, Sir Arthur and Lady Lawley were visited by the Governor of South Australia, Lord Tennyson, and his wife. They discussed the projected plans for a new railroad linking Perth to Adelaide.[16] On Friday June 28th, Sir Arthur Lawley, as Governor, opened the First Session of the Fourth Parliament of Western Australia. During his speech he said,

> *"No great volume of new legislation will be proposed to you during this session, but you will be asked to pass laws dealing with the Consent of the State to the construction of a Trans-continental Railway through this State by the Federal Government."*

On Wednesday July 3rd, the new Governor and his wife made their first official visit to Fremantle at the invitation of the Mayor and Councillors of the port. The High Street was decorated with evergreens and flags for the occasion. The Vice-regal party travelled down from Perth on the River Swan in the steam launch "Black-eyed Susan". Disembarking at the South Quay, Sir Arthur and Lady Lawley were met by an escort of the Fremantle Mounted Infantry. A large crowd had gathered in front of the Town Hall. Here a Guard of Honour of the Fremantle Infantry and Artillery was drawn up, and as the Lawleys alighted from their carriage, they were received by a salute from the soldiery and cheers from the crowd. After the Civic Reception, the ladies of Fremantle served afternoon tea.[17]

Royal Visit to Western Australia

On Saturday July 20th, the Duke and Duchess of York and Cornwall were due to visit Perth. However, due to storm at sea, the R.M.S. Ophir and its Royal Navy escorts were unable to get into Fremantle and had to return to the Port of Albany. Two cruisers, the H.M.S. Juno and the H.M.S. St George with their escorting warships accompanied the Ophir on the Royal Tour. At Albany, the Duke and Duchess were met by the Royal Train which took them to Perth, where they arrived a day late. They stayed with the Lawleys in Government House. Accompanying them were the two Ladies in Waiting, Lady Margaret Lygon and Lady Katherine Coke, Lord Wenlock who was Head of the Royal Household, the Honourable Derek Keppel, Equerry, and Mrs Keppel and Lt. Colonel Sir Arthur Biggs. Lord Wenlock was Arthur Lawley's eldest brother and Derek Keppel's sister in law, Alice, was Edward VII's mistress.

Figure 65: The Royal Train which brought the Duke and Duchess from Albany to Perth.

Figure 66: Government House, Perth.

Figure 67: The Royal Party at Government House, Perth, Western Australia.

Second Row   *Prince George.*   *Ned (Richard Lawley).*

First Row   *Sir Arthur Lawley. Princess Mary. Lady Lawley. Beilby, Lord Wenlock.*

Sitting in front   *Cecilia and Ursula Lawley.*

Figure 68: At the Royal Pavilion.

Figure 69: The Duke and Duchess greeted by the crowds in Perth.

Figure 70: The Railway Workers' Royal Arch.

Figure 71: The Duke and Duchess arrive to open the new King's Park.

Figure 72: The Duke and Duchess of York and Cornwall with school children.

On Monday July 22nd, there was a Civic Welcome by the Mayor and Councillors in the Town Hall. The Duke in his speech said,

"Mr Mayor on behalf of the Duchess and myself, I beg to thank you and the citizens of Perth for the hearty welcome which you have extended to us. It has given us the greatest pleasure to pay this visit here and the only regret we feel is that owing to the stress of the weather, we did not arrive last Saturday."

The Royal Party then proceeded through the Citizen's Arch on Milligan Street to the Royal Pavilion where they watched a procession and a military march past. That evening there was a Dinner Party at Government Houses for the Duke and Duchess which was attended by the former Prime Minister, George Throssell, and his wife, the Mayor of Perth and his wife, the Right Reverend Gibney, Bishop of Western Australia, and other dignitaries. Then there was a reception in the Ball Room for invited citizens to meet the Royal Couple. This was followed by a moonlight carriage ride to see the illuminations and the lights of Perth by night.

The following day, Tuesday 23rd July, there was a Levée in the morning after which the Duke conferred a knighthood on Admiral Beaumont. The Duke and Duchess then drove through Perth to the new Park which they officially opened and named the King's Park. They were accompanied by the former Premier of Western Australia, Sir John Forrest, and the President of the Park Board, the Hon. J. W. Hackett. There followed the laying of the Foundation Stone of the Fallen Soldiers Memorial for the heroes who had died in the Boer War, after which there was a presentation of medals to their living comrades. That evening there was another Dinner Party at Government House followed by a citizen's reception and a concert.

On Wednesday 24th, the Duke unveiled the Memorial Tablet to the deceased soldiers in St George's Cathedral. Then the Royal Couple visited the Museum and the Western Australian Gallery of Art, where the Duke laid the foundation stone of the New Wing. They then proceeded to the mint to learn about the mining and smelting of gold in the Western Australian goldfields. In the afternoon, there was a royal reception in the gardens of Government House followed by dinner and a Fireworks Display. Later a concert was given by the Royal Marine Band in the Town Hall.

Writing home to his wife Constance on July 24th, Beilby Lord Wenlock said, "We have had a very rough time of it and could not come up in the ship to Joe's harbour Fremantle, but had to put back to Albany – a very good harbour on the south coast. From there we had fifteen hours rail up to Perth. Joe and Annie and the children were delighted to see us, but unfortunately after our first afternoon and evening here Joe had to take to his bed with a bad cold and feverish attack and there he has been for two blessed days out of the five which we are here for. It is very bad luck indeed for him and I am so sorry that he cannot enjoy the fruits of all his wearisome labours in preparing for the Royal Visit. However we have got through it very well so far and Annie has been a regular trump. But I shall be much surprised if she does not break down after we have gone. It has been very hard work for her just when she ought to have been resting completely – and I am afraid they are also worried by money difficulties. This is a most charming house with a very nice garden – but they cannot possibly live in it on the salary which is allowed. They seem wonderfully popular and have made an excellent impression to start with – but it is going to cost them more than they can afford. If they do not raise the salary they will not be able to go on living here. Ursula is wonderfully well – and looks robuster – but is quite a different child – much quieter and not nearly so full of life."

On Thursday 25th, Her Royal Highness received a presentation by the school children of Western Australia in the grounds of Government House. The gardens surrounding the house were extensive and beautifully laid out with views overlooking the River Swan. In the afternoon the Duke and Duchess paid a visit to the Zoological Gardens to see the animal life of Australia, Africa and Asia. That evening there was a Farewell Dinner Party, after which German Lieder were sung by the Perth Liedertafel. This was particularly appropriate since the Duchess came from Teck near Stuttgart in Germany. The evening ended with more spectacular illuminations.

On the morning of Friday 26th July, the Duke and Duchess embarked on the R.M.S. Ophir at Fremantle. Their visit to Australia had ended. This was a landmark Royal Tour overseas, the beginning of a tradition which has lasted ever since.[18] The Lawleys' son, Richard, sailed on the Ophir with the royal party. He disembarked at St. Vincent to join a ship of the Royal Navy and sail on to Dartmouth Naval College.

Figure 73: The RMS Ophir leaving Fremantle, Western Australia, July 26th 1901.

The Duke of York was not invested as Prince of Wales until after the Royal Party arrived back in England on November 1st. The investiture took place on November 9th 1901.

On September 6th 1901, President William McKinley was shot dead in Buffalo, New York, while attending the Pan American Exposition. McKinley had just reached out to shake hands with a well wisher in the Exposition's Temple of Music at a few minutes past four in the afternoon, when two shots rang throughout the auditorium. The first bullet struck the President in the chest while the second slammed into his abdomen. The assassin, a Polish anarchist by the name of Leon Czolgosz, was taken into custody immediately. In Perth, a Memorial Service was held for President McKinley at St George's Cathedral on the afternoon of September 13th attended by his Excellency the Governor and Lady Lawley and other dignitaries and prominent citizens.

On September 25th Sir Arthur and Lady Lawley gave their first ball at Government House. The galleries of the Ball Room were festooned with evergreens tied with huge stiffened bows of scarlet. Metcher's Band played excellent music and a most tempting supper was served on tables artistically decorated with wild flowers. Captain Wolfe Murray in his gorgeous Highland Uniform made the enjoyment of the guests his first consideration. Sir Arthur and Lady Lawley received their guests inside the main entrance and afterwards they moved about among the visitors as if in a private drawing room. It was this utter absence of stiffness and formality which made the governor and his wife so extremely popular. The two little girls were present and danced together. They enjoyed the ball as much as anybody.

Figure 74: The Ball Room Government House, Perth.

There were two main newspapers in Perth. One was the Western Mail and the other the Western Australian. A prominent figure in the city, J. W. Hackett, was the Editor of the latter. On October 10th 1901, Lady Lawley started the New Press at the Western Australian Newspaper Company. Later that month the Lawleys visited the Geraldtown Show and the town of Northam, where there was a civic reception at the Town Hall by Mayor George Throssell, formerly Premier of Western Australia, and the town councillors.

In November 1901, the Ministerialists, former supporters of Sir John Forrest, defeated Premier George Leake on a vote of no confidence in the Western Australian Legislative Assembly. George Leake was compelled to resign. The Ministerialists, at first unable to agree on a nominee for Premier, eventually chose Alfred Morgans, the member for Coolgardie, as a compromise candidate. He took office as Premier and Colonial Treasurer on 21st November 1901 despite never having previously held any ministerial post. In the required ministerial by-elections which followed supporters of Leake stood against Morgans' newly appointed cabinet and three of the six new ministers were defeated. Morgans then asked Sir Arthur Lawley for a dissolution of the Assembly, but this was refused. Alfred Morgans resigned as Premier on December 23rd 1901, and George Leake took office once more, this time with stronger support. [19]

With his enthusiasm for horses and the turf, Sir Arthur Lawley enjoyed the Race Meetings at Canning Park Turf Club. On November 6th, the Lawleys attended the

Melbourne Cup Meeting at the Perth Race Course. To show his support for the Turf Club, Sir Arthur sponsored a race of his own – the Lawley Mile. In November the family also attended the Royal Agricultural show, where Miss Ursula Lawley drove a pony cart. At the New Years Race Meeting in January 1902, Lady Lawley placed the Derby Winner's Silk Ribbon around the neck of Trionia, the winning horse.

Figure 75: Lady Lawley places the Silk Ribbon around Trionia's neck.

The Governor General's visit

On Monday December 23rd 1901, the new Governor General, Lord John Adrian Louis Hopetoun, arrived in Fremantle on board the R.M.S. Australia for an official visit. The Governor General was driven to the station at Fremantle and then boarded the train for Perth, where there was an official reception at the Railway Station. After the Civic Address, he was taken in an open carriage to Government House accompanied by Sir John Forrest, the Federal Minister of Defence, and his wife. On Christmas Eve there was a Levée in the morning at which prominent citizens were presented to the Governor. Lord Hopetoun spent Christmas with Sir Arthur Lawley and his family. He was a personal friend of Sir Arthur. They had been at Eton together.   In 1902 he became the first Marquis of Linlithgow. Sadly he was to die in 1908 at the early age of 48.[20]

On December 30th, the Governor General attended the races at Canning Park. On New Year's Eve, there was a Garden Party for Lord Hopetoun in the grounds of Government House attended by most of the prominent people in Perth. On New Year's Day the Lawleys and their guests were once again at Canning Park for the New Year Race Meeting. The following day, Lord Hopetoun accompanied by Sir Arthur and Lady Lawley visited the coal mining town of Collie and then went on to the coastal town of Bunbury, one hundred miles south of Perth, where there was a

Civic Reception at which Lord Hopetoun, Sir John Forrest, and Sir Arthur Lawley all gave speeches. The next day they went inland to the jarrah and karri forests near the small town of Mornington. Here they saw the lumber jacks at work and visited the saw mills.[21]

On January 4th 1902, the Governor General's party visited the Zoological Gardens in Perth. They were met at the entrance by Mr. J.W. Hackett, the President of the Parks Committee. Lord Hopetoun, Sir John Forrest, and Sir Arthur and Lady Lawley all planted trees. Lady Lawley and her daughters then went on to see the Zoo's big cats and were given the chance to play with three baby tigers. The cubs were very young and playful.[22]

On January 7th, the Vice-regal party left by rail for the interior. They stopped overnight at Northam before travelling on to the Western Australian Goldfields. On January 8th, there was a Civic Reception in Kalgoorlie with Four Pipers in Highland Uniform and a Guard of Honour from the Goldfields' Battalion of Infantry. In his speech, the Governor General said that a prominent Australian statesman had asked him whether he thought Sir Arthur would do as Governor. Lord Hopetoun replied, "You go back and thank God that you have such a man and such a woman as Sir Arthur Lawley and his wife in Western Australia." The Vice-regal party spent two days at Kalgoorlie seeing all aspects of gold mining and refining. On January 10th, the new Governor General drove in the first stake of the new Kalgoorlie Tramway.[23] The following day there was a civic reception at Coolgardie when the Governor General congratulated the town on being granted its new Waterworks Project. On January 12th, there was a visit to Fremantle and a Civic Reception at the Town Hall. The next day it was the turn of Perth to lay on a Civic Reception which was followed by a concert in the evening. On Wednesday 15th, Lord Hopetoun embarked on the R.M.S. China at Fremantle for his return voyage to Melbourne.[24]

Figure 76: The Governor General, Lord Hopetoun, Sir Arthur and Lady Lawley greet their guests at the Garden Party at Government House, Perth.

Figure 77: Lumber Jacks in the jarrah and karri forest.

Figure 78: Lady Lawley at the Zoo entrance with the Governor General of Australia, Lord Hopetoun, and the President of the Park Board, the Hon. J.W. Hackett.

Figure 79: Lady Lawley, Ursula and Cecilia play with tiger cubs at Perth zoo.

Figure 80: Annie Lawley panning for gold at Laverton.

Figure 81: Lord Hopetoun, Sir Arthur and Lady Lawley, family and friends.

The Governor and Lady Lawley lead the way

On February 9th 1902, Sir Arthur and Lady Lawley travelled by special train to the town of Albany. They had been invited to celebrate Albany Week. The Premier, Mr George Leake, with a team of his Ministers accompanied the party. They were met by the Government Resident in Albany, Mr Morgan and his wife, and by the town's Mayor and Councillors. The Albany Volunteer Artillery formed the Guard of Honour. On the following afternoon the Governor opened Albany's new park on Brunswick Road, which was named Lawley Park in his honour. The next day there was a sports meeting on the Ulster Recreation Ground. The port of Albany was very strategically located and could often be accessed when Fremantle was inaccessible because of storms at sea. At the end of February the new Cape to Australia undersea cable was landed at Cottesloe Beach. It had been laid by the Cable Ship S.S. Scotia, which forty years previously had been launched as a luxury Cunard Liner. Western Australia was becoming more accessible to the outside world.

On Thursday 10th April, Sir Arthur Lawley accompanied by his private secretary, Gerald Parker, set sail for Melbourne on the R.M.S. Rome for a three week private visit.[25] He stayed with his friends John and Hersey, Lord and Lady Hopetoun. Lord Hopetoun was having problems with the new Federal Parliament with regard to the expenses of the office of Governor General. He found himself obliged to use his own money to meet many of these costs. On May 14th 1902, he tended his resignation to the Australian Government and to the government in London. In a telegram to Joseph Chamberlain, Secretary of State to the Colonies, he wrote, "I have already strained my private resources beyond all justification. The position is impossible and after grave consideration, I think that you had better recall me after the Coronation."[26] In July Lord Hopetoun was made Marquis of Linlithgow in recognition of his services, the name coming from his birth place – Linlithgow to the west of Edinburgh.[27]

Figure 82: Sir Arthur Lawley as the Governor of Western Australia, 1901 to 1902.

On Wednesday 21st May a Fancy Dress Ball was held in the Ballroom of Government House. Sigma wrote in the Western Mail, "At nine o'clock the Governor who was in Court Dress and Lady Lawley entered the room. Lady Lawley wore a dress of pale pink satin covered with silvered net, a very long court train of white and silver brocade and white ostrich feathers from which fell a fine tulle veil ornamenting her hair. A diamond tiara, necklet and ornaments finished an extremely handsome costume. Lady Lawley's two little girls, who acted as train bearers to their mother, both wore Watteau dresses with paniers and Watteau backs of pink and white silk brocade, white skirts bordered with pale pink roses, and a wreath of the same roses in their powdered hair, which was dressed on the top of their heads. They made pretty little shepherdesses and entered into the spirit of the ball with complete childish enjoyment."[28]

Figure 83: Lady Lawley and her two daughters, Ursula Mary, standing behind, and Margaret Cecilia, Perth, Australia, 1902.

As Governor, Sir Arthur Lawley was said to have embraced the social life of Western Australia with an outgoing and friendly manner and an interest in people and events. The Lawleys travelled widely within the state even journeying from Coolgardie to the Laverton Gold Field, 700 kilometres north east of Perth, on Sikh driven camels imported from Rajasthan. They also visited the Salt Lakes in the interior.[29]

Lady Lawley identified herself with community welfare issues and charitable organisations. She founded the Lady Lawley Children's Cottage Hospital beside the sea at Cottesloe. This was a convalescent home for children who had been seriously ill. The sum of £2500 was collected for the Home from the school children, the miners in the gold fields, dances and other entertainments, the ladies of Perth and the general public. £500 was subscribed by the Government of Western Australia. The Home was opened in 1904 by Lady Bedford. Bishop Riley described how the movement for a home had been commenced by Lady Lawley, who was greatly impressed by the need for a home where children could go after an illness to regain their strength. Lady Lawley's zeal and earnestness had inspired all with whom she had come into contact. On the 28th September 1927, during a trip to Australia, Sir Arthur and Lady Lawley visited the Children's Cottage. She wrote in the Visitors' Book, "I am perfectly enchanted with the Cottage by the Sea and very proud to have my name associated with such a fine work". The Australian Red Cross now manage Lady Lawley's Children's Cottage and the wife of the Governor of Western Australia is by tradition the Patroness.[30]

There were cultural attractions in Western Australia. In 1897, the musician, Joseph Summers arrived in Perth. He was persuaded by the local musicians to form a new musical society, the Philharmonic, which had fifty members. He also conducted the Liedertafel group of singers. The Rev. James Duff commissioned him to compose music to his dramatized version of Milton's *Paradise Lost* and *Paradise Regained*, entitled *The Two Worlds*. It was completed after fifteen months' work, and was first performed for a private audience at the Bishop's Palace. The work was well received, and was later performed in the Ball Room of Government House by the Williamson's Royal Opera Company for Sir Arthur and Lady Lawley, with one reviewer claiming that 'it was glorious music'. [31]

Figure 84: Sir Arthur Lawley laying the foundation stone of the Supreme Court of Western Australia.

On June 2nd 1902, Sir Arthur Lawley, as State Governor, laid the foundation stone of the new Supreme Court of Western Australia. At about 11 o'clock in the morning the news came through of the signing of the Peace of Vereeniging on May 31st, ending the War in South Africa. Sir Arthur announced the news to the large crowd assembled for the stone laying ceremony. "The loud cheering with which the announcement was received was an indication of the satisfaction with which the news was received everywhere".[32] The stone laying was witnessed by all the Judges and 70 members of the bar.[33] Work was completed in May 1903 and the Supreme Court was opened on 8th June 1903 by the then Governor, Sir Frederick Bedford.[34]

The Governor had his own summer residence on Rottnest Island to the west of Fremantle. From 1848 to 1913, this was for the exclusive use of the Governor, his family and his guests. Here the Lawleys would go fishing, sailing and swimming. [35]

Sir Arthur Lawley was an early supporter of the idea of National Parks. After correspondence from the South Australian national parks campaigner, A. F. Robin, the Natural History Society successfully applied to have an area of 65,000 hectares between Pinjarra, North Dandalup and the Bannister River proclaimed as a flora and fauna reserve in 1894. The ambiguity of Sir John Forrest's position as premier and supporter of economic development and as nature conservationist soon came to the fore. After requests to cut timber from the reserve, Forrest recommended its cancellation in 1898. The Natural History Society objected. Bernard Woodward, secretary to the society and director of the West Australian Museum, called for the area to be declared a national park; he was supported by the governor, Sir Arthur Lawley, and the Anglican Bishop Charles Riley, a society member.[36]

Figure 85: Ursula and Sir Arthur relaxing in true Australian style.

Figure 86: Captain Wolfe Murray, Ursula, Cecilia and Annie in the Salt Lake on Rottnest Island.

Figure 87: Sir Arthur and Ursula - a swimming lesson.

On June 24th 1902, the Premier of Western Australia, Mr George Leake died. His deputy Mr W. Kingsmill took his place, an interim arrangement until a new Premier was chosen. On July 5th, Mr Walter James formed a new ministry with Mr Kingsmill as Colonial Secretary and Minister of Education. On July 17th 1902, Sir Arthur Lawley opened the second session of the fourth parliament in the history of Western Australia. He spoke with sadness of the death of the late Premier. He reported on the steady advance in agriculture, mining and industry. He highlighted the new Government Scheme to provide water to Coolgardie in the goldfields. He was also able to report that the financial position of the state had improved from a deficit of £75 thousand the previous year to a surplus of £123 thousand that year.[37]

Following the signing of the Peace at the end of the Boer War on May 31st 1902, Sir Arthur Lawley was offered the appointment of Lieutenant-Governor of the Transvaal by the British Secretary of State for the Colonies, Joseph Chamberlain. He accepted and was therefore obliged to give notice of the termination of his period of service as Governor of Western Australia.

Figure 88: Laying the Foundation Stone for the Western Australian Parliament Building.

Au revoir Australia

On July 31st 1902, Sir Arthur Lawley laid the foundation stone for the new Western Australian Parliament Buildings in Perth. They were to be built at the top of Saint George's terrace on a spacious plot of land commanding an extensive view of the city. The stone laying ceremony had been delayed by the death of the Premier, Mr George Leake, and by the illness of Edward VII, which also delayed the Coronation. In his speech Sir Arthur said:

> *"For Lady Lawley and for me our time in Western Australia has been all too short. I know that a single line in history will suffice to record the sum total of our achievements, and our very position makes it impossible to hope for more than that, but I can assure you that the very deep sympathy that Lady Lawley and I have always felt in the aspirations of our fellow citizens will last long after we have left these shores, and we shall watch with the kindliest interest the development and expansion of Western Australia and the prosperity of its citizens."*

That evening, the Western Australian Parliament gave a Farewell Dinner for His Excellency the Governor, Sir Arthur Lawley and Lady Lawley. The new Premier, Mr. W. James, said in his speech proposing the toast:

"The people of Western Australia desire to express their regret that Sir Arthur Lawley, who has been with them for so short a time, and who has endeared himself to them all, is now leaving them. The impression he has made during his stay in the State is that he is an ideal Governor. Sir Arthur has a great charm of character, which has appealed to all those who came into contact with him. In all the speeches he has delivered in all parts of the state, there were always elevated thoughts and wise counsels...It is to be regretted that Australia is to be deprived of a man who is capable of giving such speeches and expressing such thoughts....Sir Arthur came among us at a time when we had political trouble – he having in twelve months seen four Premiers. He leaves us with a great knowledge of constitutional law and an experience which rarely falls to the lot of any Governor. Sir Arthur leaves behind a reputation of having exhibited the most admirable tact during that trying period and he leaves behind a government strong in the affections of Parliament and the people. Although we are sorry to lose him, Sir Arthur's was one of those personalities that it was better to have known and lost than never to have known at all."

The Perth Newspaper, "The Western Australian"[38], described the great esteem in which Sir Arthur and Lady Lawley were held. "In act and speech Sir Arthur Lawley has under circumstances of peculiar difficulty, proved himself an ideal Constitutional Governor. As our first State Governor he has, in fact, set an admirable example to his successors. Western Australia may, indeed, count herself singularly fortunate in having possessed, during a critical period in her history, the services of so capable an administrator. Sir Arthur's coming among us coincided with the opening of a new reign and a new era in Australian annals... This was his first colonial governorship. He has, nevertheless, performed his duties, whether official or social, as if to the manner born. Both His Excellency and Lady Lawley are gifted with a charm of manner which must, wherever duty may call them, largely contribute to their popularity. For a Governor, however, something more than mere qualifications for social success are needed. Prudence and tact will always count for much. A wide knowledge of Constitutional principles that are not always too well defined; ability to act wisely and well in cases of political emergency; the faculty of complete detachment from party prejudices are still more essential, and Sir Arthur has in all these respects proved himself to be admirably equipped. His Excellency will best be remembered by his public speeches. No matter what the occasion, these, in both their form and substance have been admirable. Sir Arthur combines in no mean degree the merits of the scholar and the statesman."

Sir Arthur Lawley reluctantly relinquished the post of Governor of Western Australia on August 14th 1902, and set sail for Southern Africa to take up his important new position in the Transvaal.[39] On the Saturday before they left, the Lawleys threw an "At Home" in the Government House Ballroom. The Morning Herald stated, "There were hundreds of people anxious to pay their respects to the most popular Governor and Lady that Western Australia has had...The Misses Lawley entertained a party of young people during the afternoon."[40]

Figure 89: Guests arriving for the Farewell "At Home" at Government House, Perth.

Figure 90: Captain Wolfe Murray in his Highland Uniform says Farewell.

Figure 91: Sir Arthur and Lady Lawley say Good'bye at the Port of Fremantle,

Figure 92: The crowds wish Sir Arthur and Lady Lawley "Farewell".

Nearly 20,000 volunteers had gone from Australia to fight for the British Empire in the Boer War. Hence there was a real Australian interest in a constructive and effective peace in the Transvaal. Thus a very large crowd of four thousand gathered at the Port of Fremantle to wish the Lawleys farewell as they sailed on the RMS Sophocles for South Africa.[41]

The Lawleys were not forgotten and a modern suburb of Perth, Mount Lawley, is named after Sir Arthur. Nor did the Lawley family forget Australia. Walking knee deep through blankets of spring flowers after the winter rains, encountering aborigines in the outback, playing with baby kangaroos on Rottnest Island, watching the lion dances of the Chinese community of Perth to greet important visitors, riding camels from Rajasthan across the outback – these were unforgettable experiences. Indeed Sir Arthur and Lady Lawley were later to become involved with Western Australia in a totally different way and would revisit the state on their last great journey together.

[1]   Western Mail. Perth. May 11th 1901. Speech of Sir Arthur Lawley, K.C.M.G., Governor on opening the First Session of the Fourth Parliament, 28th June 1901.
[2]   Encyclopaedia Britannica. 2002.
[3]   The Constitutional Centre of Western Australia. Governors. List of Governors. Government House. Western Australia.
[4]   Queen Mary. James Pope-Hennessy. George Allen and Unwin. London. 1959. Page 365
[5]   The Times. January 30th 1901. Page 7. Column E.
[6]   The Western Mail. Perth. Australia. 4th May 1901.
[7]   Research Essay on the Royal Party to the first Australian Parliament. Dr Jacqueline Hollingworth. AGORA, Volume 34, No 3, 1999. Pages 32 to 35. RMS Ophir. Keeble Antiques Website.
[8]   The Royal Archives Windsor. Letter of June 14th 2004.
[9]   The Forbes Adam Archive. Brymor Jones Library. University of Hull. Lord Wenlock's correspondence – May 7th 1901.
[10] Krakatoa. Simon Winchester. Viking. London. 2003. Page 189.
[11] Parliamentary Education Office, Parliament House, Canberra, ACT, Australia, 2600.
[12] Western Mail. Perth. May 11th 1901.
[13] Eustace Lord Wraxall's "Lawley" Albums in the Empire and Commonwealth Museum. Bristol. UK
[14] World Wide Web. govhouse.wa.gov.au/cgi-bin/speeches
[15] Western Mail. Perth. June 8th 1901.
[16] Western Mail. Perth. June 15th 1901. Speech of Sir Arthur Lawley, K.C.M.G., Governor on opening the First Session of the Fourth Parliament, 28th June 1901.
[17] Western Mail. Perth. July 6th 1901.
[18] Western Mail. Perth. July 27th 1901.
[19] Wikipedia Encyclopaedia.
[20] World Wide Web. The Peerage.com.
[21] Western Mail. Perth. January 4th 1902.
[22] Eustace Lord Wraxall's "Lawley" Albums in the Empire and Commonwealth Museum. Bristol. UK
[23] Western Mail. Perth. January 11th 1902.
[24] Western Mail. Perth. January 18th 1902.
[25] Western Mail. Perth. April 12th 1902.
[26] Western Mail. Perth. May 17th 1902.
[27] Western Mail. Perth. July 5th 1902.
[28] Western Mail. Perth. May 24th 1902.
[29] Eustace Lord Wraxall's "Lawley" Albums in the Empire and Commonwealth Museum. Bristol. UK
[30] Lorraine Hayes. Lady Lawley Cottage. Western Australian Red Cross. 2006
[31] Western Australian Musical Memoirs on line.
[32] Western Mail, 7th June 1902
[33] Western Mail, 3rd June 1902.
[34] www.ntwa.com.au/convention/paper D Malcolm.rtf .
[35] Rottnest Island Brochure.

[36] History of the Australian Environment Movement by Drew Hutton: Cambridge University Press; (1999) ISBN: 052145686X

[37] Australian Trading World. 24th July 1902. Opening of the West Australian Parliament. Speech of Sir Arthur Lawley, K.C.M.G., Governor on opening the First Session of the Fourth Parliament, 17th July 1902.

[38] The Western Australian. August 15th 1902. Perth. Western Australia.

[39] Research Essay on the Royal Party to the first Australian Parliament. Dr Jacqueline Hollingworth. AGORA, Volume 34, No 3, 1999. Pages 32 to 35.

[40] Morning Herald. Perth Australia. August 1902.

[41] The Times. Friday August 15th 1902.

Chapter 4
South Africa – Peace and Reconciliation

At the urgent request of Lord Alfred Milner, Sir Arthur Lawley had been transferred to Southern Africa. He arrived in Pretoria on August 31st 1902. On Monday 1st September there was an official reception for the new Lieutenant-Governor at the Government Buildings in Pretoria.[1] In welcoming him, Mr Loveday, the Chairman of the Town Council said, "We gratefully appreciate the sacrifice Your Excellency has made in relinquishing the office of Governor in a settled and prosperous colony to assume the burdens of Lieutenant-Governor in one just emerging from a devastating war. The next few years in this country can scarcely fail to be of an epoch making character and of unique interest not only to South Africa, but to the whole Empire. In addition to the work of resettlement and reorganisation, which is going on, there will be the still greater one of developing the enormous resources of a country rich in mineral, pastoral and agricultural wealth." In his reply Sir Arthur said that it was his earnest desire to aid in the restoration of the country to peace, prosperity, freedom and strength. He promised to devote himself to the welfare and happiness of every section of the community.

Sir Alfred Milner, who ascended to the peerage in May 1901 as Lord Milner, was Governor of the Cape of Good Hope from 1897 to 1901 and High Commissioner for South Africa from 1897 to 1905. From 1902 to 1905 he relinquished the governorship of the Cape to become the Governor of the Orange River Colony (formerly the Orange Free State) and the Transvaal. Sir Arthur Lawley was appointed as Lieutenant-Governor of the Transvaal. This meant that he took special responsibility for the Transvaal under the overall leadership of Lord Milner.

In a letter of April 29th 1902, Lord Milner gave his reasons for recommending Sir Arthur as Lieutenant-Governor.[2] He said, "My selection if I had to select would be Lawley. I know him well and know he would take responsibility yet play to my lead. He knows South Africa and is immensely popular with all classes of its inhabitants. He has had to deal in Rhodesia with problems of the same kind though certainly not of the same size *as in the Transvaal,* and has shown a statesman's tact in dealing with them. He has a charming and capable wife. The social side, which I cannot supply, has its importance. The lack of a first class Englishwoman in a high position is greatly felt and will be increasingly felt if ever we have peace." When he was Administrator of Matabeleland, Captain Arthur Lawley had corresponded regularly with Sir Alfred Milner and kept him informed of events in Rhodesia. Indeed when Cecil Rhodes was besieged in Kimberley, Arthur Lawley had used the funds of the British South Africa Company to establish an effective force to defend Rhodesia from the Boers. In this he had collaborated with Milner and was therefore able to make a vital contribution to the eventual Relief of Mafeking in 1900.[3]

The Cape of Good Hope, which was settled by Dutch colonists, had been occupied by Britain at the invitation of the Prince of Orange in 1795. He had been driven off the throne by Dutch republicans supported by the French. Between 1802 and 1806, the territory was ceded to the Republic of Batavia. In 1806, the Cape was reoccupied by the British as the Napoleonic Wars continued. At the Congress of Vienna, in 1815, the Cape of Good Hope with its 16,000 Dutch colonists was ceded to Great Britain. British immigrants moved into the Cape of Good Hope in 1820, and later into Natal.

The Dutch settlers and farmers, unhappy with British rule, decided to move north on to the great open plateau of the High Veldt in the Great Trek of 1836. They called themselves Afrikaners, and their dialect of the Dutch language Afrikaans. They founded two new Afrikaner states – the Transvaal and the Orange Free State. These were recognised as independent states by Britain in 1852 and 1853. Natal became a separate Crown Colony in 1853. [4] There were wars with the Zulus, but the indigenous population was not as numerous as today and there was plenty of empty land. In 1853, the discovery of gold deposits in the Transvaal led to a gradual influx of prospectors and fortune seekers. In 1886, the rich goldfields of the Witwatersrand were opened up, a gold rush occurred, and the major gold mining corporations grew from then onwards. In December 1895, the Jameson Raid, an attempted invasion of the Transvaal to incite a rebellion, failed disastrously. As has already been observed, the forces involved were associated with the British South Africa Company and Cecil Rhodes.

The Boer War was a bitter struggle between the Dutch Afrikaner republics of the Transvaal and Orange Free State on the one hand and Britain with the Cape of Good Hope and Natal on the other. There were also British settlers called 'Uitlanders' in the Boer republics, and Dutch inhabitants in the Cape and Natal. These Dutch settlers formed a group known as the Bond. The War broke out two days after the Transvaal gave the British an ultimatum on October 9th 1899 demanding the withdrawal of British troop reinforcements that had been sent to the Cape.

Figure 93: Field Marshall Roberts.

Figure 94: General Kitchener painted by Sir Hubert Von Herkomer, 1890.

The war was hard fought and the Afrikaners were a resourceful and relentless foe. After an initial period of severe defeats by the Boers, the British under Field Marshall Sir Frederick Roberts and General Horatio Kitchener were able to take the capital cities of the Orange Free State and the Transvaal. The British, including Captain

George Abraham Gibbs of Tyntesfield serving with the North Somerset Yeomanry,[K] occupied the capital of the Transvaal, Pretoria, in June 1900 and in September Britain formally annexed the territory. The Afrikaners then took to guerrilla warfare with considerable success. In November 1900, Kitchener succeeded Roberts as Commander in Chief. During the last 18 months of the war, Kitchener combated guerrilla resistance by such methods as burning Boer farms and herding Boer women and children into disease-ridden concentration camps. Kitchener divided the country into sectors with great barbed wire fences. The strategic construction of a network of blockhouses across the country localized and isolated the Boers' forces and steadily weakened their resistance. The indigenous population was also herded into camps.

Fighting between the Boers and British continued until the resources of both Boer republics had been broken by unceasing strain against superior forces. The Boer War ended with the signing of the Peace Treaty of Vereeniging at Melrose House in Pretoria on May 31st 1902. The treaty ended the independence of the Transvaal and Orange Free State, which became British crown colonies.

On returning to England after the British victory in the Boer War, despite severe criticism of his strategy of barbed wire and concentration camps, Kitchener was made a viscount in July 1902, and was appointed as Commander in Chief of the Army of India (1902 - 1909).[5]

After the Boer War, the British High Commissioner for South Africa, Lord Alfred Milner, dedicated himself to the tasks of building the peace and reviving the economy. Milner's financial policies aided economic recovery in South Africa where he remained in until the end of March 1905, working for the assimilation of the Boer territories into a South African federation firmly linked to Britain. During this period he gathered around him a group of able young administrators, including Leo Amery, Robert Brand, John Buchan, the author and later Governor General of Canada, Lionel Curtis, Philip Kerr, and Geoffrey Robinson, who changed his name to Dawson in 1917 in order to inherit a family estate. These men became known as "Milner's kindergarten". Geoffrey Robinson was Milner's secretary in South Africa (1901-1905), Editor of the Johannesburg Star (1905-1910) and then editor of the Times in London from 1912 to 1919 and from 1922 to 1941. Philip Henry Kerr (1882-1940), the 11th Marquess of Lothian in 1930, journalist and statesman, was educated at New College, Oxford. He went in 1902 to South Africa as private secretary to Sir Arthur Lawley.[6] He was the British ambassador in Washington in 1940 at the time of his death.

Sir Arthur Lawley's post as the Lieutenant-Governor of the Transvaal was a most important one. The Transvaal contained the world's largest gold field and very valuable diamond mines. After the Boer War, the administration concentrated on restoring the mines to full working capacity and on settling British immigrants in rural areas to create a balance between the British and the Boers. At heart a moderate and humane man, Sir Arthur had the difficult task of reconciling the British and the Afrikaners. In this he was received constructive criticism and co-operation from his former enemy, Jan Christian Smuts. Smuts had concluded that an alliance of Boer and British communities was essential for the future of South Africa, and he joined with Louis Botha, the former commander of the Boer forces, to achieve this.[7] Indeed Smuts' contribution to the resolution of the conflict between the Boers and the British was to lead to much improved relations between the two communities.

[K] Captain Gibbs later married the Lawley's elder daughter, Ursula.

On Saturday 25th October 1902, there was a Banquet at the Wanderers Club to officially welcome Sir Arthur Lawley to the Transvaal. The Municipality, the Chamber of Mines, the Chambers of Trade and Commerce and the Stock Exchange combined forces to make this a sumptuous and memorable evening. It was a men only occasion. Over three hundred of the leading citizens of Pretoria and Johannesburg attended the dinner. In his reply to the "Toast of Welcome", Sir Arthur said, "I confess I do not find it easy to find words simple enough or strong enough to give adequate expression to my recognition of the honour which you have done me this evening…It is a source of very great gratification to me that so many representatives of all that is most distinguished in the social, the political and the professional life of the Transvaal should have united in so cordial a demonstration of goodwill towards me." Referring to the recent Boer War and to Lord Milner's part in the conflict, he continued, "The hurricane of war is now over, but thank God that the man, who held the rudder through the roughest weather of it all, is still here; and believe me it is no mean honour to be flag lieutenant to such an admiral." Sir Arthur went on to outline the problems facing the Transvaal, problems of the repatriation and resettlement of the Boers, of the closing of the Burgher Camps, of assisting agriculture and of promoting agricultural improvement. He discussed the restoration of normality to the indigenous population after the excesses of war and suggested that the dignity of labour should unite the black man and the white man. He concluded by saying, "The one goal in view is the establishment of a just, fair and stable Government – a just Government that we may interpret aright the mandate given to us by the British nation; a firm Government that we may establish a sense of security and of confidence in the minds of the inhabitants of this Colony; and a stable Government that we may make practical application of that popular democratic system which has come to be recognised as the most perfect form of constitutional government which the world has ever seen."[8]

Concentration Camps

Although interested in promoting the well being of the indigenous population of the Transvaal, this was not the top priority for Sir Arthur Lawley after all the bitterness of the Boer war. The most important tasks were reconciliation of the former enemies and post-war reconstruction. The Boers, Afrikaners of Dutch origin, had seen the British army commanded by Lord Kitchener divide their countryside into sectors with barbed wire fences and herd their people into concentration camps, where many children and old people, men and women died due to lack of adequate food, shelter and sanitation. According to a British journalist, W.T. Stead, the concentration camps were nothing more than a cruel torture machine. He regarded the policy of herding the civilian population into tented camps surrounded by barbed wire as perverse and evil. He wrote:

"Every one of these children, who died as a result of the halving of their rations, thereby exerting pressure on to their family still on the battlefield, was purposefully murdered. The system of half rations stands exposed and stark and unshamefully as a cold-blooded deed of state policy employed with the purpose of ensuring the surrender of people whom we were not able to defeat on the battlefield."

Emily Hobhouse, a Quaker aid worker visiting the camps, wrote:

"I soon found out that there was a scarcity of essential provisions. The accommodation was wholly inadequate. When the eight, ten or twelve people who

lived in the bell tent were squeezed into it to find shelter against the heat of the sun, the dust or the rain, there was no room to stir and the air in the tent was beyond description, even though the flaps were rolled up properly and fastened. Soap was an article that was not dispensed. The water supply was inadequate. No bedstead or mattress was procurable. Fuel was scarce and had to be collected from the green bushes on the slopes of the kopjes by the people themselves. The rations were extremely meagre and when, as I frequently experienced, the actual quantity dispensed fell short of the amount prescribed, it simply meant famine. What most distressed the women were the sufferings of their undernourished children. Sicknesses such as measles, bronchitis, pneumonia, dysentery and typhoid had already invaded the camp with fatal results."

"I saw families huddled up close to the railway line near Warrenton and Fourteen Streams. I saw an overcrowded train crawling along to Kimberley throughout a whole long night. I saw people, old and young, bundled in open trucks under a scorching sun near a station building without anything to eat. At midnight they were transported to empty tents where they groped about in the dark, looking for their little bundles. They went to sleep without any provision having been made for them and without anything to eat or to drink. I saw crowds of them along railway lines in bitterly cold weather, in pouring rain - hungry, sick, dying and dead." [9]

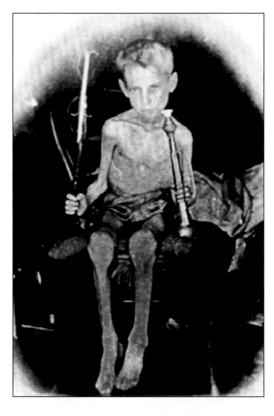

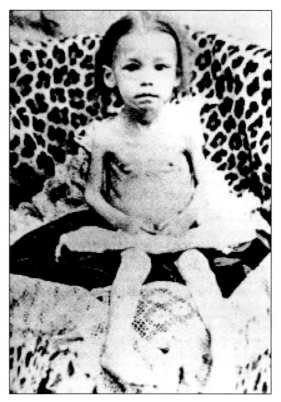

Figure 95: Abraham Carel Wessels.   **Figure 96: Starving little girl.**

Child starvation in British Concentration Camps, South Africa, 1901.

There were 110,000 prisoners in the camps in 1902 and deaths averaged 250 a week. 27,000 people died in British Concentration Camps, many of them women and children. The Dutch were understandably very bitter and deeply resented the British invasion and annexation of their lands. Not only were the Boers imprisoned, but also the indigenous population, and in fact there were 65 Black Concentration Camps, which is many more than the 47 Boer Camps. The statistics above do not include the African camps.

Figure 97: The Concentration Camp at Norvalspont.

A group of Quakers led by Lawrence Richardson arrived in South Africa to see what could be done to assist the beleaguered Boers. They got an introduction to the private secretary of Sir Arthur Lawley, which led to an interview with Mr Patrick Duncan, the Treasurer of the Transvaal, who was head of the repatriation work in the colony and who gave them full information as to how this work was being managed. They also had a letter from Sir Arthur Lawley asking magistrates and camp superintendents to give them full facilities for seeing things. Lawrence Richardson was extremely glad to have thus got on the right side of the officials and be able to go about freely. He hoped to be able to keep on good terms with the officials and with the Dutch as well. There was no doubt that the officials were doing their best towards the rebuilding of the country and were achieving a great deal. Nevertheless the work of repatriation was so gigantic that it was not to be wondered at if hitches and breakdowns occurred.

The country had been swept bare, away from the railways hardly a house had retained its roof, and most of the livestock had been destroyed. A reliable authority, Howard Pim, estimated that the Boers had lost five sixths of their property to the value of £25,000,000. The railways were unable to bring in all the stores that were wanted and they were seriously behind schedule. The transportation of cattle was a still more serious question. It was estimated that only 100,000 cattle were left in the Orange River Colony and 50,000 in the Transvaal, and that these were in such poor condition that a trek to an out-lying district might have taken a fortnight where it ought to have taken a week. Ploughing could only be done by lending animals round from one farm to another. All sorts of dangers lay ahead - rinderpest, horse sickness and other diseases, failure of the mealie crop from too little rain or impassable highways from too much rain. Nevertheless the work of repatriation was going forward and over half the people had returned to their farms. Those that were still left in the camps were mostly 'bywoners' (poor landless whites) and widows. These were the people with most problems and there was a great danger that a pauper class would be formed - and South Africa as yet had no poorhouses.[10]

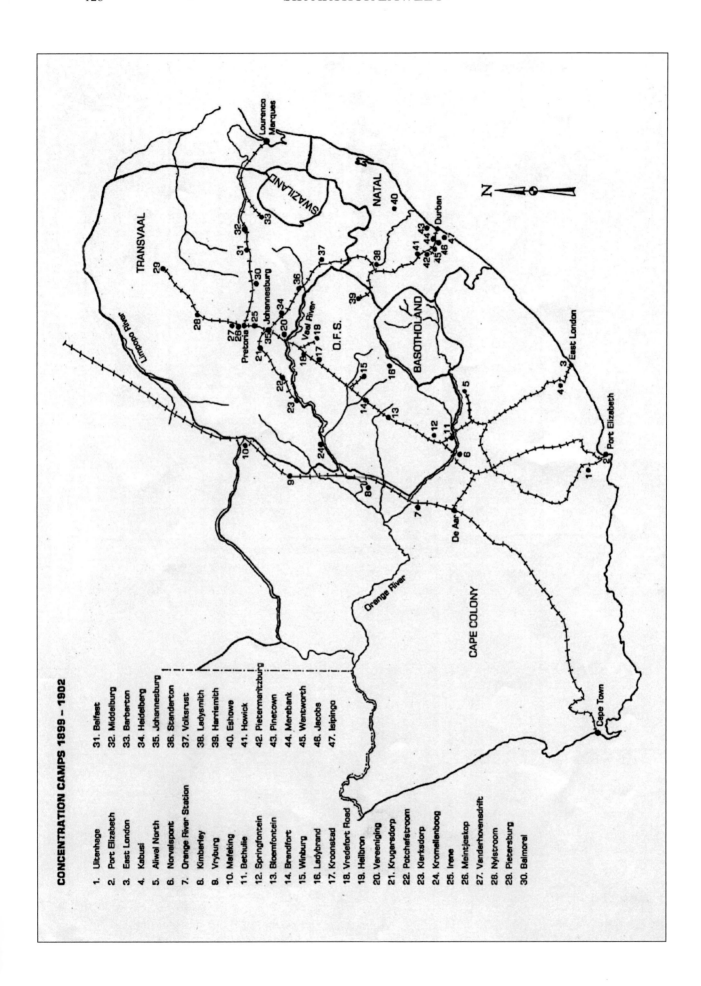

CONCENTRATION CAMPS 1899 – 1902

1. Uitenhage
2. Port Elizabeth
3. East London
4. Kabusi
5. Aliwal North
6. Norvalspont
7. Orange River Station
8. Kimberley
9. Vryburg
10. Mafeking
11. Bethulie
12. Springfontein
13. Bloemfontein
14. Brandfort
15. Winburg
16. Ladybrand
17. Kroonstad
18. Vredefort Road
19. Heilbron
20. Vereeniging
21. Krugersdorp
22. Potchefstroom
23. Klerksdorp
24. Kromellenboog
25. Irene
26. Meintjeskop
27. Vanderhovensdrift
28. Nylstroom
29. Pietersburg
30. Balmoral
31. Belfast
32. Middelburg
33. Barberton
34. Heidelberg
35. Johannesburg
36. Standerton
37. Volksrust
38. Ladysmith
39. Harrismith
40. Eshowe
41. Howick
42. Pietermaritzburg
43. Pinetown
44. Merebank
45. Wentworth
46. Jacobs
47. Isipingo

Figure 98: British soldiers destroy a Boer Farm; part of Kitchener's scorched earth policy.

In London, following Emily Hobhouse's reports, in 1902 the Fawcett Commission of the British Parliament reported on the state of the Camps in South Africa. This was a Committee of Ladies appointed by the Secretary of State for War. Lady Millicent Garrett Fawcett was the President and Lucy A.E. Deane was the Secretary. This Commission represented an important step on the road to political rights for women.

Sir Arthur Lawley was responsible for implementing the Commission's recommendations in order to endeavour to resolve the crisis. The Fawcett Commission required the provsion of education for the children of school age, proper medical care for the sick, an improved and balanced diet, and work for the men and women who sought employment. The inmates of the camps were to be resettled in their home areas as soon as possible with the means to rebuild their houses and their farms.[11] Doctors, nurses and teachers were recruited in Britain, Australia and New Zealand.

Gradually African and Boer families were brought back from the concentration camps to be rehabilitated on their own lands. On being released from the camps, the people were allowed to take away their tents, bedsteads, cooking utensils and personal effects. They were also given a month's rations free. A wagon and oxen were lent just to take them home. Anything else they required – ploughs, seeds, cattle for their own use, further supplies of food, building materials and so forth – these were supplied by the Repatriation Board for their local district. Only what we would now consider the very barest necessities were supplied and thus they had to live in tents, while getting the ground ploughed and sown, and then set to work to repair their houses with sun-dried bricks and corrugated iron. They managed to make a start, where English people would have starved helplessly. On October 14th 1902, a deputation of influential Boer farmers visited Sir Arthur Lawley to seek cash loans to enable the burghers to purchase livestock, tools, seed and farm machinery where these were not available from Repatriation Boards. The authorities arranged to grant loans of £200 to each of the burghers to enable them to make these purchases.[12]   On October 17th, the same delegation saw the Lieutenant-Governor again, and was told that half a million sterling was to be made available for the restocking of the country in the form of a loan at 4½ per cent against security of the land. Sir Arthur said that the Government hoped that by November 1st it would have at its disposal nearly ten thousand cattle, five thousand horses, three thousand mules and one thousand donkeys.[13] The loans were to be distributed through the local Repatriation Commissions acting in consultation with the farmers themselves. The farmers were encouraged on receipt of their loans to proceed by rail to Natal or Cape Province to purchase livestock, trekking back with the cattle if they so wished. This was just the beginning of what would be an extensive programme of rehabilitation after the Boer War. By 1907, Britain had paid out more than £9,500,000 in compensation to the Boers.

Figure 99: A Boer Family returns home, Rietfontein.

Empire Builders

This was an age of Empire Builders, who believed that the British had a God given right to rule much of the world. This would now be regarded as racist and 'politically incorrect', but then it was the spirit of the age. The British were jingoistic and full of confidence. Joseph Chamberlain set the tone in a speech in Toronto in the winter of 1887. During this speech he said:

> *"I must emphasize the greatness and importance of the distinction reserved for the Anglo-Saxon race, that proud, persistent, self-asserting and resolute stock which no change of climate or condition can alter, and which is infallibly bound to be the predominant force in the future history and civilisation of the world......The interest of true democracy is not towards anarchy or disintegration of the Empire, but rather to uniting together of kindred races with similar objectives......If Imperial Federation is a dream, it is a grand idea. It is one to stimulate the patriotism and*

statesmanship of every man who loves his country; and whether it be destined or not to perfect realisation, at least let us do all in our power to promote it."[14]

Lord Alfred Milner, summed this up in May 1913 when he wrote,

"The British race has become responsible for the peace and order, and just and humane government of nearly four hundred million people.... The Pax Britannica is essential to the maintenance of civilised conditions of existence among two fifths of the human race.... Our share of the white man's burden is an exceptional share...and we can bear it...only if we bring to the task the individual strength of the British race throughout the world, with all its immense possibilities of growth.... There is not the slightest reason to limit increase, provided that the stock be sound and as long as there are vast undeveloped areas under our own flag simply clamouring for more inhabitants.... I have emphasised the importance of the racial bond. From my point of view, that is fundamental. It is the British race that built the Empire, and it is the undivided British race which can alone uphold it."[15]

Figure 100: General Jan Christian Smuts with his Boer War horse "Charlie".

Chamberlain and Milner wanted to see British immigrants settle the vast empty spaces on the Veldt plateau of Southern and Central Africa. As far as the rights of the indigenous people were concerned, Milner wrote, in 1901, "that a distinction must be drawn in the case of natives between personal and political rights. A political equality of white and black is impossible, and I do not think that in any South African parliament the interest of blacks should be specially represented."[16] This now seems an extraordinary statement. Milner was ambivalent in his attitude towards race, asserting the idea of the British right to rule, while at the same time feeling uncomfortable at the notion that this assertion might deprive others of their legitimate rights.

Writing to Joseph Chamberlain on Boxing Day 1902, he further clarified his stance. "I should be very sorry and ashamed to see the policy of the new government towards Coloured Persons and Asiatics characterised by the same arbitrariness and even brutality as that of President Kruger.....I think that a compromise is perfectly possible which, while ensuring a decent status both to the Coloured Person and the Indian and as full protection of his rights as of those of any other class of the community, will nevertheless neither give him equality with the white man not allow him to swamp the white man." These provocative statements show the extent to which the assumption of British racial superiority prevailed.

Figure 101: Lord Alfred Milner.   **Figure 102: Joseph Chamberlain.**

Because of the post-war situation which faced Sir Arthur Lawley from 1902 to 1905, consideration of the rights of the African peoples was sadly not a priority. Sir Arthur reported that the Africans in the Transvaal had hoped that 'the old position of master and servant would be altered'. However the settlers and the British officials made every effort 'to maintain the relative position of the races as it existed in past days'. Milner and Lawley wanted to extend the municipal vote to aliens and also to coloured British subjects, who could pass an education test. This was in line with Cecil Rhodes' ideas as later expressed by Milner in 1905:

"I hold the view that the right lines on the colour question are based on the principle of Mr. Rhodes – equal rights for all civilised men. You may learn that the essence of wisdom is to be discriminating; not to throw all people of colour into one indistinguishable heap – but to follow closely the difference of race, of circumstance, and of degree of civilisation, and to adopt your policy intelligently and sympathetically to the several requirements of each."[17] Hence for Milner and Lawley education not race was the key to the franchise.

The Johannesburg municipal council, which consisted wholly of nominated white members, objected strongly to the coloured franchise. The administration wishing to reconcile the British and the Boers gave in to these objections. Because under the terms of the Peace of Vereeniging the franchise issue was to be left to an elected assembly, Sir Arthur Lawley was not empowered to legislate on this question. He was therefore not prepared to try to impose a franchise 'in opposition to the most deep-rooted sentiments of the white population'. He considered it unwise to endeavour to enforce 'a principle repudiated no less by the British inhabitants than by the Dutch'. His government was not ready to grant aliens a privilege denied to coloured British subjects, and so it excluded both, although a strong body of white opinion favoured the franchise for white aliens.[18]

Joseph Chamberlain, the Colonial Secretary, protested that he could not justify a continuation of the Boer Republic's discrimination, but Milner chose not to act upon Chamberlain's advice and continued the discriminatory policies. He did this to avoid antagonising the defeated Boers and to accommodate the prejudices of the White League, an organisation of shopkeepers and traders. Milner's main consideration was the maintenance of British supremacy. Such attitudes would be unacceptable and described as racist in modern society, but in late Victorian and Edwardian England they were accepted by many as being in keeping with the idea of Empire.

The visit of Joseph Chamberlain

The visit of Joseph Chamberlain, the Colonial Secretary, to South Africa helped to improve relations between the British and the Boers. Mr. Chamberlain and his wife arrived in Durban in the cruiser H.M.S. Good Hope on December 26th 1902.[19] Before leaving Durban, Chamberlain met an Indian delegation led by Mohandas Gandhi. "Unaware of the momentousness of the occasion, Chamberlain thus presided over a confrontation between Milnerite imperialism and its evolving Gandhian antithesis."[20] Joseph and Mary Chamberlain were met by Lord Milner and Sir Arthur Lawley on the Transvaal border on January 3rd 1903. Thence they travelled together by rail to Pretoria.

The Chamberlains and Lord Milner stayed with Sir Arthur and Lady Lawley at their official residence. On Monday 5th January, Lady Lawley threw a Garden Party at her home in Pretoria, which was attended by the Chamberlains and most of the leading political, commercial and social figures in the Transvaal. On January 6th, there was a Great banquet in Pretoria for Joseph Chamberlain given by the Chairman of the Municipal Council, Mr Loveday. Lord Milner, General De la Rey, Sir Arthur Lawley, General Louis Botha, General Baden-Powell and Sir Neville Lyttelton were all there. Joseph Chamberlain made an impassioned appeal for peace and reconciliation which was well received by all the guests.[21]

The next morning, in the capital of the Transvaal, Chamberlain received a Boer delegation with Jan Christian Smuts acting as their spokesman. He listened to their grievances and indicated that some concessions might be made with regard to language, education and policy towards the native peoples. Following these discussions, the Lieutenant-Governor, Sir Arthur Lawley, the Transvaal Colonial Secretary, W.R. Davidson and the Treasurer, Patrick Duncan met the Boer delegation which included Generals Botha and De la Rey, Commandant Boyers, Mr. Schalk Burger and their advocate, Jan Christian Smuts.[22] Sir Arthur opened the meeting by saying:

"I should like to assure you of the very great pleasure it gives me to see so many of your representatives this afternoon, and I hope the results of our conversation will be all that we desire for the advance and settlement of the country. I think it is the one object which we all have in view and I am only too glad of the advice which you have given me. If I can in any way facilitate and expedite that settlement by means that you may legitimately ask, I can assure you that it would give me the greatest pleasure to do so. I think from what little I have seen I shall be able to make a reply on almost every point. I shall be glad to know exactly what you propose."

Mr Burger raised the issue of the £3,000,000 promised by the British for the relief of people who could not help themselves – service personnel, police and landless labourers who were now unemployed. There was also concern about transport of goods. Sir Arthur said that hauliers and carriers would be given mules on loan from the Government so that these men could cease working in the mines and return to their normal trade, but that trolleys were in short supply. The delegates expressed their approval of the reduced freight rates on the railway and hoped that more could be done to facilitate the cheap transportation of replacement livestock by rail. The delegation considered that under the terms of the Peace Treaty aid should not be limited to farmers and that townsfolk should also receive financial assistance. There had been talk of the work of the Repatriation Commission being terminated and the Boers were anxious that this should not happen until the Government was satisfied that the rendering of any further assistance was unnecessary.

Sir Arthur informed the delegates that small land holders would in future be included in compensation schemes. Mr Burger said that most farmers had received six mules and eight oxen, but that the condition of the animals was so poor that little work could be expected from them. Sir Arthur announced that more animals would be given to larger farms to enable the farmers to lease some land and loan some animals to bywoners – landless labourers. However Mr. Burger pointed out that some of the animals delivered were too weak to work or were sick and had been later shot by the police. There were cases where oxen to be delivered had died on the road and farmers refusing these animals were told they would get no further assistance from the Repatriation Commission. Mr de Klerk suggested that animals should be branded to identify their owners. He then raised the question of the £200 limit on assistance for each farmer. He requested that the farmer be allowed to borrow an additional £500 on security of his land. Sir Arthur said the Government was prepared to raise the limit on assistance to £400. The Boer delegation wanted to see the importation of cattle on a much larger scale. They wanted to encourage private as well as government importation of livestock, but to discourage profiteering and speculators. Sir Arthur said that 85,000 head of cattle would be imported by May 31st 1903, but that caution was needed since protection against diseased animals was vital.

Sir Arthur also emphasized his desire to see as many people as possible earning their own living. The question of pre-war Transvaal Government Bonds, Government Notes, Cheques and Postal Orders was raised. Sir Arthur, suspecting that Transvaal State Reserves had been sent abroad during the war, delayed a decision on this. General Botha said, "With reference to the charge that we sent out millions of pounds during the War, I can give the assurance that no money has been sent out to my knowledge. I discussed this question with Mr Chamberlain and I hope the matter will be settled and we can come to a proper agreement about it." Sir Arthur replied that his Treasurer was preparing a statement and was currently ascertaining the assets of the late government, but that if Mr Smuts would prepare a statement on the arrears of salary of individual officials, the government would consider these on their own merits. The Boer delegation requested the new government to take over all the assets and official debts of the former government. They also wished to ensure that the British Army paid the monies due under its contracts and promissory notes.

Sir Arthur raised the problem of war orphans and asked for the views of the Boer delegation. Commandant Boyers expressed concern about unsatisfactory guardians and said that the Afrikaner Community would like to take control of the children. Mr Botha and General De la Rey wished to see the church supervise the upbringing and education of the orphans in the vicinity of their former homes. They were concerned about institutionalisation in large orphanages. They said that Mr Chamberlain had expressed his support for their suggestions. The British had said that they would support widows and orphans from the war. The Boer delegates wished to know what that support would be.

The question of land tenure was raised and Sir Arthur said that there were three categories of land occupancy:-

1. Where there was proper title and the conditions of occupancy were fulfilled.
2. Where the land was occupied by squatters and conditions were not fulfilled.
3. Where the land was held without condition and it would be necessary for a Committee to establish the position of the occupants.

Where necessary a time extension could be granted to resolve the question of property rights.

Mr Smuts raised the question of punishment for crimes committed during the recent war. He drew the Lieutenant-Governor's attention to a case in the Middleburg District where two men had murdered another man. Sir Arthur promised to look into this matter. Mr Smuts also raised the question of the new Liquor Law which prohibited distillation by a farmer from his own vineyard. Sir Arthur promised to raise this issue when the legislation was formulated for consideration by the assembly.

Jan Smuts also asked that the Government Gazette be published in Afrikaans as well as English. He raised too, the issue of Burghers who were living in exile and wished to return to the Transvaal. A Transvaal delegation to Europe was also being refused repatriation. He emphasized that the Afrikaner community would vouch for their good conduct. The cases of ex-Commandant Malan, a wounded prisoner who had surrendered to the British, and of Willie Mangle, who was also seriously injured were raised. General Botha emphasized that according to the Peace Treaty Afrikaners should be permitted to return to their homes and families.

In thanking the delegation for their suggestions and advice, Sir Arthur emphasized that the Administration wished to resolve the issues raised and provide satisfactory solutions to the problems discussed. He hoped that this would be the first of many such meetings.

On the 8th January there was a great meeting in the Randsaal, where Paul Kruger used to preside over the Transvaal Parliament. At 11.00 am Joseph Chamberlain, Lord Milner, Sir Arthur Lawley, General De la Rey and General Louis Botha entered the chamber and went on to the raised platform. Chamberlain addressed the gathering and announced the measures that were to be taken to bring peace, reconciliation, reconstruction, social stability and prosperity to the people of the Transvaal. He said that the British Government would provide between £10 million and £15 million to meet the costs involved. Botha had thanked the Europeans for the £100,000 they had donated but had not thanked Chamberlain, which caused him considerable annoyance. Chamberlain accepted the invitation to tour the Western Transvaal and visit Mafeking. [23]

Figure 103: Joseph and Mary Chamberlain at the Lawleys' residence in Pretoria.

From Pretoria, on Saturday 10th January, the Chamberlains continued their journey to Johannesburg, where they spent a fortnight with Lord Milner at Sunnyside, the High Commissioner's residence and headquarters. Together they discussed plans for the future of South Africa. "The spirit of reconciliation ran throughout Chamberlain's remarks in South Africa, always accompanied by a note of firmness in upholding the gains Britain had fought to achieve. In his first major speech on December 27th 1902, he had announced that his aim in South Africa was to see if "out of these two great kindred races we cannot make a fusion – a nation stronger in its unity than either of its parts would be alone."[24]

On Wednesday 14th January, Lord Milner threw a Garden Party in the grounds of his residence, Sunnyside, for Joseph Chamberlain and his wife. Geoffrey Robinson in his diary described it as "a great success with a thousand people there and Joseph Chamberlain with Lord Milner out on the lawn talking to people all the time."[25] On Saturday 17th January, there was a great dinner given for Joseph Chamberlain at the Wanderers Sports Club attended by six hundred guests at which Mr. Chamberlain gave a tremendous oration encouraging a union of the peoples of South Africa and announcing the settlement of the War Debt. He praised the British Empire and encouraged all South Africans to participate in the imperial venture. He concluded his speech by saying,

"The day of small kingdoms with petty jealousies is past. The future is with the great empires. There is no greater empire than the British Empire. The Mother Country has set the example. She has thrown off the apathy and indifference of past generations. No longer do we hear from statesmen to whom separation from the colonies is almost an object of desire. The colonies, on their part, have reciprocated that feeling. They have abandoned provincialism and are agreed to play their part in the glorious empire which is theirs as well as ours. They are ready to undertake the obligations which go with the privileges. That is the spirit which exists and which I desire shall continue. Let us say with the colonial poet:

Unite the Empire, make it stand compact,
Shoulder to shoulder; let its members feel
The touch of human brotherhood and act
As one great nation, true and strong as steel."

Lord Milner and Sir Arthur Lawley in their speeches in response adopted a similar vein.[26]

Figure 104: Sunnyside, Johannesburg, Lord Milner's Home, with Lawley and Farrar girls.

On the morning of Thursday January 22nd, Joseph and Mary Chamberlain, Lord Milner and Sir Arthur Lawley left Park Station by Special Train amid the cheers of large crowds assembled on the platform and outside the station. At Krugersdorp, where they stopped for half an hour, Mr Chamberlain spoke to the assembled crowd. He regretted the losses incurred on both sides during the war and said that the future prosperity of the country depended on the co-operation of all. The Chamberlains spent the night at Potchefstroom, which lay in a predominantly Boer region, where the visitors were the guests of a Dutch resident, Mr. Jooste. The following day they received a spontaneous and hearty welcome from the citizens of Potchefstroom many of whom had surrendered early rather than continue the guerrilla war. In the afternoon they visited General Andries Cronje's farm where triumphal arches and decorations welcomed Joseph Chamberlain, who was quite astonished when some of the Boers unhitched the horses from his carriage and "dragged him in triumph past the long line of wagons outspanned along the main approach." General Cronje headed a Boer Land Syndicate to resettle dispossessed Boers on the land and to enable them to earn their own livelihood.

Figure 105: General J.H. De la Rey.

Figure 106: General Louis Botha.

Figure 107: Mr Chamberlain steps down from the wagon on the trek to Mafeking,

Joseph Chamberlain spoke to the assembled crowd expressing the hope that many of the Boers who had been landless bywoners in the past would now have the opportunity of keeping themselves and their children on their own farms. This was greeted by loud cheers. Mr Chamberlain concluded his visit on the morning of January 24th, by going to see forty British farmers who had recently settled to the south of Potchefstroom. He encouraged them to persevere with their venture assuring them that the government would help as far as possible.

Mr Chamberlain and his wife, joined by Sir Arthur Lawley and Major General Baden-Powell, then set out on their wagon trek from Potchestroom to Mafeking. They travelled in a Cape cart or covered wagon. They were well looked after.[27] The tents in which they sometimes slept were carpeted and well furnished, "veritable palaces of Aladdin in the middle of the rural simplicity of the Dutch township." Five hundred pounds of ice were sent ahead to each halting place. Chamberlain and his party were surprised by the warm welcome they received from the Boers both former collaborators and former foes. Mr. Chamberlain was deeply moved by "the mystery and beauty of the veldt," and affected more than he anticipated by the ravages of the recent war. En route, they were met just outside Ventersdorp by a commando of Boers, who accompanied them into town. The Colonial Secretary was escorted to the house of the district magistrate, where the Boer commando formed a semi-circle. Mrs. Mary Chamberlain was presented with a bouquet of flowers while Mr. Joseph Chamberlain was cordially greeted by General De la Rey. The Colonial Secretary congratulated the Boers on being the comrades of so great and gallant a man as General De la Rey and then said, "I hope he is my friend and I hope you are all my friends. We fought a good fight and there is nothing to be ashamed of on either side." General De la Rey made a speech in Dutch. He thanked his hearers for coming together to welcome Mr Chamberlain, and said that as soon as he met him in London, he recognized that he was a strong man, and felt sure that if anyone could do good service to South Africa it was Mr. Chamberlain. He hoped that the Boers would be as good subjects to the new government as they had been to the old.

Together they journeyed on through Lichtenburg to Ottoshoop near Mafeking.[28] After a brief visit to the local schools, Mr and Mrs Chamberlain, Sir Arthur Lawley and General Baden-Powell drove to the Court House. Here an address of welcome was read from the farmers of Zeerust and district expressing their confidence in the Government and their satisfaction about what had already been done for the country. It also urged that railway connections should be provided to Zeerust. Mr Chamberlain replied with a speech encouraging progressive development and peaceful co-operation between the British and the Boers.[29]

Then they travelled on to Mafeking, where the Chamberlains were met by the Bulawayo and Mafeking Cadets, who were drawn up outside the house where they were going to stay. Joseph Chamberlain congratulated them on having taken part at such a young age in the defence of the Empire. The following morning, Mr and Mrs Chamberlain were shown around the siege works at Mafeking by General Baden-Powell. Then they continued their journey by rail to the city of Bloemfontein in the Orange River Colony and thence through Port Elizabeth and Grahamstown in the Eastern Cape Colony to Cape Town, where they embarked on the Union Castle steamer S.S. Norman on February 25th 1903 to sail home to England.

On February 16th 1903, the only Boers left in concentration camps were at Brandford Camp and they were due to leave soon. On March 5th, arrangements were put in place for Boer prisoners in India to be repatriated. Concern had been expressed about the treatment of Boer prisoners of war at Fort Gorindgarth in India. On March 18th, Major Pretorius set sale for Bermuda to persuade recalcitrant Boer prisoners of war to make a Declaration of Allegiance and return home.[30]

Gandhi and the birth of Satyagraha

Mohandas Gandhi had arrived in Natal in May 1893 intending to try his luck as a lawyer in South Africa. He had established himself in legal practice defending the rights of the minority Indian population in Natal and the Transvaal. In 1900, Gandhi had said he "must do his bit in the war" and started an Indian Ambulance Corps. He left Natal to join the army with a small band of Indian stretcher-bearers. Nearly 1,100 Indians served in Gandhi's Ambulance Corps caring for wounded British and Empire troops during the war against the Boer Republics.

Figure 108: Mohandas K. Gandhi, Barrister at Law.

After the Boer War, Gandhi thought that Britain had betrayed the hopes of the Indians who had helped them. The specific reasons given for legislation to restrict the Asian community were flimsy and contradictory. Indians were said to have unsanitary habits and to live in squalor, but so did many poor whites in the slums of Fordsburg and Vrededorp and they were never segregated by law. Asian immigration was said to threaten white supremacy. Yet Lord Milner, Sir Arthur Lawley and the mine owners imported 43,000 Chinese for the mines against protests from South Africans of all races. On the other hand, Indians were accused of out-trading whites and using their 'immense wealth', as Lawley described it, to buy out the 'credulous and ignorant Dutch farmer'. According to Sir Arthur Lawley, whites were to be protected against Indians in what he called a 'struggle between East and West for the inheritance of the semi-vacant territories of South Africa'.[31] This statement was in line with Lord

Milner's belief that British settlers should move into the vast open spaces of Southern Africa.

Gandhi often came into conflict with the white supremacist attitudes of the British administration. Summarising white prejudices, Gandhi noted that "the very qualities of Indians count for defects in South Africa. They were disliked for their simplicity, patience, perseverance, frugality and other-worldliness". A voiceless minority numbering less than five per cent of the white population of the Transvaal, the Indians were not politically represented either municipally or provincially. Yet their modest claim to reasonable treatment as civilised citizens of the Empire was callously disregarded. "The promises held out to them in the pre-war days by professed champions of their cause" were, according to Sir Arthur Lawley, "now more broken than kept".[32]

In his book "Satyagraha", M.K. Gandhi describes his experiences in South Africa. "I was now confronted by a dilemma even more difficult than the one which faced me in 1894. From one standpoint, it seemed I could return to India as soon as Mr Chamberlain left South Africa. On the other hand I could clearly see that if I returned with the vain fancy of serving on a larger field in India while I was fully aware of the great danger which stared the South African Indians in the face, the spirit of service which I had acquired would be stultified. I thought that even if that meant living in South Africa all my life, I must remain there until the gathering clouds were dispersed or until they broke upon us and swept us all away, all our counteracting efforts notwithstanding. This is how I spoke to the Indian leaders. Now, as in 1894, I declared my intention to maintain myself by legal practice. As for the community, this was precisely what they wanted.

"I soon applied for admission to practise in the Transvaal. There was some apprehension that the Law Society here too would oppose my application, but it proved groundless. I was enrolled as an attorney of the Supreme Court, and opened an office in Johannesburg. Of all places in the Transvaal, Johannesburg had the largest population of Indians and was therefore well suited for me to settle in, from the standpoint of public work as well as of my own maintenance. I was daily gaining bitter experience of the corruption of the Asiatic Department, and the best efforts of the Transvaal British Indian Association were directed to finding a remedy for this disease. The immediate aim was limited to saving ourselves from the on-rushing flood in shape of this Asiatic Department.

"Indian deputations waited upon Lord Milner, upon Lord Selborne who had come there, upon Sir Arthur Lawley who was Lieutenant-Governor of the Transvaal and who subsequently became Governor of Madras, and upon officers of lesser dignity. I often used to see Government officers. We obtained some slight relief here and there, but it was all patchwork. We used to receive some such satisfaction as is experienced by a man who has been deprived of his all by robbers and who by beseeching the robbers induces them to return something of very small value. Our misgivings as regards the restrictions on Indian immigration proved correct. Permits were no longer required from Europeans, while they continued to be demanded from Indians". [33]

The Asiatic Department had been set up by the Transvaal Government in 1902 to deal with Indian affairs. It was staffed in the main by British Army Officers who had come from India during the Boer War and had decided to stay on in South Africa. "Their mentality was that of white Sahibs in a colony of coloured inferiors." Gandhi knew that many of the Department's officials accepted bribes from Indians. When

Gandhi tried to convince Lionel Curtis of the Asiatic Department of the qualities of the Indians in South Africa, Curtis replied, "Mr Gandhi, you are preaching to the converted. It is not the vices of the Indians that Europeans in this country fear, but their virtues".[34]

Sir Arthur Lawley viewed the Indian position from an Empire perspective. Some of the support for the Indian cause in South Africa was due to calculations of political advantage within India. As Lord Curzon, the Viceroy of India from 1898 to 1905, explained, "the educated classes in India, who most resented the treatment of Indians in Africa, attached great value to those principles of freedom and equality which they had learnt to regard as the right of a British subject; and though not without its inconveniences, which are indeed daily becoming more obvious, it constitutes almost the only basis upon which an active loyalty to the rule of an alien conqueror is likely to be developed".

Support of Indian rights overseas was not caused by a belief in racial equality, but was rather a means of containing the challenge that the idea of equal human rights posed to British supremacy in India. Indeed Lord Curzon was careful to limit his claims on behalf of his Indian subjects. "We do not for one moment suggest", he told the Indian secretary, "nor do we regard it as possible, that Indians should enjoy in an African colony an absolute equality of right with the white colonists, for such equality does not exist even in India.. We do not, for instance, claim for them admission to the franchise, or inclusion on the general jury roll, for these institutions are foreign to their ideas." Curzon was unwilling to accept the view that "all citizens of the Empire, whatever their colour or origin, ought to be at liberty to live and labour in all parts of it on the same footing, unhampered by any racial disabilities or social and economic restrictions".

Only in England itself, where several Indians were elected to parliament during the 1890s, were Indians able to claim their full political rights, and to gain unhampered rights of immigration. Yet even there, as Sir Arthur Lawley observed, ideals of equality flourished only because Indian migration posed no threat to the livelihood of the English people. "As India is protected by her climate against Europeans", he wrote, "so England is protected by the same agency against the invasion of the Asiatic, to which South Africa is subject. But if it were not so, would the faith of those pledges of equal treatment be held to entitle the Indian shop-keeper to eliminate from English society the small shop-keeper and farmer?" Such views would be regarded as reprehensibly racist today. In the days of the Empire the British regarded themselves as a chosen elite superior to the indigenous peoples whom they ruled.[35]

The Indians in South Africa were most unhappy with the approach of Lord Milner and Sir Arthur Lawley. In November 1905, British Indians at Heidelburg presented a loyal address to Sir Arthur as the Lieutenant-Governor of the Transvaal, and in so doing drew his attention to the recently decided Test Case of *Habib Motan versus the Transvaal Government* on the Law of 1885. Following this test case, the position of Indians in the Transvaal as defined in Law 3 of 1885 (amended in 1886) was:

1. An Indian could immigrate into the colony without restriction.
2. He could trade anywhere he liked within the colony. Locations could be set aside for him, but the law could not enforce him only to reside in these locations because there was no sanction provided in the Law for this.
3. He could not become a burgher.
4. He could not own landed property except in locations.

5. He had to pay a registration fee of £3 on entering the colony.

The Indians of Heidelburg wanted their rights respected as was promised before the recent war. The Transvaal Indians has an influential friend in London with whom Gandhi corresponded frequently. This was Sir M.M. Bhownaggree, the Member of Parliament for Bethnal Green North East. On Wednesday June 7th 1905, he tabled a motion in the House of Commons which said, "This house regards with disapproval the degrading and harsh measures adopted in respect of his Majesty's Indian subjects in several British colonies, notably in South Africa, and considers them to be inconsistent with the reasonable claims of the people of India as subjects of the British Empire to fair treatment." [36] On June 21st 1905, Sir M.M. Bhownaggree complained in the House of Commons about the failure of the Transvaal Administration to keep promises made before the Boer War. He said that since the establishment of British rule in the Transvaal the state of British Indians in that colony had been worse than it was before. [37]

Figure 109: Heidelburg, Transvaal, 1903.

Dealing with the status of Indians in the Transvaal, Sir Arthur was very guarded and no wonder. He said that nothing could be done by the Government until sanction was received from the Colonial Secretary. Sir Arthur praised the industriousness and loyalty of the Indian community, but stressed that he sympathised very much with the desire of the white inhabitants not to be non-plussed by Asiatic traders. He made the British position clear in his memorandum of 13 April 1904 on the need for new legislation to control Indian trade and immigration.

The Opening of the Transvaal Legislative Council

On May 20th 1903, Sir Arthur Lawley as Lieutenant-Governor opened the Legislative Council in the Randsaal, Pretoria. This was the first British parliament in the Transvaal.[38] There was a full chamber with military officials, judges, clergy and civil authorities all dressed in uniforms or robes. In the Legislative Council, there were sixteen official members including the Lieutenant-Governor, who was the president, and fourteen unofficial members including six from the Rand and three Boers.[39] Many of the Boers who had been invited were conspicuously absent from this occasion."[40]

Figure 110: The first British Transvaal parliament in the Randsaal, Pretoria. To the right of Sir Arthur Lawley sit Prince Arthur of Connaught and General Lyttelton.

After the members had been sworn in, the Lieutenant-Governor delivered his inaugural address. In welcoming the new and enlarged Legislative Council, Sir Arthur said,

> *"The Transvaal has but recently emerged from a protracted period of storm and stress, of social upheaval and political convulsion. It is my earnest hope that all traces of the great struggle which has rent this country might subside. It is with the desire that this political consummation may be achieved, that a political institution has been so framed that while the various territories and different industries of this colony may as far as possible be represented in the Legislative body, such representative element may be introduced without recourse being had to a popular election, which would inevitably give rise to the bitterness of political and racial strife at a time when the country cries aloud for rest."*

Sir Arthur described the progress which had been made with repatriation and resettlement of Boer families and soldiers returning home after the war. He discussed payment of compensation and explained why some delays had occurred. He described the improved fiscal situation helped by the customs duties on imported goods, by a 10 per cent tax on the profits of the Gold Mines, and by increased railway revenues. He outlined the structure of the new judiciary with a Supreme Court sitting in Pretoria and a Witwatersrand High Court. The Government intended to introduce a system of Circuit Courts in districts beyond the main urban centres. There were also to be resident magistrates in each district.

Arrangements had been made for the creation of an Inter Colonial Council embracing the Transvaal and the Orange River Colony, which the High Commissioner would chair. This Council would be responsible for the public services which were common to the two colonies, in particular South African Railways and the South African Constabulary. This Council was the first step in the movement towards the creation of the Union of South Africa.

The Lieutenant-Governor reviewed the work accomplished, described the work to be done in the fields of transport, health, education, mining and the resettlement of the indigenous population, and outlined important measures for local self-government and heavy expenditure in the extension of railroads and other public works. He promised as far as possible to meet local sentiment with regard to education, saying that the Government recognized the rising generation as an asset to be developed to the highest degree. Provision would be made to teach the Dutch language, in accordance with the letter of the peace terms. Sir Arthur outlined the consideration being given to the establishment of a University in the Transvaal and said that a Commission had been established to "inquire into this question in connection especially with technical and agricultural education." He summed up his own sentiments by saying, "The idea of a South African University appeals to me as being one to the realisation of which the co-operation of the South African Colonies would be worthily devoted."

Sir Arthur also described the precautions which were to be taken to meet the danger of an outbreak of bubonic plague, cases of which had already occurred in neighbouring colonies. The fact that there had been an increase in cases of leprosy from 50 in June 1900 to 250 in May 1903 was a cause for concern which would require special attention.

There was considerable interest in the Transvaal's new diamond discoveries. Sir Arthur acknowledged this when he said, "Investigations have brought to light the existence of a diamond field, which bids fair to rival any field which has hitherto been discovered." Illicit diamond buying was one of several problems encountered by the South African diamond mines. Planned new legislation included an amended Diamond Law and also a revised Gold Law. Plans for the development of new iron ore and copper finds were also outlined. [41]

The Lieutenant-Governor spoke at length on Native Affairs. He said. "Recent events have had a very disturbing effect on the natives generally, resulting in the removal of many from their old dwelling places, the loss of much of their stock and a general disintegration and demoralisation. It has been deemed advisable to allow gradual resettlement to take place without any precipitate action on the part of the Government. Every encouragement has been given to the natives to return as tenants to their former landlords and to retain the relative position of the races as it existed in past days....I do not think that there is at the present time in the Transvaal any large surplus of natives to be reckoned on as available for increasing the existing labour supply....The general advancement and development of the natives will be stimulated and encouraged by the Government, but the process will naturally be gradual." The emphasis of this discourse was on the indigenous population as a source of labour supply, although some consideration was given to making farmland available for settlement and to providing food depots in districts where the recent harvest had been a failure.

Figure 111: Captain King, Sir Arthur Lawley, Major Geoffrey Glyn and Ned on the steps of Governement House before the meeting of the 1904 Legislative Council.

Sir Arthur concluded by saying that the exhibition of patience and courage by Briton and Boer inspired him with the hope that the scars of the recent struggle were not indelible and that all feelings of resentment might disappear when the people of the country realised that the interest which bound them together were far stronger than any difference which might keep them asunder. He expressed the wish that they should become a peaceful, prosperous and united people.

In the Legislative Council of 1903, seats had been offered to the Boer leaders, Botha, Smuts and De la Rey, but they had declined this offer.[42] Later they were to participate. Sir Arthur Lawley as President of the Legislative Council opened each of the sessions of that council. Opening the third session of the Legislative Council on June the 23rd 1904, Sir Arthur was able to say in his opening speech, "In spite of the continued depression there has been a marked return to normal conditions. The work of repatriation has been completed, and the majority of those concerned are now independent of Government Relief." By the time he opened the fifth session on Saturday July 8th 1905, the "Het Volk" party was in the ascendancy and in due course this party would form the first elected government of the British colony of the Transvaal.

Work and Leisure

Sir Arthur Lawley worked closely with Lord Milner, and the Lawleys frequently dined with the High Commissioner. There were regular meetings of the Inter-Colonial Conference, the Customs Conference, the Railway Extension Conference, the Education Conference and the Health Conference.[43] At some of these Lord Milner would preside, at others Sir Arthur Lawley would take the chair. Sir Arthur was a member of the Inter-Colonial Conference, the Chairman of the Executive Council and the President of the Legislative Council of the Transvaal.[44]

Lady Lawley threw garden parties and dinner parties, presented prizes and laid foundation stones. On Thursday July 2nd 1903, Lady Lawley, whom the Dawson diary describes as a "gay thing", laid the foundation stone of the New Club. On Tuesday March 29th 1904, Sir Arthur Lawley opened the Technical Institute in Johannesburg. On April 30th 1904, Lady Lawley gave away the prizes at the Transvaal Bisley Shooting Contest. Important guests would arrive from time to time. For example on October 26th 1904, Lord and Lady Roberts and their two daughters arrived to visit the Transvaal.[45] Lord Roberts, the Field Marshal who had commanded the British armies during the Boer War, was known as "Bob" and his considerate treatment of his troops led to the phrase, "Bob's your uncle". Lord Roberts and Sir Arthur Lawley shared the same enthusiasm for the well-being of the army and the welfare of the individual soldier.

Figure 112: Lady Lawley and the Members of the Women's Loyal Guild at the Lieutenant-Governor's House in February 1904.

In May 1903, Lady Lawley, her sister, Jeannette Leatham, and Jeannette's daughter, Lorna Priscilla, made a journey to Ladysmith in order to visit the battle fields and the war graves of the recent Boer War and to pay homage to the dead soldiers. They went to the Tugela River, Colenso, Wagon Hill, Harts Hill, Railway Hill, and Spion Kop. They also visited Majuba Hill, the scene of a famous British defeat in February 1881 during the First Boer War.[46] At Green Hill they placed a wreath on the new memorial cross sited on the lower slopes. Beneath the cross was inscribed, "Pro Patria – In loving memory of our comrades of the 2nd Battalion of the King's Own Lancaster Regiment who fell in action over Ounderbroeck Spruit on the 22nd, 23rd and 24th February and at Pieter's Hill on the 27th February 1900".

Lady Lawley was the Transvaal Patron of the Guild of Loyal Women which had branches all over South Africa and did good works for the sick, the aged, the less advantaged and the poorer members of the community.[47] The Guild was interested in education and arranged lecture tours. It supported Lady Lawley in her scheme for the establishment of school libraries. During the last week of February 1904, Lady Lawley held a Garden Party attended by over 300 members of the Guild in the grounds of Government House. The Star reported that "Sir Arthur and Lady Lawley entertained their guests in the charming manner for which they are well known."[48]

Figure 113: Dressing up for a party. Cecilia Lawley, Hermione Lyttelton and Ursula Lawley with Gholi their dog.

On Friday October 9th 1903, the Lieutenant-Governor and Lady Lawley threw their first ball at Government House, Sunnyside, Pretoria. Nearly fifteen hundred invitations were sent out and over a thousand guests came from the civilian, military, social and commercial ranks of Transvaal society. The Star reporter wrote, "The grounds looking their very best and sweet with the scent of thousands of roses everywhere were thronged with strollers the entire evening. The house was brilliant with lights and gay with pretty frocks and handsome uniforms with the strong dash of neutral smartness imparted by the presence of up-to-date men in civilian attire." Sir Arthur and Lady Lawley received their guests on a superbly decorated raised dais surrounded by ferns and flowers at one end of the ball room.

"The Band of the Transvaal Town Police provided the music and the ballroom (120 feet by 55 feet) was thronged with revellers. There were ferns and palm trees at the doors. The walls were lined with potted privet hedges and ropes garlanded with roses hung festooned from above. The programme of dances began with a Square Dance led by Lady Lawley and General Lyttelton and ended with a gallop. The floor was packed for every dance and the guests participated with much enthusiasm. Tea and supper were served in the reception rooms of the Residency and there was even a card room in a marquee on the lawn for those who did not care to dance.

Lady Lawley wore an elegant gown of pink Singapore satin and chiffon of a colour that had a suggestion of heliotrope. This was complemented by a diamond and emerald tiara and a diamond collar. The Star reported, "The Misses Lawley wore white muslin frocks with blue sashes and black bows on their soft, fair hair. The Honourable Mrs Algernon Lawley was in cream panne, a lovely gown worn with many diamonds."

The report from the Johannesburg Star concluded, "Every element necessary to perfect enjoyment was present; the ball was brilliant, successful and enjoyable. The first dance at Government House, Pretoria may fairly be said to have been one of the most successful ever held in the sub-continent." Most of the guests from Johannesburg had arrived by special train from Park Station and there were two special trains at 12.30 am and at 3.30 am to take the Rand revellers home.

The social life in Pretoria and Johannesburg was focused on Social Clubs like the Athenaeum and the New Club, and Sports Clubs like the Wanderers, where Test Matches were played with visiting cricket teams. In 1902, the first Test Match was played against Australia, in which the Transvaal was soundly beaten.[49] Many people played bridge and there were theatres in both cities. The two leading theatres – the Gaiety and His Majesty's Theatre – were in Johannesburg. On November 28th the Star's Weekly Edition advertised a play called "The Schoolgirl" at His Majesty's Theatre. There were frequent dinner parties and a very active social life. There was even a music hall in Johannesburg – The Empire Palace of Varieties.

Annie Lawley derived great pleasure from going for a drive in the Lawley's new De Dion Bouton car. This was not always plain sailing. On Saturday 18th November 1905, Sir Arthur Lawley visited Gezina near Pretoria to open a Wild Flower Show. He began his speech by saying, "My only regret is that Lady Lawley is not with me today; but unfortunately even motor cars are not infallible, and although she started from Johannesburg, she did not get very far on the way here."[50]

Lieutenant Colonel H. F. Trew was an Australian who served in the South African Constabulary from 1901 to 1908. He described the Lawleys' love of the great

outdoors. Early in 1903, Lieutenant Colonel Trew reported that he had been told by
Baden-Powell to make arrangements for Sir Arthur and Lady Lawley to stay at
Pilgrim's Rest in the Transvaal and to then accompany them on a tour of the District.
Mr Stein, the hotel keeper, gave them the use of his own house for their visit. As
there were no guns for a salute, the local people got some dynamite from the nearby
mines and fired twenty one dynamite blasts from the mountainside to welcome their
guests. The tour was to be made on horse back with a Cape Cart to carry their
camping gear. Trew lent Lady Lawley his polo pony and they had a wonderful trip
through the mountains to Kruger's Post. Trew wrote, "Sir Arthur and Lady Lawley
took all hearts by storm, for they proved to be a very charming couple." The local
farmers invited the Lawleys to lunch, and Lady Lawley was concerned because she
was to meet Abel Erasmus, whom Sir Garnet Wolesley had described in a book she
had just read as "a fiend in human form." After lunch, Lady Lawley said that she
could not understand how Sir Garnet Wolesley could be so mistaken about Mr
Erasmus. She said that she thought that Abel Erasmus looked like one of the old
patriarchs out of the Bible and that she liked him very much.

Figure 114: Lady Lawley driving the De Dion Bouton car.

Later Lieutenant Colonel Trew was transferred to Pretoria where one of his
subalterns, Harold Fitzclarence, was the son of the Earl of Munster, a great friend of
Sir Arthur Lawley's. As Harold was hard up, Sir Arthur arranged for him to live in a
cottage at Sunnyside, (Government House, Pretoria). Coming home late one night
after a murder investigation, they were informed by Mrs Fitzclarence that the whisky
had run out. Harold suggested that they should go over to Government House and tap
on the butler's window to see if they could borrow a bottle of His Excellency's
whisky. They crept along the path beside the house and knocked on a window. After
a time a light was turned on and to their horror they saw the Lieutenant-Governor in
his pyjamas. They both stood to attention and saluted. Sir Arthur said, "Well

gentlemen, to what do I owe the honour of this visit?" Harold made a happy-go-lucky apology and explained what they needed. Sir Arthur said, "Well you fellows wait here whilst I go and forage and see if I can find some whisky." He returned in a few minutes with half a bottle, which he handed to them through the window saying, "I don't know what the guard would say if they saw this performance."[51] They thanked him and crept back to the cottage mutually agreeing that Sir Arthur was a good sport.[52]

On another occasion at a dinner at Government House, one of the guests was a senior Civil Servant who was noted for the amount of liquor he could put away. A discussion of hobbies began at the dinner table and the guests were describing their pastimes. Lady Lawley said to the senior Civil Servant, "What is your hobby?" "Drink, madam!" he replied to the amusement of the hosts and all the other guests.

Sir Arthur Lawley was a keen huntsman with a love for the open wilderness of the African plains. When the opportunity arose he would go on safari. With his enthusiasm for wild life and his love of the natural world, one of the acts of his administration was to provide for the establishment of a game sanctuary in the North East Transvaal. The details were published in the Government Gazette of September 1903. This game sanctuary was later to become Kruger National Park.[53]

On 22nd July 1904, Lady Lawley set out with her friend, Lady Farrar, and Cecil Rhodes' brother, Arthur, to visit Rhodesia. They travelled by rail via Potchefstroom and Mafeking to Bulawayo. Here they saw the new statue of Cecil John Rhodes, which had been unveiled, on July 7th, by the Mayor of Bulawayo.[54]

Figure 115: Lady Lawley crosses the Zambesi Gorge below the Victoria Falls – July 1904.

The Administrator of Rhodesia, Sir William Milton, and his wife and Colonel Frank Rhodes were the principal guests at the unveiling. Cecil Rhodes had died on March 26th 1902 and had been buried in the Matopos Hills near Bulawayo. Lady Lawley, Lady Farrar and Arthur Rhodes visited the grave at World's View.[55]

Beyond Bulawayo, Lady Lawley and her party journeyed along the new railway line northwest towards the Victoria Falls. Just below the Falls a new railway bridge was being built over the Zambesi Gorge. There was a cable across the gorge with a chair on a pulley in which Lady Lawley crossed from one side to the other. Lady Farrar then crossed too. They also visited the different parts of the Falls – the Devil's Cataract, the Main Falls, the Rainbow Falls and the Eastern Cataract on the far side of the Zambesi. They took a launch out to Livingstone Island and watched hippos cavorting in the Zambesi, which is a mile wide above the Falls. The party stayed in the new Victoria Falls Hotel. Sir George and Lady Farrar had a large new Colonial Dutch style house and a farm near Pretoria. Sir George was a leading member of the new Progressive Party. They were close friends of the Lawleys.[56]

Figure 116: Jack Tar, the first engine to cross the Victoria Falls Bridge in August 1905.

Chinese Imported Labour

On October 2nd 1903, Walter J. Stubbs, a Mining Engineer and Metallurgist, wrote to Sir Arthur Lawley complaining about the "monstrous demand of South African mining speculators to import hordes of Chinamen at low wages to work in the Rand, when this work could be carried out by all white labour at current rates of pay and at costs not exceeding 30 shillings a short ton. The favourable conditions on the Witwatersrand – little water underground, almost total absence of timbering required underground, very cheap fuel, easily workable ores and exceptionally cheap mine labour – meant that mining costs should be lower. He stated that in Western Australia where conditions were far less favourable gold was mined at a cost of 18 shillings a short ton. In the Transvaal the cost per short ton from 1890 to 1899 averaged 32½ shillings a short ton. Stubbs stated, "I am lost in amazement at the costliness of this work and am quite unable to realize how it was possible to squander money to this extent unless the grossest extravagance and criminal incompetence ran riot."

In December 1900, he brought these facts to the attention of Sir Alfred Milner. He also wrote to the Department of Mines in Victoria, Australia, which provided facts and figures bearing out all his statements. In May 1902 he wrote to the Imperial Government in London, to the Colonial secretary and to Lord Milner appraising them of the situation. He also wrote to several London and provincial newspapers. The rate of pay for miners in the Australian colonies and New Zealand ranged between 7½ and 16 shillings for an eight hour day as compared with 2 to 2½ shillings on the Rand Goldfield in the Transvaal for African labourers doing the same job. He suggested that the gold could be mined using all white labour paid at 20 shillings a day under competent management and still produce the gold at 30 shillings per short ton. The essence of this protest was not to defend the work of African mine labourers, but to create more jobs for Boer and British workers on the Rand.

The main reason for importing Chinese Indentured Labour was the chronic labour shortage in the gold mines of the Witwatersrand. On October 19th 1903, Sir Arthur Lawley wrote to Lord Milner, "The mining industry before the war was producing gold at the rate of £20 million per annum. Owing to the scarcity of labour, not only has it not recovered from the effects of the war but its present output is little over half that rate and is increasing very slowly. It is impossible to overrate the depressing effect which this stagnation of the mining industry has upon all business in this colony. The condition of the agricultural industry at the present is almost desperate and is for some time to come more likely to cause a drain on public funds than to be a source of wealth. The process of recovery from the devastation of war has been impeded by a severe and prolonged drought."[57]

The severity of the crisis was emphasized in two telegrams sent to Milner on October 28th 1903 in which Lawley stated, "Mining groups think that it is most important to make preliminary arrangements for the emigration and reception of Chinese indentured labourers. It is essential that they should have experienced assistance and they are anxious to procure Evans, Protector of the Chinese Straits Settlement, who is recommended as the best man for the purpose." The second telegram said, "Perry is sailing on November 4th going to China via London to arrange on behalf of the mining group for the first lot of Chinese.....The Government must instruct British officials in China not to hinder us." [58] To underline his concern Sir Arthur sent Milner another telegram on October 30th in which he wrote, "Distress among all classes increases daily and delay now in a solution of the labour problem would...inevitably bring about a general financial crisis here and would render the raising of our new loan of £10 million most difficult.... The labour shortage is the most pressing and important question before us and I feel your presence at the Colonial Office will expedite matters enormously."[59]

Yet Sir Arthur Lawley had earlier that year expressed the view that the Transvaal Government instead of raising taxes above ten per cent might purchase gold mining shares to profit both from rising income and capital gains. "Gold shares here are going up by leaps and bounds and we ought to say what we intend to have before the public buys them at prices which will leave no room for profit if we subsequently put on heavy taxation….. There can be no possible objection to the State obtaining a much greater share of the new mining wealth and also of the rise in value," he wrote in two telegrams to Lord Milner.[60] Hence Lawley was looking to a more prosperous future even while the crisis was at its height.

On February 10th 1904, the Transvaal Legislative Council approved an Ordinance for the Importing of Chinese Indentured Labour to work in the gold mines. That same month, in response to this decision, a protest signed by fourteen Boer leaders, including Botha and Smuts, was handed to Sir Arthur Lawley. It read, "The question" of indentured Chinese labour "has never been submitted to the approval of the people…the overall majority of whom are unalterably opposed to the introduction of Asiatic labour…under whatever restrictions…We are most anxious that His Majesty's Government…shall not remain under the mistaken impression that the Boer population is in favour of a measure which it looks upon as a public calamity of the first magnitude." Sir Arthur was requested to forward this protest to the Secretary of State. The first 600 Chinese labourers arrived in Durban from Hong Kong on 18th June 1904 and began working on the Rand gold mines on July 2nd. The labourers were engaged on three year contracts. They were placed under the supervision of the Transvaal government from recruitment to repatriation. The imported labour did enable the gold mines to increase their output and revenue substantially, but it was deeply unpopular with the people of South Africa.[61]

Shortly before leaving South Africa in 1905, Lord Milner had approved a decision allowing employers to inflict corporal punishment on their Chinese labourers without reference to a magistrate in cases of violence or unruliness in the mine compounds. In June 1905, Sir Arthur Lawley as Acting High Commissioner, hearing of abuses by the Mine Foremen, withdrew the permission for corporal punishment and reported the matter to the Colonial Secretary. There was an investigation which expressed disapproval of Milner's decision and approval of Sir Arthur's actions. Indeed Milner himself admitted that he had made an error of judgement. By March 1905, there were 35,000 Chinese mine workers in the Transvaal. The number of African mine workers was then 105,184.

The impact of the additional work force was to increase gold production from £15½ million in 1904 to £29 million in 1905. In March 1904, it was doubted that the Transvaal government would be able to meet its expenses for the current financial year ending on June 30th without assistance from the United Kingdom. On June 30th 1905, the Transvaal government had a surplus of £347,000. However, given that by 1910 there were 183,000 African workers in the mines of the Transvaal, it is quite possible that the mine owners hoodwinked Lord Milner into obtaining Chinese indentured labour in order to depress African wages in the mines.[62]

In England the importation of Chinese labour for the mines of the Transvaal caused uproar. The Swanley, a vessel bringing Chinese workers from Hong Kong to South Africa, was shipwrecked. The crew and all the passengers were drowned. The British and Foreign Anti-Slavery Society passed a resolution at the Meeting of its Committee protesting against the servile conditions under which it was proposed to introduce Chinese labour and asking the Government not to consent to the Labour Importation Ordinance. The Transvaal administration suggested that in order to obtain the views of the Chinese Minister on the proposed legislation, the best course would be to send him a copy of the Ordinance with the suggestion that a Committee of the Chinese Legation should discuss the matter. The Transvaal appointed its own Representative to China. Chinese Labour Regulations were introduced into the Transvaal to control the price of goods sold on the compounds, the pay for piece work and wages, the sale of intoxicants to Chinese workers, medical care, precautions against bubonic plague, and religious instruction. In the British parliamentary election at the end of 1905, the import of Chinese Labour into South Africa was one of the issues which led to the defeat of the Conservatives by Campbell Bannerman's Liberal Party.[63]

Post-war Recovery

Among the casualties of the Boer War were large numbers of dead horses and it was vital to replace the lost horses as rapidly as possible. Sir Arthur Lawley was a very skilled horseman, having been a cavalry officer in the Tenth Hussars. He was also an enthusiastic huntsman. He took a great interest in the Government Stud Farm at Standerton, which was managed by Captain Blackburn D.S.O. In the April of 1905, he visited the stud farm and expressed a wish that the Hackneys be broken to harness and sold. Otherwise he was very pleased indeed with the thoroughbred horses and not displeased with the farm in general. Following his visit he wrote:

"I found at Beginsel a number of stallions, mostly thoroughbreds, and in addition a Yorkshire coaching horse of no great merit, an Arab and two hackneys. The majority of the thoroughbred stallions are of a very high class and they are bound to do good in the country, but there are one or two of them which I think might be dispensed with to advantage. My own idea is that, as a Government, we should go in for quality and introduce strains of blood which, from experience in other countries, we know are likely to improve the general breed of horses. With thoroughbred stock we are quite safe. The introduction of good Arab blood, in a country such as this is, will be certain to be beneficial, but I am distinctly opposed to the introduction of coaching and hackney blood."

Figure 117: Horse riding near Pretoria Cecilia, Sir Arthur, Ursula, Lady Lawley, Geoffrey Glyn, and Ned Lawley

"The mares which I saw are a very mixed lot, and I think that a great deal of weeding out is required. We have a few thoroughbred mares, a few hunting mares of fair merit, and a good many colonial bred and other nondescript animals, which do not seem to me likely to do much towards improving the breed of horses in this country. My policy would be to get rid of all the odds and ends of mares, and to confine our enterprise solely to thoroughbred mares, though I should not object to the retention of some of the best hunting mares."

"I think it is one of our duties to educate the Dutchman to the principle that if you have good stock they are worth taking care of. This opens up the question of our Model Farms. The farm at Potchefstroom is not what a government farm should be in the matter of buildings, and I hope that it will not be long before we are able to give an object lesson in the way in which valuable stock should be both housed and cared for."

As a result of this advice, Captain Blackburn was instructed to sell the inferior stock and with the money raised to buy thoroughbred mares already in foal. Some of the original mares were, however, kept for breeding purposes with the eventual aim of removing them by natural wastage and gradually replacing them with thoroughbred animals. With the agreement of the Commissioner of Lands and the Lieutenant-Governor, a good herd of cattle and a fine flock of sheep were established on the farm at Standerton. Improvements to the buildings were effected providing concrete floors and better roofing. To restock the farms of South Africa cattle were imported from the United States, Austria and Hungary.[64]

With so much devastation caused by war, the farm animals of South Africa were prone to disease. On September 28th 1903, Sir Arthur Lawley wrote to Lord Milner, "We have had a series of calamities in our various Stock Departments. We've lost since the beginning of June 255 brood mares at the Stud Farm, 920 mules from pyrozoma, and now we have an outbreak of Rhodesian Redwater among our choice herd of Texan cattle. Last week we lost 160 in one day. Fowke told me that my speech at Klip River has been well received much to the chagrin of Botha and Smuts and that they have determined to go for me."[65]

East Coast Fever broke out on the cattle farms of the Transvaal and Rhodesia in 1904 and 1905. A veterinary officer, Stockman, said that when the farmers finally realized that the disease was "one of location" they also recognized that "if they moved their cattle on to fresh ground after each outbreak, the sick ones dropped out, and they eventually left the disease behind them." This might have been done safely, but "each man was a law unto himself, and he left a trail of infection behind him for the cattle of his unsuspecting neighbours to pick up." Although an infected animal might travel on the roads for 20 days and carry the disease for 200 miles, observation had shown that the disease did not ordinarily take longer leaps than 65 miles, except by rail. Later in the report Stockman said, "One must admit that the stock-owner will do everything in his power to protect his property once he knows how science can assist him". The opinions of Stockman about the Boer farmers' independence were amply confirmed on March 10, 1905, when a group of Boer leaders went over the heads of the veterinarians and the officials of the Department of Agriculture to complain to Sir Arthur Lawley as the Lieutenant - Governor of the Transvaal. The Boer delegation was headed by two men who were to become the first and second Prime Ministers of the Union of South Africa, Louis Botha and Jan Christian Smuts.[66]

Sir Arthur Lawley's administration was also interested in the industrial development of the Transvaal. Sir Arthur's legal team negotiated a six year mining lease in the Lydenburg area (about one hundred miles east of Pretoria) granted to Henry Horace Wright who had discovered iron ore, limestone and dolomite there. The deposits were on government farms at Magnet Heights, Steelport Drift and Grootkop, all in the vicinity of Lydenburg. The lease, which also included separate portions of the farm at Doornkop, was approved by the Commissioner of Mines and the Surveyor General. The lease included the right to use water from the Steelpoort River and permission to construct a railway line linked to the Central South African Railway. Henry Horace Wright undertook to spend one million pounds sterling over six years on developing the railway, mines and other facilities. He also undertook to smelt the iron ore to make pig iron or steel in reduction plants or furnaces on the leased land. There then followed a 99 year lease dependent on continuing steel production and government satisfaction that the lease was being respected. This was the first initiative to develop the South African steel industry.[67]

Sir Arthur was also keen to promote prospecting for new minerals. For example in April 1904, the government received a report showing about 30,000 new pegging of mining claims in the Barberton district near Swaziland, and 46,500 mining claims around Pietersburg in the Northern Transvaal. At the same time two other areas around Zoutspansberg and Komati, which had pressured for some time to have their districts opened up for prospecting, were given the go-ahead in April 1904. In due course Barberton developed gold, iron ore, copper and phosphate mines, Pietersburg asbestos mining, Lydenburg chrome and platinum mines and Komati coal mining.[68]

Figure 118: Barberton.

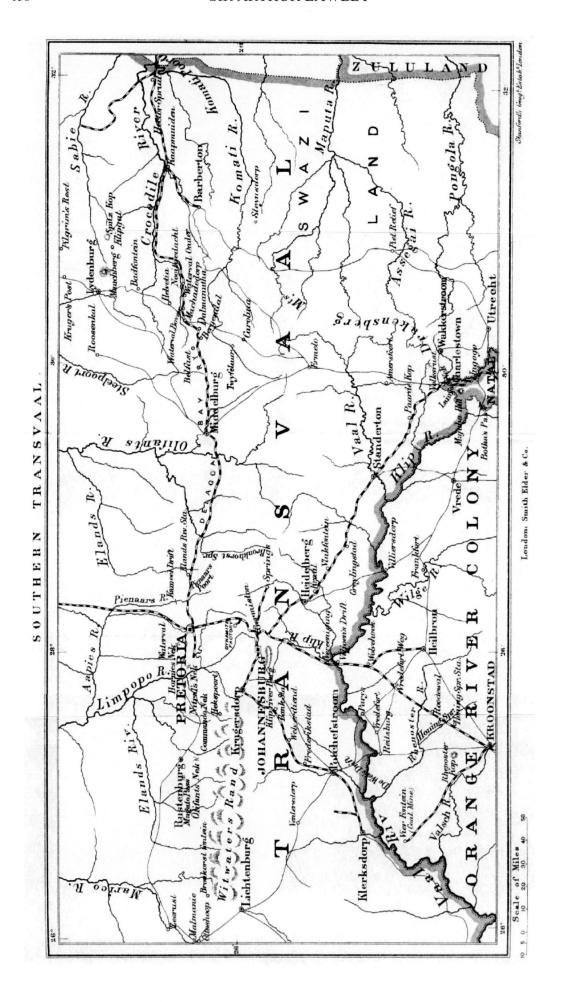

Sir Arthur Lawley had been involved in the construction of the railway from Kimberley in Cape Province to Bulawayo in Rhodesia in the 1890s. In the Transvaal and Orange River Colony, between 1902 and 1905, £22 million were spent on restocking and rehabilitating the railway system and on constructing 800 miles of new track.[69]

Figure 119: Gone Fishing - Colonel Holdsworth, Gholi and Cecilia.

There were also some significant developments in education. A new initiative was an education system for Africans, which offered eight years of primary schooling as opposed to the seven years given in the European and Asian school systems.[70] However Bishop William Marlborough Carter complained that more money was being spent by the Transvaal Government on the Pretoria Zoo than on African Education. He persuaded the Mirfield Fathers of the Community of the Resurrection and the Wantage Sisters to send out missionaries and found schools in the Transvaal.[71] Trevor Huddleston was a Mirfield Father and Desmond Tutu, the Archbishop of Cape Town, was a pupil at one of the Community's schools. Bishop

Carter had been Head of the Eton Mission when Sir Arthur Lawley's brother, Algy, was working there after his ordination in 1881. William Carter, the famous big game hunter Alfred Pease, and the Rev. Algernon Lawley had all studied together at Trinity College Cambridge.[72]

To further education in the English language, in February 1903 the Transvaal advertised in the United Kingdom for fully certificated kindergarten and elementary teachers on salaries of £240 and £300 respectively.[73] The teachers were to be employed in Farm Schools and Town Schools. With regard to tertiary education, an official was sent to England, in September 1903, for discussions with the Education Board and the Royal College of Science about the introduction of post-graduate courses for the planned new Technical Institute in Johannesburg.[74] In the Education Commission's report to Lord Milner on this issue, Sir Arthur Lawley wrote, "The most urgent need of this community is the immediate provision of a high school, efficient in every respect, and of a scientific University specialized according to the needs of the great industries of the community. I can hardly doubt that an appeal to the local patriotism of those, who have made their fortune here, will not be without its effect and that before long Johannesburg will possess a University which on its own lines will be superior to anything that now exists in the world."[75] The Commission recommended that a Technical Institute should be established and that simultaneous steps should be taken to lay the foundation for a University too. Thus was born the University of Witwatersrand.

In 1903, in Potchefstroom, the oldest town in the Transvaal, Potchefstroom Central Primary School was founded. That same year, the citizens urged their Lieutenant-Governor, Sir Arthur Lawley, to establish an English medium boys' high school in the town to serve the needs of the Western Transvaal. The town council offered a 40-acre site. The secondary school was then built. On 31 January 1905, accompanied by the band of the Border Regiment, Sir Richard Solomon, acting as Lieutenant-Governor of the Transvaal while Sir Arthur was on leave, opened Potchefstroom College.[76] On instructions from the education department the name of the school was soon changed to Potchefstroom High School for Boys. This became a school famed for its prowess at rugby. The site for the school had been an infamous concentration camp during the Boer War. The first school on this land was for the children interned in that camp.

Between 1904 and 1905, the Victoria League sent eight thousand books to the Transvaal to encourage the setting up of public libraries and school libraries to promote English language and literature. They had close co-operation from their committee in Pretoria, which included Lord Milner and Sir Arthur and Lady Lawley. The Victoria League in London were in regular close contact with Lady Lawley who was took great interest in their work. Local communities also collected money to open libraries and purchase books for their shelves. [77]

During the first three months of 1903, there was an outbreak of pneumonic plague in the Witwatersrand. Mohandas K. Gandhi had been on two Plague Committees and had been a volunteer nurse for plague patients for two years. He acted swiftly on behalf of the Indian community. The Government Entrepôt in Station Road, Johannesburg was fitted out as a temporary hospital. Out of the twenty five patients admitted only five remained alive on the Saturday night of March 21st. Gandhi said that the Indian community had done everything it possibly could to prevent the spread of the disease and that every case had been reported. He considered that if proper precautions were taken, the spread of the disease could be averted. In an interview with the Star, he said, "In my opinion the plague has broken out entirely owing to the insanitary and overcrowded conditions of the area aggravated by the recent wet weather. I do not think that the germ must necessarily have been imported; the plague is nothing more than an acute form of pneumonia. The Indian Community is not at all to blame for the outbreak. It is the machinery of government that is faulty, and I say with all due deference that if the Public Health Committee had been more practical there would have been no outbreak. The only thing now to be done is to burn the whole of the buildings in the insanitary area, and move the people to a temporary camp and feed them. This would entail expense, but it would be well worth incurring." The Star reported that Mr Gandhi made an appeal for funds which was liberally responded to, and that he was rendering valuable assistance to the authorities. There were also cases of plague among the African and Chinese workers in the Gold Mines. All cases were isolated and quarantine was imposed to contain the outbreak.[78]

Beyond politics there were other duties for the Governor to perform. In 1903 he attended the inauguration of St Andrew's Presbyterian Church, in Fairview. This attractive little brick-built, iron-roofed church was associated with the Second Transvaal Scottish Volunteers. On the foundation stone are the words, "Laid in 1903 by His Excellency the Lieutenant-Governor Sir Arthur Lawley KCMG., the same official who in 1902 ratified the appointment of Gordon Sandilands as first Officer Commanding the Transvaal Scottish Volunteers". Members of the St Andrew's congregation fought in the 4th South African Infantry Regiment (S.A. Scottish) during World War I. Their names were listed on the congregation's own memorial rather than on the special Transvaal Scottish or South African Scottish plaques. During the First World War the Rev Ian Macdonald, the Minister of this Church, served in the Highland Division and was severely wounded at Delville Wood, where he lay for three days before being found. He was later cared for by a sixteen-year-old nurse, Elizabeth Bowes-Lyon, who became Her Majesty Queen Elizabeth the Queen Mother.[79]

The Lawleys were very keen on riding and indeed Sir Arthur was a most accomplished horseman. In the Transvaal they would ride out over the veldt to visit friends or just for relaxation. In the June of 1903, they were joined by their son Ned – Richard Lawley – who came out on sick leave from HMS Britannia. The family took a short holiday together, trekking on horseback to the S.A.C. Camp at Losberg and then on to the River Vaal.[80] The doctor recommended that Ned should stay in South Africa until the end of the year, but Ned sailed back from Cape Town to resume his duties on July 31st.[81] Geoffrey Robinson sometimes accompanied the Lawleys on outings. His diaries refer to going for rides with the Lawley girls and to playing charades with the Curtis family and the Lawley girls. On February 16th 1905, he rode with Sir Arthur and his secretary, Geoffrey Carr-Glyn, to a picnic tea organized by Mrs Pennant. On November 18th 1905, Geoffrey Robinson went for a ride after lunch with Lady Lawley and the girls to draw Emily Hobhouse, the Quaker activist who had brought the conditions in the British Concentration Camps in South Africa to the notice of the U.K. government in London. Sadly Miss Hobhouse was indisposed.

Major General Baden-Powell was in South Africa both during and after the Boer War. Indeed, it was at the siege of Mafeking that he made his name. The Relief of Mafeking on May 17th 1900 after a siege of 217 days caused euphoria and mass hysteria in Britain leading to a new phrase "Making Mafeking". Later Baden-Powell was responsible for setting up the South African Constabulary for keeping law and order in the Transvaal and the Orange River Colony in the aftermath of the Boer War.

Originally 10,000 strong, the force was reduced to 6,000, and then to 4,000, as peace and order were restored. Robert Baden-Powell worked closely on police matters with the Lieutenant-Governor.

Figure 120: The South African Constabulary.

C.B.S. photo.

Col. J. S. Nicholson.   Gen. Baden Powell.

Figure 121: General Baden-Powell with Colonel J. S. Nicholson.

When Baden-Powell left South Africa he wrote: "My own connection with South African Constabulary came to a sudden end early in 1903. I received the announcement that I had been appointed Inspector-General of Cavalry for Great Britain and Ireland. Here was another bombshell! A promotion, which I had never expected, especially as I was already employed on active work in South Africa! I at once put myself in the hands of Lord Milner, since I was serving under him, as to whether I should accept the step or not.   He replied very generously stating that the appointment was, as he termed it, 'the Blue Riband' of the Cavalry, and that as the SAC was now in good working order, I might accept it with a clear conscience. With mixed feelings of elation and regret, I accepted accordingly. I made a farewell round of my Divisions and eventually handed over my Command of the Constabulary to Colonel J. Nicholson. It was only then that I realised how hard it was to break away from one's own child, but my regret was tempered by the kindly greetings I got, not only from the Constabulary but from friends, civil and military, British and Boer as well. As consolation, I had a wonderful tribute from Lord Milner, written in his own hand, to the efficiency and value of the force, and also a very high appreciation from Sir Arthur Lawley, Governor of the Transvaal". [82]

The collaboration between Sir Arthur Lawley and Lord Baden-Powell developed into a close association between the Lawley family and the Boy Scouts and the Girl Guides. This led Sir Arthur's grandson, Richard, the second Lord Wraxall, to assist generously with many Scouting and Guiding events in Bristol and North Somerset and to give full support to Scout and Guide camps on his estate at Tyntesfield.

On August 19th 1903, Sir Arthur wrote to Lord Milner, "I am off to Swaziland tomorrow and shall be glad of the breath of the Veldt to blow away the relics of the flu which has again laid me low. I had a short interview with Botha and Smuts today on the subject of Prisoners of War." There were Africans in the Police Force in Swaziland and on Sunday August 24th 1903, Sir Arthur Lawley inspected the Zulu policemen at Embabaan Police Camp. There was a resident British Commissioner in Swaziland and the Zulu Police came under his jurisdiction.[83]

Figure 122: Sir Arthur Lawley crossing the Komati River on his way to Swaziland.

Sir Arthur and Lady Lawley trekked with Arthur's brother, Algy, and his sister in law, May, from Barberton to Swaziland. They forded the Komati River on horse back. At Embabaan the Queen Regent of Swaziland came with a large following to meet the Lieutenant-Governor and his party. Sir Arthur later received a deputation of British residents wising to discuss local affairs.

In June 1903, by an Order in Council under the Foreign Jurisdiction Act, the Governor of the Transvaal had been empowered to administer Swaziland and to legislate by proclamation. It was this piece of legislation by the British government which necessitated Sir Arthur Lawley's visit.[84]

At the first meeting with Sir Arthur, the Queen Regent got up from her chair and walked to the table at which His Excellency sat. Leaning over she explained in a stage whisper which was audible on every side, "I don't want to talk loudly about it. I just whisper in your ear, but it is good I should tell you that before the war we used to receive money. Our beer pots are now empty."

At the end of this interview in taking her leave, the dowager remarked, "We could have given you a welcome in cattle, but we are poor. All I have is one cow. It is so small that I will not call it a cow; I will call it a goat. Therefore I say I give you a goat." Sir Arthur responded by saying that he would give her three oxen as food for her people.[85]

Figure 123: Sir Arthur Lawley inspects the Zulu Police.

The Queen arriving for the indaba with her followers. Aug 24th 1903.

Figure 124: The Queen Regent of Swaziland comes to meet Sir Arthur Lawley.

The general demeanour of the Queen Regent was not very courteous and the size of her entourage was very limited. Enquiries found that the reason for this was that many young men feared they would be asked why they had not paid the "Hut Tax", while others thought they might be asked why they were not at work. On the Tuesday morning, the Queen was equally sour, but following a private meeting with Sir Arthur her demeanour changed, and in the afternoon she became very effusive and anxious to please. She dragged about with her a toy elephant which Lady Lawley had given to one of the late king's sons.

A prominent chief was asked why it was that the people made such a poor show. His reply was, "show me a herd of bull elephants led by a cow and I will answer you". The young men, encouraged by the younger chiefs, did not obey the Queen Regent, who without bloodshed could not enforce her authority. Her attempt to assume authority at the interviews was rather a failure.

Sir Arthur gave the Swazi Queen a Cape Cart as a present from the Transvaal Government. As her own special gift for the Swazi Queen, Lady Lawley brought a velvet robe intricately embroidered on the cape over the shoulders and around the hem beneath the knees.[86] The tone of the later meetings between the Africans and the Europeans was very gratifying.[87]

On Saturday 19th September 1903, there was a great Military Review at the Klip River Camp. The review before Lieutenant-General Sir Neville Lyttelton and Sir Arthur Lawley was the largest ever held in South Africa and was a most impressive sight. Nearly ten thousand troops were on parade including five batteries of horse and field artillery, three cavalry regiments, a troop of the constabulary and five battalions of infantry.

A large number of Boer farmers and their families witnessed the review and a few spectators even came out from the Rand. The troops began to assemble at nine o'clock, and when the Lieutenant-Governor and General Lyttelton arrived, all the units were drawn up in a line extending for over a mile. Sir Arthur and General Lyttelton rode up and down the line and then returned to the Saluting Point ready for the march past to begin. The massed mounted bands led the procession and then fell out opposite the saluting point to play their music as the cavalry passed by. Then came the Seventh and Eighth Hussars followed by the Queens Bays. The three field batteries were next in line followed by the Eighth Mounted Infantry and the Mounted Constabulary.

Then the infantry marched past. Massed Infantry Bands replaced the mounted musicians. The Royal Irish led the column of infantry. Then the Inniskilling Fusiliers marched past to the music of "The British Grenadiers". The Welsh Regiment led by their famous white goat was next in line followed by the Leinsters, who marched past to the strains of "Come back to Erin". The pipers then stepped to the front and played their comrades of the Scottish Rifles past the saluting point. The brilliant colours of military reviews at home were replaced by serviceable khaki, but the gleaming steel of their weapons and the polished brass on their webbing glinted in the South African sunshine. Lady Lawley, Lady Lyttelton and the other ladies watched from a viewing platform nearby. [88]

Sir Arthur then spoke to the Boer farmers who had come to watch the Military Review. He said,

"I am pleased to have the opportunity to meet with the farmers of this district face to face. I know that you are men whose traditions, whose lives, whose hearts are deeply rooted in the soil of the Transvaal. Your fathers lived here before you, and I hope that for many years and many generations to come your sons and grandsons will live after you on the same land, and will realise a development of its resources and an accumulation of its riches that they have not hitherto dreamed of. I should like also, if I might, to say, as your Governor, how much I appreciate the generous and ready spirit in which the proposal to exercise the troops was welcomed by you, and to thank you for the courtesy and cordiality with which they have been received. Time was gentlemen when the khaki was not so welcome on your farms, but I hope those days are past and with them every, or at least some of the traces of resentment which the grim presence of war cannot fail to engender. I have set before myself as my duty and my aspiration to obliterate all such traces, and I welcome your presence here today as some indication on your part that you are ready to join me in my endeavour."

Figure 125: Sir Arthur Lawley with General Neville Lyttelton at the Review of British troops at Klip River Camp in September 1903.

Writing to Lord Milner the following day he said, "I went down to Klip River yesterday to attend a Review of the Troops who have been manoeuvring in that region for the past three weeks, but more to attend a luncheon for the farmers of this district, and took the opportunity to say a few words in counterblast to the Emily Hobhouse screech. I was studiously moderate as I think that steadily dropping a fire of facts will be the best response, and an occasional recital of what reparation has really achieved is a better answer than violent rhetoric." [89]

In May 1904, a Boer Congress took place in the Randsaal, the Council Chamber, in Pretoria. The delegates were introduced by General Botha, who stated that it was the desire of the Boers to co-operate with the Government. Sir Arthur Lawley welcomed the delegates and expressed his appreciation of the personal courtesy and kindness he had always received from the Boers. While the Government's administration might be unfamiliar, he said, its motives were honest and good. Boer representatives from twenty one centres gathered to complete their political organization, to criticize the Government and to put forward the policies they would like to see adopted in the country. The Congress lasted for three days. On the final day, they presented their resolutions to the Lieutenant-Governor, who replied in detail in a speech lasting for over two hours. The Boers protested about the imposition of a War Tax, which Sir Arthur explained the government did not intend to enforce at a time when the country can ill afford to pay it. In any event no such measure was about to be put to the Legislative Council. There were protests about the removing of magistrates' courts from some districts, which Sir Arthur explained was a temporary measure to save expenditure. When challenged on the question of the three million pounds compensation promised by the British Government, Sir Arthur said,

"Not a penny of the three millions has gone on administration. The whole and a great deal more has gone in restoring the ravages of the war.... There is a further grant from the Imperial Authorities of two millions for compensation to British subjects, foreign subjects and natives. There is also a sum of five millions for the guaranteed loan to be devoted to repatriation. There are two other funds. The first of these is the sum of two millions sterling, given to us by the War Office, to pay out to certain burghers with whom the military authorities had entered into special agreement, and who are entitled to a more liberal scale of compensation than the rest of the burghers. The second is the sum of two and a half millions, which was placed into our hands to pay the military receipts which were given out by the military during the war, so that altogether a sum of fourteen and a half millions has been devoted to the restoration of this country."

The subject of cattle disease was raised by the Boers and Sir Arthur pleaded for the farmers to co-operate with the scientific experts who were doing all in their power to control the disease – East Coast Fever. He warned them that one or two obstinate men, unless the Government had the power to overcome their ignorance and prejudice, might keep this disease alive in the country for years. The Boers had raised a grievance relating to the danger faced by farmers living in districts with large indigenous African populations who were not allowed to carry rifles. Sir Arthur pointed out that the possession of a rifle was allowed to any person who required one for protection.

The Boers then protested about the passing of the Diamond Law and it was explained to them that this law was necessary to allow for the development of the Premier Diamond Mine west of Pretoria. In any event the law could be amended when self government was granted. The conference then went on to consider education, war widows and orphans, the unemployed and the native question. Sir Arthur explained that while education would be given special consideration later, funds donated by European nations to the Boers and British money were already available for widows and orphans. The government was employing many poorer Boers in reconstruction and other projects. Sir Arthur pointed out that a Commission representing all the South African colonies was actively considering the native question in its entirety. Questions relating to Swaziland and Asiatic legislation were then raised and Sir Arthur explained that he would have to await sanction from the Colonial Secretary in London on these issues. The request by the Boers for Divisional Councils in each region of the Transvaal was favourably received. On May 26th, the Johannesburg Star stated that "all that patient explanation, complete mastery of the facts, and ready sympathy could do was done yesterday by Sir Arthur Lawley." [90]

At the end of the Congress General Louis Botha delivered a Farewell Address in which he expressed warm appreciation of Sir Arthur Lawley's speech. He said that it gave him great satisfaction to note that the Government was willing to co-operate with the Boers. Then the Congress went to Government House where Lady Lawley had arranged a lavish Garden Party for the members of the Congress.

Figure 126: Pretoria – Sir Arthur and Lady Lawley, the Rev. Algy and May Lawley, Sir Alfred and Lady Pease, Colonel and Mrs Archdale and Dr Carter, the Bishop of Pretoria.

On August 30th 1904, Sir Arthur and Lady Lawley and their two daughters, and Mr Patrick Duncan, the Colonial Secretary, went on leave for four months to England. During Sir Arthur's absence, Sir Richard Solomon, the Attorney General, became the Acting Lieutenant-Governor of the Transvaal. The Lawley family sailed from Cape Town on board the Union Castle steamer Kenilworth Castle and arrived at Southampton on Saturday 17th September.[91] On September 18th, Sir Arthur Lawley visited the Colonial Office.[92] The Times had reported on June 22nd, "It is expected that Sir Arthur Lawley will take extended leave of absence after this session of the Legislative Council owing to the state of his health." This was probably the reason why Sir Arthur extended his leave to nearly five months. [93]

On Monday October 17th 1904, Sir Arthur Lawley visited his brother the Rev. Algernon Lawley in Hackney, where the St John at Hackney Church Institute had just been rebuilt at a cost of £3000. Another brother, Colonel Richard Thompson Lawley, was there too. A new hall had also been erected in honour of the late Lady Wenlock, who had died in December 1899. She was the mother of the Lawley brothers, who were there for the official opening ceremony. An anonymous family member had donated £1000 to meet the cost of its construction. Sir Arthur seconded the vote of thanks to Lord Amherst of Hackney who opened the new buildings. He spoke at length about what was happening in the Transvaal. To commemorate his visit he planted a plane tree in the courtyard outside.[94]

It was not until the 20th January 1905, that Sir Arthur Lawley had the customary audience with King Edward VII at Buckingham Palace and then called at the Colonial Office prior to taking the Mail Train from Waterloo to Southampton en route back to South Africa.[95] He sailed on the Union Castle steamer Carisbrooke Castle accompanied by his Private Secretary, Philip Kerr.[96] Lady Lawley and her two daughters stayed on for a while in England. On April 28th, they sailed from Trieste on the Austrian Lloyd's mail steamer "Bohemia" bound for Delgoa Bay.[97]

On the morning of February 14th 1905, Sir Arthur Lawley was driven to Government Building in Pretoria with an escort of the South African Constabulary. Here he was met by the Mayor of Pretoria and Members of the Town Council and the Chamber of Commerce, who delivered an official welcome to the Lieutenant-Governor. During his speech of acknowledgement, Sir Arthur said, "On returning here I notice that even in the short time I have been away, considerable changes have taken place and I think they are mostly, if not all, for the better. I have had the opportunity of gauging the position by two indications of coming prosperity, which are the extraordinary advance made in the development of the Premier Diamond Mine and the steady and continuing advance of the great industry on which the future welfare of this country so much depends." (Gold mining) "I start my new spell of work imbued with hope and confidence in the future."[98]

Figure 127: A Garden Party at Government House, Sunnyside, Pretoria.

On Sunday March 21st 1905, there was a Farewell Garden Party at Government House, Sunnyside, in Pretoria given by Sir Arthur Lawley for Lord Milner, who was finishing his term as High Commissioner. It was a glorious day and perhaps 1500 people participated. Lieutenant-Colonel H. F. Trew tells an amusing anecdote about the Garden Party.

Colonel Sam Steele, formerly of the North West Mounted Police and Strathcona's Horse, was an immense figure of a man, six feet four tall and weighing fifteen stone. He was a tough character who had lived on the Canadian Western Frontier all his life and had been involved in fighting Indians, outlaws and horse rustlers. In addition he was the quickest and most deadly revolver shot that Trew had ever seen. To everyone's astonishment Sam Steele arrived at the Farewell Garden Party dressed in an old fashioned top hat and a frock coat which was much too tight for him. Saluting him, Trew said, "Well this is a surprise. I thought you would be in uniform." "Well Trew", he replied, "Mrs Steele insisted that I should wear my old plug hat and frock coat, but I feel like a darned fool in them." Later an A.D.C. came up and said that Lord Milner would like to speak to him. Lord Milner took his arm and they started to walk along a path in the garden. Disaster could be seen coming because a fruit tree grew beside the path with a branch stretched across at the perfect angle to catch Steele's top hat. Sure enough the branch caught the hat and knocked it off. Because the tight coat would not allow Steele to bend down, Trew picked up the hat and gave it to him. Steele thanked him and said, "I guess I'm too big for these fancy gardens." Then he turned to Lord Milner and said, "Sir, if this darned plug hat falls off again, I'll kick the top off it."

Slowly the two paced backwards and forwards along the path, the Colonel remembering to duck each time they passed the cherry tree. Finally, however, he got so interested in the conversation that he forgot to duck and off fell the hat again. The Colonel gave it a running kick like an accomplished rugby player, and the plug hat sailed into the air and landed in a flower bed, whence it was recovered by a shocked Aide de Camp.[99]

On Friday March 31st, the City of Johannesburg threw a splendid Farewell Dinner for Lord Alfred Milner. The following day Sir Arthur Lawley and Geoffrey Carr-Glyn accompanied Lord Milner on his journey down to the port of Lourenzo Marques in Portuguese East Africa, where he embarked on April 3rd on the S.S. Haerber to sail, via the Suez Canal, home to England.[100]

The new South African High Commissioner, Lord Selborne, did not arrive in Cape Town until May 16th.[101] Lord Milner had told Balfour, the British Prime Minister, in February 1904, that if his successor were to come from the Colonial Service, he would recommend Sir Arthur Lawley for the post. Indeed, when Lord Milner was on leave or visiting England, Sir Arthur deputised for him as Acting High Commissioner. The longest such period of leave was from 7th August to 12th December 1903. In 1905, Sir Arthur once more assumed the post of Acting High Commissioner from April 2nd onwards while he awaited the arrival of Lord Selborne.[102] Lord Selborne then decided to go on tour around the Transvaal and Orange River Colony to get to know the region, leaving Sir Arthur in charge of the administration.[103]

Meanwhile a new Government House was near to completion in Pretoria. It had been designed by the architect Sir Herbert Baker in 1902 as the official residence of the Lieutenant-Governor of the Transvaal Colony. The new abode was a magnificent Colonial Dutch mansion with extensive and beautiful gardens. Although the Lawleys often visited this mansion, they never lived there and in due course it was occupied in 1906 by Sir Arthur's successor.

Figure 128: The new Government House in Pretoria in 1905, later used as official residence for the State President of the Republic of South Africa.

Towards the middle of May, Lady Lawley and her two daughters disembarked at Mombasa on their way back to South Africa. Sir Arthur wrote to Lord Milner on May 29th, "My wife when she got to Mombasa made up her mind to see something of Uganda and is spending a fortnight or three weeks in that country so she will not be here till the middle of next month."[104] Winston Churchill in his book, "My African Journey", described the railway journey from Mombasa to Uganda. The line had been built between 1896 and 1902 and the Lawley ladies made their journey two years before Churchill. They were visiting unspoilt Africa. Churchill wrote, "After Makindu station the traveller enters upon a region of grass. Here is presented the wonderful and unique spectacle which the Uganda Railway offers to the European. The plains are crowded with wild animals. From the windows of the carriage the whole zoological garden can be seen disporting itself. Herds of antelope and gazelle, troops of zebra – sometimes four or five hundred together – watch the train pass with placid assurance, or scamper a hundred yards further away, and turn again. Many are quite close to the line. With field glasses one can distinguish long files of black wildebeest and herds of red kongoni and wild ostriches walking sedately in twos and threes, and every kind of small deer and gazelle. The zebras come close enough for their stripes to be admired with the naked eye. We have arrived at Shimba, 'The Place of Lions", and there is no reason why the passengers should not see one, or even half a dozen, stalking across the plain." [105] The journey continued past Mount Kenya, across the Great Rift Valley, over the White Highlands to Kisumu on Lake Victoria, and across the lake by steamboat to Entebbe and Kampala in Uganda. After this thrilling journey Lady Lawley and her girls arrived back in Pretoria on Wednesday June 14th.[106]

One June 25th 1905, Frederick Wells discovered the Cullinan Diamond at the Premier Mine near Pretoria. It was the largest gem quality diamond ever found at 3,106.75 carats. There was much excitement in Pretoria and Mr. Wells received a reward of £3500. [107] In 1907, the Transvaal Government purchased the diamond and gave it to King Edward VII.[108] Several gems cut from this diamond, the Stars of Africa, are now in the British Crown Jewels.

During the first week of October 1905, Sir Arthur and Lady Lawley set out on a trek around the North of the Transvaal visiting Potgietersrus, Pietersburg, Louis Trichard and other towns. On Thursday 5th October, Sir Arthur met a body of 40 Boer farmers from the local branch of Het Volk in Zoutpansberg. Receiving the deputation he listened to their grievances attentively. One significant request was that the hut tax for native workers on the farms be reduced. Before the war it had been 12/6d for farm labourers as opposed to £2 for the African men who chose not to leave their villages. The effect of this had been to encourage men to leave their villages to work on the farms. On this matter Sir Arthur said that something might be done the following year, but that this could not be a reduction to the pre-war level of hut tax for farm workers. For the rest, he said that the Government was fully aware of the distress among some sections of the farming community, and that before he left some means would be decided to improve their lot. However the amount the Government could spend was limited and therefore where possible he encouraged a spirit of self reliance. Sir Arthur and Lady Lawley visited several farms and Lady Lawley spoke in Dutch with the farmers' wives.[109]

Figure 129: Lord Selborne, the new High Commissioner, arrives in Pretoria.

On Wednesday 11th October they were in Pietersburg to visit the Elim Hospital run by a group of Swiss Medical Missionaries to serve the needs of African patients. The Head of the hospital suggested that the Government should provide itinerant doctors to give medical advice to the indigenous population. Lady Lawley, much concerned about the well-being and health of the native peoples, agreed to be the patroness of the hospital.

On Saturday 17th, the Lawleys arrived in Louis Trichard. Here the town was decorated in their honour and there was a civic reception. After this Chief Mpefu and three hundred of his followers voiced two deep "Inkoses" as the Governor and his wife made their way to their camp. In the afternoon there were lengthy discussions with the town committees, including the committee concerned with the extension of the railway network. The citizens of Louis Trichard wanted the railway line from Pretoria to Pietersburg to be continued to Salisbury in Rhodesia. Sir Arthur said that he thought the Chartered Company would not agree to this because the line would compete with Rhodesia's own railway. However it might well be possible to extend the railway line from Pietersburg to Louis Trichard.

Figure 130: Lord Selborne, Sir Arthur Lawley and accompanying officers in Pretoria before the meeting of the July 1905 Legislative Council.

On Friday 3rd November, the Lawleys were back in Pietersburg. In the morning they visited the Government Orphanage, the hospital and the school. Lady Lawley discussed with the ladies of Pietersburg the possibility of starting domestic industries like spinning and weaving for the girls of the town. Sir Arthur met the townsfolk and farmers at 11.30 am in the Court House, where addresses in English and Dutch expressed the loyalty of the local population and their appreciation for all that had been done to help them. Sir Arthur said that he had been much impressed by what he had seen during his visit. Many people had undergone privations and were still experiencing them, but some, by an exercise of common sense, great courage and application had forced aside their difficulties and by degrees were attaining to a condition of prosperity. He said that he had every sympathy with such people and would try to give them any assistance that the Government could provide. The farmers of the district were concerned at being undercut by cheap imported grains and requested an increase in tariffs. They also wanted the right to have their own distilleries on their farms. In response, Sir Arthur said that there was already a tariff of two shillings a bag on imported grain and heavier rail freight charges. However the subject would be discussed at the next Customs Conference. The question of farm distilleries involved the payment of excise duties and was for the Representative Assembly to decide. The people of Pietersburg were concerned at the increase in the Indian population in the Transvaal, but Sir Arthur responded by saying that according to official figures the Indian population was similar to that before the war. Asked about extensions to the railway network, he responded positively, but expressed reservations about the economic feasibility of extending the railway line as far as the Rhodesian border.[110]

The Lawley's trek was reported in the Johannesburg Star, whose new editor was Geoffrey Robinson – Geoffrey Dawson from 1917 onwards.[111] He was recommended for this editorship by Lord Milner and remained Editor of the Johannesburg Star and the Times Correspondent in South Africa until November 1910. On November 24th 1905, Geoffrey Robinson wrote in his diary; "The sensation of the day – Sir Arthur Lawley's appointment to Madras – a horrid loss." On Monday December 4th, the entry read – "To the station to say good bye to the Lawleys – very sad their going."

The Indian Community and Lord Selborne

When Lord Selborne replaced Lord Milner as High Commissioner and Governor of the Transvaal and Orange River Colony, the Indian Community, sensing the impending political changes in London, once more raised the issue of the status of Indians in the Transvaal. The Indians' Deputation to Lord Selborne in 1905 was a spirited defence of Indian rights. The delegates stated:

"As to the new legislation to replace Transvaal Law 3 of 1885, the dispatch drawn by Sir Arthur Lawley has caused us a very great deal of pain. It insists on legislation affecting British Indians or Asiatics, as such. It also insists on the principle of compulsory segregation, both of which are in conflict with the repeated assurances given to British Indians. Sir Arthur Lawley, I wish to say with the greatest deference, has allowed himself to be led astray by what he saw in Natal. Natal has been held up as an example of what the Transvaal should be, but the responsible politicians in Natal have always admitted that Indians have been the saving of the Colony. Sir James Hulett stated before the Native Affairs Commission that the Indian, even as a trader, was a desirable citizen, and formed a better link between the white wholesale merchant and the native. Sir Arthur Lawley had also stated that, even if promises were made to British Indians, they were made in ignorance of the facts as they now are, and therefore it would be a greater duty to break them than to carry them out. With the greatest deference, I venture to submit that this is a wrong view to take of the promises. We are not dealing with promises that were made fifty years ago, though we undoubtedly rely upon the Proclamation of 1858 as our 'Magna Carta'." This was the proclamation of direct rule under the British Crown made after the Indian Mutiny of 1857. "That Proclamation has been re-affirmed more than once. Viceroy after Viceroy has stated emphatically that it was a promise to be acted upon. At the conference of the Colonial Premiers, Mr. Chamberlain laid down the same doctrine and told the Premiers that no legislation affecting British Indians outside India as such would be countenanced by Her late Majesty's Government, that it would be putting an affront quite unnecessarily on millions of the loyal subjects of the Crown.…."

On the subject of immigration and the perceived threat of mass migration from India, Gandhi himself later wrote, "The British Indian Association accepts Sir Arthur Lawley's proposal as to the introduction of an Immigration Ordinance on the Cape of Good Hope model, and makes a suggestion whereby the objectors themselves, namely the local authorities, would have virtual control over the issue of new licences." [112]

Mohandas Gandhi and the British Indian Association were formidable defenders of Indian rights. However, Gandhi was much more preoccupied with defending the civil, commercial and property rights of the Indian community than with the rights of the indigenous peoples of South Africa. Sadly, in the years which followed the Boer War, British policies were entrenching that racial segregation which led to the policy of apartheid. The native population, whose lands had been occupied by the white settlers, continued to be exploited as a source of cheap labour. The rights of the African peoples, who formed the majority of the population of South Africa, were not given proper consideration as the discussion focused upon the human, commercial and political rights of the Indian immigrant population.

Mohandas K. Gandhi founded his Tolstoy model farm near the town of Lawley in the Transvaal. He undoubtedly would have been amused by the location next to a township named after the Lieutenant-Governor. Today there is still a street in Pretoria – Lawley Street – named after Sir Arthur. On December 4th 1905, Gandhi, as Secretary of the British Indian Association, bade farewell to Sir Arthur Lawley, who left South Africa to become Governor of Madras. [113]

Gandhi wrote, "We congratulate Sir Arthur Lawley on his appointment as Governor of Madras. It is a distinction well deserved by His Excellency. Sir Arthur is always kindly, courteous and solicitous for the welfare of those whose interests are entrusted to him. His views on Indians are strange, and we have been often obliged to comment upon many inaccuracies into which he has been led in considering this question, but we have always believed these views to be honestly held. Moreover, wrongly though we consider it to be so, Sir Arthur has believed that in upholding the anti-Indian policy, he would best serve the interests of the European inhabitants of the Transvaal. The mere fact, however, that Sir Arthur has been led to hold such views, owing to his extreme anxiety to serve the European interests in the Transvaal, may be his strength in Madras, for his kindliness, his courtesy, his sympathy and his anxiety have now to be transferred to the millions of Indians over whose destiny he is to preside for the next five years. Sir Arthur is to fill the place vacated by Lord Ampthill, who has so endeared himself to the people of the Madras Presidency. We hope that Sir Arthur will continue the tradition he inherits." [114]

Farewell

Upon his departure, speeches from men of all races spoke of the tact, kindliness, courage and straight dealing which made Sir Arthur's departure felt as a personal loss to South Africa. He had achieved much. The concentration camps were closed, the population resettled, the farms and mines, railways and towns were in the process of recovering. Law and order were restored, and the economy was steadily improving. The Boers and the British were increasingly working together. The conquered lands were soon to become self-governing provinces of the Union of South Africa. The Orange River Colony would once more be named the Orange Free State. The Indian immigrant population had achieved some improvement in its' commercial, legal and political position. Sir Arthur's defence of the interests of the British and Boer shopkeepers was motivated by the desire to restore their commercial viability after the disastrous effects of the Boer War. Although the Indian population was peripheral to the recent armed struggle, they had previously been stoutly defended by Joseph Chamberlain, who at the Diamond Jubilee Conference of Colonial Premiers in 1897 said: "We ask you to bear in mind the traditions of the British Empire, which make no distinction in favour or against race or colour, and to exclude, by reason of their colour or by reason of their race, all Her Majesty's Indian subjects, or even all of the Asiatics, would be an act so offensive to those peoples, that it would be most painful to Her Majesty to have to sanction it."[115]

Figure 131: Sir Arthur and Lady Lawley, Lord and Lady Selborne, Colonel Geoffrey Carr-Glyn, Sir George and Lady Farrar and their daughters.

In July 1904, Alfred Lyttelton, who had replaced Joseph Chamberlain as Secretary of State for the Colonies in the autumn of 1903, promised representative government for the Transvaal. The Lyttelton Constitution was published in February 1905. It provided for an elected majority in the legislature and an executive council dominated by British officials. The constitutional issue was settled by a change of government in Britain. Balfour's conservative ministry fell in December 1905. In January 1906, Campbell-Bannerman won an election unique in British politics for the prominence given to a colonial issue - the importation of Chinese labour into the Transvaal. The new Liberal cabinet scrapped Lyttelton's constitution and decided to give the

Transvaal a constitution with a nominated upper chamber and a legislative assembly of sixty-nine white members elected by white men only.[116]

This caused great concern to Sir Arthur Lawley, who expressed his views in a letter addressed to the new Secretary of State for the Colonies, Lord Elgin, on January 12th 1906 written at the Coburg Hotel in Grosvenor Square, London.[117] He said that the Transvaal was settling down satisfactorily and that the Boers were not indisposed to accept the situation and to work with the Government to restore the country to a condition of material prosperity. He had visited all parts of the country and met representatives of every section of the community, and was firmly convinced that if left alone the Boers would gradually acquiesce in the existing order. However the Boer political leaders had suggested that a change of government in Britain would be followed by an immediate reversal in policy, encouraging "the idea that the incoming of a Liberal Government must of necessity mean the advancement of Dutch as opposed to British ideals."

Sir Arthur felt that if the constituencies were based on the total population and not on the number of eligible voters, the Boers with their large families would be favoured over the British whose population included many single young men. He described "the bitterness with which the British section of the population in the Transvaal" would "regard any action on the part of Her Majesty's Government tending to alter the existing condition of things in a direction inimical to the British interests."

He then explained how there was "a feeling of great soreness among the British population of the Transvaal in consequence of the extreme lengths to which the anti-Chinese agitation had been carried at home." He wrote, "I am not now thinking of reasonable criticism directed against the policy of Chinese labour, but of the extravagant abuse of a large class of British people in the Transvaal in which many of the opponents of Chinese labour had indulged."

Sir Arthur asked Her Majesty's Government, "Is it conceivable that the British section should be expected to acquiesce in the reversal of the Lyttelton Constitution, which has now been in course of being carried into effect for nearly a year, without being allowed as full an expression of their views on the proposed revolution as was permitted to the Boers and everybody else with regard to the original settlement?"

Nevertheless the Lyttelton Constitution was abandoned and the new constitution was undoubtedly more favourable to the Boers. The African, Asian and Cape Coloured peoples were not included in this settlement. Sir Arthur wrote in his letter, "The question of granting the franchise to any of the coloured races must be left to the Representative Assembly of the Transvaal in accordance with the Terms of Surrender." In these circumstances it was most unlikely that full adult male suffrage would have been granted.

Lord Milner admitted that he regretted the agreement to leave the native franchise to the decision of an elected responsible government. He told Lord Selborne, "If I had known then as well as I know now the extravagance of the prejudice on the part of the whites against any concession to any coloured man, however civilised, I should never have agreed to so absolute an exclusion, not only for natives, but of the whole coloured population, from any rights of citizenship, even in municipal affairs."[118]

On Wednesday November 29th 1905, the Mayor of Johannesburg held a banquet attended by Lord Selborne and the retiring Lieutenant-Governor, who was the guest of honour. In his after dinner speech, Sir Arthur spoke about the native peoples of South Africa. He said that the racial question was the only one which darkened the future of this land. At the conclusion of his speech he said, "The natives in element are good if moulded aright. See to this question, for it is the greatest problem you have to face."[119]

On Thursday afternoon, November 30th, Lady Farrar held a reception to say farewell to Sir Arthur and Lady Lawley. The Johannesburg Star reported;

"At Bedford Farm, the beautiful country residence of Sir George and Lady Farrar, there was held one of the most successful functions of the season. It was a reception which constitutes Johannesburg's farewell to Sir Arthur and Lady Lawley who leave on Monday next for a new sphere of duties in Madras. In all ways the affair was distinctly successful.... Lady Lawley, who carried a bunch of flowers gathered on the estate, walked everywhere after the reception: she seemed to be taking a farewell of the surroundings as well as of the friends to whom she spoke. More than once she expressed her regret at leaving South Africa and added, "I am really sorry to go; people may not believe it, but I am." The Misses Lawley with the four pretty daughters of Lady Farrar and the small daughter of the Chinese Consul formed a pretty group during a great part of the afternoon, flitting in the brilliant sunshine and exploring nooks of the garden."

Figure 132: Johannesburg 1904.

On Friday December 1st 1905, there was a Farewell Banquet given in honour of Sir Arthur Lawley at the Grand Hotel in Pretoria. It was attended by General Louis Botha, Patrick Duncan (Colonial Secretary), General Sir H. T. Hildyard (G.O.C. British Forces in South Africa), Sir Richard Solomon (Attorney General), Dr Carter (the Bishop of Pretoria), Lionel Curtis and numerous other guests. [120]   During a Farewell Speech, Sir Arthur Lawley said:

> *"Gentlemen, I have seen this country writhing under the grip of the war demon, and, when that grip has been relaxed, I have seen her exhausted, her homes deserted, her hearths desolate; the whole face of the land bored, blasted and blackened to a cinder, and here and there against the black, the ruggedness of stone marking where some soldier lay in his last sleep; for them a brother perhaps, maybe a friend, or probably a father or a son.*

> *"Men whom I have laughed with and lived with, men whom I have loved – they lie there too, and today, tomorrow and in the days to come, these little graves are they growing? Are they building themselves up as a community to bury suspicion and distrust, race prejudice and vindictive hate, or are they yet so low that across them, from either side, we may stretch out our hands until finger touches finger, till palm meets palm, and in one hand grip we swear to forget and forgive – for believe me gentlemen in this respect there is much for both sides still to do. That is the first step. It looks so easy. It seems so simple; but it is not easy, it is not simple. Have we taken it you and I? For remember it is not on this government or that on whom your ultimate responsibility lies, but on your children and the generations yet unborn. Are we not all of us road makers laying the track over which the footfalls of posterity must pass; and I put it to you that when your last day's work is done, when in the winter of your life you look back upon the task which you have rendered, what will you see? Will it be a tangled network of race lines, running one athwart the other, the most tortuous paths of political intrigue, or will it be the bright and level road of progress prosperity and peace? It should be so to all men to whom the words South Africa represent all that is meant by home....*

> *"Gentlemen, once more, on behalf of my wife and myself, I thank you most sincerely for all the courtesy, all the consideration, all the kindness that you have shown me, and my last words are that God may bring peace to this land and that He may pour down upon your country the abundant blessings which lie in His right hand."*

General Louis Botha in his reply said,

> *"I am accustomed, if I am charged, either to run away or to defend myself. It seems to me this evening that there is no chance of running away. Gentlemen, I have listened with attention to what has been said here tonight, and the words of advice which His Excellency gave certainly impressed every one of us. I am particularly glad with regard to the advice of co-operation which he has given us and I am certain that as far as I am personally concerned and the Afrikaner people we desire to have perpetual peace in South Africa. There are large and most important questions regarding South Africa, and so long as the two white races in this country do not heartily co-operate and work together then you will have no chance of settling those questions amicably. Today there is no room for quarrels in South Africa and we must no longer look upon South Africa as a land of different colonies. We must look upon South Africa as one land, and the population of this country must deal with the questions and interests of this country as if it were one country. Only when we leave distress and co-operate and work together, only then can we expect that God will bless this country. I only wish to say this, that although I wish Sir Arthur Lawley all success on his promotion, still I have a grievance against the British Government for taking him away now that we*

*know him. Gentlemen, I will conclude by saying that in the future which lies
before us, I trust that I will be one of those who will assist in bringing about peace
and co-operation in South Africa."*

The British restored internal self-government to the Transvaal in 1906. In elections
held in 1907, under the colony's new constitution, the former commander of the
Transvaal's forces in the war, General Louis Botha, led his Het Volk party to a
majority and became prime minister with the support of Jan Christian Smuts. Their
government promoted unity between the Afrikaners and the British, and in 1910, the
Transvaal became a province of the Union of South Africa.[121] After the Second World
War, the Afrikaner Nationalist Party became dominant. This led to the policy of
Apartheid, which brutally suppressed the human rights of the majority of the
population. They would have to wait until 27th April 1994 to vote in a free election
and attain their full human rights as Nelson Mandela completed his "Long Walk to
Freedom".

Sir Arthur Lawley was on the horns of a dilemma in the Transvaal. His
instructions were to focus on reconciling the British and the Afrikaners following the
Boer War. If, therefore, he appeared at times to be unsympathetic to the requests of
the minority Indian population, this was not because he was racially prejudiced, but
because he was unsure of his position. The ambivalence of the Colonial Office in
London and of Milner in Johannesburg did not help. His position was fraught with all
the complexities, which the evolution of the racial politics of South Africa was later to
reveal. Speaking at the Agricultural Show in Pietersburg in May 1905, Sir Arthur
Lawley said:

*"Of all the difficulties which present themselves to the Government at the present
time, none is harder than that dealing with the status of British Indians in this
country. The Government realises the conspicuous and splendid services which
have been rendered to the Empire by them in India and in other parts. The
Government appreciates the value of these services fully. People in this country,
however, recognise that the conditions governing the Indians are not the same as
those existing in the land from which the latter came. Here prejudices have arisen
in the minds of the people owing to past history, and the question of the Indian
presence is looked on from an entirely different standpoint. I am sure the Indians
must recognise this. The Government is asked to hold the scales of justice
impartially, and the question is still a matter of correspondence between the Home
Government and the Colonial administration."[122]*

Sir Arthur would have been irritated, intrigued and imperceptibly influenced by
his dealings with Mohandas Gandhi, who developed his policy of "Satyagraha" or
passive resistance in South Africa. His understanding of Indian people had increased
and when he returned to the India he had served in as a young soldier, it was with a
deeper appreciation of the aspirations and ambitions of the peoples of India.

On Saturday 2nd December 1905, there was a Garden Party given by Sir Arthur and
Lady Lawley at Government House, Sunnyside, to say good'bye to the citizens of
Pretoria. Sadly there was a heavy downpour at the beginning of the afternoon, but
eventually the sun reappeared. The Band of the Queen's Own Cameron Highlanders
occupied a picturesque spot near the orchard and struck up their music at 4 o'clock to
persuade the guests to leave their shelter and come out and enjoy the garden. Tea was
served on the tennis courts and groups of military officers in dress uniform leant
colour to the occasion. Lady Lawley chatted affably with her guests and her smile

cheered away the mournful feelings of her friends. All the leading residents of Pretoria attended the Garden Party, including representatives of the Dutch community from General Botha downwards, members of the military, political, social and commercial world.

Figure 133: Guard of Honour for the Departure of Sir Arthur and Lady Lawley from Pretoria, December 1905.

On the following Monday, the Lawleys were given a splendid send off at Pretoria Railway Station. On the platform were a large number of officers, NCOs, and men of the Northern Rifles who had come to say good'bye to their Honorary Colonel – Sir Arthur Lawley. Accompanying their parents were Richard, Ursula and Cecilia Lawley.

In his address to Sir Arthur and Lady Lawley the Mayor of Pretoria said,

"Your Excellency. Upon your departure we desire on behalf of the towns-people of Pretoria to express the regret which is uppermost in our minds at the loss we are suffering. We recognise the great service which you have rendered to this Colony, to our King and Country during a most difficult and arduous period of reconstructive work after a long and devastating war.

Under these circumstances it is no small achievement that Your Excellency has so successfully carried out the task committed to you under the most difficult and trying of circumstances. It is with great pleasure that we assure Your Excellency that your efforts are recognised by all classes of the community and we are confident that you will not only be remembered with the highest respect, but also with the deepest affection and regard.

We beg to tender you our sincere congratulations on the promotion to the high office to which you have been appointed by His Majesty the King and to wish you continued success in your new sphere of government. We pray that Your Excellency and Lady Lawley may enjoy long life and every happiness."

During the course of his reply Sir Arthur said,

"It is to my wife and myself a source of deep regret that now we have to bid you farewell. I value most highly the generous way in which you have spoken of the way in which I have done my work here, and if there is any merit in my services, I am more than rewarded when I see here so many faces whose sympathy and help

have never been withheld from me in the many difficulties with which I have been surrounded. I shall always remember the way in which I have been supported by the representatives of this city. We both hope that for you there is waiting an era of prosperous seasons and prosperous days, and of all that may tend to exalt a nation and its people. We wish you good-bye."[123]

Figure 134. Cartoon from the Transvaal Critic of Sir Arthur Lawley's departure.

The Lawley's special train stopped for an hour in Johannesburg en route to Cape Town. The Transvaal Leader wrote an article entitled, "Johannesburg's Farewell to Sir Arthur Lawley."[124] It said, "At 11.35 a.m. the special train to convey Sir Arthur Lawley and Lady Lawley to Cape Town arrived at Park Station. The Town's address was read by the Town Clerk.

"We desire to express the very great regret which is felt at the departure from this country of Your Excellency and Lady Lawley. During the past three years Your Excellency has shared with the Governor the arduous task of building up anew the fabric of government in this colony and the conditions essential to material prosperity. The wise statesmanship, the single hearted devotion and the steadfastness of purpose which Your Excellency has brought to the accomplishment of this task have earned universal admiration, while the sympathy and consideration which you have always shown in dealing with individuals have smoothed away many difficulties and inspired very deep feelings of personal regard in which Lady Lawley is associated with yourself."

In his speech replying, Sir Arthur thanked the Mayor and Councillors of Johannesburg on behalf of himself and his wife.

"I thank you for the flattering references which you have made to my past work. No reference thereto would have been quite complete unless you had treated it as you have done – namely as a part of the great work which was undertaken by Lord

Milner. If my own individual efforts and my personal influence have helped in that work, I am indeed more than rewarded, though I know that I have only to thank the example which he set me and the inspiration which he gave me."

The Lawley family embarked on a Union Castle liner at Cape Town to sail to Southampton and be in England in time for Christmas.

[1]   The Star, Weekly Edition. Johannesburg. Saturday September 6th 1902.

[2]   The Milner Papers. Bodleian Library Oxford. Dep. 171. Fols 41/230. Johannesburg, 29th April 1902. Milner to Ommaney.

[3]   The Milner Papers. Bodleian Library Oxford. Dep. 171, Folios 189 to 191.

[4]   The Nation and The Empire. Lord Alfred Milner. Constable. London, 1913.

[5]   Encyclopaedia Britannica. 2002.
      The Collected Essays of Bernard Makhosezwe Magubane, Africa World Press, Trenton, New Jersey, 1996.

[6]   "Milner's Kindergarten", Carroll Quigley. "The Anglo-American Establishment," written in 1949 and not published until 1981.
      Times Obituary for Geoffrey Dawson, Wednesday, Nov 8th 1944.

[7]   "Jan Christian Smuts" by his son J.C. Smuts. Cassell and Co. Ltd. Cape Town. 1952

[8]   The Star. Weekly Edition. Johannesburg. Saturday November 1st 1902.

[9]   Emily Hobhouse: The Brunt of War and where it fell. Methuen. London.1902

[10] Lawrence Richardson. Selected Correspondence (1902 – 1903). Edited by Arthur Davey.

[11] Report on the Concentration Camps in South Africa by the Committee of Ladies appointed by the Secretary of State for War. Her Majesty's Stationery Office, London. 1902. Presented to both Houses of Parliament by Command of His Majesty.

[12] The Times. October 15th. Page 3. Column B.

[13] The Times. Monday October 20th 1902. Page 3. Column A.

[14] Joseph Chamberlain, Entrepreneur in Politics. Peter T. Marsh. Yale. 1994. ISBN 0 300 05801 2 Pages 294 and 295.

[15] Milner, Apostle of Empire. John Marlowe. Hamish Hamilton. London. 1976.

[16] The Making of a Racist State: British Imperialism and the Making of South Africa. Bernard Makhosezwe Magubane, Africa World Press, Trenton, New Jersey, 1996 Pages 132 and 325

[17] Milner, Apostle of Empire. John Marlowe. Hamish Hamilton. London. 1976. Pages 153 and 154.

[18] "Gold Miners and the Imperial War". ANC Website. South Africa.

[19] The Good Hope was sunk at the Battle of Coronel off Chile in 1914.

[20] Joseph Chamberlain, Entrepreneur in Politics. Peter T. Marsh. Yale 1994. ISBN 0 300 05801 2. Page 347.

[21] The Times. Thursday January 8th. Page 3. Column A

[22] South African National Archives, Volume 76, System 01. Reference 84. Boers and Burghers Interview with Sir Arthur Lawley. 07.01.1903

[23] The Times. Monday January 12th 1903. Page 3. Column B.

[24] Mr Chamberlain's speeches. December 27th 1902. (Edited by C.W. Boyd London 1914).

[25] Geoffrey Dawson's Diary – entry for January 14th 1903. Bodleian Library Oxford

[26] The Times. Monday 19th January 1903. Page 5. Column A.

[27] With Chamberlain in South Africa, Central News Agency. 1903. Page 47 from "Joseph Chamberlain, Entrepreneur in Politics". Peter T. Marsh. Yale 1994. Page 553.

[28] Washington Post. January 26th 1903, page 1. Milner, Apostle of Empire. John Marlowe. Hamish Hamilton. London. 1976. Page 145. The Times. January 26th 1903. Page 5. Column D.

[29] The Times. 28th January 1903.

[30] Colonial Office Despatches CO 510/4 – 8627, 10321 and 12726. National Archives. Kew

[31] Mahatma Gandhi and Sir Arthur Lawley. www.sahistory.org. 2002

[32] British Indians and the Transvaal by L.W. Ritch. www.mkgandhi.org

[33] Satygraha in South Africa by M.K. Gandhi. Navajivan Trust. 1928

[34] The Life of Mahatma Gandhi by Louis Fischer. Jonathan Cape. London 1951. Page 78.

[35] Ideologies of the Raj (The New Cambridge History of India) by Thomas R. Metcalf, et al: Cambridge University Press; New Ed edition (1997) ISBN: 0521589371 Page 218.

[36] The Times. Thursday 8th June 1905. Page 6. Column A.

[37] The Times. Thursday June 22nd 1905. Page 6. Column A.

[38] The Star, Weekly Edition. Johannesburg. Saturday May 23rd 1903.

39 The Nation and The Empire. Lord Alfred Milner. Constable. London, 1913.

40 New York Times. May 21st 1903, page 5.

41 The Times. Thursday May 22nd 1903. Page 5. Column A.

42 "Jan Christian Smuts" by his son J.C. Smuts. Cassell and Co. Ltd. Cape Town. 1952

43 Geoffrey Dawson's Diaries for 1902 to 1905. Bodleian Library Oxford.

44 Colonial Office List for 1911. National Archives. Kew.

45 Dawson diary for 1904. Bodleian Library. Oxford.

46 Lord Wraxall's albums at the Empire and Commonwealth Museum. Bristol. UK.

47 The Star, Weekly Edition. Johannesburg. Saturday November 7th 1903.

48 The Star, Weekly Edition. Johannesburg. Saturday February 27th 1904.

49 Geoffrey Dawson's Diary – entry for October 21st 1902. Bodleian Library Oxford

50 Johannesburg Star. 20th November 1905.

51 Source: Anglo-Boer War Museum

52 Lt.-Col. H.F. Trew. African Man Hunts. London. 1938.

53 The Star, Weekly Edition. Johannesburg. Saturday September 19th 1903.

54 Dawson diary for 1904. Bodleian Library. Oxford.

55 The Bulawayo Chronicle. Saturday July 9th 1904.

56 Lord Wraxall's Photo Albums. Empire and Commonwealth Museum. Bristol. Sir George and Lady Farrar's Photo Albums. Rhodes House. Oxford. M.K. Gandhi. "Johannesburg Letter" June 26th 1907. www.mkgandhi.org

57 The Milner Papers. Bodleian Library Oxford. Dep 322. Fols 312/3. October 19th 1903.

58 The Milner Papers. Bodleian Library Oxford. Dep 322. Fols 323/6. October 28th 1903.

59 The Milner Papers. Bodleian Library Oxford. Dep 322. Fols 327/8. October 30th 1903.

60 The Milner Papers. Bodleian Library Oxford. Dep 323. Fols 133/7. February 19th and 27th 1903.

61 Milner, Apostle of Empire. John Marlowe. Hamish Hamilton. London. 1976. Page 164.

62 Milner, Apostle of Empire. John Marlowe. Hamish Hamilton. London. 1976. Chapter 7.

63 Colonial Office Despatches CO 510/6 – 3559, 9246 and Chinese Labour Regulations. National Archives. Kew.

64 South African National Archives, Volume 667, System 01. Reference G2924/9. Standerton Stud Farm. Visit of Sir Arthur Lawley to Farm. Suggestions re Class of Stock to be raised etc. 1905. Colonial Office Despatches CO 510/5 – 5090 and 6066. National Archives. Kew.

65 The Milner Papers. Bodleian Library Oxford. Dep 237. Fols 148/152. September 28th 1903.

66 Science and Empire : East Coast Fever in Rhodesia and the Transvaal (Cambridge Studies in the History of Medicine) by Paul F. Cranefield, Editors: Charles Rosenberg and Colin Jones: Cambridge University Press; New Ed. (2002) ISBN: 0521524490.

67 South African National Archives, Volume Seven, System 01. Reference P/LC3/03. Papers laid on the Table, 2nd Session, Memorandum of Agreement of Lease between Sir Arthur Lawley KCMG and Henry Horace Wright. 1903.

68 South African National Archives, Volume Seven, System 01. Reference P/LC3/03. Papers laid on the Table, 2nd Session, Memorandum of Agreement of Lease between Sir Arthur Lawley KCMG and Henry Horace Wright. 1903.
    South African National Archives, Volume 45, System 01. Reference CM 1046/04. Sir Arthur Lawley. Proclamation Komati and Northern Districts. 15.04.1904.

69 The Nation and The Empire. Lord Alfred Milner. Constable. London, 1913.

70 Elusive Equity: Education Reform in Post Apartheid South Africa by Edward B. Fiske, Helen F. Ladd

71 Doctorial Thesis. M.S.J. Ledwaba. University of Pretoria 1905.

72 Algy Lawley. Latimer Trend and Co. Plymouth. 1933.

73 Colonial Office Despatches CO 510/6 4791 and 23294. National Archives. Kew.

74 Colonial Office Despatches CO 510/6 September 5th 1903. National Archives. Kew.

75 The Times. Monday August 17th 1903. Page 8. column F.

76 World Wide Web.potchboyshigh.co.za/hist.htm

77 The Times. Thursday April 18th 1905. Page 15. Column C.

78 The Star, Weekly Edition. Johannesburg. Saturday March 25th 1904.

79 "Transvaal Scottish Related Monuments" by James H. Mitchell. 1999.

80 Lord Wraxall's albums at the Empire and Commonwealth Museum. Bristol. UK.

81 Colonial Office Despatches CO 510/5 27099, 28422, 28423 National Archives. Kew.

82 Lessons from the Varsity of Life by Lord Baden-Powell of Gilwell.
    Chapter 8. The South African Constabulary.

[83] The Milner Papers. Bodleian Library Oxford. Dep. 237. Fols 144/5. Letter of August 19th 1903.

[84] Encyclopaedia Britannica – Swaziland.

[85] The Star, Weekly Edition. Johannesburg. Saturday September 5th 1903.

[86] Lord Wraxall's albums at the Empire and Commonwealth Museum. Bristol. UK.

[87] The Times. Tuesday 25th August 1903. Page 3. Column E.
The Star, Weekly Edition. Johannesburg. Saturday September 5th 1903.

[88] The Star, Weekly Edition. Johannesburg. Saturday September 26th 1903.

[89] The Milner Papers. Bodleian Library Oxford. Dep. 237. Fols 146/7. Letter of September 20th 1903.

[90] The Times. Thursday May 26th 1904. Page 3. Column C.
The Times. May 27th 1904. Page 3. Column D.
The Times. Wednesday July 6th 1904. Page 6. Column A.

[91] The Times. Tuesday August 30th. Page 3. Column D, and Monday 19th September.

[92] The Times. Wednesday September 21st 1904. Page 7. Column F.

[93] The Times. Wednesday June 22nd 1904. Page 12. Column A.

[94] The Times. Monday October 17th 1904. Page 5. Column B.

[95] The Times. Saturday January 21st 1905. Page 11. Column E.

[96] The Times. Saturday January 23rd 1905. Page 10. Column A.

[97] The Times. Saturday March 4th 1905. Page 9. Column E.

[98] The Star, Weekly Edition. Johannesburg. Saturday February 18th 1905.

[99] Lt.-Col. H.F. Trew. African Man Hunts. London. 1938.

[100] Geoffrey Dawson diary for 1905. Bodleian Library, Oxford.

[101] The Times. Wednesday 17th May 1907. Page 5. Column C.

[102] South African National Archives, Volume 57, System 01. Reference 84/04. Sir Arthur Lawley administering the Government in Viscount Milner's absence. 05.02.1905. Incoming Despatches.
The Times. April 3rd 1905. Page 4. Column B.

[103] Milner, Apostle of Empire. John Marlowe. Hamish Hamilton. London. 1976.
Telegram to Joseph Chamberlain. August 6th 1903.
South African National Archives, Volume 49, System 01. Reference 64/3. Appointment of Governor and High Commissioner Sir Arthur Lawley, starting 1903 ending 1905.
South African National Archives, Volume 57, System 01. Reference 84/04. Sir Arthur Lawley administering the Government in Viscount Milner's absence. 05.02.1905. Incoming Despatches.

[104] The Milner Papers. Dep 189. Letter of May 29th 1905 from Sir Arthur Lawley to Lord Milner.

[105] My Africa Journey. Winston Churchill. Hodder and Stoughton. London 1908. Page 11.

[106] The Milner Papers. Dep 189. Letter of June 12th 1905 from Sir Arthur Lawley to Lord Milner.

[107] Wikpedia Encyclopaedia. Encyclopaedia Britannica. Diamond vues.com.

[108] The Times. Tuesday August 20th 1907. Page 3. Column A.

[109] The Star, Weekly Edition. Johannesburg. Saturday October 14th 1905.

[110] The Star, Weekly Edition. Johannesburg. Saturday November 4th 1905.

[111] Geoffrey Dawson diary for 1905. Bodleian Library, Oxford.
The Star, Johannesburg, Transvaal. October 25th 1905.

[112] M. K. Gandhi. The Star. Johannesburg. 10th September 1904.

[113] Mahatma Gandhi Media and Research Service. Chronology 1905

[114] Indian Opinion, 2nd December 1905.

[115] Mr Chamberlain's speeches. December 27th 1902. (Edited by C.W. Boyd London 1914).

[116] Class & Colour in South Africa 1850-1950, Chapter 5. International Defence and Aid Fund for Southern Africa (January, 1983) ISBN: 0904759520

[117] Transvaal Constitution; letter from Sir Arthur Lawley to the Earl of Elgin – National Archives Kew. Reference: CO 879/91/9

[118] Milner, Apostle of Empire. John Marlowe. Hamish Hamilton. London. 1976.

[119] The Times. November 30th 1905. Page 5. Column C.

[120] Johannesburg Star December 2nd 1905. Pages 9 and 10.

[121] "Jan Christian Smuts" by his son J.C. Smuts. Cassell and Co. Ltd. Cape Town. 1952.

[122] The Collected Works of Mahatma Gandhi. Page 268.

[123] The Star, Weekly Edition. Johannesburg. Saturday December 9th 1905

[124] The Transvaal Leader. Tuesday December 5th 1905.

Chapter 5
Ruler of the Raj

The Madras Presidency

On March 5th 1906, Sir Arthur and Lady Lawley left Victoria Station in London by the Ostend boat train to visit their son Ned (Richard Lawley) who was convalescing in Germany. Sir Arthur Lawley then proceeded to Marseilles to embark on the P. and O. steamship "Himalaya" and sail to India. He had just been dubbed Knight Grand Commander of the Order of the Indian Empire. Leaving the "Himalaya" at Port Said, the new Governor of Madras arrived in Bombay aboard the Mail Steamer "Oriental" on Monday March 23rd. A guard of honour of the Royal Scots was mounted at Bunder Head. Sir Arthur was accompanied by Major G. Carr Glyn D.S.O., his Military Secretary, and Captain Duff, his A.D.C. On the 28th March, Sir Arthur assumed the office of Governor of Fort St. George and its dependencies.[1] Other new appointments were then made. On July 17th, the Madras Gazette announced that Mr Murray Hammick was to be the Chief Secretary, and Mr. J. N. Atkinson the Secretary to the Government Revenue Department.[2] The main Government Departments at Fort St George were the Public, the Ecclesiastical, the Judicial, the Legislative, the Revenue and the Public Works Departments. Other departments covered Education, Agriculture, Forestry, Public Health, Medicine, and Marine, Ports and Harbours. There were two main organs of Government – the Executive Council and the Legislative Council. The Governor was President of both the Councils. The Madras Presidency governed 40 million people.

Figure 135: His Excellency the Governor arriving at Fort St. George on May 28th 1906.

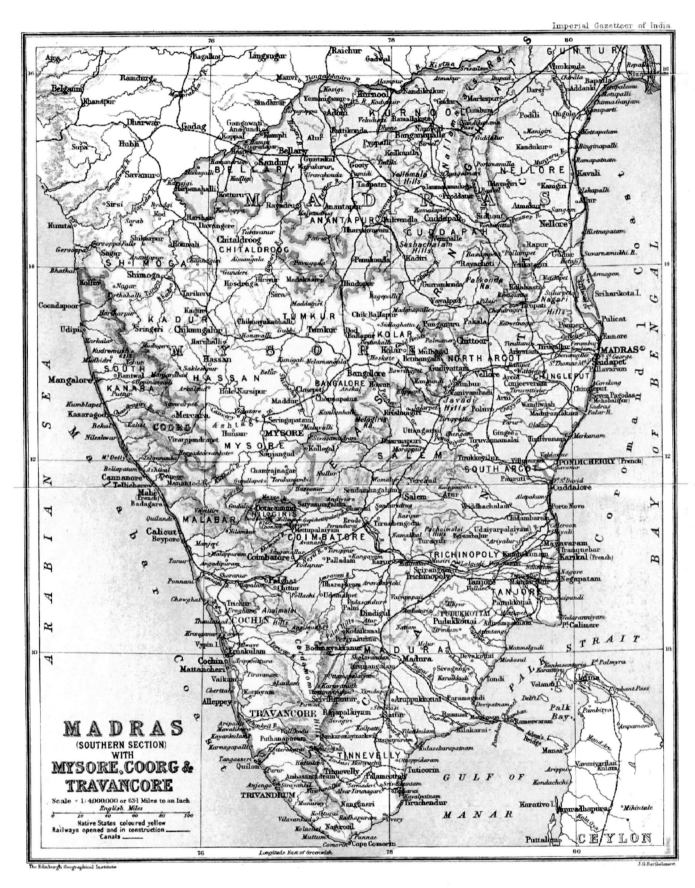

Figure 136: The Madras Presidency (Southern Section).

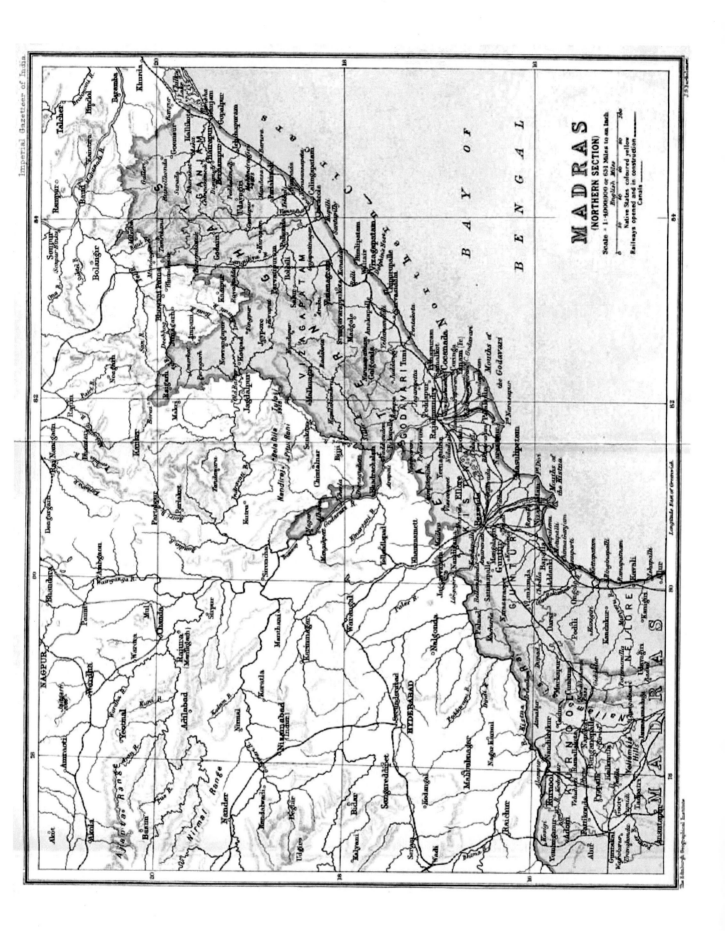

Figure 137: The Madras Presidency (Northern Section).

Figure 138: Madras: Government House (left) and the Banqueting Hall (right).

Lady Lawley, concerned about the health of their son who was due to go to Oxford, stayed on for a while in England.[3] On Friday 26th October, she and her two daughters embarked on the steamship Caledonia at Marseilles to sail to Colombo.[4]

Sir Arthur's brother Beilby Lawley, the third Baron Wenlock, had been the Governor of Madras between January 1891 and March 1896. The Governor lived in Government House, Fort St George, a palatial residence with numerous servants, and had an official Daimler car at his disposal. There was a Head Butler called Muniswami, who ruled with a rod of iron. For the governor's ceremonial use, there was a glittering coach with prancing horses, accompanied by a bodyguard of Indian troopers with red uniforms, glittering steel accoutrements and pennoned lances. There was also Guindy, a spacious and elegant country home on the outskirts of Madras, surrounded by an extensive park. Nearby were a golf course, hockey pitches, riding stables and the Guindy Horse Racing Track.

From May to October each year during the hot season, the Madras Government and its officials, the Governor and his family went to Government House in the hill station of Ooty or Ootacamund in the Nilgiri Hills. Sir Arthur was an accomplished horseman, a quality admired by the Indian princes of the Madras Presidency. He enjoyed hunting with the Ooty hounds and was frequently joined by close friends like the Maharajah of Mysore. "Hunting, which had been the passion of his youth in England, probably appealed to him more than any other form of recreation, and he was a fine shot with a rifle and brought home many of the trophies – tiger, panther and bison – for which the Southern Indian jungles are well renowned." [5]

The English presence in what later became the Province of Madras started in 1639, when English traders acquired some lands for the purpose of erecting a fort at

Madras-patnam on the East Coast of India. In the course of the years which followed, Fort St. George became the centre of all British activities in the region, and gradually its authority – first limited to some coastal settlements – was extended to include all the territories under direct or indirect British rule in South Eastern and Southern India.

Figure 139: Government House, Madras.

Unlike elsewhere in India – where many Indian Princely States continued to exist as Protectorates – most States under the suzerainty of the British-Indian Government of Madras were gradually annexed to the Province.[6]

The new Governor introduced the Morley-Minto reforms, which gave more democratic participation in government to the Indians. As President and the leader of the Legislature, Sir Arthur Lawley's tact, geniality, candour, sincerity and skill at public speaking won him widespread respect. He brought in a Land Estates Act protecting the rights of tenants against over exploitative landlords. He appointed the Maharaja of Bobbili to be the first Indian to have membership of the Executive. Sir Arthur also did much for the development of Madras industries and commerce.[7] During the last week of June 1906, the Madras Industrial Conference was held in the Centennary Hall at Palamkottah. The Governor gave this his full support.[8]

During the summer of 1906, Sir Arthur Lawley first visited his official residence, Government House in the hill station of Ootacamund. Sir Arthur attended the Annual Breakfast of the Ootacamund Club on Saturday 4th July 1906, where one hundred club members led by General Sir Charles and Lady Eggerton, Sir James Thompson, and

Mr G.S. Forbes I.C.S. welcomed him to Ooty.[9] Later that month, Sir Arthur and the Eggertons attended an excellent concert and play in the Armoury in aid of St Stephen's Orphanage and Poor School. St Stephen's was the Anglican Church in Ooty attended by the officials and bureaucracy of the Madras Presidency.

Figure 140: His Excellency the Governor at his Investiture in March 1906 with two Indian Princes, the son of Kumaraja Venkatagiri on the left and the son of the Rajah of Kurupam on the right.

The Maharajah of Mysore

On October 13th 1906, Sir Arthur paid his first visit to the Maharajah of Mysore, who was to become a close personal friend. That first day there was an exchange of official visits, the Maharajah to the British Residency and the Governor to the Maharajah's Palace. The following morning, Sir Arthur was taken on a carriage ride

with the Maharajah through the streets of Mysore to see the main sights of the city.
The Maharajah then took the Governor to see his riding stables where there were 130
horses and some of these were later saddled up and mounted to give a display of show
jumping for the visitors. Then the party visited the Zoological Gardens before
proceeding to see the New Palace, which had been under construction for eight years,
and was nearly completed. The following day the visit culminated with a tiger hunt. [10]
While this official tour was under way, a crisis was breaking in Madras.

Figure 141: Krishnaraja Wodeyar IV, the Maharaja of Mysore (1902-1940).

The Bankrupt Bank

In 1906, one of the major Banks in Madras, Arbuthnot and Company, went bankrupt and in the ensuing crash many people lost a great deal of money. Indeed even Sir Arthur Lawley himself sustained some losses in what was the biggest crash in Indian banking history. Sir George Gough Arbuthnot was the head of Arbuthnot and Company when the crash occurred. He was a member of the Madras Legislative Council and a prominent figure in Madras society at that time. Sir George's social position had a good deal to do with the problems which confronted the firm. Because he was well known and highly esteemed he brought in numerous deposits, but unfortunately used these for speculation and personal advantage. Much money was spent on searching for gold in the Nilgiri and Anamalais Hills, on investment in American railway projects, on new South African gold fields and in the plantation crops of the West Indies. Arbuthnot and Company were drained dry. P. Macfadyen, the senior partner of Macfadyen and Co. in London, Arbuthnot's correspondent and associate in England and an old Madras hand, committed suicide on October 20th, 1906. Then the crisis broke. Both firms petitioned the courts on the 22nd to be declared insolvent. The auditors appointed by the Official Assignee estimated that Arbuthnot's liabilities were 27 million rupees and its assets only 7½ million rupees. The firm had 2,300 operating accounts in India with balances of 2¾ million rupees and about 4,000 fixed deposits with claims amounting to over 25 million rupees. With the assets being described as being only on paper and "beyond all belief, worthless, crumbling to dust when touched", there was no way to meet the claims of the depositors, who included almost everyone in Madras who had savings or some money to invest.

In the aftermath of the crash, Sir Arthur Lawley as the Governor of Madras, who had lost £1200 in the bankruptcy of the company, launched a public fund to raise money to help the weaker sections who had lost everything in Arbuthnot's. The Madras Times reported on November 15th that His Excellency the Governor had donated 1000 rupees to the Arbuthnot Relief Fund. [11]

The family arrive

Lady Lawley, with her son and her daughters, had spent the summer and autumn of 1906 in England. On November 19th, Sir Arthur said in a speech during his Tour of Madura and Trichinopoly, "I shall soon have the pleasure of welcoming again my wife and children from whom I have been separated for so long." That afternoon Lady Lawley and her daughters arrived in Madura to join Sir Arthur. They were accompanied by Lady Lawley's sister Mamie (Mrs Mary Gosling), Sir Arthur's brother Dick (Colonel the Hon. Richard Thompson Lawley C.B.), Colonel Geoffrey Glyn and Mrs Glyn. In the evening the whole party went to see the great banyan tree in the compound of the old judge's house. [12] During the course of this tour, Sir Arthur showed an interest in encouraging industry in Southern India. In a speech in Madura, he said,

> "In regard to your weaving industry which is, I know, an important element in the life of the community here, I can assure you that the Government is anxious to carry on a forward and progressive policy towards not only this but also towards other industries in this country." [13]

Figure 142: Banyan tree in the compound of the old judge's house, Madura.

Figure 143: Lady Lawley and Mrs Mary Gosling take an afternoon stroll.

Sir Arthur had retained the services of his A.D.C. and Secretary from the Transvaal, Colonel Geoffrey Carr Glyn D.S.O. Geoffrey Glyn served as the Governor's Military Secretary. He and his wife were trusted friends. As Geoffrey Glyn was recovering from typhoid fever caught in Bangalore, Colonel Richard Lawley had agreed to act as temporary Military Secretary to the Governor. He knew the ropes because had been Lord Wenlock's Military Secretary when he was Governor of Madras.[14]

On the morning of Saturday December 20th 1906, Colonel Richard T. Lawley and Lady Lawley visited the Buckingham Textile Mills in Perambore, where about four thousand men and boys were engaged in spinning, weaving, dyeing, bleaching and finished work. This demonstrated further support from the Lawley family for the cotton textile industry of Southern India.

Another great interest of the Lawleys was in Indian education. The Indian Universities Act was published in December 1906. "It was held that the University Curricula did not lay sufficient emphasis on the importance of English, a sound knowledge of which is the only avenue to a liberal education". At the University of Madras, an honours course of three years and a pass course of two years were introduced. A more prominent place was given in the Scheme of Studies to the English language. It was planned to establish a University Library. The Teachers College at Saldapet was to be reorganised.[15]

R. T. L.   W.   A. L.

January 1907.

Figure 144: The Lawley Brothers – Richard, Beilby and Arthur.

Sir Arthur Lawley's eldest brother was expected for Christmas in 1906. At 7.42 a.m. on Saturday morning December 24th 1906, Beilby Lord Wenlock accompanied by the Hon. Mrs Portman, the Hon. Mrs Forbes and Miss Martineau arrived at Egmore Station, Madras, from Colombo. Beilby had been the Governor of Madras during the 1890s. Red baize was spread on the station platform and a guard of honour consisting of 100 rank and file with regimental band and colours was provided by the Madras Volunteer Guards. Lord Wenlock was met by his brothers Sir Arthur Lawley and Colonel Richard. T. Lawley, and by the Hon. Mr. G. S. Forbes. Lord Wenlock boarded one of the Governor's state carriages and was driven off to Government House Madras en route to Guindy escorted by a full compliment of the Governor's Body Guard. Two arches decorated the route. One said, "Mussalmans Welcome their Friend, Lord Wenlock"; the other said, "Welcome to our benefactor Lord Wenlock. God bless him."

The Madras Times reported that on Thursday December 28th, "the Prince of Arcot gave a garden party for Their Excellencies Sir Arthur and Lady Lawley and Lord Wenlock at his Adyar residence – "Prince's Lodge". His Excellency the Governor was accompanied by Lord Wenlock in the first carriage escorted by the Body Guard. They were followed by two other carriages in which sat Lady Lawley and her daughters, and Colonel Richard T. Lawley with Mrs Mary Gosling. There was a glittering gathering of the Mahommedans and the élite of the city. After the introductions, their Excellencies walked around the grounds and took a lively interest in the several amusements provided by the prince."[16]

The Taj Mahal

On New Year's Day the Lawley brothers, Lady Lawley and her daughters went to a State Reception in the Banqueting Hall in Madras and the following evening there was a State Ball.[17] On Wednesday 9th January, Beilby accompanied Lady Lawley on a visit to the General Hospital. That evening Lord Wenlock left Madras on the Bombay Mail Train on a visit to Agra. He took with him Ursula and Cecilia Lawley, the Hon. Mrs Portman, the Hon. Mrs Forbes, Miss Martineau and Mrs Mary Gosling. In Agra, they not only saw the sepulchral splendour of the Taj Mahal, but also witnessed an orchestrated display of imperial power laid on by Lord Kitchener to impress the Amir of Afghanistan.

Beilby wrote to his wife, Constance, from Lucknow on January 16th, "We had a very good time of it in Camp at Agra. Everything was most beautifully done – and Lady Minto puts on all the airs and graces of Royalty. Her three daughters are most pretty and charming and all the A.D.Cs and 'detrimentals' out here are head over heels in love with them. She is bringing them home for two months of the London season and I have no doubt would be only too pleased if she had not to take them back. We had any number of full dress dinners, reviews, functions and fireworks…."

The Amir of Afghanistan was in Agra and there was a review of 30,000 troops which he witnessed with considerable impact. Lord Wenlock wrote, "Many of the Indian Rajahs think that we are doing too much for him – but I think it is the right game to make him friendly and so far he has enjoyed himself immensely. He has taken very much to Lord Kitchener who apparently has much influence over him. He actually played the piano the other night – which I hardly expected from an Afghan Potentate. He is to be in India altogether about two months, and I hope he will be thoroughly impressed with all he will see. We got away from Agra at midnight on the 14th and after spending a night in Cawnpore, came on here to Lucknow. We leave tomorrow night for Benares and so by Calcutta back to Madras where we are due on the 22nd." [18]

Figure 145: The Taj Mahal - 1907.

On his return to Madras, Beilby wrote to Constance, "Everything is so much what we used to know so well – the surf on the beach and the evening glow. A dinner and a dance tonight and I shall try to get a rubber of bridge."[19]

Later that month, Sir Arthur Lawley and his two brothers left for an official tour of Cochin and Travancore, which lasted from January 25th to February 14th. On January 26th, they were met by His Highness the Rajah of Cochin who gave a State Dinner in their honour at Ernakulam. The return visit to the British Residency in Cochin, where the Lawleys were staying, was on the following day.

Lord Wenlock wrote to his wife from Cochin, "We got to this enchanting fairyland on Saturday 26th and are well lodged in an excellent Residency set in the flashing waters which come in fresh from the Arabian Sea, and amidst a mass of palm covered islands. The party are delighted with it and the Rajah and his people do everything in our honour – banquets, fireworks, expeditions, garden parties – all in brilliant sunshine by day and moonlight by night, and though we are in a land of perpetual summer, the nights are still quite cold."[20]

The Governor's party journeyed south by launch along the coastal canals and lagoons of Travancore. The Madras Times reported on January 31st, "The entertainment given in honour of Lord Wenlock by Rajah Bahadur P. Ananda Charlu at his residence "Lakeside" yesterday proved a very successful one in every way....

Lord Wenlock arrived with their Excellencies Sir Arthur and Lady Lawley and Miss Ursula Lawley."

In his speech thanking his host, Lord Wenlock said,

Figure 146: Sir Arthur Lawley, Mrs. Portman and Lord Wenlock in Travancore.

Figure 147: Buffalo Racing - Cochin.

"I wish particularly to thank you for the extremely kind manner in which you have received me here this afternoon especially for the kind words which you have addressed to me on my visit to Madras, the scene of my former labours, where I am glad to think that my own brother has taken the place I once occupied. I sincerely hope that he will have as pleasant and happy a time in Madras as I have had myself. It has given me extreme pleasure to come back and to renew many old friendships and acquaintanceships. I really think that I have seldom had such an opportunity of meeting so many of my old friends together."

At the end of their visit, Lord Wenlock and Sir Arthur and Lady Lawley were garlanded and then bade farewell to the Rajah and his family.[21]

Lord Wenlock and Sir Arthur continued their journey south through Trivandrum before going on to a shooting camp in the hills. Beilby wrote to Constance from the Camp at Periyar on February 5th, "We got here last night to find a regular town of grass huts most beautifully finished with verandahs, bathrooms, mess rooms and everything we could want made out of bamboo – writing tables, bedsteads and panels to the walls worked with all kinds of different designs. It has taken months to construct. Then we go out into different shooting camps all beautifully constructed. Annie, Mamie Gosling and Mrs Carr have also come while the others have gone on to Madras….. The jungle is all round us and most of last night anyone who was awake could hear a tiger and a sambur close by – one roaring and the other belling – all night…. We are about three thousand feet up here and the air is much fresher than down below."[22]

The hunting party returned to Madras on February 20th. That evening Lord Wenlock accompanied by the Hon. Mrs Portland left Madras by the North West Mail Train of Madras Railways for Bombay en route to England. Sir Arthur, Ursula and Cecilia Lawley were on the platform to bid farewell to Lord Wenlock and Mrs Portland and wish them 'bon voyage'.[23]

Colonel Richard Thompson Lawley, Dick, stayed on at Ootacamund for a while, having booked his passage to England for May 12th 1907.[24] On April 25th 1907, Sir Arthur Lawley opened a new Pasteur Institute in Coonoor to deal with the victims of rabies and persons who had been bitten by rabid animals.[25]

South Canara

In November 1907, Sir Arthur and Lady Lawley and their two daughters went on an official tour of South Canara. The Lawleys were enthusiastic supporters of medical missionary endeavours. One of the first Jesuit Missionaries to come to Mangalore, the main urban centre in South Canara, was a German, Father Müller.[26] He arrived in Mangalore on 31st December 1878 and later joined the staff of the newly established Saint Aloysius College there. By then he was a fully trained Homoeopathic Physician. He had brought with him a small chest of Homeopathic medicines from the firm of Catellan in Paris, and with these he started treating his students in Saint Aloysius College. The fame of his successful treatment grew rapidly, thus forcing him to open a regular dispensary in 1880, which he called the Homeopathic Poor Dispensary. The philanthropic work of Father Müller did not stop with the Dispensary. In 1890, he started the Saint Joseph's Leprosy Hospital and Asylum to house and treat poor leprosy patients shunned by society.

In 1895 Father Müller started work on a General Hospital, and by 1901 there were two wards, one for men and the other for women. In 1902, when bubonic plague broke out in Mangalore, Father Müller reacted immediately. In spite of the heavy downpour of the monsoon rains, he constructed a Plague Hospital in a record time of four weeks so that he could take proper care of the patients and their treatment.

For his services to India Father Müller was awarded the Kaiser-i-Hindi Medal. Before pinning the medal on the Father's breast in November 1907, Sir Arthur Lawley, as Governor of Madras, said,

"I take it that the purpose in view when the bestowal of the medal is determined on, is to make known, as widely as possible, the recognition of services of exceptional merit rendered to India and her peoples. I feel that the phrase which I have used of exceptional merit is a most inadequate description of the work, which you have done in this district. The Church to which you belong has been for decade after decade a practical and living exposition of the teachings of Christ, of self-sacrifice, self-obliteration, and self-devotion to the welfare of others. And, Ladies and Gentlemen, no exponent of these doctrines has been more faithful, more consistent, and more conspicuous than Father Müller."

Figure 148: Mr P. F. Saldhana's De Dion car in which the Lawley girls drove to Karkala.

During their visit to Mangalore, Sir Arthur and Lady Lawley, and their daughters, Ursula and Cecilia, found themselves in need of additional transport.[27] The Governor had his own Daimler, which could not accommodate the entire party, so Mr P. F. X. Saldanha offered the loan of his brand new De Dion car. The De Dion was an 8-10 HP single cylinder automobile, and was the first ever motor car to negotiate the narrow, winding and undulating roads of the coastal city of Mangalore, which was then a sleepy town, almost like an overgrown village. The De Dion proved to be very suitable for the young ladies as it was able to keep pace with the Governor's high powered car.

The De Dion was brought from Paris by Mr Saldanha (1860-1938), a pioneer of the coffee curing industry in Mangalore. The car was shipped to the port town in the month of October, 1906. Its arrival created a sensation in the town and crowds used to flock regularly to Mr Saldanha's house to gaze at this four-wheeled miracle on wheels. The car was used sparingly, for though there was no petrol rationing, petrol was a commodity for which there was no use and therefore was not readily available. Petrol had to be ferried by boat all the way from Madras (Chennai) to Bombay (Mumbai) in five or ten gallon drums, under a special licence. The petrol was then brought from Bombay to Mangalore, which is on the coast 300 kilometres south of Goa. Mangalore was on the west coast of the Madras Presidency. The De Dion car had a cruising speed of 19 kms per hour. On November 8th, Mr Saldanha loaned his car to Sir Arthur's two daughters to motor up to Karkala, 33 miles from Mangalore, where there is an historic monolithic statue of Bahubali revered by the Jain ascetics who follow the path of spiritual purity and enlightenment. On his return to Madras, Sir Arthur wrote a special letter of thanks to Mr Saldanha for the loan of his car. The whole incident is reminiscent of E.M. Forster's "Passage to India".[28]

There were Jain shrines at several locations – Danavulapad in the Cuddapah District, Sankaram in the Vizagapatam District and Rahathirtham near Vizianagram. These were the responsibility of the Archaeological Survey of India which was reorganised in 1906. At that time an archaeological excavation of an Amaravati stupa in the Guntur District was under way. During the five years of Sir Arthur's Presidency, three thousand inscriptions from stones and 63 from ancient copper plates were copied by experts in epigraphy.[29]

Figure 149: Lady Lawley and he daughter, Ursula, about to be taken for a drive.

Figure 150: "A tank in Mysore with Canarese women drawing water". Lady Lawley.

Figure 151: Early morning on Lake Ootacamund, Nilgiri Hills. Lady Lawley.

Lady Lawley's water colours of the staff at Government House.

Figure 152: Governor's Bodyguard.

Figure 153: Head Coachman.

Figure 154: The Cook.

Figure 155: Muniswami – The Butler.

Accomplished artist

Lady Lawley was an accomplished artist especially in water colours. She had learned to paint at the Académie Julian in Paris in the early 1880s, where Tony Robert Fleury and William Bouguereau were teaching at the time. Her cousins were the Emmet sisters – Rosina, Lydia and Jane – who became famous American artists and also studied at the Académie Julian. The academy's students included Henri Matisse, Alphons Mucha and Pierre Bonnard. Lady Lawley's grand mother, Jane Erin McEvers, was herself an artist. She took a particular interest in Annie's studies.[30] There are books of sketches that Jane Erin drew in France and Germany in the early 1860s kept at Tyntesfield in Somerset.[31] She came from the American branch of the Emmet family, which was descended from her father, Irish patriot Thomas Addis Emmet, the brother of the renowned Irish martyr Robert Emmet. The family included many artists, physicians, lawyers, and writers among its ranks including Henry James. At the time of her birth, Jane Erin's father was in prison at Fort George in Scotland for the part he played in the United Irishmen movement. Her mother accompanied her father to prison and so Jane Erin was born in gaol on the 18th April 1802, just a few months prior to her parents' release.[32] Thomas Addis Emmet was banished from Britain and went to live in Brussels for a while before emigrating to America.

Lady Lawley made records of her experiences in India with her brush and pencil. Some of her work has reached the public in her book on "Southern India", for which the text was written by F. E. Penny. The book was first published in 1914 and contains fifty of Lady Lawley's water colours of Indian life and landscapes.[33] So impressive are these paintings that the book is still in publication. It was the people of India that attracted Annie Lawley most, and her paintings of the Cook and of the Head Coachman at Government House contrast with water colours of a Saddhu, a Learned Ascetic, a Hindu Pariah beggar and a Tamil girl. She also painted scenes of rural life such as "A Tank in Mysore with Canarese Women drawing water." With the peoples of India both she and her husband established relations of warm friendship, and she took a special and sustained interest in every movement for the welfare of Indian women.[34]

In 1907 Sir Arthur Lawley became the Governor of the Government School of Art. This was reorganised to include i) Pure Design and ii) Design as applied to industry – metal work, lacquer ware, wood carving and commercial art.[35]

Law and order

Sir Arthur Lawley was characteristically judicious and firm when handling unrest. In 1908, in riots at Tinnevelly, a mob was for some hours in command of the situation, but the Governor's combination of decisive firmness and understanding calmed the rioting crowd. The need for law and order led to a thorough reform of the state police, railway police and city police with a more logical structure and more efficient administration, backed by better pay and career prospects. A Criminal Investigation Department was set up. Police training schools were established at Vellore, Vizianagram and Coimbatore. In 1909, the King's Police Medal was created and awarded to eight members of the force on the recommendation of His Excellency the Governor in Council. At the presentation of the new medal at the Police School in the interesting old town of Vellore in 1911, Sir Arthur Lawley said, "What I would especially urge on the recipients is never to forget that this is the King's Medal, that it is a mark of royal favour, a token of our King Emperor's confidence and trust in their loyalty, their courage and sense of duty."

To administer justice two additional Judges were appointed by H.E. the Governor to the High Court Bench. The High Court handled such cases as the failure of Arbuthnot's Bank. There was also a Madras Magistrates Court which dealt with lesser cases. Additional support was given by the Governor to the Law College in Madras. Sir Arthur always visited the gaols whenever he was on tour to acquaint himself with the health and general condition of the prisoners. Measures to improve the accommodation and health of prisoners were undertaken. Buildings were given better ventilation, clean water and improved drainage. Prisoners were given more food and a more balanced diet. Elementary education was made available with industrial training for young offenders. There was improved pay for prison warders.[36]

Figure 156: The forces of Law and Order. Officers and men of the Madras Police.

Education

During Sir Arthur's governorship primary and secondary education were made more effective and were better funded. The length of the course for the training of elementary school teachers was raised from one to two years. In 1908, a directive was given out that fourteen elementary teacher training schools and ten higher elementary teacher training classes were to be established. In addition six new secondary teacher training classes were to be attached for preference to the secondary departments of Arts Colleges, if not to secondary schools. Over a thousand teachers were to be trained annually of whom one hundred were for secondary, 240 for higher elementary and 800 for elementary schools. Five hundred and sixty teachers each year were already trained in other institutions. Because of the difficulty in securing the services of women teachers, two new schools were to be built in Rajahmundry and Mangalore for the training of Telugu and Canarese lady teachers. The Presidency Training School for Mistresses was to be supplemented by six new government Ladies Teacher Training Schools, two for Tamils, one for Canarese, one for Telugu and two for

Moslems. The small secondary school attached to the Training School for Mistresses in Madras was to be developed into a separate secondary school for girls.

Elsewhere the Government Girls School at Cannamore and the model school attached to the Training School for Mistresses at Coimbatore were to be raised to upper secondary grade. New Government Schools for educating Mohammedan girls were opened in Mylapore, Mangalore, Trinchinopoly and Satyamangalam. The Mohammedan Lady Teachers Training School was reorganised, improved and moved to a new site at Guntur. Special provision was made for education of the hills tribes – Khonds, Jatapus, Savaras, Panos and Koyas. New schools were opened where required. Also a school for the blind was built at Palamcottah. A new Code of Regulations was introduced for European schools on April 1st 1906. The grants made to European schools were generous and rose by 50 per cent between 1906 and 1910.[37]

Social whirl and sacred cows

Life for the British in India was privileged and the social whirl could at times be heady. The Lawleys were in the highest echelons of Raj society. On December 18th 1907, the Prince of Arcot gave a dinner party followed by a dance at his residence the "Amir Mahal" in honour of Their Excellencies Sir Arthur and Lady Lawley. The entrance gate to the grounds was magnificently illuminated with coloured lights with "Welcome to Their Excellencies" across the top of the arch.[38]

On January 9th 1908, Lady Lawley's sister, Jeannette, and her brother, Gordon Cunard, arrived in Madras from Calcutta.[39] Gordon was accompanied by his wife, Edith. Jeannette's daughter, Lorna, came too. As Lady Lawley was a Cunard, her family had the shipping connections which enabled them to organise ambitious voyages to distant lands. Not surprisingly they visited the family in India.[40]

Caryl Annesley . W.A.Duff . Ursula . A.A.L. Gordon . Edith . Jeannette . Lorna .

Figure 157: Visitors from England. Ursula and Lady Lawley with her sister, Jeannette Leatham, her niece, Lorna Leatham, her brother, Gordon Cunard, and his wife, Edith. January 1908.

Sir Arthur Lawley was fully aware of the importance of the sacred cow to Hindus and therefore when the opportunity came to open a Pinjrapole or home for abandoned cows, he was only too ready to do so. On Saturday 11th January 1908, Sir Arthur opened the new Pinjrapole in the City of Madras.[41] His family and visitors joined him. The Madras Times reported, "His Excellency arrived with Lady Lawley and a large party from Government House and was received at the entrance by Mr Justice Boddam, the President, and the members of the Society for the Prevention of Cruelty to Animals. His Highness the Maharajah of Kurnarika presented His Excellency with an ornamental key."

A description of the on-going work of the centre was given recently in the local press. "On entering the Pinjrapole, a shelter for the cows, one got a feeling of entering Brindhavan." Brindhavan is the birth place of Lord Krishna. "As far as the eye could see, cows grazed in the open ground and came running to grab the grass from the hands of the visitors. The cows, 1314 of them, were quite literally dragged out from the jaws of death. Indeed, they had landed in the Pinjrapole after being rescued from slaughterhouses. 'These cows are saved by merciful persons who pay a large sum of money to drive them alive from the slaughter houses and donate them here,' said Suresh, the manager of the Pinjrapole. The 12-acre site on the Konnur High Road was a donation from the Chathurbhujdas family, who were wealthy members of the business community of Vijayanagaram, and animal lovers in the city."

"We not only maintain the cows here, but also provide emergency medication in case they are ill. When the illness is severe, doctors at the veterinary hospital give free treatment to them,' explained Suresh. The cow maintenance centre is bustling with activities early in the morning with 80 workers cleaning the sheds and taking milk from 135 milk-yielding cows. 500 litres of milk thus collected are sold to the donors who pay 1,500 rupees per month. Activities are at their peak on new moon days, when many North Indians visit this place and feed the cows with greens, as a sign of providing food to their dead ancestors. Also during the 'Mattupongal' celebrations, the place will be filled with visitors, who donate heaps of fodder for the animals, and spend the day here".[42]

On January 13th 1908, the Prince of Arcot gave a Garden Party at the "Amir Mahal" in honour of Their Excellencies Sir Arthur and Lady Lawley and His Highness the Maharajah of Mysore. There were a large number of guests. Sir Arthur and his wife arrived in a splendid carriage drawn by a pair of horses and escorted by the Governor's Body Guard. There was a large red carpet on one side of the lawn where the Governor and Lady Lawley took up their seats on gilded chairs and were soon joined by the Maharajah with whom they conversed amicably. The afternoon was beautifully bright and cool and the gaily decorated grounds and many ladies moving about in their smart frocks with here and there an Indian gentleman in picturesque Oriental costume made a very fetching scene. Lady Lawley wore a white dress with a black hat and Miss Lawley was also in white with a black hat.[43] What Gordon and Edith Cunard and Jeannette and Lorna Leatham thought of all this splendour can only be imagined, but it must have created a lasting impression.

On Thursday 30th January, the second day of the Madras Races at Guindy, the only event which attracted a large number of entries was the Lawley Cup. The Lawley family and the Maharajah of Mysore attended the races that afternoon.[44] There were several riding stables at Guindy and the Madras Hounds were also based there.

Figure 158: The Main Stand at the Race Course in Mysore.

Figure 159: Cecila Lawley with a Greyling at Guindy Stables.

An experimental farm

Gordon and Edith Cunard accompanied Sir Arthur and Lady Lawley and their daughters on the Governor's Eighth Tour of Cuddalore and Tanjore between the 19th and the 28th of February 1908. During this tour the Governor, his wife and guests visited an interesting agrarian development which was fostering links between medicine and agriculture. In order to develop medicinal plants, Abraham Pandithar, a Medicinal Practitioner, established an experimental farm at Karunanandapuram in

Tanjore on 370 acres of land purchased in November 1899. Gradually he increased the size of this farm to nearly 550 acres. He created a beautiful orchard of rare and exotic trees and shrubs. The soil which was stony and sterile had to be supplemented by imported good soil and the addition of manure. He planted mangoes, jacks, figs, pomegranates, peaches, plantains and coconuts.

He sunk two wells – one 40 feet deep and pumped by a diesel engine, and another 75 feet deep and pumped by a windmill. These were supplemented by a third well in 1907. All three were used for irrigation as well as water supply. He also transformed the farm into a multi-purpose agricultural endeavour to promote modern scientific farming. He established a rose garden and developed new varieties of rose. There were experiments with rubber, mangosteens, nutmegs and cloves. He developed several strains of sugar cane and during his research he discovered a new sport-cane variety which was taken by Mr. C. A. Barber, the then Government Botanist, for use in the Government farm at Palur. In the agricultural exhibitions of South India, the sugar canes from the Karunananda farm were invariably awarded the first prize. Twelve new varieties of maize, including Himalayan maize, were also introduced successfully. Australian golden maize was imported and used for cross breeding to create new hybrids. Arrowroot, mango-ginger, the king yam, potatoes and cabbages were also grown.

Three hundred acres were allocated to ryots, peasant farmers, who were advised by Mr. Pandithar and encouraged to implement the best farming practices by the award of annual prizes.

Sir Arthur and Lady Lawley visited the farm on the 22nd of February 1908. In his entry in the visitor's book Sir Arthur praised Abraham Pandithar's contribution to the cause of scientific farming in South India, Sir Arthur wrote:

"I have spent a thoroughly enjoyable morning at Mr Abraham Pandithar's farm, who kindly invited me to see the various works which he has already carried out and personally explained to me the various experiments which he is now conducting.

Herein is a tale of diligence, enterprise and skill in the field of agriculture which is unique in my Indian experience and therefore the more interesting.

It is an object lesson of which the exponent and the members of his family may well be proud. I carry away with me a most delightful memory of my visit the charm of which was enhanced by the courtesy of my host and hostess and the charming entertainment of which we were the recipients." [45]

In recognition of his public services, the title of Rao Sahib was conferred upon Abraham Pandithar on the 25th of June 1909. [46]

Sir Arthur Lawley was very concerned about the welfare of the rural peasants or ryots in the agricultural districts of the Presidency. On July 1st 1908, the Estates Land Act passed into law. This recognised the ryot tenant's occupancy rights which were declared heritable and transferable. The tenant was given the security of a fair and equitable rent and the domain in which the tenant exercised his property rights was protected and conserved for inheritance purposes. This Act also made the landowner responsible for the maintenance of his irrigation works. Estates were to be surveyed and records kept. To demonstrate that landlords also had rights, measures were put in place for the recovery of arrears in rent. [47]

Ooty

Ootacamund was the summer capital of the British Raj in Southern India. Founded in 1822 by the district administrator, John Sullivan, Ooty is situated at an altitude of about 7000 feet above sea level. Each year between May and the end of October, the Government of Madras moved to Ootacamund. The Governor's Residence, Government House, was the focus of activity and there was a splendid Club House with a fine golf course, polo, swimming and tennis. Snooker is said to have originated on the billiard tables of the Ootacamund Club, invented by an army officer – Sir Neville Francis Fitzgerald Chamberlain. There was also a cricket ground with regular matches played between teams from the Army, the Indian Civil Service and the business sector. Visiting teams would come from various parts of India as well as from the island of Ceylon. There were riding stables and kennels at Ooty and the Ootacamund Hounds hunted across the surrounding countryside and the open grasslands of the Wenlock Downs, named after Sir Arthur's brother Beilby Lord Wenlock. There were Point to Point Races and Gymkhanas, and horse riding was a very popular pastime.

Figure 160: Cecilia and Ursula Lawley riding at Ooty.

The maharajas, the business fraternity and the senior civil servants had summer cottages at Ooty. There were churches like St Stephen's and St Thomas's and traditional inns. It was in many ways a re-creation of Old England. When the Governor was in residence the Union Jack flew over Government House and a six gun salute would announce his arrival and departure. The misty blue haze of the Nilgiri Hills, and the fragrant mountain rains were a welcome change from the sultry heat of Madras.[48] The smaller hill resorts adjoining Ooty - Coonoor and Kotagiri - had the same dewy fresh mornings and breezy calm evenings as Ooty. The botanical gardens were established by the Marquis of Tweeddale in 1847 and still are a major attraction.

The Ooty Flower Show was held annually and fishing became a popular sport. Lady Lawley painted an evocative water colour of the lake at Ootacamund. (Figure 151)

Figure 161: Government House, Ootacamund, 1908.

Figure 162: Guests and Hunting Party at Government House, Ootacamund, 1908.

Figure 163. Sir Arthur and Lady Lawley in India.

Figure 164. Ursula and Cecilia Lawley at Government House.

Figure 165: The railway to Ootacamund.

Figure 166: The Ootacamund Hounds in the monsoonal rain.

Sir Arthur Lawley had a keen interest in the natural world, and around Ooty there was an attempt to recreate England in the Highlands of India. He and his daughters,

Ursula and Cecilia, frequently hunted with the Ootacamund Hounds. The Nilgiri Game Protection Association succeeded in introducing British game birds to the Nilgiris as well as the spaniels and other bird dogs used to hunt them. It also attempted to stock the streams in the Nilgiri Hills with trout. This was a Herculean endeavour subsequently assumed by the Madras government, which imported eggs from Germany, Wales and New Zealand. Mr. Wilson, a piscicultural expert, introduced rainbow trout into the rivers of the Nilgiri District. Fish farms were also established in various locations. Sir Arthur Lawley declared the first trout season open in 1911.[49]

Figure 167: Sir Arthur Lawley on horse back at Ooty.

Ninety miles from Coimbatore, at the southern tip of the Palani Hills, lay Kodaikanal. Dense greenery, crystal clear springs, water falls and misty cool air made Kodai one of the most popular hill stations in South India. The hill sides abounded with the Kurinji flower which blooms once in 12 years. For orchid lovers, there was an orchidorium in the vicinity, with more than 300 varieties of orchid. Favourite walks were to the Bear Shola Falls, the Silver Cascade, Kodai Lake, Bryant Park, Coaker's Walk and Kukkai Cave.

Figure 168: The Wenlock Downs, Ootacamund.

Figure 169: Toda Tribesmen in the Nilgiri Hills.

Railways

These hill stations were opened up by the British as a refuge from the heat of Madras and the coastal plains. The first Sanatorium was built in the Nilgiri Hills during the 1830s. In due course the mountain railway was built which was linked to the main railway line from Madras. In 1882, a Swiss engineer named Arthur Riggenbach came to the Nilgiri Hills on an invitation from Government of India and he submitted detailed estimates for a line costing £132,000. A local company named "The Nilgiri Rigi Railway Co. Ltd." was formed, and the Government offered it free land. This company insisted on a guaranteed return of 4%, which was not acceptable, and the proposed railway, once again, had to be shelved. In 1885, another Nilgiri Railway Company was formed and, in 1886, planning work commenced, using the Swiss Rigi Mountain system with a one metre gauge. The work on the line commenced in August 1891 when Sir Arthur Lawley's brother, Beilby Lord Wenlock, the then Governor of Madras, turned the first turf to begin construction. The Mettupalayam-Coonoor section of the track was opened for traffic on 15th June 1899. In January 1903, the Indian Government purchased the line, and took over the construction of the new extension from Coonoor to Ooty. The Nilgiri Mountain Railway was operated by the former Madras Railway Company until 31st December 1907 on the behalf of the Government. In January 1908, the railway line was handed over to South Indian Railways. Construction continued. The line from Coonoor to Fernhill was completed on 15th September 1908 and reached Ooty, one month later. Towards the end of October, Sir Arthur Lawley officiated at the opening ceremony of the new railway to Ootacamund.

Figure 170: The Official Opening of the Ootacamund Railway in October 1908.

Sir Arthur was a great railway enthusiast. He was involved with the construction of new railway lines in Rhodesia and South Africa. In Western Australia he was involved in the preliminary planning of the railway link across the Nullarbor Plain from Perth to Adelaide. In the Madras Presidency, the South Indian Railway and the Madras and Southern Mahratta Railway operated the rail network. The Madras Administration encouraged District Boards to build branch lines, but in the event only one was actually constructed from Bezwanda to Masulipatam Port. This was opened by Sir Arthur on February 4th 1908.[50] In his speech replying to the District Board of Tanjore's address on February 20th 1908, Sir Arthur said:

> "I should like to say a word to the District Board on their enterprise in the construction of their District Board Railway and to congratulate them also on the success which has attended their efforts. It has been I know an enormous boon to the district and I am glad to know that it has also proved commercially a success. I only wish that I could see the policy of construction of railways by District Boards more universally adopted and I can conceive of no object to which your energies can better be devoted in the interests of the country than the extension of the railway system."

On February 25th 1908, the Lawleys visited the South Indian Railway Workshops in Negapatam, where they saw the Boiler Shop, the Smith Shop, the Foundry, the Machine Shop, the Saw Mill, the Carriage Body Shop, the Painting and Finishing Shop, and the Waggon Shop.[51]

During Sir Arthur's Presidency (1906-1911) altogether ten new lines were added to the network. These were:

- Bezwanda to Masulipatam Port (in the North East)

- Dhone to Kurnool (linking Kurnool to the main line).

- Coonor to Ootacamund (completing the line to Ooty).

- Pamban to Dhanashkodi (towards Adam's Bridge and Ceylon).

- Azhikkal to Mangalore (along the West coast).

- Vizianagram to Parvatipur (in the North East).

- Kanevihalli branch line

- Arantangi Quarry Siding

- The North East Line was given access to the Central Station by a new line from Koprukupet to Basin Bridge

- The Loop Line from Washermanpet to Basin Bridge

Another major transport achievement was the construction of Napier Bridge where the River Cooum crosses the Madras Coastal Marina to enter the Bay of Bengal.

Indian summer

In the summer of 1908, Sir Arthur and Lady Lawley's son, Richard, came out to live in India with the family. At Ootacamund on October 3rd, there was an amateur dramatic performance at Government House in which he played a part. The play performed was "H.E. the Governor", which is set on an island in the Indian Ocean. The Madras Times wrote, "We have never seen a play better staged on private boards, better rehearsed and better acted.... The far end of the ball room at Government House was converted into a stage and a heavy yellow brocade curtain in keeping with the hangings of the room was hung from pillar to pillar.... Miss Ursula Lawley as Miss Carlton, the daughter of the Colonial Secretary, left nothing to be desired. She looked radiantly pretty and happy, a very great step towards the successful acting of the part of a young lady who wins the hearts of the A.D.C., the Private Secretary and H.E. himself, and was natural and unaffected, and altogether winsome.... Mr Richard Lawley also was excellent. It was a simple part for him to do as he had only to personate a charming young A.D.C., which he does every day of his life, and to fall in love gracefully and naturally, an art which he has now acquired and the part was complete. He could not have done it more naturally than he did." [52]

Richard Lawley, known to the family as Ned, also accompanied his parents on a tour to the Cochin Forests and Shikar from 20th to 25th October.[53]

Figure 171: Ned, Richard Lawley, and Ursula rehearse their lines for a play at Ooty.

Sir Arthur's administration wished to encourage the participation of young Indian men of good education in the Civil Service. The key posts of Collector and Divisional Officer were filled by British civil servants. However many posts were open to Indians. For example in the Inland Revenue Clerical Service there were two grades filled by indigenous officers – a lower and a higher. Taxation policy was designed to meet the circumstances encountered. For example the Salt Tax was reduced to increase consumption, and there was some consideration of the use of fiscal measures to reduce the high prices of grain given the good harvests between 1906 and 1910.

November 1st 1908 was the fiftieth anniversary of Queen Victoria's Proclamation bringing India under the control of the British Crown and promising that her government would treat all its subjects equally, uphold the rights of princes and respect the religions of India. Two of the most powerful Indian Princes in the sphere of the Madras Presidency were the Maharajah of Mysore, who was a close friend of Sir Arthur, and the Nizam of Hyderabad, who was less liked by the family. The Nizam and the Maharajah managed to retain independent power by being allied to the British, and having a British political officer resident in their state. Mysore had a Representative Assembly established in 1881. [54]

Figure 172: The Nizam of Hyderabad.

On the 2nd November 1908, there was a Celebration of the Jubilee of the Royal Proclamation in Madras. Sir Arthur in his speech emphasised the role of Queen Victoria as the Empress of India. He said:

"We are assembled here today to celebrate the occasion of the assumption by the Crown of the direct control of the destinies of the various peoples of this continent. It was a remarkable event in the History of India – an incident of momentous import in the life of our late Queen-Empress. I believe it would be difficult to exaggerate the devotion in the hearts of the Indians of all castes and of all creeds, sects and races to the throne and person of Queen Victoria. It was more than mere reverence for an august Sovereign or respect for a sagacious Ruler. It was love for a noble Queen by whom that love – love for India and her Indian subjects – was deeply reciprocated.

Her letters which have recently been published show us how – before the issue of that very Proclamation of which this is the jubilee – how deep and tender was Her Majesty's concern for the preservation of the rights and religions of the millions who then passed more directly under her sway and how great was her own personal insistence on the preservation of their sanctity.

In the spirit of tolerance and sympathy which the Proclamation itself makes manifest we trace the Queen's own handiwork. It evinces a desire on her part to fulfil faithfully her duty – a desire which was evinced in every act of hers and which so immeasurably enhanced the splendour of the Crown which she wore." [55]

Figure 173: The Maharajah's Junior Guard.

In 1906, Sir John Morley had been appointed the Secretary of State for India and the Earl of Minto, Viceroy of India by the new Liberal Prime Minister, Campbell-Bannerman. They chose November 1st 1908 to announce the Morley-Minto Reforms. These were embodied in the Indian Councils Act which passed into law in 1909. Sixty Indian representatives were to be elected to the Viceroy's Executive and between thirty and fifty to the Provincial Legislative Councils, where they would assist with the framing of laws and policies. The electoral system was designed to achieve a balance of all minority interests. No one was disbarred from standing for election even extremists. Many liberal Indians did indeed decide to participate in the government in the interests of their own people. This had the effect of isolating the more militant nationalists.[56]

Sir Arthur Lawley made occasional State Visits to Indian Princes like the Nizam of Hyderabad and the Maharajah of Mysore. The Governor and his party would stay in the British Residency, where they could entertain the Princes of the Raj. In the cool dry months between November and April, many rajahs came to the city of Madras for the Social Season. They had their own palaces there. As Governor, Sir Arthur Lawley would also visit the capital city of the British Raj, Calcutta, to consult with the Viceroy, Earl Minto, with Lord Kitchener, who commanded the Army of India at that time, and with other important personages. Delhi did not become the capital city until December 1911.

Official tours

During each year of his stay in India, the Governor, sometimes accompanied by his wife, his son and daughters, went on official tours to various parts of the Madras Presidency. There were fifteen such tours altogether, and each was recorded in a leather bound book published by the Madras Government Press. There were specially printed Survey of India maps enclosed in the sleeves of each book to indicate the route taken by the Governor and his party. These beautifully printed and detailed reports cover:

- The First Tour of Coimbatore and Salem Districts – 23rd September to 4th October 1906;

- The Second Tour of Mysore State and North Arcot and Chingleput Districts –

  12th to 26th October and 3rd November 1906;

- The Third Tour of Madura and Trichinopoly – 18th to 28th November 1906;

- The Fourth Tour of Cochin and Travancore – 25th January to 14th February 1907;

- The Fifth Tour of Malabar – 13th to 24th September 1907;

- The Sixth Tour of South Canara – 3rd to 10th November 1907;

- The Seventh Tour of Bezwada, Masulipatam and Nellore – 3rd to 11th February 1908.

- The Eighth Tour of Tanjore – 19th to 28th February 1908;

- The Ninth Tour of Cochin Forests and Shikar – 20th to 25th October 1908;

- The Tenth Tour of Tinnevelly and Palamcottah (joined on 25th November by the Governor of Ceylon, Sir Henry McCallum, to consider the proposed rail link with Ceylon) – 22nd November to 3rd December 1908;

- The Eleventh Tour of Cuddapah, Kurnool and Guntur – 15th to 22nd December 1908;

- The Twelfth Tour of Vizianagram, Chatrapur, Ganjan and Vizagapatam (interrupted by a visit to Calcutta) - 26th to 29th January, and 3rd to 15th February 1909;[57]

- The Thirteenth Tour of Vellore – 1st to 3rd November 1909; this tour was cut short by the indisposition of Lady Lawley.

- The Fourteenth Tour of Mysore, Hospet, Bellary, Anantapur, and Hyderabad – 20th October to 17th November 1910;

- The Fifteenth Tour of South Arcot – 6th to 9th February 1911.

Figure 174: Rajah's had palaces in the city of Madras like the Old Carnatic Palace, Chepauk.

Figure 175: Sir Arthur Lawley and friends with a tiger kill.

Figure 176: Crossing the Karempoja River in Malabar by Ferry, Fifth Tour, September 1907.

During the Second Tour, Sir Arthur Lawley went on a tiger hunt with the Maharajah of Mysore, who drove him to a shooting camp at Antarsanti, 40 miles from Mysore. "After breakfast the party proceeded a short distance further along the road and then entered the forest on elephants and proceeded to the machans (raised platforms used for tiger hunts). When the parties had taken up their positions, the beat commenced. A tiger was driven up to the machans, but would not break into the open and turned back. His Excellency and Major Glyn then moved to a machan on a broad ride cut in the forest. The tiger was driven across the ride. Major Glyn wounded him and Sir Arthur had another shot at him and hit him as the beast bounded across the ride. Sir Arthur, Major Glyn and Mr Fraser then went after him on elephants into the jungle. By the time the tiger was found, he was very nearly dead and Mr Fraser dispatched him." After the hunt, His Highness the Maharajah drove His Excellency Sir Arthur Lawley back to Government House in his motor car.[58]

As an illustration of the kind of regal progress that official tours entailed, it is informative to look at one in more detail. Here are some of the events which occurred during the Eleventh Tour of Cuddapah, Kurnool and Guntur in December 1908.[59]

In each region there was a British Officer called the Collector, who administered the region and collected the taxes, except in the Princely States like Hyderabad, where there was a British Resident who worked alongside the Nizam and lived in a rather fine Residency with a classical portico. There were also District Superintendents of Police, Judges and District Officers upon whom the Raj relied for day to day local administration. Each tour would include these British officials and the Indian Princes of the regions through which the Governor and his party journeyed.

Transport was by rail where possible, but there was a problem with two different gauges on the railway lines – one of 5 feet 6 inches and another of one metre. Hence it was occasionally necessary to change trains. The Governor had his own private railway coach or saloon. Where suitable rail transport was not available, the Governor used his own car, a Daimler. When rail and road transport were combined, cars would be rented. For example, on December 17th 1908, cars were hired by Mr. J.W. Hughes I.C.S., Collector of Kurnool, for the journey from Gooty Station to Kurnool. These were a 30 horse power Dennis for the Governor's official party and a 9HP De Dion which followed in case of accidents. [60]

Figure 177: Sir Arthur Lawley with a Flower Garland and Bouquet.

The Governor would be formally greeted by each municipality or district through which he passed. Usually the Collector, a British official of the Indian Civil Service, who was responsible for tax collection and local administration, would preside. For example in Cuddapah on December 16th 1908, the Governor was greeted by the Collector, Mr J.G.D. Partridge I.C.S. Quite frequently "His Excellency the Governor" was garlanded with flowers as a welcoming gesture. On December 17th, Sir Arthur Lawley was met and garlanded by some of the principal inhabitants of Gooty at the railway station.

Figure 178: The Collector addresses a Public Meeting in Cuddalore (Fifteenth Tour, 1911).

Municipal and District addresses would be given by the Chairman of the Municipal Council or the District Board. Some of the topics frequently raised were:-

i) Loyalty, ii) Law and order, iii) History, iv) Population, v) Sanitation and drainage, vi) Water supply, vii) Free compulsory Primary Education, viii) High School Education, ix) Hospitals and health provision, x) Electoral issues, xi) Local self-government and the extension of the franchise, xii) Railways, telegraphs, roads, tracks, bridges and transport, xiii) Farming and agricultural education and research facilities, and xiv) Finance and taxation. There was usually a request for financial help from the Central Madras Government. The Governor would reply to the speeches of each district and municipality.

In Cuddapah he said,

> *"Gentlemen. I look upon you as partners in the work of administration – we as a central government, you as local government. We are engaged upon similar tasks and the degree to which the Central Government is ready to assist you is limited not by our wishes but by our resources."*

This would generally be followed by the granting of the requests for which the central government had already made provision and the considering of requests which were on the Madras Government's agenda for discussion. Expensive demands such as that for free primary education were politely declined as being unaffordable without raising the levels of taxation.

Frequently there would be Christian missionaries and ministers of religion in attendance. Other religions also had claims to make. The request for a Hindu Girls High School in Kurnool similar to the already existing "Muhammadan Girls High School" showed the importance of the role of religion in education in India.

On December 17th 1908, Sir Arthur Lawley visited Coles Memorial High School near Kurnool, which was run by the American Baptist Mission. He was received by the Rev. W.A. Stanton and the Rev. J. Newcomb. US$10,000 had been generously donated by Dr Abraham Coles of New Jersey to build the school and a further US$1,900 to equip it. Observing the Union Jack and the Stars and Stripes side by side, Sir Arthur said:

"The scions of the Anglo-Saxon race look at these two flags which bid us remember what is the mission of the race in life. Surely it is that we should ever strive to carry the light of Christianity to the darkest quarters of the earth; that we should restrain and push back...the encroachment of poverty, ignorance and sin; that we should strive ever day by day...to attain to a higher plane and to a nobler ideal of thought and action alike."

The Governor also visited schools, hospitals, experimental farms, water works and other projects. At Kurnool he paid a visit to the tomb of a 17th century warrior prince, Abdul Waham Khan. At Banganapalle, on December 18th 1908, he visited a diamond mine and later opened the new Lawley Municipal Market. Tickled to have a market named Lawley, Sir Arthur said:

"It is my earnest wish that this market may be the scene of great commercial activity bringing prosperity and wealth to the citizens of this town."

As he proceeded through the Presidency, Sir Arthur Lawley would stop at every village he passed through to speak with the village officers and ryots (peasants). He would listen attentively to their complaints and suggestions.

Figure 179: Sir Arthur Lawley installing the Nawab of Banganapalle.

The Governor was also a King Maker with extraordinary powers. He came to Banganapalle to invest the new Nawab as ruler of the principality. The control of Banganapalle was handed over to the British by the Nizam in 1800. Internal disorder from time to time had called for the intervention of the Madras Government. Sayyid Fath-i-Ali Khan, the Nawab of Banganapalle since 1868, had been a model ruler during the early years of his reign. Alas, financial mismanagement during his latter years had reduced the state to the brink of insolvency.[61] Therefore in 1904, the Government had removed the Nawab from power only a few months before his death in 1905, and replaced him by a British Resident, Mr. J.C. Molony, I.C.S.

Sayyid Ghulam Muhammad Ali Khan III succeeded his father as a minor in 1905, but was invested with full ruling powers three years later, after the finances and administration had been reformed. His reign saw momentous changes and was, by most accounts, stable and effective. He died in 1922 leaving his little state to his eldest son. At the 1908 ceremony installing the new Nawab, Sir Arthur Lawley said,

> *"Secure under the sheltering arm of the paramount power, the people of this state may devote themselves to the arts of peace and the development of the resources of the country.... The Nawab takes up the reins of office under conditions that seem altogether set fair...."*

Addressing the Nawab he continued,

> *"You have the capacity no less than the desire to be numbered among those rulers whose names will be held hereafter in affectionate reverence and respect.... I pray that your rule may be long, prosperous and happy."*

At the close of this speech His Excellency the Governor placed the Nawab on the Gadi (throne) and presented him with the sanad (legal title) of his succession to the jaghir (dynastic lands) and with a khilat (ceremonial present) consisting of a sword and cloths. That evening the Nawab gave a State Dinner in honour of Sir Arthur.

The British missionary endeavours included the Society for the Promotion of the Gospel. On Sunday 20th December, the Governor attended Divine Service at the S.P.G. Church and visited the S.P.G. School with the Rev. A.F.R. Bird. The S.P.G. said there were 18,000 Christians in the districts of Kurnool and Cuddapeh. The School had 272 pupils with 124 in the Primary, 107 in the Lower Secondary and 41 in the Higher Secondary. The boys were 60 per cent Christian, 20 per cent Brahman, 15 per cent other Hindu castes and 5 per cent Moslem. To date 18 students had matriculated, two of whom were Native Pastors and a further two who were preparing for Holy Orders at the Society's Theological College. There was also a local S.P.G. Medical Mission with a European doctor which provided a dispensary and medical care for the school's pupils.

At Guntur, Sir Arthur Lawley visited the American Evangelical Lutheran Mission Hospital for Women and Children. There were three American physicians who were working in the hospital. From September 1907 to September 1908, they had performed 403 major operations. There were two branch dispensaries in the district and a Nurses Training School attached to the hospital run by a lady graduate of the University of Pennsylvania Hospital.

Sir Arthur Lawley then visited the Municipal Hospital where the very old buildings were inadequate and there were plans to build a new hospital. Sir Arthur wrote, "The Municipal Hospital, which I visited this morning, is in the matter of structure quite unsuited for the purposes of a hospital. It is inadequate and incommodious. I hope very much that the erection of a new hospital may not be long delayed. The wards were clean and tidy and I am sure that Captain Illius and his staff do all that is possible for the patients."

Figure 180: Cecily Blair, Sir Arthur and Lady Lawley and Ursula in Tanjore, February 1908.

The Governor's tours had a purpose and that was to discover the needs of the people on the ground and to make provision for improvements where these seemed to be required. Sir Arthur wished to become acquainted with all the regions of the Presidency and meet the Princes, officials, civil servants, members of the business community, councillors and people of Southern India. He had a particular interest in education and visited numerous schools and colleges. He also supported the work of Christian missionaries and encouraged their efforts in the fields of education and medicine. The welfare of the ryots or Indian peasants was a particular concern. He would take the trouble to meet them individually as he toured through the many and varied regions of the Presidency. Sir Arthur liked to observe things first hand for himself rather than rely on reports which might be biased. He sought a thorough in-depth knowledge of the lands and peoples he ruled.

After a visit by the Governor, there would usually be a Garden Party and a Public Entertainment in honour of His Excellency. At Guntur on December 21st 1908, a Garden Party was given in his honour by M. R. Ry Toleti Appa Rao Garu in the compound of the Collector's house. He was shown in turn some conjuring, a kollattam dance, an ashtavadhanam performance, and a Lambadi dance. Kollattam is the name of a charming dance practised by a group of young girls, with two wooden sticks artistically painted in red and green striking against each other. Ashtavadhanam is an imaginative Telugu poetry event with eight participants or Prucchakas. Five of these Prucchakas set poetic challenges to an Avadhani sitting in their midst. He has to construct the poems. Each poem has four lines.

After tea, Sir Arthur proceeded to the next compound where there was music and entertainments, and M. R. Ry Toleti Appa Rao Garu, the Telugu Pandit of Rajahmundry College, read a Telugu poem which had been composed by Vaddadi Subbarayudu in honour of Sir Arthur Lawley. This is an English translation of the poem:

The Telugu Pandit's Poem

In the Bhartavarsha full plains and forests
Rendered holy by the ever flowing waters
Of the deep Ganges, Godavari and other rivers,
Enriched by the Himalayas and other high mountains
Full of inexhaustible stores of diamonds,
Gold, silver and other metals;
Glorified in their immortal poems
By saints like Valmiki and Vyasa
And protected by the mighty arm
Of Sreerama, Bharata and other sovereigns
Of the Solar and Lunar races,
Lies the large province of Madras
In shape like the constellation of the Great Bear
Over which rules Sir Arthur Lawley
Enjoying the popularity of his subjects.
The town of Guntur which has become noted
As having been ruled over
By the illustrious grandfather of the great poet
Who composed in language of nectar sweetness
The whole of the Mahabharata
Except one or two of its earlier chapters
Has now the fortune of being visited
By the Governor, Sir Arthur Lawley,
Having become the capital
Of the new district
To which it has given its name.

Governor Lawley has been restoring vigour
To the tree of industry,
The several branches of which have by the effect of time,
Ceased to sprout and yield wealth distributing fruit.
Do thou God Indra, Ruler of the Clouds,
And Governor Lawley partaker of the nature of gods
By acting in concert and giving order
To the water-giving clouds and engineers
To supply water to the thirsting crops,
Mercifully check the stream of tears
Of the cultivator heaving with his long sighs.
A little below four crores* of men and women
Have been contentedly enjoying happiness
Under your benign rule, O Governor Lawley.
May the Great God in his mercy
Grant you long life and health.

Vaddadi Subbarayudu, the Telugu Pandit of Rajamundry,
Out of his deep loyalty, offers to thee these lines
Just as a thread is offered when the Moon
Newly appears in the West.
So O thou, Lord Lawley, the Moon of Governors,
Pray graciously accept this humble offering.

*a crore is an Indian term for ten million.

[1] The Madras Times. March 29th 1906.
[2] The Madras Times. July 19th 1906.
[3] The Times. Tuesday March 6th 1906. Page 10. Column A.
      The Times. Tuesday 7th October 1909. Page 11. Column D.
[4] The Times. Tuesday 23rd October 1906. Page 9. Column E.
[5] Times Obituary for Lord Wenlock, Wednesday June 15th 1932
[6] British India, Madras States. Geocities. Bob Hilkens 2000. B. Schemmel: Rulers.org. 1995-2004
[7] "Raj. The Making and Unmaking of British India". Lawrence James. Little, Brown and Co. 1997.
      British India, Madras States. Geocities. Bob Hilkens 2000.
      Times Obituary for Lord Wenlock, Wednesday June 15th 1932
[8] Madras Times. June 28th 1906.
[9] Madras Times. July 9th 1906.
[10] The Second Tour of Mysore State and North Arcot and Chingleput Districts – 12 to 26 Oct and 3
      Nov 1906. Madras Government Press. 1909.
[11] "The crash of Arbuthnott and Co." Arbuthnott Family Association.. www.Arbuthnott.org.
      "Building a bank, the MCt. Way." The Hindu, Monday April 12th 2004.
      Letter from Lord Wenlock to his wife Constance on Christmas Day 1906. Hull University –
      Brynmor Jones Library. Forbes Adam Archive.
      The Madras Times. November 15th 1906.
[12] Madras Times. November 20th 1906. The Third Tour of Sir Arthur Lawley to Madura and
      Trinchinopoly. November 19th to 26th 1906. Madras Government Press.
[13] The Third Tour to Madura and Trichinopoly. November 18th to 26th, 1906. Madras Government
      Press. Pages 39 and 45
[14] Letter from Lord Wenlock to his wife Constance on Christmas Day 1906. Hull University –
      Brynmor Jones Library. Forbes Adam Archive.
[15] Notes on the administration of His Excellency the Honourable Sir Arthur Lawley, Governor of
      Madras, 1906-11. Madras Government Press. 1912.
[16] The Madras Times. January 3rd 1907.
[17] Letter from Lord Wenlock to his wife Constance on Christmas Day 1906. Hull University –
      Brynmor Jones Library. Forbes Adam Archive
[18] Letter from Lord Wenlock in Lucknow to his wife Constance on January 16th 1907. Hull
      University – Brynmor Jones Library. Forbes Adam Archive
[19] Letter from Lord Wenlock to his wife Constance on January 23rd 1907. Hull University – Brynmor
      Jones Library. Forbes Adam Archive
[20] Letter from Lord Wenlock to his wife Constance on January 29th 1907. Hull University – Brynmor
      Jones Library. Forbes Adam Archive
[21] Madras Times. January 31st 1907.
[22] Letter from Lord Wenlock to his wife Constance on February 5th 1907. Hull University – Brynmor
      Jones Library. Forbes Adam Archive
[23] Madras Times. February 21st 1907.
[24] Letter from Dick Lawley in Bangalore 17th February 1907. Forbes Adam Archive. Brynmor Jones
      Library. University of Hull.
[25] Notes on the administration of His Excellency the Honourable Sir Arthur Lawley, Governor of
      Madras, 1906-11. Madras Government Press. 1912.
[26] http://lewfh.tripod.com/frmullershomeopathicdispensaryforthepoor
      The Sixth Tour of South Canara – 3 to 10 Nov 1907. Madras Government Press. 1909.
[27] The Sixth Tour of South Canara by Sir Arthur Lawley. Madras Government Press. 1909.
[28] "Miracle on Wheels". Living, Deccan Herald. Saturday July 12th 2003.

[29] Notes on the administration of His Excellency the Honourable Sir Arthur Lawley, Governor of Madras, 1906-11. Madras Government Press. 1912.

[30] Eustace Lord Wraxall in conversation, September 10th 2004.
Emmet Papers, Smithsonian Institute, Washington D.C., U.S.A.

[31] National Trust. Tyntesfield. Somerset. 2004.

[32] Eustace Lord Wraxall in conversation, September 10th 2004.
Emmet Papers, Smithsonian Institute, Washington D.C., U.S.A.
Thomas Addis Emmet: "The Emmet Family: With Some Incidents Relating to Irish History." (New York privately printed in 1898).
World Wide Web. RootsWeb's World Connect Project Emmet Family 2.htm

[33] Lady Lawley and Penny F.E. (Fanny Emily) Southern India, Painted by Lady Lawley. A&C Black. London. 1914.

[34] Times Obituary for Lady Wenlock, Monday 30th April 1944.

[35] Notes on the administration of His Excellency the Honourable Sir Arthur Lawley, Governor of Madras, 1906-11. Madras Government Press. 1912.

[36] Notes on the administration of His Excellency the Honourable Sir Arthur Lawley, Governor of Madras, 1906-11. Madras Government Press. 1912. Pages 21 to 23.
Sir Arthur Lawley to Lord Crewe. 15th February 1911. Cambridge University Library.

[37] Notes on the administration of His Excellency the Honourable Sir Arthur Lawley, Governor of Madras, 1906-11. Madras Government Press. 1912.

[38] Madras Times. January 2nd 1908.

[39] Madras Times. January 9th 1908.

[40] Lord Wraxall's Albums. Empire and Commonwealth Museum, Bristol.

[41] Madras Times. January 9th 1908.

[42] http://www.chennaionline.com/society/animal.asp

[43] Madras Times. January 23rd 1908.

[44] Madras Times. January 30th 1908.

[45] The Eighth Tour of Sir Arthur Lawley to Tanjore – 19 to 28 Feb 1908 – Madras Government Press.

[46] Abraham Pandithar- The father of Tamizh Isai. /www.sangeetham.com.

[47] Notes on the administration of His Excellency the Honourable Sir Arthur Lawley, Governor of Madras, 1906-11. Madras Government Press. 1912.

[48] History of Ootacamund (Ooty). www.ooty.com.
History of Ootacamund by Sir Frederick Price. 1908.
Nilgiri Mountain Railways – http://www.railmuseum.org/nmr/.
Nilgiri Railway http://www.indiainvites.com/Trains_files/Ooty.htm.
The Magic Mountains: Hill Stations and the British Raj by Dane Keith Kennedy: University of California Press: (1996).
Lord Wraxall's Albums. Empire and Commonwealth Museum, Bristol.
"My First School Days in Ootacamund, the Queen of Hill Stations" Rodney Hall. Obantech Web Page.

[49] Notes on the administration of His Excellency the Honourable Sir Arthur Lawley, Governor of Madras, 1906-11. Madras Government Press. 1912.

[50] Madras Times. February 6th 1908.

[51] The Eighth Tour of Sir Arthur Lawley to Tanjore – 19 to 28 Feb 1908 – Madras Government Press.

[52] Madras Times. 8th October 1908.

[53] Madras Times. 22nd October 1908.

[54] Madras Times. 4th October 1906.

[55] Lawley, Sir Arthur, Speeches delivered by His Excellency the Honourable Sir Arthur Lawley while Governor of Madras, 1906-11. Madras Government Press. India Office. 1912.

[56] "Raj. The Making and Unmaking of British India". Lawrence James. Little, Brown and Co. 1997. Page 432.

[57] Madras Times. February 4th and February 11th 1909.

[58] The Second Tour of Mysore State and North Arcot and Chingleput Districts – 12 to 26 Oct and 3 Nov 1906.

[59] The Eleventh Tour of H.E. The Hon. Sir Arthur Lawley, G.C.I.E. K.C.M.G., Governor of Madras. Cuddapah, Kurnool and Guntur. December 15th to 22nd 1908. Madras Government Press. 1909.

[60] The Eleventh Tour of H.E. The Hon. Sir Arthur Lawley, G.C.I.E. K.C.M.G., Governor of Madras. Cuddapah, Kurnool and Guntur. December 15th to 22nd 1908. Madras Government Press. 1909

[61] Banganapalle Brief History. World Wide Web. 4dw.net/royalark/India/banganapalle.htm

Chapter 6
Catastrophe, Conspiracy, Celebration

The Benefits of Empire

The construction of the National Art Gallery in Madras was completed in 1909. The new building, with a stunning facade, was built of pink sandstone brought from Sathyavedu, and formed part of the Madras Museum campus. It was opened on January 23rd 1909, by the Governor of Fort St. George, Sir Arthur Lawley, and called the Victoria Memorial Hall after the Queen-Empress Victoria.[1] In March, a new Central Records Building was opened in Madras.

Figure 181: Victoria Memorial Hall, Madras, opened by Sir Arthur Lawley in 1909.

On February 12th, Sir Arthur spoke to the students at a Training College for teachers. The Madras Times reported, "The personal reminiscences of his life as a small schoolboy or 'Scug' at Eton in which Sir Arthur Lawley indulged when addressing the students at the Training College at Rajamundry were introduced in a particularly felicitous way. It must have deeply impressed the future schoolmasters of

South India to hear how the mighty and puissant Governor was once a 'Scug' living in awe of 'Swells' and masters."[2]

Commenting on the Twelfth Tour of Vizianagram, Chatrapur, Ganjan and Vizagapatam (26th January to 15th February 1909), the Madras Times stated:

"Sir Arthur Lawley has that most useful quality of being able to inspire with cordial liking those to whom he talks confidentially. He has the happy knack of saying the right thing in the right way. His sympathetic attention to grievances and his friendly interchange of views seem to win all hearts, and, after all is said and done, it is as invaluable an attribute of a Governor, especially among a sentimental and emotional people, as the power of ruling wisely."[3]

On this tour Sir Arthur was accompanied by his wife and his son, Richard.

Figure 182: The Madras Agricultural College and Research Institute, Coimbatore.

In July 1909, Sir Arthur then opened the new Madras Agricultural College and Research Institute in Coimbatore. This is one of the oldest Institutes of Agriculture Education in India and was originally started in 1868 at Saidapet, Madras, and later established at Coimbatore in 1906. The first batch of eight students was admitted to the Licentiate in Agriculture in 1908. The building with its British Colonial architecture depicts symbolically the lofty ideals of Agricultural Education in the days of the Raj. The college is now the Tamil Nadu Agricultural University.[4]

During Sir Arthur's term as governor, much was done to improve agriculture. Seven agricultural research stations were set up. The first two were in the Tanjore and Vizagapatam districts. At Tinnevelly and Karunganni, research focused on the development of cotton production. At other stations, new strands of sugar cane were introduced from Mauritius. Improved ploughs and seed drills were also introduced. Experimental model farms disseminated the innovations. The cultivation of the cinchona trees to obtain quinine was fostered under government control and output was increased with the beneficial effect of helping to combat malaria. In 1909, the Government sanctioned the building of a Bacteriological Laboratory for the Madras Veterinary College, which had been set up in 1903.[5]

The first Survey of Fisheries had been undertaken by Sir Frederick Nicholson in 1905. The stocks of fish were found to be abundant, but the development was limited and restricted by inadequate fishing vessels and out-dated methods. The fishermen would not venture far from the shore. Following a fact finding tour, Sir Frederick established an experimental marine station at Enmore on the East Coast in 1908. In 1909, a new experimental station with an improved location was completed at Cannamore. The government encouraged associated industries like the manufacture of fish oil and guano. To improve the efficiency of the fishing vessels experiments were conducted in catching and preserving fish using better designed and larger boats with improved nets.[6]

Sir Arthur Lawley was very keen on the advancement of science. The leading institution for Technical and Industrial Education was the College of Engineering in Madras. Here the length of study for the B.A. degree was increased from two to four years. Plans were drawn up to move the college from its rather small campus to a new site at Guindy on the southern outskirts of the city. Here there were to be new workshops and laboratories, hostels for the students and residences for the principal and professors.

In a speech at the Convocation of the Madras University on March 26th 1909, Sir Arthur said:

"Western though, western science and western knowledge have been made known to India by the medium of English literature. That is a record of the history, the politics, the religions, the enterprises, the romance of the English people for 300 years told...by all the masters of poetry and prose. And among all the authors, the historians, the essayists, the bards and the teachers there is one creed, one doctrine, one faith and that is liberty of thought. It is in striking contrast to Indian teaching in the past of which the prevailing characteristic has been unquestioning acceptance of the master's teaching, uncomplaining submission to authority.

It seems to me that a new garden as it were has been opened in which the Indian intellect may roam at large, a garden in which the rustling of the trees, the murmur of the streams, the song of the birds, the scent of the flowers are akin in that in all of them the scent, the breath, the essence is the same:

Liberty, Liberty, Liberty!

Independence of judgement, freedom of ideas, emancipation from slavery to authority, liberty of thought – that is the spirit of the garden – the spirit which has been engendered in the minds of Indians by English literature."

These were the very ideas which Gandhi and Nehru were to espouse in their quest for independence for India and the ending of British rule. Democracy, liberal ideals and Empire were uneasy bed fellows.

Catastrophe

Sadly, 1909 was a year of great tragedy for Sir Arthur and Lady Lawley. On September 4th, their only son, Richard Edward (known as "Ned"), was killed in a riding accident, while hunting at Coonoor in the Nilgiri Hills near the hill station of Ooty. The Madras Times reported, "Mr R.E. Lawley met with his death on the hunting field late this afternoon. He fell at a jump over a ditch at Chemmund Shola. No on witnessed the accident. He was discovered by his sister Ursula[7] with his mount on top of him and his neck broken; and he must have been there for at least half an hour before he was discovered. Majors Hinge and Slater were on the golf links and were summoned. His Excellency was also golfing at the time and the sad news was broken to him by Major Duff. Major Duff was one of the first to arrive at the scene of the accident. The accident occurred at 4.30 pm and the body was conveyed to Government House by Majors Duff, Hinge and Slater about 7.50 pm. A stretcher of branches of trees and red coats was improvised to convey the body to the motor car. Her Excellency was not out hunting but the Miss Lawleys were. Mr. Lawley had only arrived the previous day from Secunderabad."

Figure 183: Richard Edward Lawley 1887 – 1909. A posthumous portrait by W.E. Miller.

The Editorial of the Madras Times of September 9th stated, "It is impossible after a tragedy of this kind to express sufficiently sympathy with their Excellencies and their unhappy family. Young Mr Lawley who had returned to Ootacamund from Secunderabad on Thursday last (September 2nd) was killed out hunting on Saturday afternoon. He had come back with his health quite restored. In fact he had said that he had not felt so well for a long time and was cheerfully looking forward to training his horses for the Point to Point races. But on Saturday his horse slipped and fell heavily, breaking Mr Lawley's neck in his fall. It is a case where the fewest words are the best expression of the real sense of sympathy and sorrow which everyone in the Presidency must feel for His Excellency the Governor and his family."

Richard Edward Lawley was born on May 9th 1887 and was educated by a private tutor. In 1901, he returned from Australia with the Royal Party on the R.M.S. Ophir, accompanying them as far as St Vincent. Thence he sailed home with the Royal Navy to begin his studies at Dartmouth on the training ship HMS Britannia at the Royal Naval College. In 1903, he visited his family in the Transvaal, where the doctors expressed their concern about his medical condition and advised prolonged sick leave.[8] Later he withdrew from the navy because of ill health and spent some time at Oxford before proceeding to India. He was 22 years old.[9] Messages of sympathy and condolences arrived from all sections of the community and from all parts of the Presidency.[10] On September 8th 1909, a Public Meeting was held to express the condolences of the people of Ootacamund to Sir Arthur and Lady Lawley. The Civil Court Building was crowded and standing room was not available for late comers. During his opening speech, the Chairman, Mr F. Rowlanson, said:

"Nowhere in the world I believe, gentlemen, are the ties which knit families in unity better realised and more warmly cherished than in this land of India. They are markedly observed and honoured by you who are native to this country, and we others, to whom our residence here has some of the painful characteristics of exile from the homeland of our birth, run you close in our recognition of the value of those ties... For several years now each hot weather has sent up to our beloved half English Nilgiri climate our Governor, his Lady and their charming family. Each year we have become more familiar with the personalities of Their Excellencies and their children, and each year has taught us to feel a warmer interest in their welfare."

Judge Fernandez in moving the proposed message of sympathy said:

"The occasion which has brought us together this evening is sad beyond expression, and the duty we have to perform is a very mournful one indeed. The snapping of a young life of great potential and full of bright promise always evokes in the human breast the deepest sympathy, but when to this is conjoined the fact that the death of a young man whose untimely end has sent a thrill of sorrow and grief through the land has made desolate the erstwhile happy hearth and home of our beloved Governor, His Excellency Sir Arthur Lawley, and that a noble English House which gave us another Governor in the person of Lord Wenlock has thereby been deprived of a prop to its honour and traditions, the outpouring of sympathy must be correspondingly greater. Grief such as that of Their Excellencies the Governor and Lady Lawley at the loss of their only son under such distressing circumstances must be too great to be easily assuaged."

Judge Fernandez went on to move the resolution that "this meeting of the residents of Ootacamund desires to convey to Their Excellencies Sir Arthur and Lady Lawley and the members of their family its respectful and heartfelt sympathy with them in their sorrow occasioned by the sudden and painful death of Mr Richard Lawley on Saturday the 4th day of September 1909." [11]

The funeral took place on September 6th. The coffin and hearse were completely covered with the innumerable wreaths sent by friends and sympathisers. The sad procession was led by two Sowars of His Excellency's Bodyguard, then came the hearse drawn by four horses with postillion riders. The members of His Excellency's staff walked on each side of the hearse. Immediately behind followed the Government House carriage with Their Excellencies and the Misses Lawley with the Bodyguard to the front and rear. The European Subordinate Staff came next followed by His Excellency's Band in full dress uniform. Sir James Wolfe Murray, Mrs Douglas and the two members of the Council followed. Six servants attached to Government House came next, and then followed an immense line of carriages, a strong body of police and last a very large but orderly and respectful crowd of native Indians... As the cortege turned the corner of the Gymkhana it was viewed by a very large number of the European population, who awaited its arrival at the church and paid their last respects to the son of our respected Governor and Lady Lawley. At the gate of the cemetery the party was received by the full choir of St Stephen's Church headed by the Right Reverend Lord Bishop of Madras. Their Excellencies and the Misses Lawley came immediately behind the coffin bearers and were followed by all the Government officials, civil and military, and the entire European population of Ootacamund as well as many Parsi ladies and gentlemen, the leading Native Officials and the Government House staff. In St Stephen's Church the service was read by the Bishop of Madras and very many were moved to tears as the hymn – "Just as I am without one plea" – was sung. At the graveside the scene was most impressive. Here also the Service was read by the Bishop of Madras, and the hymn – "Jesus lives no longer now" – was sung. On the conclusion of the Burial Service, Their Excellencies were conducted to their carriage by Major Duff, the Military Secretary. The whole funeral party remained at the grave side until their Excellencies had left.[12]

There is a memorial to Richard Lawley in St Helen's Church, Escrick a few miles south of the city of York. When in 1928, his eldest sister, Ursula Mary Lady Wraxall, had her first baby, a boy, she named him George Richard Lawley Gibbs after his father George and the uncle the baby boy would never know – Richard Lawley.

From November 1st to 3rd, Sir Arthur and Lady Lawley accompanied by their daughters undertook the Thirteenth Official Tour of Vellore. They motored to Vellore accompanied by Captain Heseltine. Sir Arthur visited the Fort and the Central Jail, but Lady Lawley was unwell with the result that she was not able to pay a visit to either the American Mission Hospital or the Fort. The people of Vellore expressed universal sympathy with Their Excellencies at their bereavement. They left Vellore on the morning of November 3rd arriving at Guindy in time for lunch.[13]

Visit of the Viceroy

In November and December 1909, the Indian Viceroy and his wife, the Earl and Countess of Minto, visited Mysore and Madras. They arrived in Mysore City on November 25th and the Maharaja laid on a State Banquet to welcome them. On November 28th, the Maharaja and the Viceroy travelled to Kheddah Camp to see the elephants. The Viceroy and his wife went into the jungle and crossed the Kabani River by the foot ferry to reach the elephant school. There they watched the mahouts breaking in a group of wild elephants. Two days later they saw the spectacle of the capture and taming of the elephants and then watched as elephants were trained to enter and cross rivers. On December 3rd, the Viceregal Party visited Bangalore and the following day they went to the Kolar Goldfield, known as the Johannesburg of India. Here they were greeted by Dr Smeeth, the Mysore State geologist. [14]

Figure 184: The Countess of Minto and other guests crossing the Kabani River.

Figure 185: Wild Elephants watch the Countess of Minto at the Elephant Taming School.

Figure 186: The arrival of the Earl and Countess of Minto in Madras.

Figure 187: The Earl and Countess of Minto arrive at the Banqueting Hall, Madras.

Figure 188: The Visit of the Viceroy. The Earl and Countess of Minto are in the centre. Lady Lawley is to their left and Sir Arthur to their right. Cecilia Lawley is on the far left and Ursula Lawley on the far right.

The Viceregal visit, although official, was also an occasion for The Earl and Countess of Minto to express their condolences at the tragic death of the Lawley's son. Lord Minto's A.D.C. was Colonel John Evelyn Gibbs, the brother of George Abraham Gibbs of Tyntesfield.[15] On Friday December 10th, Sir Arthur and Lady Lawley met the Viceregal party at Madras Central Station. During the morning Lord Minto, accompanied by Lieutenant-General Sir James Wolfe Murray, presented new colours to the Second Battalion of the Dorset Regiment. In the afternoon there was a drive through the City of Madras with a guard of honour provided by the Dorset Regiment. Lady Minto and Lady Lawley visited the Gosha Hospital. Then the Maharaja of Travancore and Lord Minto exchanged visits – a very Indian form of courtesy – while Lady Minto accompanied by Sir Arthur and Lady Lawley paid a visit to the Technical Institute. That evening there was a Reception for the Earl and Countess of Minto at Government House.

On the morning of Saturday 11th, the Earl of Minto laid the foundation stone of the New Municipal Buildings accompanied by Sir Arthur Lawley. After lunch at Fort St George the Viceregal party accompanied by the Governor and his wife drove to Guindy along the Marina and the Promenade of St Thomé. The route was beautifully decorated and lined with cheering children. After a day of rest on the Sunday, the Countess of Minto, accompanied by Sir Arthur and Lady Lawley, attended a Garden Party thrown by the Prince of Arcot on the afternoon of Monday 13th. Lord Minto was unwell and remained at the Governor's Residence at Guindy. The Viceroy and his wife departed by an official train at 10.30 p.m. that evening.

Because the Earl and Countess had been unable to visit Trinchinopoly to see the festivities laid on in their honour, Sir Arthur and Lady Lawley went later in their place. On Thursday 18th December, accompanied by their daughters Ursula and Cecilia, they saw the celebrations, which culminated in the spectacular Illumination of the Rock – the highlight of this visit.

In January 1910, life began to return to normal and the Lawleys attended the opening of the Annual Gymkhana in Madras of which Sir Arthur was the patron. They had missed "HMS Pinafore" in Ootacamund in October 1909, but in January 1910 they attended the Madras Dramatic Society's production of "Les Cloches de Corneville".

Charity and Industry

In the political arena the Transvaal Indian question came back to haunt Sir Arthur Lawley in May 1910, when, by a strange twist of fate, some eighty Indians were deported from South Africa by the Transvaal Government. The Madras Presidency responded by issuing orders for the provision of temporary relief and assisted them with their repatriation.

It was in the year 1910, that the Rev. J. Breeden, a Missionary Worker, first thought of the establishment of a Home for Orphan and Destitute Anglo-Indian children in South India. In October 1910, the Rev. Breeden addressed the Madras Missionary Conference in the city of Madras, and at the meeting the first appeal for the establishment of St. George's Homes was made by him. A committee of influential citizens was formed with the Rev. J. Breeden at its head, in order to raise the necessary finances for the establishment of the Homes. The committee unanimously voted that the most suitable location for the Homes was in the neighbourhood of Kodaikanal in the Pulney Hills. On February 10, 1911 the Government offered a site of some 900 acres in Kodaikanal, a distance of about 4 miles from the actual town. On March 16, 1911, Sir Arthur Lawley, Governor of Madras, became the first President of the Homes.[16]

The promotion of local industry was another concern of Sir Arthur's Presidency. To encourage local textile and leather manufacturers, the Madura Technical Institute was established, teaching dyeing, weaving and leather working skills. There were growing industries in these fields. A Department for Industry had been set up in 1905 with Mr. A. Chatterton as its first director. Chrome tanning for leather and improved weaving looms were some early innovations. Improved drills for boring wells and motor driven pumps for raising water enabled irrigation to be much extended. In 1908, there was an Industrial Conference at Ootacamund opened by Sir Arthur Lawley on September 14th, which led to developments in education and training and to further industrial growth.

Booth Tucker, a Salvation Army officer who had been in the Indian Civil Service, was eager to promote the silk industry. He wished to see sericulture established as a cottage industry. Sir Arthur considered that India ought to be a great silk producing country, especially since silk production would not bring the interests of the Indian ryot into collision with those of the Lancashire mill hand. He also thought that Swadeshi (self-help) Sericulture might help with the problem of what to do to assist the Eurasian community of Madras.[17]

There were two sides to Swadeshi. Sir Arthur Lawley said that "if Swadeshi meant self-help, if it meant encouragement of local enterprise, if it meant the development of Indian industries and the exploitation of the marvellous resources at her command, then the movement had his entire sympathy. If on the other hand it meant the adoption of methods which included the boycott of British goods and imposing on the poor the necessity to buy an inferior article in a dearer market, then he had no sympathy with it whatsoever."[18]

Great improvements were undertaken in Madras Harbour during Sir Arthur's Presidency. A new harbour entrance was constructed to the North East protected by a 400 metre long breakwater. A new ship wharf was built over 100 metres long with a 10 metre depth of water alongside.

Figure 189: Spectators watching a Polo Match.

Figure 190: Cecilia Lawley, Caryl Annesley and Cecily Blair at the Governor's Country Seat at Guindy Park just south of the City of Madras.

The Yuvaraja's Marriage

In June 1910, the Maharaja of Mysore's son and heir apparent to the throne, the Yuvaraja of Mysore, was married. The Maharaja was a close personal friend and he and Sir Arthur enjoyed hunting together. The wedding ceremony, procession and festivities were truly regal. The new palace in Mysore had just been completed and was sumptuously decorated for the occasion.

Figure 191: Crowds outside the New Palace for the Wedding of the Yuvaraja of Mysore.

The preliminary religious ceremonies began at the Jagan Mohan Palace on June 15th when the Yuvaraja performed the "stambba puja" (flag raising ceremony). The following morning the "upanayanam" or thread ceremony was performed in the Marriage Pavilion of the New Palace when between four or five thousand people were present. The sacred thread used for the ceremony consists of three strands, joined by a knot known as Brahmagranthi or the knot of Brahma. The three strands may symbolise the Hindu trinity – Shiva, Vishnu and Brahma or the three qualities known as sattva, rajas and tamas; past, present and the future or the three states - wakefulness, dream and deep sleep. Some even say that they represent the three dimensions known as heaven (swarga), earth (martyaloka) and nether regions (patala). The ceremony is only for the three upper Hindu castes and symbolizes the transition from boyhood to manhood.

The ceremony was followed by a Durbar which lasted about two hours or more. Over 200 guests – maharajas, rajas, merchant princes and British dignitaries arrived from beyond the borders of Mysore. About 1400 other guests came from all parts of the state. On the afternoon of June 17th, departing at about 1.30 pm, His Highness the Maharaja and his eldest son, the Yuvaraja, went in procession from the New Palace to the Jagan Mohan Palace. The approaches from the Karikal Thoti to the Jagan Mohan were packed with men women and children. Thousands of His Highness's subjects from all parts of the kingdom came to get a glimpse of royalty and to testify to their loyalty to the Maharaja.

Figure 192: Regal Elephants convey the Maharaja and Yuvaraja to the Jagan Mohan Palace

Figure 193: His Highness the Yuvaraja within the Marriage Mantap supported on either side by Their Highnesses the Maharaja and Maharani of Mysore.

Figure 194: The Yuvaraja of Mysore and his bride in the Jagan Mohan Palace.

Figure 195: The Wedding Presents.

The Jagan Mohan was a sight to behold and the marriage pavilion was a magnificent creation in gold, silver and many coloured silks. His Highness accompanied by Major General Pertab Singh and the Yuvaraja with Mr. Gopalraj Urs rode on richly caparisoned elephants festooned with jewellery and precious stones. There was a military escort with bands playing and the High State Officials following on foot. The numerous costly presents of silks, jewellery and silver were conveyed in palanquins and by bearers from the Palace to the Jagan Mohan. On arrival at the Jagan Mohan, His Highness and party were received by Mr. D. Devaraj Urs and conducted to their seats. After the private ceremonies had been performed in purdah, the young bride arrayed in cloth of gold and loaded with gems of rich and rare brilliance made her appearance to the public amid a round of applause.

The Yuvaraja was seated on the right of H.H. the Maharaja and to his left were General Pertab Singh and the Thakore Sahib of Muri, a young prince of striking features. Their Excellencies Sir Arthur and Lady Lawley and their daughters accompanied by the British Resident and his wife, and by Mr A.Y.G. Campbell, the Governor's private secretary, viewed the proceedings from a balcony above on the left. On the balcony to the right were the ladies of the palace concealed behind purdahs. Outside on both sides of the building were galleries for Indian ladies which were literally crammed with Indian beauties of all shades dressed in the most valuable of cloths and wearing loads of costly gold jewellery with sparkling gems.

After the mantras were pronounced by the Gurus in purdah, the bride made her appearance amid a round of applause from the guests. The marriage proper, which consisted of the tying of the Tosli by the Yuvaraja around the bride's neck, took place at 2.30 p.m. The presentation of the Robes of Honour or Khilats followed with the deputation from Baroda leading. Then came Benares, Cooch Behar, Bhavnagar and other princely states all presenting robes of honour to the Yuvaraja and his bride. The proceeding ended at about 4.30 pm.[19]

Visitors from home

In October 1910, Lady Lawley's youngest sister, Caroline Margaret, came out to visit India with her husband the Honourable Athole Hay. They stayed with the Lawleys at Ootacamund and on Thursday October 20th set out with Sir Arthur on the Governor's Fourteenth Tour.[20] Mrs Hay was known to family and friends as Maggie. To begin the tour the men went to a shooting camp at Hascanur in the Coimbatore District. Sir Arthur did not shoot but Athole Hay shot two large bull bisons. They stayed at the Camp until Wednesday 26th when they drove to Mysore arriving at about 3 p.m. Other members of the party either took the train or motored to Mysore. The military commander, General Sir James Wolfe Murray, accompanied the party. His Highness the Maharaja of Mysore loaned the Governor two cars in which Lady Lawley and her daughters, Ursula and Cecilia, Mrs Hay, and Miss Allen were driven to Mysore. There the Governor and his party assembled as guests of the Maharaja. Their host had hounds specially transported from the Ooty kennels and fine horses ready for a hunt at 6.00 a.m. on the morning of Thursday 27th. That afternoon the Maharaja's guests visited an Industrial and Agricultural Exhibition. The Maharaja and his son, the Yuvaraja, then took their guests to the stables to inspect the fine thoroughbred horses which were the Maharajah's pride and joy. That evening the Governor and his party dined at the British Residency with Colonel Daly, the Resident, and his wife and daughter. The next morning after breakfast, there was display of jujitsu by two Indian pupils of an expert Japanese instructor. Lady Lawley,

Colonel Daly, and a large party motored to the Cauvery Falls near Shivasamudram and inspected the bridge and the hydro-electric power station there. They returned that evening to Mysore where the Maharaja had taken Sir Arthur for a drive that afternoon in one of his luxury limousines.

On the morning of Saturday 29th, the hounds met again and some excellent sport was provided. In the afternoon the Maharaja called at Government House with a carriage and team of horses to drive Sir Arthur and Lady Lawley, Colonel Daly and Mr and Mrs Athole Hay to the New Palace for a guided tour. His Highness was their guide and the visitors were able to inspect the jewels used on state occasions which were laid out in one of the Durbar Halls. The host then took his guests to the top of one of the New Palace towers from which there was an impressive view of the city and the surrounding countryside. Finally the Maharaja took his visitors on a carriage ride around the streets of Mysore.

On the Sunday morning, Lady Lawley motored over to Seringapatam where she spent the day sketching and painting in water colours. The others went to the Jagan Mohan Palace to see another display of jujitsu. Then the Hays and the Lawley girls motored over to Seringapatam with Colonel and Mrs Daly. Sir Arthur and his aides went to see the Maharajah and his mother, the Dowager Maharani. After this visit His Highness, His Excellency and their party also drove over to Seringapatam to join the others. While Lady Lawley was painting the other visitors had been to see Tipu Sultan's tomb and the Seringapatam Fort. That evening the whole party motored back to Mysore. Very early on the morning of Monday 31st October there was another hunting party which met at the new Race Course and then after breakfast the Maharaja and Yuvaraja came over to Government House to bid Sir Arthur and Lady Lawley and their party farewell.

The Governor's party then travelled on through the state of Mysore. Lady Lawley took several opportunities to sketch and paint at the village of Siravanti and the Gersoppa Waterfalls. There the Maharaja had instructed his men to erect a tented camp for the visitors near to the Mysore Bungalow. The Maharaja could not have been a more kind or considerate host.

Sir Arthur and Lady Lawley and their party then travelled on to Hospet, the seat of the Raja of Anagundi, where the Governor undertook official duties while his guests did some sight seeing with Lady Lawley. Thence they proceeded, on November 7th, to Bellary to be greeted by a large crowd outside the Town Hall, where entertainments were provided – a Lambadi dance, a bazaar drama, music, gymnastics, juggling and a sword dance. A military band provided the music and at the end of the evening there was a firework display. The next morning, Sir Arthur inspected the prison and later went with his wife to visit the Municipal Hospital and Government Training School. Meetings with local gentry and dignitaries were followed by lunch and a visit in the afternoon to the S.P.C.A. Missionary Hospital. Then the customary "Feeding of the Poor" took place when three thousand destitute people were assembled and fed in honour of His Excellency the Governor. A visit to Bellary Fort was followed by a dinner party given by Sir Arthur and Lady Lawley for the leading European ladies and gentlemen of Bellary.

The following morning the Governor inspected the troops. The Garrison consisted of the second wing of the Dorset Regiment and the 63rd Palamcottah Light Infantry. Sir Arthur then visited the Convent of the Good Shepherd and the associated orphanages and Girls High School. Lady Lawley was indisposed and so her daughters, Ursula and Cecilia, watched the programme of songs and exercises so as not to disappoint the children. Sir Arthur then visited the Dorset Regimental Lines, where the troops gave an energetic and skilled gymnastics display. He then walked over to the Station Hospital, built in 1880 and extremely spacious, where 72 beds were available for sick soldiers. In the afternoon, an inspection of the Police Force was accompanied by pinning the King's Medal on Head Constable Behmiah for his outstanding bravery in plunging into the waters of the Tongabadra River in order to secure the arrest of a prisoner who was about to escape. That afternoon the Collector, Mr J.A. Cummings, gave a Garden Party for the Governor and his party, and in the evening they all dined in the Dorset Regiment's Officers Mess together with the European residents of Bellary.

Figure 196: The Dorset Regiment with Regimental Band on parade in Madras.

Sadly Maggie Hay was taken ill there and so her husband, Athole Hay, and her niece, Ursula Lawley, stayed on in Bellary to look after her, while the rest of the party proceeded on their journey. The Governor's party then travelled by first class rail to visit Anantapur and Guntakal where a similar range of official and informal events were on their programme. Thence they journeyed on to Hyderabad by rail arriving at the main station at 8 o'clock on the morning of November 12th.

The Nizam of Hyderabad

Sir Arthur and Lady Lawley, Cecilia and Miss Allen were met by the British Resident and the senior civilian and military officials. General Sir James Wolfe Murray was there to greet the visitors. Then Sir Arthur inspected the Guard of Honour of the Second Hyderabad Infantry on the platform, and later the Governor and his party were driven through the streets of Hyderabad to the Falaknama Castle, a sumptuous Palace which the Nizam had made available for their use during their stay.

They were escorted by a Squadron of the First Hyderabad Lancers. At the Castle they were welcomed by Sir Afsar-ul-Mulk, the Nizam's Military Chief of Staff. After breakfast Sir Arthur and his party set off in motor cars through Hyderabad and past the extensive lake known as the Hussein Sagar Tank, which connects the twin cities of Hyderabad and Secunderabad. They drove on to the United Services Club at Secunderabad where drinks were served. When he returned to Falaknama Castle, Sir Arthur received Sir Kishen Prasad, the poet and Prime Minister of Hyderabad. Meanwhile the other members of the Governor's party went on a more extensive motor tour on through Trimulgherry, where the 13th Hussars, a British regiment then serving there with the army of India, was based, and on to Bolarum where there was a large British cantonment. That evening His Highness the Nizam accompanied by his Prime Minister, Sir Kishen Prasad, and Sir Afsar-ul-Mulk called on Their Excellencies Sir Arthur and Lady Lawley at Falkanama Castle and stayed for tea. A Guard of Honour was furnished by the Third Hyderabad Infantry.

Figure 197: Sir Arthur Lawley inspects the Guard of Honour at Hyderabad Station.

Figure 198: H.E. The Governor and Lady Lawley welcomed in Hyderabad.

Figure 199: Arrival at Falaknama Castle.

Figure 200: Drawing Room, Falaknama Castle.

Figure 201: Marble Hall and Fountain, Falaknama Castle.

Figure 202: United Services Club Secunderabad.

Figure 203: The guests of His Highness the Nizam. Miss Allen, Lady Lawley, Sir Arthur Lawley, General Wolfe Murray and Cecilia Lawley in the front row. A.Y.G. Campbell is behind Sir Arthur.

Figure 204: The Nizam's Chowmahala Palace in Hyderabad.

Figure 205: Sir Arthur and Lady Lawley, Cecilia Lawley and Miss Allen arrive at the Afzal Mahal within the Chowmahala Palace.

Figure 206: The British Residency, Hyderabad.

On Sunday 13th November in the morning, Sir Arthur and Lady Lawley and their party were driven out to Golconda to see the old fortress and ancient tombs. They were met there by Sir Afsar-ul-Mulk. Unfortunately a heavy shower of rain prevented the visitors from climbing to the top of the hill to see the view.

After Sunday lunch at Falaknama Castle, Sir Arthur and Lady Lawley's party motored through Hyderabad to Secunderabad and on to Bolarum and later took tea with the Nizam, Sir Kishen Prasad, and Sir Afsar-ul-Mulk at Chowmahala Palace. After tea Their Excellencies attended Divine Service at All Saints Church, Trimulgherry, a wonderful Victorian Gothic building.

On the Sunday evening, Sir Arthur and Lady Lawley and party dined with the Nizam at his Chowmahala Palace. Covers were laid for nearly one hundred guests and His Highness proposed the toast of His Majesty the King Emperor and of Their Excellencies. Sir Arthur proposed the toast to His Highness the Nizam and took the opportunity of expressing in a few words his gratitude to the Nizam for his generous and kindly hospitality.

After breakfast on Monday morning, November 14th, Sir Arthur Lawley and some of his party motored out again to Golconda. This time they were fortunate with the weather. They walked to the top of the hill and obtained an excellent view of the fort and the surrounding countryside from the roof of the Bala Hissar or keep. Later that morning, Sir Afsar-ul-Mulk arranged a hunting party at Bisgunta. First there was a cheetah hunt with one of the Nizam's cheetahs chasing a black buck. The cheetah travelled in a specially designed cart. There were plenty of black buck and two runs by the cheetah both resulted in a kill. The first run was exceptionally good. Afterwards there was some hawking and black buck catching by a tame black buck.

Figure 207: Golconda Tombs and Fort.

Figure 208: The Nizam of Hyderabad's hunting cheetahs.

Figure 209: Sir Arthur, Lady Lawley and Cecilia leave for the Garden Party.

Figure 210: The Iron Bungalow in the Public Gardens Hyderabad.

In the afternoon Their Excellencies attended a Garden Party given by the Prime Minister in the Public Gardens. There was a large gathering to meet them and the function was a very pleasant one. The Gardens were prettily illuminated after sunset. That evening, Sir Arthur and Lady Lawley dined with the British Resident, Richard Temple, at the Residency. At 8.30 am on Tuesday 15th November, Sir Arthur Lawley and his party left by a special train which was due to arrive in Madras early on the following morning. Lady Lawley took the train to Bellary to join her sick sister Maggie, and Athole Hay and Ursula who were looking after her. Together they travelled back to Madras.[21]

The Earl of Crewe

On November 3rd 1910, Robert Crewe-Milnes, the first Earl of Crewe, was appointed Secretary of State for India. He was an old friend of Sir Arthur Lawley. In February 1911, Sir Arthur Lawley wrote to Lord Crewe:

"The Legislative Council last week... asked my government to invite a reconsideration at your hands of the Secretary of State's decision to refuse our request for the creation of a Government Department of Industries.... There is no doubt that any evidence of a desire on our part to show practical sympathy with industrial development in India would be welcomed very warmly by Indians of every creed and caste".[22]

Sir Arthur wrote a long letter from Government House, Guindy to congratulate Lord Crewe on his appointment as Secretary for State for India.[23] Here is part of the letter he wrote:

"I am delighted to think of you as my chief. It was very nice indeed to get your telegram telling me of your instalment in the India Office... Fortunately I can say that "All's well" from the Madras Watchtower....It happens that this year we have had an altogether phenomenal rainfall. For you, who know of Indian life and conditions, know also how attenuated is the margin between bare existence and

*starvation for the silent millions on the land and can appreciate how totally
important is the otherwise twaddly topic of the weather. Last year the North East
Monsoon failed. This year it has been everywhere abundant and so we are
content....*"

*I have been away on a somewhat protracted tour.... I left Ootacamund – our hill
station – just about a month ago and have only just got back to Madras. I "did" a
couple of Mysore Districts – Bellary and Anantapur, two of the smallest and least
important of the Districts of the Presidency. The usual programme of addresses,
speeches, Inspections of Schools and Institutions and all sorts of garden parties
etc. etc. etc. I put in a week at Mysore, the province of the little Maharaja to whom
I am sincerely attached and who showers on me every mark of friendship – we
had a delightful time and I hope that it was not altogether wasted. The little man is
very lonely and it is I think desirable that if he makes friends it should be with
Englishmen who appreciate his many excellent qualities and who are ready to help
him whenever they can. He is very ready to confide in me although of course he is
not in any way under the Madras Government, and perhaps I am able to be of use
quite unofficially of course."*

"*A new Resident has recently been sent to Mysore – one Daly – who was a
contemporary and friend and is a particularly nice person who already enjoys the
Maharaja's confidence to a wonderful degree. Thence we went to Hyderabad, a
contrast indeed. In matters of Religion, of Rulers and I might add of Residents as
the poles asunder. A most unattractive person is the Nizam, in appearance, in
manners and character! But he seems to be desirous to show me courtesy so I
have no reason to be ought but satisfied. Certainly I had a most interesting visit
there.*"

There was an outbreak of Bubonic Plague in Madras towards the end of 1910. Sir
Arthur Lawley informed Lord Crewe about this.[24] From Government House Guindy
he wrote:

"*Since I last wrote to you I have been to Salem, the Head Quarters of one of the
most flourishing Districts, where Plague has been rather bad. I was anxious to see
whether anything more could be done...to check its' rapid increases. I rode all
round the town and very depressing it was to see the more than semi-deserted
streets from which the plague and famine stricken people have fled. Out of a total
of 80 thousand more than 50 thousand have migrated out spreading the disease, I
fear, far and wide. The Brahminics are always the first to go and their quarter was
totally deserted. In several others not a soul was to be seen. Very dreary the
whole place seemed to be. Weavers of the poorest class are left. They cannot
afford to go and leave their home behind. The sad thing is that there is no market
whereat they can sell their goods...... I am trying to devise some means of helping
these poor folk.*"

In due course, Sir Arthur persuaded a large business house in Madras to help the
weavers find a market for their textiles and their situation improved.[25] The letter
continues:

"*I had a motor so seized the opportunity of seeing as much as possible of the
country thereabouts. Never was the prospect more pleasing. It is hard that it
should be marred by this cruel inrush of disease and death.... I am only afraid that
we may be in for a more serious outbreak than has yet visited this Presidency. The*

number of places reporting plague is increasing fast and as these terrors thicken,
people fly. North, south, east and west they are bound in some cases to carry the
disease with them. One pleasing feature of the Salem outbreak is the marked
readiness of the citizens to get themselves inoculated."

Figure 211: St George's Cathedral Madras.

In December 1910, the Maharaja of Bobbili told Sir Arthur that he felt unable to continue as a member of the Executive Council. Sir Arthur recommended Mr Justice V. Krishnaswamy Iyer as his replacement. He was conspicuous among the Indians for his ability and public spirit.[26] He was in due course appointed. Thus there continued to be an Indian representative on the Executive Council. The Legislative Council had about 24 members – twelve British and twelve Indian – although the numbers varied. The Indian members were mainly businessmen, but the Indian Princes were represented with the Nawab Muhamed Raza Khan, the Raja of Kurrupam and the Raja of Kollengode being among the princely members. [27]

As Christmas 1910 approached there was a wedding in St George's Cathedral. Sir Arthur Lawley's Private Secretary, Archibald Y. G. Campbell, who had been with him for five years, married Miss Frances Young. Miss Young's sister and Ursula Lawley were the bridesmaids and there were two pages, Master Allen Campbell (with Sir Arthur in the photograph) and Master Weston Leach (with the bride's mother). The bride was given away by her brother Captain Hugh Young and Major Duff was the best man. The service was conducted by His Lordship the Bishop of Madras. The Reception was in the Banqueting Hall and His Excellency and Lady Lawley were "at home" to honour the occasion. "A very large number of ladies and gentlemen were present and the gathering was one of the biggest and most influential that has ever been seen at the Banqueting Hall." [28]

Miss Young   *Major Duff*   *Captain Hugh Young*

Figure 212: The Wedding of Sir Arthur Lawley's Private Secretary, Archibald Campbell, to Miss Frances Young on December 21st 1910 in St George's Cathedral, Madras.

Second Row   *Cecilia.   Maggie Hay.   Mr Campbell. Frances.   Lady Lawley. Athole Hay.*

Front Row   *Mrs Campbell.   Sir Arthur Lawley.   Mrs Young.   Ursula.*

Sir Arthur Lawley expected to leave his post on March 28th 1911,[29] but, because his successor was not yet ready, was granted an extension until November 4th 1911. After Christmas 1910, Sir Arthur wrote to Lord Crewe from Government House, Ootacamund:

> *"We have had a very quiet and a very sad Christmas. My wife and I are here alone and I know that it will be a great effort to her to say good bye to Ooty."* [30]

In January 1911, Sir Arthur Lawley began to show signs of weariness. He wrote to Lord Crewe:

> *"We are ploughing our way through the quagmire of the Madras "Season" – a very fatiguing process but I suppose inevitable. I generally start at 7.00 am and work all day preliminary to a big Dinner Party. In this climate somewhat exhausting. Night's long shadows bring a merciful respite. The thermometer bids us pare in life's pleasures. Already the nights wax hot and the thinnest of sheets is a burden. But for all the sunshine is glorious."* [31]

Yet later that month he wrote:

"I find the work intensely interesting and though there are moments when the idea of a holiday is attractive, yet I know that I shall be sorry when I have to lay down the reins and have to contemplate the possibility of enforced idleness." [32]

Medicine and Public Health

Sir Arthur's government did much to improve medical services during his five years in office. In March 1911 the Presidency's government resolved to create a special Malaria Board to take measures to control the disease. In 1910, Sir Arthur and Lady Lawley had laid the foundation stone of a new hospital at Coonoor. The Madras Maternity Hospital was thoroughly renovated and modernized. Electricity was installed and a new School Block to accommodate and train 100 medical students was added. The Government Ophthalmic Hospital had a new out-patients department and additional wards. Their official opening by Lady Lawley was unusual. There was a large brass padlock with a ceremonial key. On the padlock were inscribed the words – Lady Lawley Wards at Government Ophthalmic Hospital, Madras, February 13th 1911. The padlock and key are inside an engraved brass box which was presented to Sir Arthur Lawley by Himayatul Islam Sabha in Calicut in 1907. Both are now in the National Trust Victorian Country House of Tyntesfield.

Figure 213: The Lawleys are guests of Mr Aziz ud Din, Cuddalore February 6th 1911.

The Medical College and Medical Schools were placed under the control of the Surgeon General. Training Schools for Nurses were fostered and encouraged. New Physiological and Hygiene Laboratories were constructed and it was planned to build a new Pathological Laboratory. Provisions were made for the mentally ill, lepers and TB sufferers and there were plans for new Sanatoria. Support was given to municipal and district hospitals throughout the Presidency. Fifty thousand rupees were donated to St Bartholomew's Hospital in Ootacamund. There were proposals to move the Government General Hospital to a new healthier site near Guindy outside Madras.[33]

Public Health and sanitation were given due priority with special attention paid to the hazards of bubonic plague and cholera. Schemes to improve the water supply, drainage and sewage disposal were supported. Standing water and pools were drained and mosquito larvae were killed with kerosene oil. Quinine was produced within the Presidency of Madras and the drug was administered to combat malaria in affected patients.

Another major concern was forest preservation. There were plans to establish a Forestry College at Coimbatore to train Indian foresters in forest management. The forests were used as a source of fuel, building materials and a location for grazing. Hence they would require careful management. At Banjam district and elsewhere, shifting cultivators practised Podu, moving around the forest and clearing fresh land every few years. This needed to be managed sensitively.[34]

Sir Arthur Lawley was very popular with the Islamic citizens of Madras to whom he showed particular friendship and consideration. On April 3rd 1911, His Excellency the Governor laid the foundation stone of the Lawley Hall for the Anjuman Mohammedan Community. This was the recognition by the Moslems of Madras of the work done by Sir Arthur.

Conspiracy

The Madras Presidency exercised political control over five native states – Travancore, Cochin, Pudukkottai, Banganapalle and Sandur. Not surprisingly the people of these states did not all endorse British rule. In Tinnevelly resistance was particularly active. Men like Babo Bepin and Chandra Pal preached Swaraj (self government) and Swadeshi in the sense of resistance and boycott. There were incidences of violence. The European Club at Cocanda was attacked and seriously damaged on May 31st 1907. In 1909 a mob in Tinnevelly was incited to riot by provocative speeches from the political activists, Chidambaram Pillai and Subramanya Siva. They invaded the Church Missionary Society's College and the Munsif's Court, burned the Municipal Offices and the Police Station, and destroyed some furniture in the hospital. The police were ordered to open fire on the crowd by the Superintendent of Police and the District Magistrate. Four people were killed and several others injured. Chidambaram Pillai and Subramanya Siva were prosecuted for inciting violence and sentenced to imprisonment. In another incident at Tuticorin, the Divisional Officer and the police were assaulted by a mob which did not disperse until the police opened fire. Several persons were injured.[35]

In May the Presidency submitted its estimates for the cost of the Madras Camp at the Delhi Durbar. There were to be one hundred Europeans and fifty Indians to represent 41 million people. Despite numerous requests from Sir Arthur Lawley, the King and Queen decided not to visit Madras. Sir Arthur reminded the India Office of the disappointment of the loyal subjects in the Madras Presidency at their Majesties inability to visit them. He also emphasized that the costs of the Durbar were well within their means since Madras was an affluent part of India.[36]

Towards the end May, after a period of illness, the Secretary of State for India, Lord Crewe, returned to work. Sir Thomas Carmichael, the Governor of the State of Victoria in Australia, who was to replace Sir Arthur Lawley as Governor of Madras, visited Colombo for a short stay at the beginning of June. Because the Government

Offices in Ootacamund usually closed in mid October and opened again a week later in Madras, it was agreed that Carmichael would arrive in Madras on October 31st.[37]

Figure 214: The members of the Executive Council – Mr Murray Hammick, Sir William Meyer, Sir Arthur Lawley, the Raja of Bobbili and Mr John Atkinson.

Life wasn't all work and during May, Sir Arthur was able to take a break to go hunting.[38] He wrote to Lord Crewe:

"I have been away into the jungle for two or three days after a mythical tiger. Even though we were disappointed in never seeing the animal, we were successful in avoiding two days of a furious hurricane which ushered in the monsoon. A tearing wind and torrents of rain. In an adjacent valley they had sixteen inches of rain in twenty four hours. We also had a spell of absolute rest and we encompassed the death of two full grown leopards."

At 10.40 a.m. on the 17th June 1911, Mr. Robert W. D'Estcourt Ashe I.C.S., the Collector and District Magistrate of the Tinnevelly district, was shot dead at Maniyachi Railway Station by a smartly dressed Brahmin aged about thirty. A

Mohammedan, who was standing nearby, thwarted an attempt by the murderer to fire a second shot at Mr Ashe. The assassin fled and eventually retreated into a latrine, where to evade capture he shot himself dead through the mouth. The murder seems to have been deliberately planned. The second class ticket found on the person of the assassin showed that he had travelled to Maniyachi by the same train as Mr and Mrs Ashe, who had changed at Maniyachi in order to catch the Madras mail train en route for Kodaikanal. Mr Ashe was a very capable officer, keen, fearless and enthusiastic in the discharge of his duties, and the sad and untimely termination of such a bright and promising career was deeply deplored His widow had only just arrived from England on June 12th. The couple had four children.[39] The Governor in Council offered his deepest sympathies.

In a letter to Lord Crewe, [40] Sir Arthur Lawley wrote:

"The murderer has been identified. As I write a telegram is handed to me from the Chief of our Criminal Investigation Department to say that as far as he can at present say the murderer appears to have been a political fanatic and seemingly a member of some secret seditious association conducting operations at Pondichery, Tuticorin and Shencottali, to which latter place the assassin belonged.... There is a very 'bad lot' of political agitators of the worst type in Pondichery."

The assassination led Sir Arthur to impose firm measures to restore law and order. "The simultaneous suggestion in nationalist circles that Sir Arthur's measures were unduly repressive, and in some of the English owned newspapers that he was too lenient, may be taken as proving that he knew how to check the growth of sedition without arousing avoidable resentment."[41] The perpetrators of the crime seem to have resided in Pondicherry, one of the remaining French enclaves in India. On July 5th, Sir Arthur wrote to Lord Crewe to inform him of the situation:

"Our Police are hard at work trying to trace the origin and growth of the movement which led up to Ashe's murder. They have seized a goodly number of documents and papers which give clear evidence of murderous plotting on the part of a small gang. Some ten or twelve persons have been arrested and of these one or two have turned approvers (informers). Pondicherry is, I think I may say undoubtedly, the centre from which the crime has been engineered.

"Pondicherry is a plague spot from which a poisonous stream of seditious literature is constantly finding its way into our towns and villages in Southern India. Lately a number of abominable pamphlets and circulars of violent tendency have been distributed to a considerable number of the usual virulent extremist type, and I think that there is no doubt that they emanate from Pondicherry. It is there that Aratudo Ghose has taken refuge and there are one or two men with him – Subramanya Bharati and others of whom Bharati only just escaped arrest when we laid Chidambaram Pillai and other seditionists by the heels. From the evidence now forthcoming it is clear that not only have they been issuing printed appeals inciting crime, but they have been sending out missionaries of extremism to one or two centres – Tuticorin, Shencottali in Travancore and elsewhere – to induce youthful " patriots" of the Vauchi Iyer type to form themselves into a band of anarchists.

"It is the Pondicherry gang which is really responsible for this crime. Of that I am quite convinced and I only wish that we could come to some arrangement with the French authorities whereby we could bring these ruffians to book.

*"Meanwhile it is sad to reflect that we have not received from Indian sources –
whether official or non-official – the slightest hint of any seditious movement being
on foot, though some knowledge of it must have existed nor does anyone come
forward to render us any real help."* [42]

As the investigation continued, Sir Arthur Lawley was able to update the India
Office in London with progress. On July 12th he wrote:

*"We have made two important arrests during the past week in connection with the
Tinnevelly murder – Neelakanta Anyar and Chidambaram Pillai – the latter is not
the same man as the Chidambaram Pillai who was the prime mover in the
Tinnevelly riots three years ago. But these are the two men who are believed to
have organised the conspiracy which led to Ashe's murder. I wish that our
evidence was ampler and stronger than it is.*

*"Brahmin influence in Travancore and Tinnevelly is very strong and, as the crime
was organized and achieved by Brahmin agency, we are not getting as much help
as we ought to get. The police are working diligently and I hope that we may
tussle out the whole plot."* [43]

By September 6th the investigation was coming to a conclusion. Sir Arthur wrote
to Lord Crewe:

*"I have been put in possession of a good deal of information concerning the doings
of the anarchist gang in Pondicherry. It consists of some 30 to 35 men, whose
names we have, of whom the leader is V.V.S. Aiyas. He was at one time a
prominent figure at India House in London. He came to Pondicherry last year and
ever since he arrived he has been very active in preaching sedition and urging the
adoption of violent methods. He has also been giving his men regular lessons in
the art of pistol and revolver shooting. He is said to be a good shot himself and to
have erected shooting galleries where regular practice is carried on. The target is
said to represent the figure of an Englishman with two or three bull's eyes on the
body. They are said to have imported some 50 or 60 revolvers and pistols from St
Etienne. I think there is no reason to doubt that Vauchi Iyer – the man who shot
Ashe – was taught to shoot at these galleries.*

*"Immediately after Ashe's murder, practice seems to have stopped for a few days,
but has since begun again and is being actively carried on. Our informants seem
to be confident that they are working up for the Durbar. Whether this be so or not,
there is no doubt that there is a pretty mischievous gang in Pondicherry and the
Durbar no doubt presents itself as a very tempting opportunity for the display of
their abominable methods. However I think that our Police are fully appreciative
of the seriousness of the situation; and I have no fear that there will be any
difficulty in keeping ourselves fully informed of what is going on and of being able
to watch these reptiles and stop their power for mischief. We shall do all that is
possible to this end and ought to be able to cope with the situation."* [44]

This whole episode demonstrates the importance of the political officers and the
police in controlling rebellious factions, sedition and opposition to the British Raj.

Celebration

On August 29th 1911, the Nizam of Hyderabad died.[45] He was the most powerful
Indian Prince in the Madras Presidency's sphere of influence. Sir Arthur Lawley, as
Governor, had a duty to ensure a smooth succession. On September 12th 1911, the

British Resident, Richard Temple, representing the Governor, attended the Coronation Durbar of the new Nizam Mir Osman Ali Khan.[46]

On September 15th, Sir Arthur laid the Foundation Stone of the Lawley Institute in Ootacamund. The Maharaja of Bobbili donated the money for its construction and furbishing. The institute was a Residential Club for Indian Gentlemen.[47] During the third week of September 1911, in the Ootacamund Hunt Races, Cecila Lawley rode the winner – "Guinevere" in the Ladies Point to Point Race and Ursula took second place on "Peggy". Both horses were owned by Sir Arthur Lawley. In the Ladies Point to Point Pony's Race, Ursula won on Mr E. Nicholson's "Beresford" while Cecila riding Mr E.G. Thompson's "Coronation" was in third place. The two girls shared their father's passion for horse riding.[48]

The Sheriff of Madras, Diwan Bahadur Govind Doss Chathoorbhooja, junior partner of the firm Chathoorbhooja Doss, Khusal Doss and Sons, offered to erect a bronze statue in Madras of George V, as Emperor, for the Delhi Durbar in 1911. Sir Arthur Lawley gave the idea to Govind Doss and he agreed to supervise the casting of the statue by an eminent artist from England. Govind Doss paid 45,000 rupees for the statue. Earlier, in 1910, when Edward VII died, he had donated 10,000 rupees for the erection of a statue of Edward VII near the Central Station in Madras.[49]

On the afternoon of October 26th, H.E. Lady Lawley accompanied by her daughters Ursula and Cecilia visited the Dowager Princess of Arcot at Amir Mahal. "All the ladies of the Arcot and Carnatic families assembled and presented a farewell address to Her Excellency". Then the Princess garlanded Lady Lawley and her daughters.[50]

On Saturday 28th October there was a Farewell Entertainment given to Their Excellencies by their numerous friends and well wishers in Southern India. The Madras Times said of Sir Arthur:

"To know him was to love and respect him. Not only in this town, but in the various rural stations where he has gone on tour hundreds of leading gentlemen have had private interviews with His Excellency and each one of them must have been impressed by his refreshing frankness and amiability of disposition, which induced in visitors the feeling that should they unburden their hearts, their representations would receive a ready and sympathetic hearing. One of the most notable traits of His Excellency's character is his extreme accessibility to people from all grades of society and from all shades of opinion, and his readiness and willingness at all times to hear patiently and to redress promptly any personal matters which might be brought to his notice."[51]

The gathering was exceedingly large for people had travelled from all parts of the Presidency to attend. A temporary pandal 200 feet in length and forty feet wide was erected with double verandahs on either side. There were a dozen chandeliers and a tapestry decorated with the Royal Coat of Arms and other devices. There were Zamindars robed in silk and lace and bedecked with diamonds and rubies, Indian ladies with their picturesque saris and jewellery, Indian gentlemen with turbans of variegated colours, military officers in their uniforms, English ladies in their rich flowing dresses. All these combined to relieve the monotony of the sombre looking black coats of the gentlemen. Both banks of the river were lit up with kerosene lamps from Government House Bridge to the Bar, and the circumference of the Island was illuminated with numerous Washington lights.

Figure 215: Sir Arthur Lawley, Governor of Madras 1906 to 1911.

Their Excellencies arrived at 9.00 p.m. accompanied by Sir Arthur's brother, the Hon. Rev. Algernon Lawley, escorted by a full compliment of the Bodyguard. The entertainment began with a theatrical performance by the New Royal Parsee Theatrical Company of Bombay. This was followed by an illusionist and an astonishing display of Indian swordsmanship. There followed a musical ride by the horsemen of the Governor's Bodyguard.

Sir Subramania Iyer then presented Lady Lawley with a loving cup in solid silver, eighteen inches in height, with exquisite workmanship by T. T. Hawker and Sons. This was in appreciation of the keen interest which Lady Lawley had shown in everything connected with Indian ladies. It was given as a souvenir of her years in Madras.

Sir Subramania Iyer then delivered the farewell oration. During the course of his speech Sir Subramania said:

"Turning to what Your Excellency and Lady Lawley have been able to accomplish during the past five years and more, you will carry with you the love, affection and gratitude of one and all without exception, and will have the satisfaction of feeling that the utmost good that could have been done has been done. Relief of suffering and care of the sick have always been to you a labour of love. There was hardly a plague infected spot which did not attract your Excellency's attention. The improvement of work of medical aid throughout the country was ever in your mind. Nothing calculated to advance the moral and material interests of the people failed to secure the hearty and influential support of Your Excellency."

In his reply Sir Arthur said

As I look round I see on all sides men of other races and other creeds than my own - Indians who have been fellow workers with me in the task of administration, loyal and devoted fellow workers and staunch comrades! Sincerely do I thank them for their generous help. I see members of the land-owning aristocracy. I see colleagues of my own in the Legislative Council representing various communities and diverse interests; men engaged in public life; and many others who while not engaged in public affairs have yet generously admitted me to the privilege of their personal friendship; all gathered here to still further increase the debt of obligation under which I already lie for manifold kindnesses received at their hands.

The beautiful entertainment which you have organized, the generous donations which have been forthcoming in order that our portraits may hang on the walls of Government House, the presentation to my wife of this beautiful cup, for which she bids me offer you in her name her most heartfelt thanks - all these are tokens of your good-will towards us which believe me we prize more highly than any poor words of mine can express.

I know that it is in your capacity as our friends that you have proffered us this mark of your regard, and it comes to recompense me for the toil and anxiety, which I have undergone in the service of India and inspires me with the hope that I have not laboured altogether in vain. The remembrance of it will always be precious to us, and again we thank you most sincerely. We pray that God's blessing may rest on this land. My heart is too full to say more." [52]

The evening concluded with another Musical Ride by the Governors Guard and then a magnificent Firework Display.

On November 1st 1911, Sir Arthur, now at the end of his Governorship, laid the Foundation Stone of the new Gifford Medical School attached to the Government Maternity Hospital. Sir Arthur and his wife then opened the Lady Lawley Nurses

Home. Their Excellencies were garlanded with extravagant garlands of flowers and Lady Lawley presented gifts of cloth to thirty Indian women.

The Indian ladies of Madras assembled later to meet with Lady Lawley. They wished to thank her for all that she had done to help them. [53] Their leader said:

> *"We, the Indian Ladies of Madras are here assembled to do honour to you on the eve of your departure to England. For over five years Your Excellency has dwelt among us and during that period you have endeared yourself to the hearts of all of us by the kindness, sympathy and courtesy which you have always extended to us. You have done much to promote the most cordial relations between Europeans and Indians and Government House during the past five years has been a meeting ground for members of both races."*

"The close of Sir Arthur Lawley's administration found the political atmosphere on the whole clearer. Criticism of the measures of Government had become more reasonable and discriminating, while the forces of order and settled government were able to array themselves more definitely and single mindedly against the extremist section."[54]

In his final letter from India to Lord Crewe Sir Arthur wrote:

> *"The sands of time are running out apace, and in a very few days I shall have retired into insignificance.*

> *"I remember very well the occasion of my embarking on my first Governorship in Australia. I went to the Colonial Office for 'instructions' and I recall the words of a distinguished official there who said to me, "If you want to be a successful governor never let me hear the mention of your name! Keep us if possible in happy oblivion of your existence!" I am sure that is very sound advice. I have always tried to act upon it and you also I hope have profited thereby inasmuch as I have always endeavoured to cause you as little unnecessary trouble as possible myself, and to give my 'subjects' as little cause as possible for appeals to you against any action or inaction on my part! It is over five and a half years now since I got up on to the box to drive the coach. In that time I have had to steer through some queerish places but I think I may claim that on the whole I have managed to keep fairly clear of the ruts, that I have not jolted the passengers unduly, and that I have not blown my horn with any unnecessary frequency!*

> *"I am sorry – very sorry – to put down the reins but I have had a long stage, and at times I realize that I want a rest. It is fascinating work this governing of India!*

> *Full of problems and one is no sooner solved than another of seemingly greater magnitude than the last at once pops up! But I have confidence in the genius of the British Race to be equal to any emergency! Well, this is alas my 'Goodbye'! I can cry 'All's well' from my watch tower with an easy mind!"*

The end of Sir Arthur Lawley's Governorship of Madras saw some controversy in the press much of it related to the murder of Mr Ashe, the Collector of Tinnevelly. The English newspapers suggested that Sir Arthur had been too lenient and liberal; the Indian press alleged that he had been too harsh and reactionary.[55]

The Indian newspaper "The Hindu" charged Sir Arthur Lawley with being responsible for the dissolution of Swadeshi enterprises, in particular the Steamship Navigation Company, for the shooting of four innocent persons on March 13th 1908, and for the conditions which led to the murder of the Tinnevelly Collector, Mr W. d'E Ashe. In fact Sir Arthur had promoted Swadeshi enterprises, restored law and order after a riot, and had in no way created the conditions which led to Mr Ashe's murder.

The citizens of Tinnevelly took the unusual step of calling a Public Meeting to protest against the attacks made in "The Hindu", a Madras newspaper, on the administration of His Excellency Sir Arthur Lawley as Governor of Madras. A resolution was unanimously passed which said,

"The citizens of Tinnevelly and Palamcottah in Public Meeting assembled place on record their deep regret that The Hindu of Madras should in its review of His Excellency Sir Arthur Lawley's administration have attacked His Excellency undeservedly and unsympathetically with reference to Tinnevelly affairs, and they further deeply deplore that the attitudes and feelings of the people of this District during its period of trouble have been inopportunely and incorrectly set forth in the said revue." [56]

Figure 216: Udaipur, the Palace from the Lake.

The Indian Patriot of Madras in a review of Sir Arthur Lawley's work said: - "Striking a balance between the achievements and errors of His Excellency's administration, and even viewing the errors in the most critical spirit, there is such an amount of good work accomplished as well justifies Sir Subramania Iyer's observations at the entertainment to His Excellency that 'he did as much good as he could.' Sir Arthur Lawley had many obstacles to face and many difficulties to overcome; and although one may think that the obstacles and difficulties might have been met in a better way, we are bound to say that the achievements effected in spite of them are large enough and substantial enough to enable us to remember his name and his administration of Madras with appreciation and gratitude. He will leave behind him hundreds of friends who have been drawn to him by his personal qualities of courtesy and kindness of heart. Those who know him well know that his views on public affairs have been very liberal; and if those views have not always prevailed the explanation is found in the limitations to which we have referred in the beginning. In saying this we feel sure that we express the feeling and opinion of all the most important sections of the Indian community, of the most influential men among them.

"There is indeed a section of our countrymen who will not agree with us. But we are convinced we are right. And now it remains to us only to wish God-speed to His Excellency and Lady Lawley, both of whom have received during the past few days signal marks of appreciation and regard. Wherever they may be, we shall remember them and we are sure that they will not forget Madras and its people."[57]

Figure 217: The Victoria Hall, Udaipur.

On November 3rd 1911, Sir Arthur finally retired from his post in India. He was succeeded by Sir Thomas Gibson Carmichael, who stayed in the governorship for only one year. Sir Arthur and Lady Lawley and their daughters decided to stay on for the Great Durbar in December. In the interim they took the opportunity to see Rajastan where they visited Udaipur, Chittorgarh and other princely cities. They were accompanied by Algy, Sir Arthur's brother, the Hon. Rev. Algernon Lawley and his wife May. Algy and May had already visited South Africa, where they had stayed with their old friend, Archbishop William Carter, in Cape Town. He had been head of the Eton Mission at Hackney Wick from 1880 to 1891, when Algy was the Mission's Curate.[58]

Figure 218: Palace of Rance Padmani from the South West, Chittorgarh.

In December 1911, Sir Arthur and Lady Lawley attended the King Emperor's Great Durbar in Delhi to acknowledge the new King George V and Queen Mary. In Delhi, Sir Arthur Lawley was dubbed Knight Grand Commander of the Star of India. In the evening of December 8th, their Imperial Majesties gave a Coronation Dinner Party. A large number of guests were invited. The guests of honour were the Viceroy and his wife, Lord and Lady Hardinge, Sir Arthur and Lady Lawley and the Earl and Countess of Sefton.[59] There were several dinner parties in the Madras Governor's Camp given by Their Excellencies Sir Thomas and Lady Carmichael. Sir Arthur and Lady Lawley, Ursula and Cecilia were among the first to receive invitations. At the dinner on Saturday 9th December, "Lady Lawley was wearing a beautiful gown in shades of silver and grey and her daughters wore very pretty dresses of pale green veiled in silver net on the corsage." On Sunday 10th December at the Durbar Divine Service, the Bishop of Madras preached the sermon on the text, "The kingdoms of this world have become the kingdom of our Lord and of His Christ," an interesting theme in a sub-continent where the majority was Hindu or Moslem by faith.[60] The Lawleys stayed on in India until after the conclusion of the Durbar.

The white man's burden

Sir Arthur Lawley held the then acceptable view of the Empire as being the "White Man's Burden". The British were responsible for the material, economic, educational, medical and social well-being of the peoples of the British Empire. There is almost a moral tone in the argument, which glosses over the subterfuge, duplicity, diplomatic intrigue, commercial ambition, avarice, imperial war-mongering, and great power rivalry which lay behind the acquisition of the Empire. When Queen Victoria became Empress of India in 1876, a self righteous, almost religious approach developed, which viewed imperial rule as a sacred duty. Now these ideas sound arrogant, racially prejudiced, intolerant and intolerable, but in late Victorian and Edwardian Britain such views were widespread among the working, middle and upper classes.

Figure 219: The Durbar at Delhi December 12th 1911.

This was the belief of Alfred Milner and is well expressed in "Credo - Lord Milner's Faith", published posthumously in the Times on July 27th 1925:

"I am a British Nationalist..... If I am also an Imperialist it is because the destiny of the English race, owing to its insular position and long supremacy at sea, has been to strike fresh roots into different parts of the world. My patriotism knows no geographical but only racial limits. I am an Imperialist and not a little Englander, because I am a British Race Patriot.... It is not the soil of England, which is essential to arouse my patriotism, but the speech, the tradition, the spiritual heritage, the principles, the aspirations of the British race. "[61]

The British imperialists regarded themselves as being born to a sacred duty of civilising mankind. They considered themselves to be superior and a cut above the rest. Such a concept was not simply misguided and inherently racist, but also dangerous because it could lead so easily to the Nazi idea of the Master Race. It is interesting to reflect that one of Hitler's favourite films was "The Lives of a Bengal Lancer" (1935), a tale of the adventures of three British officers of the 41st Regiment of the Bengal Lancers, stationed in northwest India. When the officers are captured and tortured by the treacherous Mohammed Khan, he threatens one of the three, Lieutenant Alan McGregor (Gary Cooper), with the oft-quoted line, "We have ways of making men talk". Perhaps Hitler identified with the imperial ideas of racial elitism combined with military superiority.

Figure 220: The King Emperor George V and Queen Mary at the Delhi Durbar in 1911.

The British lived separate lives from their subject peoples with their Sports Clubs, Social Clubs, theatres, hotels and Hill Stations. Gymkhanas and Polo Matches reflected their passion for horses and riding. The social round of dinner parties, concerts, whist and bridge parties, amateur dramatics and garden parties was part of the imperial life style. The church with its' missionary schools, colleges, clinics, surgeries and hospitals lent some altruism to what would otherwise have been a military, political and commercial Raj. Queen Victoria and King Edward VII gave

Imperial Rule that necessary regal ingredient. However in due course Gandhi would make it self evident that the Empire was based on false premises.

The missionary zeal of the Christian Churches in lands like India sought to make the indigenous population not merely citizens of the Empire, but also converts to Christianity. With the sword and the ledger book went the Bible. There was a precedent to this. Britain was not the first imperial power to endeavour to convert Indians. The Islamic Mogul Emperors had in previous generations done likewise. The missionaries' involvement in education and medical care undoubtedly benefited local communities, and they also built churches all over India. Although there had been a Christian church present in South India since Roman times, founded by Saint Thomas, the endeavour to convert the indigenous people was made with the assumption that the religion of the Mother Country was self evidently superior to the faiths of the subject peoples.

Sir Arthur Lawley wrote a Foreword for a book, "The Students of Asia" by G. Sherwood Eddy. The book is about the work of Christian schools in India, China and Japan. He wrote:

> *"India is stirring from her sleep of ages. For centuries ignorance has drugged her senses and numbed her comely limbs. Today her best friends bestir themselves to expel the heavy fumes of ignorance, and let in the pure sweet light of knowledge and wisdom. Foremost in this task are missionaries of Anglo-Saxon race, Christian men and women who are bearing to the farthest and darkest corners of the Eastern world the torch of civilization and progress, spreading the truths of Christian hope and Christian faith, and giving by their lives a daily example of Christian love. In the mission field of India, Americans and English are working side by side. In the densely crowded cities of the East, away from the fever-stricken jungles, amid the sweltering villages of the plains, men and women of our race are moving to their work, while all around them are rising churches, seminaries, hospitals and schools – visible tokens of a Western civilization and a higher life....*

> *"I may speak, moreover, as one who for several years in India had particular opportunities of gauging the strength of the forces which are at work in that great sub-continent, and I have no hesitation in saying that among the influences by which the social and political life in India is now being stirred to its profoundest depths, that of the missionaries is wholly for good. For many a year centrifugal forces have been at work to break through the fetters of caste and creed and custom by which Asiatic society of every grade has for centuries been manacled. We can trace with absorbing interest the growth of this movement and realize how wonderful is the opportunity which here presents itself to weave into the fabric of Indian life a strand of social and physical stability sadly lacking today, and it is in striking contrast to the brilliant display of intellectual force of which Indian students have shown themselves to be very capable....*

> *"I know how greatly all those who have at heart the "betterment of India" – Government and missionaries alike – concern themselves with the educational problem. The record of missionary achievement in this direction is indeed marvellous."* [62]

Sir Arthur later expounded his ideas on the benefits of British rule in India in a speech made in Ottawa in August 1912:

"Today India is second in the matter of population and fifth in the matter of wealth amongst the nations of the world. And yet India is hardly a nation at all, but a great congeries of peoples of multitudinous races, creeds, and castes, differing widely in type, in language, in religion, and in degrees of civilization. We found India convulsed by incessant warfare, deluged by a ceaseless stream of anarchy, bloodshed, and crime; we have given her the benefits of universal peace. We found her people a prey to injustice, corruption and oppression; we have given them a pure judiciary, and justice between man and man. We have given them the ablest, most upright, the most devoted civil service that the world has ever seen. We have undertaken vast public works in the way of railways, and roads and systems of irrigation. By this latter we have saved millions of human lives, and today, thanks thereto and to a sagacious organization, we can fight famine as we could never fight it before. The land is dotted with hospitals and schools and all of what I may call the "plant" of higher civilization. In all ways we are seeking to restrain and push back the encroachment of ignorance and poverty, and disease, and sin, and to raise the people to a higher standard of life." [63]

The use of the word "sin" has religious undertones. The Lawleys were Anglicans and the missionary author, Fanny Emily Penny, who wrote the text for Lady Lawley's book of watercolours, "Southern India", was a family friend.[64] Hence the religious connotations are understandable if perhaps inappropriate. The Indian Mutiny of 1857 had shaken British confidence and Sir Arthur's words were emphasizing the benefits of British rule. While some of these were laudable, the underlying assumptions within the Empire of British racial superiority and a god given right to rule were to be challenged most effectively by Gandhi and others in the years to come.

Before that over eight hundred thousand Indian troops would cross the sea to fight in the coming conflict of the First World War. The Arch of India in Delhi commemorates the sixty five thousand brave Indian soldiers, who died during that conflict, many of them on the Western Front or in Mesopotamia (modern Iraq).

Sir Arthur Lawley in his speeches showed an awareness of the inconsistencies and injustices of British Imperial and Dominion policies on race. His contacts with Mohandas K. Gandhi evidently made him think about the issue and he argued that throughout Britain and her Empire full rights of citizenship should be granted to all. At the same time he defended immigration policies excluding non-whites from Australia and restricting Asian immigration into Canada, which were to be primarily lands for British and European immigrants. He had an exaggerated idea of possible Indian immigration into Africa and Asian immigration into Australia. His attitude towards the subject peoples of the Empire was paternalistic, but might be regarded by some as being patronising. He revealed a readiness to take up the "white man's burden", but a reluctance to relinquish it. This ambivalence was not that of one man, but of the "Zeitgeist" of late Victorian and Edwardian England.

In his Jubilee Speech of November 1908, Sir Arthur Lawley said:

"What we all desire is to attain the 'Betterment of India'. Let that be our rallying cry and I know that the chiefs and peoples of India will rally to our standard. There are strong positions to be attacked and carried. There are problems of great magnitude, social, economic, political, which await solution…. The solution of these problems…can only be arrived at not by the estrangement of the rulers and the ruled but by co-operation and sympathy of the one with the other, not by indifference on the part of the one to the motives, susceptibilities and aspirations of

the other but by a patient endeavour to attain mutual knowledge and understanding, not by wrangling and the strife of tongues but by forbearance and good-will. If that be our intent then the hope for the future may be strong." [65]

The assumption behind the speech was that the Indians, who were aware of the increase in democratic government in Britain, would not want democracy themselves, that they would be content to remain subjects of the Raj and that the British would remain in India for ever. These inconsistencies were seized upon by Gandhi, Nehru and the Indian Congress Party and ultimately led to the independence of India and of the other British colonies. The irony was that in the case of India, the benefits of British rule probably outweighed the disadvantages. The British built roads and railways, great barrages and irrigation canals, schools and universities, agricultural research stations, public buildings and new cities. They established democracy and the rule of law. Under the British fragmented India became a united country. After independence the creation of Pakistan frustrated Gandhi's aim of a fully united sub-continent. The eventual outcome was the creation of five new Commonwealth Countries – India, Pakistan, Bangladesh, Burma and Sri Lanka. India today, with a population now exceeding 1000 million, is the world's largest democracy. Perhaps, after all, Sir Arthur Lawley's altruism was not altogether misplaced.

[1] "New for Old". Frontline. Volume 20 - Issue 14, July 05 - 18, 2003. India's National Magazine from the publishers of The Hindu

[2] Madras Times. February 18th 1909. Page 13.

[3] Madras Times. February 18th 1909. Page 27.

[4] Tamil Nadu Agricultural University. Historical Background. 2004

[5] Notes on the administration of His Excellency the Honourable Sir Arthur Lawley, Governor of Madras, 1906-11. Madras Government Press. 1912.

[6] Notes on the administration of His Excellency the Honourable Sir Arthur Lawley, Governor of Madras, 1906-11. Madras Government Press. 1912.

[7] Eustace Lord Wraxall in conversation. June 16th 2005.

[8] Transvaal Gazette 27099. 21st July 1903. National Archives. Kew. London.

[9] Times Obituary for Mr. R.E. Lawley, September 7th 1909
     The Royal Archives Windsor. Letter of June 14th 2004.

[10] Madras Mail. 14th September 1909.

[11] Madras Times. 9th September. 1909.

[12] Madras Times. 16th September 1909.

[13] Madras Mail. 4th November 1909.

[14] Lord Wraxall's "Lawley Albums". Empire and Commonwealth Museum. Bristol. UK.
      The Madras Times. 2nd December 1909.

[15] The Times Obituary to Col. Evelyn Gibbs. Wednesday October 12th 1932. Page 7. Column B.

[16] Madras History Foundation Kodaikanal Home.

[17] Sir Arthur Lawley to Lord Crewe. 26th January 1911. Cambridge University Library.

[18] The Times. Friday 19th October 1906. Page 7. Column F.

[19] The Madras Times. June 22nd 1910.

[20] The Madras Times. Thursday 20th October 1910.
      The Madras Times. November 3rd 1910.
      The Madras Times. November 10th 1910.
      Lord Wraxall's "Lawley Albums". Empire and Commonwealth Museum. Bristol. UK.

[21] The Madras Times. November 17th 1910.
      The Madras Mail. Saturday 12th, Monday 14th and Tuesday 15th November 1910.

[22] Sir Arthur Lawley to Lord Crewe. 23rd February 1911. Cambridge University Library.

[23] Sir Arthur Lawley to Lord Crewe. 17th November 1910. Cambridge University Library.

[24] Sir Arthur Lawley to Lord Crewe. 8th December 1910. Cambridge University Library.

[25] Sir Arthur Lawley to Lord Crewe. 5th January 1911. Cambridge University Library.

[26] Sir Arthur Lawley to Lord Crewe. 21st December 1910. Cambridge University Library.

[27] The Madras Times. 28th January 1909.

[28] The Madras Times. 22nd December 1910.
Lord Wraxall's "Lawley Albums". Empire and Commonwealth Museum. Bristol. UK.

[29] Sir Arthur Lawley to Lord Crewe. 22nd December 1910. Cambridge University Library.

[30] Sir Arthur Lawley to Lord Crewe. 28th December 1910. Cambridge University Library.

[31] Sir Arthur Lawley to Lord Crewe. 19th January 1911. Cambridge University Library.

[32] Sir Arthur Lawley to Lord Crewe. 26th January 1911. Cambridge University Library

[33] Notes on the administration of His Excellency the Honourable Sir Arthur Lawley, Governor of Madras, 1906-11. Madras Government Press. 1912.

[34] The Magic Mountains: Hill Stations and the British Raj by Dane Keith Kennedy: University of California Press: (1996).
Notes on the administration of His Excellency the Honourable Sir Arthur Lawley, Governor of Madras, 1906-11. Madras Government Press. 1912.

[35] Notes on the administration of His Excellency the Honourable Sir Arthur Lawley, Governor of Madras, 1906-11. Madras Government Press. 1912. Page 54

[36] Sir Arthur Lawley to Lord Crewe. 31st May 1911, and earlier letters. Cambridge University Library.

[37] Sir Arthur Lawley to Lord Crewe. 31st May 1911. Cambridge University Library.

[38] Sir Arthur Lawley to Lord Crewe. 31st May 1911. Cambridge University Library.

[39] The Madras Mail and the Madras Times. 19th June 1911.

[40] Sir Arthur Lawley to Lord Crewe. 21st June 1911. Cambridge University Library.

[41] Times Obituary for Lord Wenlock, Wednesday June 15th 1932.

[42] Sir Arthur Lawley to Lord Crewe. 5th July 1911. Cambridge University Library.

[43] Sir Arthur Lawley to Lord Crewe. 12th July 1911. Cambridge University Library.

[44] Sir Arthur Lawley to Lord Crewe. 6th September 1911. Cambridge University Library.

[45] Madras Times. Thursday 8th September 1911.

[46] Madras Times. Thursday 15th September 1911.

[47] Madras Times. Thursday September 16th 1905.

[48] The Madras Times. September 20th 1911.

[49] News Today. Chennai. 22nd June 2005.

[50] Madras Times. 26th October 1911.

[51] Madras Times. November 2nd 1902.

[52] Lawley, Sir Arthur , Speeches delivered by His Excellency the Honourable Sir Arthur Lawley while Governor of Madras, 1906-11. Madras Government Press. India Office. 1912.

[53] Madras Times. November 2nd 1911.

[54] Notes on the administration of His Excellency the Honourable Sir Arthur Lawley, Governor of Madras, 1906-11. Madras Government Press. 1912. Page 54

[55] The Times. Wednesday June 15th 1932. Page 9. Column A.

[56] The Madras Mail. Thursday November 2nd 1911. Page 3.

[57] The Madras Mail. Friday November 3rd 1911. Page 3.

[58] The Times. Friday 18th December 1908. Page 13. Column D.
Algy Lawley. Latimer, Trend and Co. Plymouth. 1933. Pages 57 and 59.

[59] The Madras Times. December 14th 1911.

[60] The Times of India. December 11th 1911.
The Madras Mail. Monday December 11th 1911.

[61] Milner, Apostle of Empire. John Marlowe. Hamish Hamilton. London. 1976.

[62] The Students of Asia. G. Sherwood Eddy. The Religious Tract Society. London. 1916.

[63] Canada and the Empire. Speeches delivered by Sir Arthur Lawley. Library and Archives of Canada. 1912.

[64] Lady Lawley and Penny F.E. (Fanny Emily) Southern India, Painted by Lady Lawley. A&C Black. London. 1914.
Lawley, Sir Arthur , Speeches delivered by His Excellency the Honourable Sir Arthur Lawley while Governor of Madras, 1906-11. Madras Government Press. India Office. 1912.

Chapter 7
Eloquent Knight Errant

Coming home

In January 1912, Sir Arthur Lawley and his family left India. They travelled home in a leisurely fashion. They sailed from Bombay on January 1st 1912 on the Australia Lloyd steamer S.S. Koerber en route to Kenya. From Mombasa they took the train to Nairobi. Thence they travelled by the railway over the Great Rift Valley and the White Highlands to Kisumu on Lake Victoria, where they embarked on a steam ship to cross the lake to the recently completed Port Bell near Entebbe and Kampala in Uganda.[1] Later on February 27th they disembarked at Beira on their way by rail to Rhodesia where they visited old haunts and old friends.[2] They then travelled on to the Transvaal in South Africa before setting sail for England. They arrived back in London in May after over six years of absence.[3]

In London, Sir Arthur found work in the city, becoming a director of the London and North West Railway, of the Yorkshire Insurance Company, of the London Bank of Australia and of the Forestal Land, Timber and Railways Company. Given his enthusiasm for railways in Rhodesia, Australia, the Transvaal and India, the directorship of the London and North West Railway was particularly appropriate. Sir Arthur also owned shares in the Central Argentinian Railroad.[4]

At the Delhi Durbar, Sir Arthur's daughter, Ursula Mary, had impressed Queen Mary and in April 1912, she was appointed as Lady in Waiting to the Queen.[5] The Americans were much pleased by Ursula's appointment. On April 24th, The Washington Post reported:

> *"Although it has been hinted more than once that American women would be less welcome at the court of St. James during the present reign than they were when King Edward was on the throne, Queen Mary has just given another proof that she is not prejudiced against those whose antecedents and relationships connect them with this side of the Atlantic.*

> *For she has just appointed as her maid of honour Miss Ursula Lawley, who although not actually American, can certainly claim American ancestry on one side of the house. Her father, Sir Arthur Lawley, married Annie Cunard daughter of Sir Edward Cunard, who wedded Mary, daughter of Bache McEvers of New York."*

On May 8th 1912, the Philadelphia Telegraph reported:

> *"Miss Ursula Lawley, who has been appointed maid of honour by Queen Mary of England, claims American ancestry. Her grandmother, Mary Lady Cunard was a daughter of Bache McEvers, of New York, while her grandfather, Sir Edward Cunard was the son of Sir Samuel Cunard, who was the son of Abraham Cunard, a prominent merchant of Philadelphia."*

Bache McEvers was descended from John McEvers, a Dublin merchant who emigrated from Ireland in 1716 to 1717. John McEvers' son, Charles made a fortune during the Seven Years War (1756 to 1763). He imported rum from the West Indies to sell to the soldiers and he purchased French ships taken as prizes in the Caribbean and brought them back to New York. Here they were repaired, and the ships and their cargoes were then sold at a profit. Charles McEvers' son, also named Charles, was Bache McEvers' father. He founded the New York Insurance Company. He married Mary Bache, daughter of Theophylact Bache and Ann Dorothy Barclay. Hence their son was called Bache McEvers. The McEvers family attended Trinity Church, Broadway and the family vault is in the Churchyard very close to Ground Zero in Manhatten. Annie Lawley's parents were buried there.

Abraham Cunard was the great grandson of Thones Kunreds. Thones was born in Mönchen Gladbach in Germany in 1653. He emigrated from nearby Krefeld to Pennsylvania in 1683. He was a Quaker and in 1688, the first protest against slavery in the New World was drafted at his house in Germantown, Philadelphia. He died in 1729. Abraham's grandfather, Henry (1689-1758), changed the family name to Cunreds. His father, Samuel (1731-1792), changed it again to Cunard. Abraham Cunard was born in 1755. He left Philadelphia in 1783 and settled in Halifax, Nova Scotia, Canada. His wife, Margaret Murphy, came from Ireland. Abraham Cunard died in 1824.[6] His son, Sir Samuel Cunard, founded the Cunard Shipping Line. With such ancestry, it is little wonder that the Washington Post and the Philadelphia Telegraph regarded Ursula as being almost American.[7]

Figure 221: Broadway and Trinity Church in 1830 by John William Hill.

On June 2nd, Sir Arthur and Lady Lawley attended the National India Association Dinner in support of the thousand Indian students studying in London. There was much concern for their welfare and their need for financial support.[8]

On June 12th, the Lawleys attended the Fourth Rhodesia Dinner held at the Connaught Rooms. Sir Arthur Lawley proposed the toast, "Rhodesia". In his speech, "he praised the ever present vision of the great Cecil Rhodes himself." He said that "heathenism and barbarism with all their hideous accessories had been driven back, that railways had been opened throughout the territory and that the Chartered Company had striven to work hand in hand with the pioneers of every industry."

Later that summer Sir Arthur Lawley went to Canada, where he addressed audiences in Ottawa on August 27th and Winnipeg on September 2nd on the theme of "Canada, the Royal Navy and the Empire".[9] During the years preceding the First World War, a very costly armaments race had been taking place. As far as Britain was concerned, the construction of giant battleships known as "Dreadnoughts" by Germany posed a threat to British supremacy at sea. In October 1911, Winston Churchill was appointed First Lord of the Admiralty. Churchill thought Canada might be persuaded to build dreadnoughts for the Royal Navy.[10] Sir Arthur Lawley chose the title of his speeches with this in mind.

Addressing a distinguished audience in Ottawa, including the Conservative Prime Minister, Sir Robert Borden, and the Liberal Leader of the Opposition, Sir Wilfrid Laurier, Sir Arthur said,

> *"I look at Europe and I see one vast armed camp. I see the greatest military power on the continent, which is at the same time the second greatest naval power of the world, straining every nerve, making every possible sacrifice to increase her efficiency as a fighting machine. And when I reflect that all this effort is being made for no ostensible reason or visible purpose, I find it impossible ...to escape the conviction that at any moment England may find herself embarked in a struggle of colossal magnitude in which her very existence as a nation may be at stake."*

Speaking to another audience in Winnipeg, Sir Arthur said,

> *"England's temper today is that no challenge of her naval supremacy shall find her unprepared to meet it, that no sacrifice is too great, that no expenditure is too onerous, to secure the maintenance of her superiority at sea. - In no spirit of militarism, nor for any aggressive purpose, nor for any ambitious schemes of self aggrandisement, but for the fulfilment of the noblest mission of our Race, and that is for the maintenance of the Peace of the World. For this insurance England is able and willing to pay the full premium.... I deplore, as greatly as any man, the expenditure of millions yearly on the construction of battleships and other impedimenta of war which are in themselves economically unremunerative, but I believe that the material things of life are not all that God has revealed to man, and in the very sacrifice made I see a strengthening of the moral fibre of the nation. This, you may say, is a fantastic notion in which case I will point out that there is material satisfaction to be gained in contemplating the work which has been done in the past and is being done today by the Navy of Great Britain."*

An Imperial Conference in London in 1911 had discussed the co-ordination of Dominion fleets under the command of the Royal Navy. Australia and New Zealand had both agreed to build a Dreadnought each, but insisted on retaining the autonomy of their own fleets.[11] In Canada, the Conservative Party under Sir Robert Borden won the election of 1911. As prime minister, Borden's major interest was Anglo-Canadian relations. He had long argued for the establishment of a Canadian voice in Imperial Policy.

Sir Robert Borden as the new Canadian Prime Minister received Churchill's proposal that Canada construct dreadnoughts for the Royal Navy favorably. To strengthen his hand in the Canadian Parliament, the British Admiralty prepared a statement on sea power which said, "Naval supremacy is of two kinds: general and local. General naval supremacy consists in the power to defeat in battle and drive from the seas the strongest hostile navy or combination of hostile navies wherever they may be found.… It is the general naval supremacy of Great Britain which is the primary safeguard of the security and interests of the great Dominions of the Crown."

On December 5, 1912, Borden introduced into the Canadian Parliament a Naval Bill asking for £7 million to build three dreadnoughts to be controlled and maintained by the Royal Navy for the common defence of the Empire. The bill created a political storm. The Liberal opposition declared that it perceived no danger to Canada. If the ships were to be built, the opposition said, they should be constructed in Canadian shipyards, manned by Canadian seamen, and controlled by the Canadian government. Churchill pointed out to Borden that no building yards capable of constructing dreadnoughts existed in Canada and that it would cost £15 million to create one. Under such circumstances, the laying of the first keel would wait four years. Invoking this argument, Borden managed to get the bill through the Canadian House in February 1913, but in May it was killed by the Canadian Senate. In November, the Malay States joined Australia and New Zealand by offering to pay for a dreadnought, but no Canadian capital ships were available to the Admiralty at the beginning of the First World War.[12]

Celebrating peace and preparing for war

As the First World War approached, Sir Arthur threw himself energetically into Lord Robert's Campaign for National Training and addressed a number of mass meetings in various parts of England.[13] On February 15th, Lord Roberts spoke in Bristol in favour of the National Service League. Sir Arthur Lawley spoke in his support. He said there was a real need for Universal Service for Home Defence. He emphasized that such National Service existed in France, Australia and New Zealand, countries which had deliberately adopted universal service prompted by instincts of self preservation and recognising that citizenship of a democracy carried grave responsibilities as well as great advantages.

On April 18th, Lord Roberts spoke at the Town Hall in Leeds to encourage young men to join the National Service League. Sir Arthur followed with a speech strong in Imperial sentiment and in the power and virility of its message. He said,

> *"We might dream of an era of universal peace, but are we doing our duty as Englishmen if we deliberately ignore what is going on in Europe today? Can we shut our eyes to what is passing just across the Channel, the feverish activity in every barrack, dockyard and arsenal? Can we shut our ears to the throb of the war drum and the thunder of the guns? Can we flatter ourselves into the belief that England can for ever steer clear of European complications and enjoy permanent immunity from all risk of war?…. God forbid that we should lay such flattering unction to our souls. Let us be honest and face the position. At any moment we might be enveloped in a conflict in which our very existence as a nation might be at stake."* [14]

In 1913, the movement for the promotion of Anglo-American friendship and understanding was strong and Sir Arthur Lawley was an ardent supporter. To celebrate the centenary of the Treaty of Ghent, after the War of 1812, Earl Grey persuaded Sir Arthur Lawley to accompany the first British delegation, as deputy leader, on a visit to the United States. George V and Queen Mary hosted a Farewell Dinner for the delegates at Buckingham Palace.

The British delegates arrived in New York on May 5th on board the Cunard liner, Caronia. The following day the visiting delegations from Britain, Canada,

Newfoundland, Australia and Ghent in Belgium were entertained for lunch at the Hotel Plaza by Mayor Gaynor. Ex-president Taft, Andrew Carnegie and Cornelius Vanderbilt were present at the luncheon.[15] On May 7th the delegates met to discuss monuments to peace along the border between Canada and the United States. These would include – the building of the Niagara Falls Memorial Bridge and the erection of Arches along the international border on major highways – Los Angeles to Vancouver, Miami to Quebec – and the building of a tunnel between Detroit, Michigan and Windsor, Ontario[16]. In London, Britain proposed to erect a statue of Abraham Lincoln in Parliament Square. On May 8th, the delegates took lunch with Colonel Roosevelt at "Sagamore Hill".[17]

In Washington, the visiting delegations visited President Wilson in the White House. They then attended a luncheon given by Colonel and Mrs Robert M. Thompson at their home in Sheridan Circle.[18] In the afternoon, they were then taken to Capitol Hill where they visited the Congressional Library, were escorted to the gallery of the House of Representatives by Speaker Clark and met Vice President Marshall.[19] In the evening there was a banquet where Senator Elihu Root gave the opening speech. He said, "In this country where all the peoples of all the races have been welcomed to share in its benefits, we have shown by the amalgamation of our various citizenships into one whole that all men of every race can live together in peace."

Figure 222: Sir Arthur Lawley in Washington D.C. in 1913.

Lord Weardale replied for the United Kingdom. He expressed Britain's intention of purchasing and restoring Sulgrave Manor, the old English home of the Washington family in Northamptonshire. "We propose making it a shrine to which all visiting Americans may make a pilgrimage", he said. He predicted that in the coming centenary celebration Germany would take a prominent part. Andrew Carnegie in a later speech declared that the United States should build fewer battleships and more embassies abroad for the housing of its diplomatic representatives. Sadly the Centennial Year of the Treaty of Ghent was 1914 when such illusions were to be sorely shattered.

On May 13th, the delegates went on to Philadelphia, where they watched a baseball game and later were guests at a civic reception and banquet.[20] Sir Arthur Lawley was the first speaker introduced by Charlemagne Tower, the former U.S. Ambassador to Germany. Sir Arthur said that he was impressed by the throwing power of the pitchers in the baseball game. He declared Washington to be the most beautiful city on earth and he described his pleasure at meeting President Wilson, who, he said, "cannot fail to add even greater luster and greater renown to an office already honoured and distinguished by his predecessors." The Secretary of State, William Jennings Bryan, bidding farewell to the guests, said, "The preparations for the peace celebrations are in the nature of building the greatest superdreadnought, and that is called friendship. Its compass is the heart, its shells carry good will, its missiles are carried by the smokeless powder of love, its captain is the Prince of Peace". Secretary Bryan was later to vehemently oppose American participation in the First World War.

The delegates then departed on a tour of the Eastern United States travelling as far west as Chicago. The leader of the British Delegation, Lord Weardale, had to go home half way through the tour and Sir Arthur then took charge and won the admiration of all by his charming courtesy, fine appearance and eloquent speeches. His address in New York on the "Anglo-Saxon Impulse" was not forgotten by those who heard it. This British visit helped to foster the friendship and support of America, which was to prove so vital in the coming war.

The original Treaty of Ghent was signed on December 24th 1814 at the time when the defeated Napoleon was exiled on the Island of Elba. In the event the celebration of the Centenary of the Treaty was overtaken by the outbreak of the First World War.

---

[1]   The Times of India. January 1st 1912.
       My African Journey. Winston Churchill. Stodder and Houghton. 1908.
       Canada and the Empire. Speeches delivered by Sir Arthur Lawley. Library and Archives of Canada. 1912.
[2]   The Times. 28th February 1912. Page 11. Column A.
[3]   Times Obituary for Lord Wenlock, Wednesday June 15th 1932.
       The Times. Wednesday May 15th 1912. Page 12. Column A.
[4]   Eustace Lord Wraxall in conversation. March 4th 2005.
[5]   The Royal Archives Windsor. Letter of 7th June 2004.
[6]   http://www.leake.dsl.pipex.com/Family/Castens_Side/Cunard/cunard.html
[7]   Washington Post. April 24th 1912, page 6.
       The New York City Directory ,1836-37 edition. The entry for Bache McEvers reads: "merchant 35, Broad Street."
       The New York City Directory ,1848-49 edition. Bache McEvers' entry reads: "President New York Insurance Co., 50, Wall Street and commercial merchant of 44, Broad Street, Home - Manhattanville."
       Thomas Addis Emmet: "The Emmet Family: With Some Incidents Relating to Irish History." (New York privately printed in 1898).
       R. Burnham Moffatt, "The Barclays of New York". (Bowie, Maryland, Heritage Books reprint: 2001)
       Henry B Zabriskie, "Family History of James McEvers 1755-1829 and Abraham Knapp 1759-1809, Their Children and Grand Children" (1980).
[8]   The Times. June 3rd 1912.
[9]   Canada and the Empire: Speeches delivered by Sir Arthur Lawley. A.M. Grenfell, Montreal, 1912. Montreal Herald. Notes: "Ottawa, August 27, 1912, Winnipeg, September 2, 1912." National Library of Canada. FC243
[10] Edwardian England. Elie Halevy. The Folio Society. London. 1997. Pages 494 and 495
[11] Edwardian England. Elie Halevy. The Folio Society. London. 1999.
[12] Dreadnought by Robert Massie. Jonathan Cape. London. 1992.
[13] Times Obituary for Lord Wenlock, Wednesday June 15th 1932.
       Re. Times Obituary for Lord Wenlock: letter from H.S. Perris, the British Peace Centenary Committee. Thursday 16th June 1932.
[14] The Times. Saturday 19th April 1913.
[15] New York Times May 5th 1913, page 4, "Peace Centenary Delegates Arrive".
[16] New York Times May 8th 1913, page 6, "Monuments To Rise To 100 Year Peace"
[17] New York Times May 9th 1913, page 1, "Roosevelt's Home - Peace Men's Mecca".
[18] Washington Post. April 28th 1913, page 6
       Washington Post. May 13th 1913, page 7.
[19] Washington Post. May 13th 1913, page 1.
[20] Washington Post May 14th 1913, page 2.

Chapter 8
Armageddon, 1914 – 1918

The War began at midnight on August 4th 1914. Two and a half months later, at 8 o'clock on the evening of Saturday November 14th, Field Marshall Lord Frederick Roberts died suddenly in France. On the day of the state funeral, Thursday 19th November, there were huge crowds in the streets of London and thousands of soldiers lined the route from Charing Cross to Saint Paul's Cathedral. Lord Roberts' only surviving son had lost his life at the Battle of Colenso during the Boer War and was awarded a posthumous Victoria Cross. Hence Sir Arthur Lawley, a close friend, met Aileen Lady Roberts at Charing Cross Station and accompanied her to St Paul's. Lord Roberts was laid to rest beside Lord Nelson and the Duke of Wellington.[1]

On February 9th 1915, Sir Arthur Lawley went to France as Commissioner of the British Red Cross Society and the Order of St John of Jerusalem. These two bodies formed what was known as the Joint Committee. Sir Arthur was given the rank of Colonel. He was to replace Sir Courtauld Thompson who had been compelled to leave by illness. There were three Chief Commissioners and six Commissioners serving in France and Belgium during the Great War. The three Chief Commissioners were Surgeon General Sir Alfred Keogh, Lieutenant-General Sir Arthur Sloggett and Lieutenant-General Sir Charles Burtchael. Shortly after arriving in France, Sir Arthur Lawley was visited by Geoffrey Dawson, Editor of the Times, and together they witnessed the midnight arrival of a hospital train with many cases of frozen feet.[2] Sir Arthur served in France until March 21st 1916 mainly at Headquarters in Boulogne. He was then replaced by the Earl of Donoughmore who remained in post until September 28th 1917.

Figure 223: Gertrude Bell.

Gertrude Bell wrote about Sir Arthur Lawley's work in a series of letters to her father and mother. She was a British archaeologist, writer and government official. She was born on July 14, 1868 in County Durham. Gertrude was educated at Lady Margaret Hall, Oxford and became the first woman to obtain a first-class honours degree there. She travelled extensively and from 1899 to 1914 made several archaeological expeditions in the Middle East. In addition, she learned to speak Persian and Arabic and wrote about her travels."

"Gertrude Bell acquired an in depth knowledge of the region which led her into service with the British intelligence during World War I. In 1915 she was appointed to the Arab Bureau in Cairo, which was involved in gathering information useful for mobilizing the Arabs against Turkey. She also joined the

Mesopotamia Expeditionary Force in Basra and Baghdad. She worked too for the Red Cross both in France and in Mesopotamia."[3]

Gertrude Bell's letters give us an insight into what life was like for the nurses and ambulance drivers who worked for the Red Cross and the Order of St. John. They also give us some indication of the concerns of Sir Arthur Lawley as a Red Cross Commissioner in France and in Mesopotamia.

10 February 1915, Boulogne. "Darling Father. I remembered when it was too late that I hadn't written to you for your birthday, with uncertain posts one loses count of days. But I send you now very, very dear love and the hope that next birthday may be a happier one; bless you dearest, dearest Father. Who do you think has turned up as Red Cross Commissioner - Sir Courtauld Thomson being ill? Sir Arthur Lawley. I went to see him today about a type writer. He dropped in to our office this afternoon and we took him out to tea....."

7 March 1915, Boulogne. "My dearest Father. I have been most ungrateful not to answer sooner about the motor. I heard Mr Malcolm was coming and I waited to see what he said. He is delighted and most grateful. He says that motor will, he thinks, do excellently. You will send Kirke I suppose? And thank you very much dearest. I haven't written a word since I came back. I have been buried in work - it's an awful business picking up the threads. Last night I dined with Ian Malcolm and Sir Arthur Lawley. Ursula Lawley was there and on her way to a hospital at Dunkerque. We went after dinner to see an ambulance train come in - that's why I didn't write yesterday; I wasn't in till 11.30 pm. And today I have a fantastic amount to do and can't write more. Your ever affectionate daughter, Gertrude."

11 March 1915, Boulogne. "Dearest Father. Lord Robert writes that we have to get the permission of the RAMC before having another car out. There is now an idea that your car would be sent to Rouen and I have therefore asked Sir Arthur Lawley to write to the R.A.M.C. there. In any case it would be advisable to send the motor out by Rouen as the port here is very much congested and the motor might not be delivered for a very long time. I had a talk with Sir Arthur about finances yesterday from which I gather that they are a serious problem. I do not think Mr Malcolm is wise in embarking on a new car before he knows what money he has at his disposal.

They say in London that a Belgian driver would not be acceptable to the French who look with suspicion on anyone with a French or Belgian name who is not in the army. I have asked Sir Arthur what he thinks.

12 March 1915, Boulogne. "Dearest Father. Mr Malcolm went to London today and I gave him a telegram to send to you, subject to the acceptance of the motor by the RAMC. Sir Arthur Lawley wrote at once to Rouen at my request and heard from the RAMC that they considered one motor enough for our office there but that the one we had was not suitable, being of too high power. Mr Malcolm seems to think that that motor car is to be withdrawn and replaced by yours which would be exactly right. I am most dreadfully sorry to give you so much trouble and to have been so uncertain but you see I didn't know that the whole thing had not been decided when I spoke to you and no one had given me any warning as to the intervention of the RAMC in the matter.

The hospitals are full here. We've had the biggest battle in which the British army has ever been engaged, do you realize? and so far the result of it is Neuve

Chapelle - important, no doubt, but the price has been colossal – 18,000 to 20,000 casualties I hear and about 700 officers. The cases coming into hospital now are the worst that have been known since the war began - men shattered, come here to die. But many do recover even so. Miss Douglas Pennant is working in my office - her brother was killed. I had to tell her, lest she should hear it casually. She is very brave - I like her so much. She will stay with me I think…. She works very hard. We are having a heavy time. We never seem to get through and the day's work isn't ended in the day but rolls up for tomorrow. Hence my insufficiency as a letter writer. Please thank Mother for her letter and bless you both. Your affectionate daughter Gertrude"

17 March 1915, Boulogne. *"Sir Arthur Lawley definitely objects to a Belgian chauffeur. He fears it will make difficulties."*

The Boulogne Hospitals

In October 1914, Boulogne was converted into a city of hospitals. The Casino and many of the hotels were converted with astonishing rapidity into fully equipped hospitals and further hospitals were quickly established at Wimereux, Le Touquet, Abbéville and other places in the neighbourhood.[4]

The suffering of the wounded men caused great concern to all those who worked in the hospitals in France. Some of the roads on which the ambulances had to be driven were pot holed or badly cobbled. Such a road led from the Gare Maritime, the railway station in Boulogne, to the military hospitals. On March 20th 1915, Sir Arthur Lawley wrote in a letter to the Honourable Arthur Stanley from Boulogne,

"Over 80 per cent of the badly wounded cases here have to be conveyed by our ambulances over a stretch of road paved with cobblestones and however carefully the chauffeurs drive their cars, the wounded men on the stretchers are severely jolted, and must suffer a very great amount of unnecessary pain.

"It has been suggested that we should repair this road so as to diminish the sufferings of these badly wounded men. I think it would be an exceedingly good piece of work to do, and a very good way to spend money intended for the relief of the wounded. It is estimated that the cost of repairing the road, about 16 feet wide, with a smooth asphalt surface would not exceed £500. If you think such a sum of money could be provided for this object, I would at once approach the local authorities with a view to obtaining their sanction to carry out the work."

Hodder and Stoughton had just published a book, "The Way of the Red Cross". They wrote to inform the British Red Cross that they would be pleased to pay the sum of £500, the first instalments from the sale of "The Way of the Red Cross", for the repair of the road to the Military Hospitals in Boulogne.[5]

These hospitals had to deal with as many as seven thousand cases in a single day. Sir Arthur Lawley cited an instance when the Joint Commission was asked at 6 o'clock in the evening for 20,000 articles. All were obtained, packed and dispatched by 10 o'clock the following morning. One Sunday morning they were told that a hospital was needed in Calais straight away. That evening a train left Victoria with the necessary personnel, with 120 beds, and with stores, motor cars and ambulances. Sir Arthur declared that in his belief the motors had saved thousands of lives and he told of their services at "Hill 60", at Neuve Chapelle and at Ypres. [6]

Sir Arthur and Lady Lawley stayed on Friday 3rd and Saturday 4th September 1915 with the King and Queen at Windsor Castle. George V and Queen Mary were most interested in the work of the Red Cross and the Order of St John in France and Belgium.[7]

Sir Arthur Lawley, with regret, resigned as Red Cross Commissioner in France on March 21st 1916. This was necessary to enable him to take up important work in London. The work was associated with German infiltration into British companies in Argentina. He continued to attend the meetings of the Red Cross Society and the Joint War Committee.[8] He also acted as their representative a meeting in Lucerne in May 1916 to negotiate with the German Red Cross.

The Forestal Company and Argentina

On Friday 16th June at the Meeting of the Forestal Land, Timber and Railways Company, Sir Arthur was elected Chairman of the Company. Sir Arthur Lawley was chosen as Chairman because it was felt that the task of tackling the problem of allegations of German influences within the company required the special attention of an expert organiser and administrator accustomed to judge and select men, whose authority and intentions in acting for the best in the national and company's interest would be unchallengeable. The company, which had been German, was purchased by an English company shortly before the war. At the outbreak of war 96 alien enemies were employed by the company. By June 1916, sixty five had already been dismissed, sixteen were being replaced and fifteen were being retained. These were experts absolutely necessary to the company's operations. German influences had been at work to try to seduce the staff from its allegiance to the company because Forestal was producing a commodity which was vital for British and Allied tanneries. The leather and tannin from Argentina were needed to provide the Allies with boots, shoes and other leather equipment for their armed forces. Sir Arthur was requested to go to Buenos Aires to investigate. He proceeded to the Argentine with full powers to make such changes in the administration as he thought immediately necessary, and to report to the board on any other changes he considered advisable. In due course the crisis ended, the necessary changes were made and the good name of the company was restored.[9]

Red Cross Commissioner, 1917 to 1919.

At the end of 1916, Sir Arthur Lawley was asked by the Joint Committee to visit Mesopotamia to make a report on the current situation. At that time the work in the hospitals there had been causing some concern. He made recommendations for helpful changes and endeavoured to improve the work being done by the Red Cross and the Order of St John. He also visited and inspected hospitals and other Joint Committee facilities in India. The Army of India formed a major component of the British Imperial force in Mesopotamia and Sir Arthur's experience in and knowledge of India were thus invaluable. Hence he spent some time in India advising the Joint Committee. Sir Arthur left England in December 1916 and returned to London in May 1917.[10] On February 26th, he wrote to Austen Chamberlain from Army Headquarters at Es Sinn.

"I left England shortly before Christmas to take up the Red Cross Commissionership which had become vacant. At the time there was a considerable amount of misgiving and uneasiness in the minds of many people in London as to the adequacy of the provision made for the welfare of the troops in Mesopotamia, and particularly for the welfare of the sick and the wounded.

"I landed in Bombay in mid-January, and went directly to Delhi where I had the opportunity of discussing the present situation with the Viceroy, Lord Chelmsford, the Commander in Chief, Sir Percy Lukis, and Surgeon General O'Donnell. On returning to Bombay, I visited several hospitals – the Lady Hardinge, Freeman Thomas, and the Officers Hospitals – all of them in the matter of structure, equipment, personnel – indeed in every particular – quite first rate. I sailed from Bombay to Basra in the hospital ship, Madras." [11]

Gertrude Bell's letters from Mesopotamia.

Gertrude Bell also served in Mesopotamia working as an officer in military intelligence and as a political advisor. She happened to be there in 1917 when Sir Arthur Lawley was visiting Basra. Her letters tell of their further friendship.

9 February 1917, Basra. *"Sir Arthur Lawley arrived here this week on a Red Cross inspection. He will be here till May, but not much in Basra, I fear. It is so delightful to have him, not only because he is a very delightful person but also because he brings a breath of home and news of the people one knows. After living for a year in a world of strangers, it is extremely pleasant to be with someone who brings one onto familiar ground. He is staying with General MacMunn. I dined with them the first night and next day spent part of the afternoon with them – showing Sir Arthur the sights. Tomorrow I'm going to take him out to Zubair for the afternoon to give him a glimpse of Arabia – for Zubair really is Arabia. And I shall bring him back to tea at my house. One morning when I rode out at dawn there was hoar frost on the ground. Sir Arthur gave me a grim account of the gloom and fog of London, which made me feel we are not so much to be pitied here."*

16 February 1917, Basra. *"The last fine day, I had a delightful jaunt with Sir Arthur Lawley. I wanted to show him something really Arab – he had seen so much of hospitals and wharves and engineer field parks, which are not typical of the country. So we motored out to Zubair, 8 miles to the west, a clean little desert town just like an Arabian oasis. In the bazaar we found a broker holding a sale and I bought a brass nailed wooden chest for my room, very pretty and capacious. And next we found the Shaikh of Zubair sitting in his afternoon assembly on one side of the open square. I introduced Sir Arthur and interpreted compliments. He insisted in carrying us off to tea at his house – he has just built a new house of which he is most proud. Sir Arthur was delighted, and we sat there, I explaining to Sir Arthur what Zubair was made of, and how it was the beginning of Arabia and not the end of Mesopotamia, and how we had started a school at the urgent request of the shaikh – while I was doing all this, in walked the shaikh's little son who had been a pupil at the new school for three months, and if you'll believe it he chattered in English of the funniest kind and was himself the best of illustrations of all I had been telling you about the Zubair people. And Sir Arthur, bless him, was deeply interested and most appreciative. We came home across the battlefield of Sha'aibah and stopped for a moment to climb onto the roof of the fortified farm house which was our H.Q. so that we might see the line of our trenches and of the Turkish attack – altogether a most satisfactory afternoon's sightseeing."*

30th March 1917, Basra. *"This last week has been made very pleasant by having Sir Arthur Lawley here – he leaves today for India and when he gets back to England towards the end of May he is coming to see you to give you news of me. He is a dear. He and Sir George MacMunn both came down from Baghdad last week and gave me accounts of it all which were deeply interesting."* [12]

A Message from Mesopotamia

Sir Arthur Lawley wrote a short book on his experiences during his visit in 1917 to the Persian Gulf and the valleys of the Tigris and Euphrates. He entitled the book, "A Message from Mesopotamia".[13] What follows is based on Sir Arthur's account.

There had been disturbing reports of "regrettable incidents" during the Mesopotamian Campaign of 1915 and 1916 and the British public were uneasy about the provision of medical services and proper treatment for British and Empire troops. In the autumn of 1915, river launches, medical supplies and clothing had been sent to Basra. In 1916, at the urgent request of the Indian Viceroy, a staff of Red Cross workers had been established in Basra and Amarah. In late 1916, Colonel Gould, who had been in charge of the Red Cross Unit at Basra, had been recalled to his military duties in India. His deputy, Major S.M. Moens remained in post. It was thought that a permanent Red Cross Commissioner should replace Colonel Gould. At this stage Sir Arthur Lawley was sent out as Red Cross Commissioner to report on the current conditions in Mesopotamia. He was also asked to investigate ways in which the work of the Red Cross could be enlarged in the region.

Figure 224: Nurses from British General Hospital No. 1. Basra.

The Madras Presidency had provided a hospital ship, "The Madras", in November 1914, which after service in East Africa was diverted in the autumn of 1915 to the Persian Gulf. It was in this ship that Sir Arthur sailed up the Persian Gulf in late January 1917. On the Hospital Ship Madras, Sir Arthur was able to see the wards, the operating theatre, the X-ray room, the stores, the bathrooms and toilets, the kitchens and the patient and service lifts. He also saw the ship in due course with a full tally of 450 wounded - British, Indian and Turkish.

Extracts from a diary of a member of the Medical Staff for 1915 revealed the very poor and inadequate provision of ambulances and medical attention for the wounded after the attack on Ctesiphon on November 22nd of that year. There were 4500 casualties from the action. The Hospital Ship Medjidiah and its two lighters, with a total of 857 casualties, were attacked by an ambush from the banks of the Tigris as they made their way down river to Kut.

Near the terminal of the Anglo-Persian Oil Company at Abadan, Sir Arthur described an Officers' Hospital located in a former Turkish house and harem surrounded by palm trees and well watered gardens. The Red Cross had contributed much furniture and equipment. At Basra there was an astounding variety of river craft including the Nile steamer which had transported General Gordon to Khartoum.

Because land transport was so problematic, particularly after winter rains, river launches were a godsend to the Red Cross. They were provided by the Order of St. John, the Indian Branch of the Joint War Committee and by the Red Cross. Seeing stores packed in flimsy huts and staff lodged in tents, Sir Arthur requested better accommodation and sent a huge order requisitioning supplies from Bombay and London. His requests were complied with very promptly.

Figure 225: Hospital Ship on the River Tigris.

Figure 226: A desert outpost of the British Red Cross and Order of St John near Kut.

In Basra, Sir Arthur inspected the Isolation Camp, the Nurses Homes, the Ambulance Car Convoy, the Turkish Prisoners' Camp, the Cemeteries, and the new hospital train running from Nazariyeh. Some hospitals were in tents, some in huts, one in a liquorice factory and another in the Sheikh of Mohammerah's Town Palace. The hospital in the palace was superb, while the hospital in the liquorice factory had rats and fleas, which could bear bubonic plague, and this required prompt remedial action. The heat of the summer, with temperatures soaring to 120 degrees Fahrenheit, was one of the main difficulties facing the hospitals.

Sir Arthur describes a visit to Zobeir with "an old and very dear friend" on a Saturday afternoon in February 1917. The friend is undoubtedly Gertrude Bell, whom Sir Arthur describes as "doing work of incalculable value in the political department."

Here is his account of his half day holiday:

"We set out on a jaunt to Zobeir. The sky is dull and grey, and a strong south wind is sweeping fitful clouds of dust across the desert. Nine miles from the present town of Basra is the site of the old Basra city – date somewhere about 650 AD....The main feature is the Northern Minaret faced with yellow bricks which have weathered many hundreds of years and are still of excellent quality. The ruined minaret is a great feature in the landscape. It leans like that of Pisa. Zobeir is a typical walled Arab town, to which desert tribes must come for the necessities as well as the luxuries of life. The desert is fringed with a scattered line of such towns, and whoever holds the towns holds the desert and the Bedouin tribes in the hollow of his hand.

"We drove through a series of narrow winding streets between high walls of sun-dried brick to the market place, where we pulled up, and at once the motor became the centre of a friendly, chattering crowd. My companion became suddenly prompted to be the possessor of a brass-bound box such as Arabs do largely affect, of which several were exposed for sale in the market square and some adjoining narrow streets. Our bargaining was conducted in a chorus of crescendo screams, in which not only the merchant, but also his neighbours and any casual passer-by took an interested and noisy part. At last the box was bought and bound to the back of the car. Then we discovered we had not enough money to pay for it. So we determined to repair to the Sheik of Zobeir – who is a "friend"! The friend was away, but we found the friend's brother in "mejliss" – which is akin to a durbar – seated at the opening of a deep alcove which seemed to combine the commercial properties of an ironmonger's shop with the ceremonial accessories of a Hall of State.

"We joined the posse of Arabs and Negroes surrounding the Sheik's brother, "all seated on the ground", and plunged (at least my companion did) into the conversation. Our host contrived to maintain a remarkable degree of dignity and at the same time to convey great cordiality in his welcome and readiness, not only to pay our bills, but to entertain us to tea at his house.

"After some time we all climbed into the motor and went off to his home, which is of quite recent construction – indeed only just finished. Outside, blank dreary mud walls, featureless and windowless, but inside most attractive. The rooms are built round a series of open courts or gardens of which one would have no suspicion from outside. The room in which we had tea was of very good proportions; the

walls of great thickness; all round the room a low lounge; on the floor carpets of gaudy hues; gimcrack tables and chairs and a few hideous lamps.

"One of the six sons appeared on the scene, a boy aged fifteen, very proud of his smattering of English which he had acquired in the last five or six months – a very sharp lad with good manners.

"We departed about five o'clock, laden with three couples of lesser bustard (our old friend the knoorhan of South Africa), but, alas in a condition hardly suitable for the table, time and expanding bullets having done their worst.

"Home over the Shaiba battlefield! We stopped at a big rambling serai of sunburnt bricks which was our headquarters at the time of the fight. The sun was setting and our chauffeur was not eager for a drive over the desert in the dark, so our visit to the roof of the serai had to be short. A vast expanse on every side, and at our feet line upon line of trenches marking the British position at the time of the battle. I longed to see the sun set in crimson splendour in the West, but our driver was inexorable, and I might not dally.

"We bumped back across the desert and through Basra city by the light of the moon. The narrow winding streets were dark and deserted, and their gloom was accentuated by the fitful flicker of an occasional oil lamp twinkling in its tiny niche. The shadowy alley ways were full of mystery and sinister suggestion. In silence we glided swiftly homewards. At such a moment speech would have been a sacrilege.

"And so ended a delightful day."

Before leaving Basra, Sir Arthur Lawley visited a British Convalescent Depot at Mohammerah where convalescing soldiers had created an English garden with vegetables, mignonettes, stocks and hollyhocks. The next day, February 14th, he went to inspect the Inland Water Transport Construction Works at Magill. Here two thousand workmen were employed building wharves and developing road and rail links thereby increasing the tonnage handled daily by the river port from 800 to 4000 tons. Stores were abundant and medical equipment in evidence on a lavish scale. Water supply and sanitation had been improved and insect control was under way. Houses, stores, electric generators, cold storage units and quaysides had been constructed. Sir Arthur pondered on the post-war situation and whether a British withdrawal might be regarded as a betrayal. He considered that the acquisition of the territory by Britain might be beneficial to Mesopotamia and the British Empire.

The following day Sir Arthur sailed up the Tigris on A.P.50 boat, which with its two barges could accommodate 600 wounded men quite comfortably. To reduce the agony in stretcher cases the decks were kept clear. This principle had been copied from the latest hospital ship, the Nabha, which had just reached Basra from Bombay. Sailing past Ezra's tomb and Al Amarah, the A.P.50 arrived on the morning of Sunday 18th February at Sheik Saad. In the distance, snow could be seen on the crest of the Kabirkuh Range to the East. Sir Arthur stayed in the quarters of the Assistant Director of Medical Services with an old friend whom he had last seen at work in the Indian Hospital, which occupied the old Jesuit College at Boulogne. At Sheik Said there were the Indian General Hospital Number 61 and the British General Hospital Number 31 to inspect. Both were in tented accommodation. In the Indian Hospital a surgeon from Yorkshire was at work in the operating theatre on the smashed thigh of a Gurkha soldier. At a nearby Casualty Clearing Station the wounded were being received as Sir Arthur arrived. The evacuation was skilful and the treatment prompt. Sheik Saad was at the head of a light railway to Es Sinn and Atab. British and Indian wounded and Turkish prisoners were coming in by rail. A Convalescent Home for one thousand men was being formed with literature, games and diversions being provided by the Red Cross. A Turkish Prison Camp was nearby.

Figure 227: Ezra's tomb on the banks of the Tigris.

On Thursday 22nd February, the British bombardment of the Turkish positions began. Sir Arthur and two British Colonels motored up to Sandy Ridge to see the action. A Red Cross flag was flying above the Riverside Advanced Dressing Station on the far side of the Tigris. At eleven o'clock they motored down to the bridge and across to the left bank where two Field Ambulances stood. They also saw the Hospital Ship Kamala. At midday, the first consignment of wounded arrived in Red Cross launches – some Seaforth Highlanders, some 92nd Punjabis and some 51st and 53rd Sikhs. A long stream of wounded kept coming in to the Riverside Advanced Station.

Sir Arthur and his colleagues returned by river in a launch filled with wounded men. Thirty five Seaforths were put into the Leopold and Dorothea launch and the Kamala with over eighty cases followed downstream. Visiting the Front Collecting Station by Ford car, Sir Arthur's party came under fire. A man was shot dead at the collecting station and all took cover. That evening the worst cases began to come in with wounds caused by bombs and other missiles. The Turkish counter attack was repulsed by the Seaforths but they took many casualties. All night the wounded and dying were evacuated and it was 6.30 a.m. before the last launch left the dressing station. By 8.00 a.m. 1,021 wounded had been brought in by two field ambulances and 550 of these had already gone down to Sheik Saad.

On Friday 23rd the news came that General Marshall's column had crossed the Tigris and completely surprised the Turks. By four in the afternoon the engineers had bridged the Tigris and the Turks were in full retreat. Sir Arthur and Major Moens moved into the Army Commander's camp and spent the next three days observing the evacuation of the wounded, mostly Hampshires and Gurkhas. Travelling by car across the desert to the Bridge of Boats, Sir Arthur and Major Moens encountered a huge concourse of troops, guns, transport vehicles, medical units and ambulances converging on the bridge. In due course the dressing Stations, Field Ambulances, and Casualty Clearing Stations moved forward with the advancing troops. The front was now beyond Al Kut and P boats soon began to arrive there to evacuate the wounded by river. The logistics of organising the Red Cross units with only one bridge across the river were complex but the task was brilliantly achieved.

Figure 228: The Arch of Ctesiphon.

Figure 229: A reconnaissance plane used to inform British Forces of the Turkish positions.

The aeroplane reconnaissance reported that the Turkish forces were in full retreat to Baghdad. The British Cavalry Division had been launched into the attack and the enemy was being routed into a retreating rabble. On February 27th, Sir Arthur resolved to return to Amarah where there was much Red Cross work to do. It was raining and miserably cold. As he left the Generals and Staff Officers moved in a large convoy of cars north to their new headquarters. Sir Arthur telegraphed for every Red Cross launch available to move upstream behind the advancing troops. He and Major Moens embarked on P. 51, a vessel packed tightly with British stretcher cases. They reached Amarah the following afternoon. The Red Cross Headquarters were in a long row of well-built brick houses facing the river front.

In Amarah, Sir Arthur accompanied by a Colonel Medical Consultant visited the British and Indian General Hospitals, the Convalescent Homes, the Isolation Hospital and the War Cemetery. He complemented the capable nursing staff on their remarkable influence in the wards of the hospitals. In every hospital there was a Red Cross Store Room. The contribution made by the Joint Committee of the Red Cross and Order of St John in Britain and by Indian charities had provided medical supplies and other requisites on a lavish scale.

Figure 230: Bridge of boats over the Tigris.

On Monday March 5th a telegram from General Frederick Stanley Maude, the Army Commander, requested Sir Arthur to join him up river with all speed.

Accompanied by his aide, Captain Stanley, he travelled upstream on board P.54 as she streamed past Sheikh Saad, Kut, the Bend of Shumran and the Arch of Ctesiphon. At 9.30 a.m. they were delayed in mid-stream for six hours by a bridge of boats over which an endless stream of troops and guns, carts and ambulances were passing. A constant boom of guns was heard towards Baghdad. About 4.00 p.m. the bridge was opened and around the next bend they found vessel P.53 and General Sir Stanley Maude who greeted them most cordially. On Saturday March 10th, after a fierce battle on the River Diala, the British troops managed to force the Turks to retreat. British engineers put a bridge across the Diala; a whole brigade was able to cross the river and advance headlong towards Baghdad. There were eight hundred casualties and their evacuation was no easy task – a cruel drive of many miles in ambulances or carts across rough and bumpy country to the Red Cross launches on the river bank.

On Sunday March 11th, Sir Arthur was on a river boat moving upstream behind the British gunboat Firefly recently recaptured from the Turks. He writes, "We pass a goodly number of troops marching on the left bank parallel to our course. At about 3.30 p.m. we steam round a bend of the river, and Baghdad is in sight. At this point the Tigris is a vast waterway, and on either hand is a long line of Arab houses backed by groves of high date palms. The city from the river is singularly picturesque, especially at sunrise or sunset. There is no path or roadway, as at Amarah, between the houses and the stream. In normal times the river swarms with boats of every kind, to which each house has access by a crazy wooden stairway leading down to the water's edge. For the moment, of course, there is an almost total disappearance of river craft.....On either bank crowds have gathered to watch our entry. They are singularly undemonstrative for the most part, though here and there we are greeted by a vigorous outburst of handclapping and waving of flags."

Figure 231: A Red Cross launch on the River Tigris.

The monitors, gunboats and following vessels dropped anchor and moored alongside the British residency where the Union Jack was flying flanked by the Red Cross flag since the residency was being used as a hospital. The British Consulate, also a hospital, was full of injured Turkish soldiers.

That night Sir Arthur slept with his colleagues on board the P 53. The next morning they went house hunting for a Red Cross Headquarters in Baghdad. He managed to get the Old Tigris Hotel on the river front – an ideal home for the Red Cross representative with ample room for the staff and the stores. The hotel has a garden beside the river with a pergola of vines and fig trees. Sir Arthur writes, "Our landlord received us with the utmost courtesy, and treated us to Turkish coffee (very savoury) and Turkish cigarettes (very much the reverse)."

The retreating Turks had destroyed power stations, landing stages and cranes and removed the bridge of boats and the railway rolling stock. There were rows of burnt out motor cars. The bazaar was empty of goods but the Arab and Jewish traders were there awaiting events. Sir Arthur visited the Turkish Military Hospital and those patients who could not be moved remained – three or four hundred. They were in the care of a Greek doctor and four French Sisters of Mercy. The patients included an Algerian who had been press ganged into the Turkish Army and a Russian prisoner of war. There were dead corpses lying around and the stench was unbearable. An officer of the Indian Medical Service had come with Sir Arthur and he arranged for the patients to be moved and the hospital thoroughly cleaned and disinfected. That afternoon, Sir Arthur went four miles by motor launch to the fine mosque at Khadimain. He writes, "The dome and four very tall slender minarets are heavily gilded, and below the gilding are very elaborate patterns of tiles of brilliant blue. The mosque is only to be viewed piecemeal by peeps through the great doors. Entrance by the infidel is absolutely forbidden."

Figure 232: Lieutenant-Colonel formerly Major Moens aboard a river vessel on the Tigris.

Sir Arthur found one of the finest houses in Baghdad for his deputy, Major Stanley, whom he appointed in charge of Red Cross operations in the city. A cable sent downstream resulted in over four hundred cases of medical supplies being sent to Baghdad. Then, having settled plans for Red Cross operations for the summer, Sir Arthur decided to leave the city. He took up his old quarters aboard P 56. There he was joined towards evening by six officers and two hundred men. They were tired, foot-sore, dirty, unshaven and travel-stained. A Red Cross doctor, two Army Sisters and a staff of British and Indian orderlies ministered to their every need. There were clean shirts, pyjamas and washing kit, clean sheets and writing material all available.

Figure 233: Red Cross Headquarters in Amarah.

Figure 234: Baghdad – the Golden Domes of Khadimain.

The P 56 left at 6.00 am and in thirty hours they reached Sheik Saad. Here some lightly wounded men were disembarked, while some seriously wounded stretcher cases took their place to be taken to hospital in Basra. Sir Arthur himself disembarked at Amarah to rejoin Moens, and complete his round of inspection.

Sir Arthur and Major Moens discussed plans for the coming summer and Red Cross policy and strategy in Iraq. They had to rely more and more on the Indian Joint Committee because communication with the Pall Mall Joint Committee Headquarters in London was increasingly difficult due to submarine warfare in the Atlantic. On Sir Arthur's recommendation, Major Moens was promoted to Lieutenant Colonel and became the Red Cross Commissioner in Mesopotamia. He was awarded the C.B.E. and the C.I.E. for his services in Iraq.

Figure 235: A family bathe in the River Tigris.

On Saturday 24th March, Sir Arthur boarded the Red Cross Launch *Wessex* and sailed down to Kurnah. Many heavily loaded mahelahs, cargo vessels propelled manually by their crews, passed on their way upstream. By 5.00 p.m. the *Wessex* reached Kurnah and Sir Arthur was able to leave the Tigris for a walk alongside the Euphrates for the two rivers join here. He writes, "Between its' banks of palm groves as far as the eye can reach the great river rolls towards us out of the crimson west, a flood of molten gold."

The following day there was an inspection of a new hospital under construction and then Sir Arthur continued his journey on the *Wessex* downstream to Basra. Just before reaching the town the steering gear on the launch broke down but they arrived at the depot to find that the new repair shop had been completed and that the steering gear could be mended. Sadly he heard that the launch P 56 had been burned in an accidental fire. On the night of Monday 25th Sir Arthur travelled by train to Nazariyeh. It took fifteen hours to cover 150 miles and at 11.30 a.m. he took a late breakfast with the General Officer Commanding, known to the Arabs as the "Father of Lions". There were two hospitals to inspect at Nazariyeh and when the inspection was completed, Sir Arthur and his host set off by car with a motor cycle escort to visit Ur of the Chaldes. The sight of the city of Abraham was a reminder of the great antiquity of this land. That night Sir Arthur made the return journey to Basra, where he learned that a passage on the Hospital Ship Madras was available to enable him to sail to India. Before his departure he arranged good housing for the Red Cross Staff in Basra to enable them to work effectively during the long hot summer. On one of his last evenings in Basra, he dined with Lieutenant-General Sir George MacMunn and Gertrude Bell, who was later to become one of Winston Churchill's most trusted advisors on Iraq. She recommended Faisal as King of Iraq, and she also founded the Archaeological Museum in Baghdad, a wing of which was named after her. She was known as the "uncrowned Queen of Iraq".[14]

Figure 236: Camels were used for delivering Medical Supplies to desert outposts.

Sir Arthur embarked on the Hospital Ship Madras, which sailed for Karachi on Friday 30th March at noon. En route for Karachi, Sir Arthur took every opportunity to visit and encourage the sick and wounded men in the wards – a handful of British officers and men, a good number of Indians and over one hundred wounded Turkish prisoners. On the morning of Wednesday 4th April, the Madras sailed into Karachi and tied up alongside the quay. The Assistant District Medical Supervisor took Sir Arthur to Number One Indian Hospital located in the Karachi Port Trust Building. The offices had been converted into a superb fully equipped hospital. St John's Ambulance and the Sind Women's War Work Depot had contributed most generously to equipping the hospital and the annex which was in a magnificent building with great wide staircases and lofty marble halls. Thence Sir Arthur went to the old Artillery Barracks, which had been converted into British General Hospital Number 37. Once again he was thoroughly impressed with the surgical and medical provision and with the facilities and equipment. In the evening he was driven back to the harbour to embark once more for the voyage south to Bombay.

Figure 237: Carrying the wounded to board a Red Cross Hospital Ship.

Figure 238: British General Hospital Number 3, Basra.

The Hospital Ship Madras reached Bombay on Good Friday 1917, nine weeks to the day after Colonel Sir Arthur Lawley departed thence for Basra. Since then a great deal of work had been undertaken on the Red Cross Hospitals which Sir Arthur visited and inspected in Bombay. The British Officers Hospital at Calaba, the nearby Home for Sick Nursing Sisters, and the Indian Officers Hospital in the New Museum – all had been given further accommodation and other improvements. Temporary buildings had been erected to the rear of the museum, which was renamed the Lady Hardinge Hospital. The new buildings constructed for the science schools of the University of Bombay had been converted into the Freeman Thomas Hospital for British Soldiers. The Gaekwad of Baroda's Palace had been equipped and opened as a hospital for British Officers. Sir Arthur writes, "It is the last word in sybaritic sumptuousness. If there is aught in environment many a wounded warrior will here be wooed back to convalescence by the very beauty of his luxurious surroundings." At Dadar impressive hospital wards were under construction for the Indian Labour Corps. Sir Arthur also visited three convalescent homes at Coonoor, where two further homes were planned to increase capacity to five thousand beds. Praise was given by Sir Arthur to Lady Willingdon and the Bombay Presidency War Works Committees, and to Major Hepper of the Red Cross who collected and distributed stores in abundance to Indian Hospitals, Hospital Ships and Ambulance Trains. A sub-committee had been formed to deal with 'wounded and missing' enquiries working with the YMCA (Young Men's Christian Association), while another committee provided for amusements, entertainment and recreation. Throughout India magnificent work was being done by the Order of St. John and the British Red Cross under the able direction of Sir Pardy Lukis. Red Cross Representatives were now assigned to the Headquarters of each Division in Mesopotamia and these worked in close co-ordination with the military in tending for the sick and wounded.

Figure 239: A Hospital Ship bound for India at Basra.

Sir Arthur concludes, "The men know that beyond the Generals and the Staff, beyond the Government and the War Office there is the great British Public, big hearted and generous, who have made the work of caring for the sick and wounded their own special concern. The task has been entrusted to Red Cross hands, and with that arrangement Thomas Atkins (the British Tommy) is well content.

"To the British Red Cross and Order of St. John will always accrue the honour of having contributed in measure incalculable to the rescue and relief of the sick and wounded during the Mesopotamian Campaign."

Lieutenant-General Sir Frederick Stanley Maude was the Commander in Chief in Mesopotamia. On March 18th 1917, he wrote to Colonel Sir Arthur Lawley:

"As you are shortly going to leave Mesopotamia on completion of your tour here, I should like to take this opportunity of sending you a line to say how much we all appreciate the excellent and thorough work which the Red Cross is doing in connection with this campaign.

"First and foremost I must mention the invaluable assistance which we have received from the fleet of motor launches which have been so kindly placed at our disposal. I can testify personally to the fact that these launches were the means of minimizing much pain and suffering during the latter part of last summer at a time when the medical arrangements were not so fully developed as they are now. But it is not only with regard to this motor transport that I have to speak. The Red Cross has earned for itself a good name, not merely in this Great War, but in connection with campaigns which have gone before; and I venture to think that the work done by it out here will bear favourable comparison with even its most brilliant efforts in other fields. Through its agency we have been supplied constantly and liberally with stores of the most necessary kind, and these stores, when asked for, have always been forthcoming at the shortest notice, and have been promptly delivered.

"I am therefore glad to have this opportunity of writing to tell you how much we are indebted to the system which obtains out here, and which was till recently under the control of Colonel Jay Gould with Major Moens acting as his subordinate. Everything possible has been done to meet our requirements, and we are accordingly one and all grateful to the Red Cross for their splendid efforts."

Figure 240: Grave of Lieutenant-General Sir Frederick Stanley Maude in Baghdad with other war graves nearby.

On March 19th 1917 after British forces had taken Baghdad, Lieutenant-General F.S. Maude made the following proclamation:

"Our military operations have as their object the defeat of the enemy.... To complete this task, I am charged with absolute and supreme control of all regions

in which British troops operate; but our armies do not come into your cities and lands as conquerors or enemies, but as liberators..... It is the wish not only of my King and his peoples, but it is also the wish of the great nations with whom he is in alliance, that you should prosper even as in the past, when your lands were fertile, when your ancestors gave to the world literature, science and art, and when Baghdad city was one of the wonders of the world.

"Between your people and the dominions of my King, there has been a close bond of interest.... The British government cannot remain indifferent as to what takes place in your country now or in the future.... It is the hope and desire of the British people and the nations in alliance with them that the Arab race may rise once more to greatness and renown among the peoples of the Earth, and that it shall bind itself together to this end in unity and concord." [15]

Lieutenant-General F.S. Maude died in Mesopotamia on November 18th 1917 from cholera caught from drinking milk. He was buried in Baghdad.

In July 1917, Colonel Sir Arthur Lawley, as Commissioner of the British Red Cross and the Order of St John in Mesopotamia, spoke to a packed meeting in Exeter. He talked about the work of the R.A.M.C. and the nursing sisters. He said, "I have always spoken and shall always speak with unstinting praise of the splendid response made by the R.A.M.C. to the stupendous demands made upon them in this great campaign. The spirit shown by the doctors and nurses has been simply splendid. There is no other word for it. They have ministered to the sick and wounded unstintingly and untiringly, and with a courage equal to that shown by the soldiers in the trenches. When the history of this Great War comes to be written no more glorious record will adorn its pages than that which will tell the story of the self sacrifice, the devotion and daring of our doctors and nursing sisters in Flanders and France – and the British Red Cross Society is proud and flattered to be welcomed by them as auxiliaries and comrades. We are the handmaid of the Army." Sir Arthur explained how he was present at the Messines Ridge shortly after the successful enterprise there, and saw many outward and visible signs of the work of the Red Cross Society in the casualty clearing stations. The universal exclamation he heard was, "What should we do were it not for the Red Cross?"[16]

During the First World War, the British Red Cross joined with the Order of St John to form the Joint War Committee. They nursed hundreds of thousands of wounded and dying soldiers each year. The Voluntary Aid Detachments gave their name to a type of nurse. VAD nurses were trained in first aid and others undertook training in nursing, cookery, hygiene and sanitation. Ursula Mary and Margaret Cecilia Lawley were VAD nurses.

On a visit to the British Expeditionary Force in France in 1917, the Editor of the Times, Geoffrey Dawson, wrote at the conclusion of his trip, while at Wimereux,

"Had an early lunch with Sir Arthur Lawley and Cecilia, who'd been on night duty".

Ursula and Cecilia Lawley were mentioned in despatches and awarded the Royal Red Cross. On New Years Day 1918, Geoffrey Dawson wrote in his diary,

"Both the Lawley girls appear in the Gazette tonight with the Royal Red Cross, and richly deserve it. They have been nursing in France with hardly a break from the beginning, doing almost inconceivable hours at a stretch and living in great

discomfort. I only wish these great outpourings of honours could be limited to people of their kind." [17]

On Thursday 13th August 1918, Geoffrey Dawson's diary entry said,

"Lunched with Sir Arthur Lawley and Cecilia in Seymour Street and saw her off to France."

On October 16th, he travelled from London via Boulogne to Wimereux, where Ursula and Cecilia Lawley were nursing. The entry for Wednesday October 23rd said,

"I went to Wimereux, to the Red Cross to say good bye to the Lawley girls."

Figure 241: Ursula Lawley in VAD uniform.

Throughout the war VADs worked in hospitals, convalescent homes, rest stations, packing centres, medical supply depots and working parties. The Joint War Committee organised the volunteers alongside technical and professional staff and also supplied the machinery and mechanisms to provide these services in Britain and in the conflict areas of Europe, the Middle East, Russia and East Africa. To cheer the wounded soldiers an American benefactor, Miss May T. Moulton, sent phonographs, records and needles through Sir Arthur Lawley to the Red Cross in France, and to other war zones.[18]

The Red Cross and Order of St John had ten hospitals at:

1. Le Touquet.
2. Rouen
3. Abbéville (the Society of Friends)
4. Wimereux (Sir Henry Norman's)
5. Wimereux (Lady Hadfield's)
6. Etaples (Liverpool Merchants)
7. Allied Forces Base Hospital
8. Baltic and Corn Exchange Hospital at Boulogne
9. Millicent Duchess of Sutherland
10. Le Tréport (Lady Murray's) Hospital

Figure 242: VAD nurses and ambulance drivers in France. Imperial War Museum.

The Medical Department employed medical assessors, doctors, trained nurses, bandage dressers for the wounded, and medical orderlies. The main stores department for the Joint Committee was in Boulogne. To transport stores they had 78 lorries, five motor cycles and ten touring cars. Food, medical and other supplies, kit and equipment all needed transport. There was also a construction and maintenance section dealing with buildings. Finance was always needed and fund raising and budgeting were significant activities. The Red Cross and Order of St John also had Post Offices to send and receive mail which had to respect the regulations on censorship. They had rest stations for both officers and other ranks. There were recreation huts and entertainment provision too. In addition there were Convalescent Homes for Serving Nurses in Cannes (2), Menton, Etretat, Le Touquet (2), Hardelot and Pernes.

The Joint War Committee was the first to supply motorised ambulances to the battlefields. The first convoy arrived in France on October 9th 1914 and proved much more effective in war terrain than the horse drawn ambulances used in previous conflicts. By the end of October a second convoy of motor ambulances arrived from England to serve round Ypres. Altogether seven convoys of motor ambulances arrived in France transporting one million five hundred thousand sick or wounded soldiers during the Great War. There were also military ambulances, military medical facilities and hospitals.

Centres for recording the wounded and missing were set up in France and British Red Cross searchers were authorised to search villages where fighting had taken place and also to search in hospitals. This work marked the start of the "Message and Tracing Service" which remains a vital part of the Society's work today.[19]

The Red Cross also looked after the welfare of prisoners of war. In this connection, Sir Arthur Lawley on behalf of the Red Cross and the Order of St John held talks in neutral Switzerland with Prince Maximilian of Baden. They met at the Hotel National in Lucerne on May 9th 1916 and discussed the treatment of British, Allied and German Prisoners of War. Prince Maximilian said that the British were not carrying out the agreements respecting the repatriation of men over 55 years of age and of all civilian prisoners between the ages of 17 and 55 years who were physically incapable of rendering military service. He cited the case of the brother of the pre-war German Chancellor, Prince Bernhard Von Bulow, who was unfit for military service.

Sir Arthur Lawley urged that ex-naval and ex-military officers who were physically incapacitated should be treated like civilians. There were also retired officers, including Brigadier General Bradley aged 63 years, who were interned in Schloss Cells. Prince Maximilian pressed for the repatriation of all German doctors. He stated that all British Medical Officers and men of the R.A.M.C. had been repatriated with a few exceptions whose whereabouts were not known. The exchange of clergymen to minister to the prisoners of war was also discussed. The exchange of the lists of missing men was raised and Sir Arthur said that the Red Cross would be glad to have a list of the needy whom the YMCA and the Red Cross might help. The YMCA had sent a large quantity of music to the Crown Prince of Sweden for Dr Harts, the YMCA representative in Germany, to distribute. Prince Maximilian von Baden offered to deliver games, books and other recreational supplies to the prisoners of war and said that in January and February 1916, POWs in the Camp at Senne had received 58,000 and 60,000 packages respectively.

On the subject of health Prince Maximilian said that Dr Elizabeth Rotten wished to copy the example of Dr Markel on the Allied side by providing work for prisoners and giving proper help to those recovering from wounds or sickness. Sir Arthur asserted that the Red Cross and Order of St John "were ready to make allowances for the large number of prisoners, but that this by no means excused the systematic brutality with which prisoners had been treated, the conditions prevailing at Wittemberg, Gardelegen, Schneidemuhl and other camps where typhus broke out nor the continued ill treatment in some other camps."

Notes of this meeting were taken by Sir Louis Mallet, who had been British Ambassador to Turkey in 1914.[20] On May 12th 1916, Prince Maximilian von Baden wrote a letter to Sir Arthur Lawley from Konstanz in Germany, an historic city which lies on Lake Constance near the Swiss border. Evidently anxious about some of the allegations made during the Lucerne Meeting he wrote:

"By chance I met yesterday a Swiss delegate who saw 40 German Camps and a Swiss Head Doctor who took part in the work of the Commission which decided on the internment of French prisoners in Switzerland. They confirmed that there is absolutely no difference made in the treatment of the prisoners of all nations represented in the German Camps.

"A kind word you said about me and the way one knew I regarded the prisoner question in all countries makes me hope that you will make use of what I have written here to alleviate the anxiety of your countrymen as far as this is possible.

"As you say Lady Lawley understands German, I enclose an article from the Berner Bund, which contains the answer of the German Government concerning the Camp at Wittenberg.

"I told you about the deaths in the Camp at Totsky in Russia. What would the English feel and do if they heard that 18,000 prisoners in one camp had died of typhus, and that in the same camp reign cholera and small pox. When the epidemic was at its height 130 persons died every day.

"During eighteen months I have gained insight into the immense amount of work which Germany has to fulfil to feed, house and occupy the 1,600,000 prisoners it has got. I know the difficulties and the shortcomings, but I also know all the good intentions and goodwill that exist. The progress is enormous, and thousands of men are untiringly at work to better the lot of the prisoners.

"As to myself, I will remember our meeting in Lucerne with pleasure and beg you to believe me to be yours very sincerely, Max, Prince of Baden."[21]

Figure 243: Prince Maximilian and Princess Maria Louise of Baden with their son Berthold and daughter Marie in 1912.

On 29th May 1916, as a result of the meeting between Sir Arthur and Prince Max, the first contingent of 304 British invalided and wounded prisoners arrived in Zurich. "All were astonished, delighted and much touched by the wonderful heartiness of the welcome they received everywhere en route as soon as they entered Switzerland, and several officers spoke with high appreciation of the courtesy shown to them by Prince Max von Baden at Constance".

At Lausanne nearly ten thousand people were at the railway station at 5.00 in the morning. The scene was incredibly moving and none felt it more than the British officers and men. They kept saying, "We never expected anything like this. It's marvellous. It's incredible. Do thank the Swiss for us. You cannot say too much." Long before they reached Montreux every compartment was overflowing with flowers, flags, cigarettes, chocolates, newspapers, magazines and presents of every kind. On every platform was a mass of cheering people, waving flags, handkerchiefs and hats and crying "Vive l'Angleterre", answered with cries from the troops of "Vive la Suisse."

They continued their journey to Chateau d'Oex above Montreux where they were to rest and recuperate from their ordeal in the care of the Red Cross and the Swiss people. When they were fully recovered they would continue their journey home to the United Kingdom. [22]

On July 21st 1916, the Government Committee on the Treatment by the enemy of British Prisoners of War reported their findings by a letter to Sir Arthur Lawley from 18 Carlton House Terrace. Sadly while conditions did improve in some instances, prisoners of war continued to suffer from mistreatment and deteriorating food both as regards to quantity and quality. The men were entirely dependent on their food parcels and but for the parcels from home they would have starved. Soap was practically unobtainable. Given that the strategy of blockade was aimed at starving the enemy into submission, none of this is surprising.[23]

The "Bureau de Secours aux Prisonniers de Guerre" at the British Legation in Berne sent a daily consignment of 6,400 loaves to Frankfurt in Germany to supply 19,200 British prisoners of war. The Bureau staff were in constant correspondence with the Prison Camp Commandants in Germany. The Bureau also dispatched a variety of foods in individual parcels and sent items of clothing to the British prisoners of war.[24]

In his memoirs, Prince Maximilian von Baden wrote about the peace movement in Britain in 1916. He said, "The great debate on peace in the House of Commons takes place on 24th May 1916. Its importance is hushed up in the British press which only publishes meagre extracts from the long speeches of the pacifists. The statesmanlike utterances of Ramsey MacDonald overshadow the humanitarian speeches of his adherents. MacDonald addresses a double meaning to Germany – if you are willing to restore Belgian integrity and Belgian sovereignty then let the talk of peace proceed."[25] Prince Maximilian would in all likelihood have discussed the possibilities for peace with Sir Louis Mallet and Sir Arthur Lawley.

Prince Maximilian of Baden was married to Princess Maria Louise of Hanover, a member of the British Royal Family. In 1907, on the death of his uncle, he became Grand Duke of Baden. From October 1914, as Honorary President of the Baden Red Cross, he dedicated himself to looking after the welfare of prisoners of war of all nationalities. In 1916, he became the Honorary President of the German-American Prisoner of War Assistance Section of the World Wide YMCA. On October 3rd 1918, because of his humanitarian reputation, he was appointed by Kaiser Wilhelm II to become the last Chancellor of Imperial Germany with instructions to negotiate an armistice. He resigned on November 9th, upon the abdication of the Kaiser.[26] During the period 1929 to 1932, Sir Arthur and Lady Lawley were frequent visitors to Freiburg in Baden where Sir Arthur went for medical treatment. They undoubtedly met the von Baden family, although sadly Prince Maximilian died in November 1929. In 1920, Prince Maximilian and Kurt Hahn founded the famous school – Salem – at the Von Baden castle, Schloss Salem, near Konstanz. Kurt Hahn, being Jewish, fled Nazi Germany in 1933 and went on to found Gordonstoun School and Outward Bound. Prince Philip was his pupil at Salem and Gordonstoun and Kurt Hahn persuaded him to undertake the Duke of Edinburgh Award Scheme. The Prince of Wales was also a pupil at Gordonstoun. Kurt Hahn was one of the leading lights behind the establishment of the United World Colleges.

In July 1918, Richard Thompson Lawley, the Fourth Lord Wenlock, died. He joined the Queen's Own 7th Hussars in 1875, retiring as Colonel of the Regiment in 1904. Richard T. Lawley served throughout the Nile Expedition of 1884-85 with the Light Camel Regiment. He took part in operations with the Desert Column, including the engagement at Abu Klea Wells, on 16th to the 17th February 1885. After service in Egypt, he played a prominent part in the Boer War, sailing for the Cape on board S.S. Templemore. He commanded the 7th Hussars from 20th December 1901 to the 22nd January 1902. Colonel Lawley was mentioned in despatches on 17th June 1902 and on 26th June he was appointed a Companion of the Order of the Bath, "in recognition of his services during operations in South Africa." Richard Thompson Lawley succeeded his brother, Beilby Lawley, as the 4th Baron Wenlock in January 1912. He died at Hestercombe, Taunton, on 25th July 1918.[27] His brother, the Reverend Algernon Lawley, succeeded to the title.[28]

Towards the end of the Great War, on March 12th 1918, Sir Arthur made a speech at the Stock Exchange in London on behalf of the Red Cross Society. He said that the comradeship of the trenches had buried many old prejudices and given birth to many broad and new sympathies. The Red Cross had over 1100 ambulances in France. He delivered amid cheers a glowing eulogy on the work of the VAD nurses and the VAD drivers, who drove over 300 ambulances. He appealed to members of the Stock Exchange to help the Society to meet its ever increasing expenditure and enable them to continue in an adequate manner their great service of mercy.[29]

In fund raising and many other activities the organisational skills and leadership of Sir Arthur Lawley were invaluable. He worked tirelessly and found scope for the use of all his old powers of tact and organisation, which had so often seemed to be wasted in the peace-time work of the City. He served on the Joint War Committee and on June 1st 1920 was awarded the title of Knight of Grace of the Order of Saint John for his services.[30]

While Sir Arthur was in France and the Middle East, his wife, Lady Lawley, was Honorary Secretary of the Queen Mary's Needlework Guild. She was a first rate organiser. The Guild knitted articles in wool for sailors and soldiers at the Front. The ladies of the Guild produced socks, scarves, woollen helmets, jerseys and cardigans. On Saturday 25th August 1917, it was announced that Lady Lawley was to be created a Dame Grand Cross of the British Empire in recognition of her work.[31]

---

[1]   The Times. Sunday November 15th 1914. Page 1. Column F.
      The Times. Friday November 20th 1914. Page 9. Column F.
[2]   Geoffrey Dawson and Our Times. Evelyn Wrench. Hutchinson. London. 1955. Page 119.
[3]   "Distinguished Women of the past." Danuta Bois, 1999.

[4] The Times. Saturday April 17th 1915. Page 9. Column G.
[5] The Times. "One short stretch of the way". March 29th 1915. Page 10. Column E.
[6] The Times. Thursday June 17th 1915. Page 9. Column A.
[7] The Times. Saturday September 4th 1915. Page 9. Column B.
     The Times. Monday September 6th 1915. Page 11. Column B.
[8] The Times. Thursday March 30th 1916. Page 6. Column G.
[9] The Times. Saturday June 17th 1916. Page 10. Column A.
     The Times. Saturday June 17th 1916. Page 11. Column F.
[10] Reports by the Joint War Committee and the Joint Finance Committee of the British Red Cross
     Society and the Order of St John of Jerusalem in England. London. 1921.
[11] The Times. Thursday April 26th 1917. Page 11. Column D.
[12] Gertrude Bell Archive. "The Letters" [10 February] , [11 March] , [12 March 1915] , [17 March
     1915] , [9 February 1917] , and [30 March 1917].
[13] A Message from Mesopotamia. Sir Arthur Lawley. Hodder and Stoughton. London. 1917.
[14] "Distinguished Women of the past." Danuta Bois, 1999.
[15] A Message from Mesopotamia. Sir Arthur Lawley. Hodder and Stoughton. London. 1917.
     Foreword
[16] The British Nursing Journal. July 21st 1917. Page 37.
[17] British Red Cross Records. Letter of 13th August 2004. Geoffrey Dawson Diaries. Bodleian
     Library. Oxford.
[18] New York Times. March 5th 1916, page 3, "Wounded Soldiers Cheered by Music."
[19] British Red Cross – History and Origins. www.redcross.org.uk
     Champions of Charity: War and the Rise of the Red Cross by John F. Hutchinson. Westview Press.
     (1997) ISBN: 0813333679.
     The Silver Jubilee Book. Oldham Press. London. 1935. Page 171
[20] Source FO 383/155. National Archives Kew. 1916
[21] Source FO 383/155. National Archives Kew. 1916
[22] The Times. May 31st 1916. Page 9. Column G.
[23] Source FO 383/156. National Archives Kew. 1916
[24] The Times. May 20th 1916. Page 5. Column E.
[25] The Memoirs of Prince Maximilian von Baden. Constable. London 1928. Volume 1 page 45.
[26] Wikipedia – "Maximilian von Baden"
[27] http://www.uga.edu/rom/nfallows/medals.htm
[28] The Times. Saturday July 27th 1918. Page 3. Column B.
[29] The Times. Wednesday March 13th 1918. Page 3. Column B.
[30] The Times. Wednesday June 2nd 1920. Page 18. Column E.
[31] Times Obituary for Lady Wenlock, Monday 30th April 1944.
     British Red Cross Records. Letter of 13th August 2004.
     The Times. Saturday 25th August 1917. Page 7. Column G.

Chapter 9
Victory and Ventures New

The Prisoners return

After November 11th 1918, the British prisoners of war were set free by the Germans and many walked back towards the Allied lines. Sir Arthur Lawley, as Red Cross Commissioner in France and Belgium, was responsible for the welfare of the prisoners who came to seek help from the Red Cross and the Order of St John. He did a great deal of work to ensure that the returning POWs were well cared for and brought home to Britain. He wrote a letter about this work on November 24th to Sir Arthur Stanley, Chairman of the Joint War Committee, in which he said:

"I have seen the released prisoners of war dribbling across the German frontier and arriving in hordes in Nancy. Later I visited them at their reception camp in Calais, after they had been washed, cleansed, clothed and fed, and although when they first come in they are indeed abject things, weary, footsore, hungry and filthy, yet in 48 hours they are new men.

"There is no doubt that these men have had a very hard time indeed, but the physical condition of the 6000 who have so far reached Calais is on the whole good, and their spirits are unbroken by the horrors and the hardships which undoubtedly they have had to go through. They all speak in terms of great gratitude for the help accorded to them by the civilian population of Belgium and France.

"When I was in Nancy, a week ago, several hundred prisoners came in during the evening and night that I was there, quite unexpectedly of course, and into a town occupied by the French. The French military authorities had prepared a large barracks for their reception. They were extremely sympathetic, and did everything in their power to alleviate the men's suffering. I went down to the barracks directly I arrived, at 7.00 pm., to find the men singing in chorus preparatory to a meal of soup, meat, bread and wine. While I was there, three lorry loads of rations arrived from the nearest British stores depot. Early next morning I found that several hundred more men had come in during the night…. Before I left Nancy, clothing, food and blankets for these men were on their way."[1]

One of the prisoners returning from Germany was Colonel John Evelyn Gibbs, who had been a prisoner of war at Starlsund, Heidelburg, Holzminden and Freiberg. After his homecoming, he married Lady Helena Frances Augusta Cambridge, Queen Mary's niece. The wedding took place in St George's Chapel Windsor on September 2nd 1919. His brother was George Abraham Gibbs of Tyntesfield and George's daughter, Doreen, was one of the bridesmaids.[2]

On December 2nd, Sir Arthur Lawley wrote once more to Sir Arthur Stanley. He said:

"Quite recently I have had demands for 25 motor ambulances to work between Tournai and Brussels, and a similar demand from the French zone in the neighbourhood of Metz. The first ten ambulances left Boulogne for Metz this morning and I am arranging to dispatch another 15 motor ambulances in the course of the next few days…. During the last few days two convalescent camps at Boulogne have been taken over as camps for officers and men returning from

*Germany. I have myself visited the camps more than once, and was present when
400 officers arrived yesterday morning. They seemed to be in good health and
spirits, and several of those to whom I have spoken tell me that in their captivity at
Mainz they were treated on the whole fairly decently. They all report, however,
that the plight of our soldiers returning in the Metz and Strasbourg
neighbourhoods is deplorable. These officers all stopped at Nancy for several
days on their way through, and they assured me that at the Nancy Camp both
officers and men receive every possible care and attention."* [3]

The Red Cross at Versailles

In 1919 the Peace Conference began at Versailles. At the same time delegates of
the Red Cross assembled in Paris. The International Red Cross in Berne announced
that there would be a Conference held in Geneva immediately after the signing of the
Peace Treaty. On Friday 21st February 1919, there was a dinner in Paris attended by
the Red Cross representatives of the United States, Great Britain, France, Italy and
Japan. Sir Arthur Stanley and Sir Arthur Lawley attended the dinner as British
representatives. The principal speakers were Sir Arthur Lawley, who represented the
British Red Cross Society, and Mr Henry P. Davison, representing the American Red
Cross and Chairman of the Committee of the Red Cross Societies.

In his speech, Henry P. Davidson put forward a grandiose plan for the Red Cross
backed by President Wilson and his advisor Colonel House.

In reply, Sir Arthur said in his speech:

*"Mr Davidson has revealed to us his conception of a great ideal, and has invited
your criticism thereupon. I would only urge that you should criticize it, not as a
cut and dried scheme, but only as an inspiration. To me the idea is a grand one,
and I feel privileged indeed that as the representative of the British Red Cross
Society, I should have been invited to assist in its development. The process of
development must be slow, but though the way may be long and the road may be
rough, yet the goal is worth the winning. We have emerged victorious from a
mighty conflict by combined effort after four years of bitter struggle. Today the
world is confronted by enemies no less powerful and ruthless, in the shape of
famine, disease and death. If these in turn are to suffer defeat, it can only be done
by combined effort on our part, by self-sacrifice, and by determination to be
daunted by no difficulty.*

*The necessary driving power will not be lacking. America will see to that for
"America is in". Those three words have meant much to us in the war that is over.
Two years ago the clouds hung darkly on every horizon. The ship to which the
Allies had committed their fat and their fortunes was making heavy weather
indeed, when suddenly the word went round, "America is in!" The whole world
held its breath. This old Ship of State of ours seemed for a moment to reel and
stagger in the trough of the sea, and then plunge forward with greater might,
greater frenzy and greater certainty of the victory which one day assuredly would
be in our grasp. America was in with her splendid manhood, her vast wealth,
marvellous intelligence and unlimited material resources, but she was in with far
more than this – in with her great traditions and high ideals, with her chivalry, her
loyalty and her valour, of which her sons have given us so magnificent a
manifestation on the field of Chateau Thierry, on the heights of St. Mihiel, and in
the Forest of Argonne.*

"And what is the conclusion of the whole matter? We sum it up in one glorious word, "Victory". Our victory and our peace; and then the aftermath of war, with its crop of problems of greater magnitude and greater difficulty than any of those by which we were confronted even in the direst stress of war. Men say to me that "the war is over and nothing else matters", and to myself I say, "Are these men blind and deaf who say these things?" For look where you may, the world is girdled with a belt of sorrow, and stricken humanity is lifting its hands to Heaven in impotent pleading for help which does not come. Is that cry to go unheeded and unheard? That is the question I put to you tonight. The answer is not far to seek, for once again America is in, with her lion heart and stern resolve to lighten the burden of suffering humanity, and she calls to us to stand by her side. Who can doubt what the answer will be?

Mr Davidson has spoken tonight of the marvellous work of the American Red Cross. It has indeed been phenomenal. He will not, I know, misunderstand me if I urge that the tally of work done by the other Red Cross Societies is hardly less remarkable. At the beginning of the war the British Red Cross Society was but a tiny organism. Today it is an organization powerful to reduce the sum of human suffering and human pain in every theatre of war. It has had financial support to the extent of many millions, contributed by all sorts and conditions of men, and the number of its voluntary workers runs to hundreds of thousands. Is this wonderful spirit of self-sacrifice which has permeated every section of society to be dissipated just at a time when the demand for such work is greater than it ever has been before? It would indeed be deplorable if all these engines powerful for good were to be flung upon the scrap heap or allowed to tumble to bits from rust and disuse. To you gentlemen we make our appeal tonight that you join us in urging that prompt and concentrated action be taken. We have to broaden the base on which the whole structure of our Red Cross activities has been built up, but, more than that, we have to bring home to men's minds that, great and terrible as are the sufferings of humanity today, yet the remedy is not beyond the power of man to devise, and that if only we can rise to a great occasion we may yet lead the stricken peoples of a greatly distracted world through the present dark night of sorrow to a golden dawning and a better day." [4]

Sir Arthur considered the American plan for the Red Cross to be unrealistic. On 24 February, Davidson received a letter marked "Private and Confidential" from Sir Arthur, the contents of which must have caused him some foreboding. The letter said:

"The Red Cross Council met today to discuss the proposals made in the Statement which you presented on Friday night in Paris, and while - generally speaking - your conception of the part which in future the Red Cross is to play in the world commends itself to that august body, discussion for the moment centres round the invitation issued by the International Committee and particularly the question of the inclusion of the Central Powers as participants in the Conference. Some of our people take the line that it is impossible for them to meet the Germans even after the peace is signed, seeing that they have grossly violated the Geneva Convention and are "beyond the pale." Whatever decision may be come to concerning that particular matter it is pretty certain that our Red Cross Society will raise the point in whatever answer they may send to the International Committee at Geneva. I feel pretty confident that the Geneva Committee will stick resolutely to their attitude of strict neutrality, so there may be some lengthy parlaying before even the Conference is assembled or at all events before the British Red Cross Society

decides to accept the invitation. Our people will I think fall into line with you all right on the general question of extending the scope of Red Cross activities during peace time and will be glad to see our Charter amended to that end. We may find them a bit sticky concerning the assembling of experts at Cannes in the near future. Sir Arthur Stanley is taking steps to sound out some of our friends quietly before there is any question of an official invitation being issued.... Both he and I are a bit anxious lest our Council should feel they are being "rushed" (this I have already told you) though they know they are not committed to any definite policy or to any cut and dried scheme. They are all of them anxious to get our Charter amended so as to enable us to undertake peacetime activities. The rest will follow!"

Sir Arthur Lawley's timely warning was a disappointment to Davidson. With considerable restraint, he replied that he was "a bit disappointed" and that "if the world is ever to become normal we must accept a peace, when signed, as a peace in fact and not a peace in theory"; he also reiterated his belief that his plan "must be done now if it is going to be done at all."

On March 2nd 1920, the International Red Cross Conference began in Geneva. The British delegates were Sir Arthur Stanley, Sir Arthur Lawley, Sir Robert Philip, and Dr F. Kay Menzies. During the deliberations at this Conference the improvement of public health and the prevention of disease were discussed and consideration was given to the programme of service in peace time. In this and succeeding conferences, the groundwork was laid down for the creation of the modern International Red Cross, which was to play an important role in peace time as well as in time of war.[5]

In April 1919, Earl Haig wrote an article in the Times on the British Army's March to the Rhine in which he said, "My thanks are due to Colonel the Honourable Sir Arthur Lawley, who as Commissioner has supervised the wonderful work done by the British Red Cross Society in France".

In May 1919, Sir Arthur Lawley as Red Cross Commissioner in France was present at the opening of the Cologne Leave Club for British soldiers serving with the Army of the Rhine. The Club House had a sitting Room for about 1500, which could also serve as a theatre, ball room or cinema. There was also a dining room for three hundred people, two bowling alleys, two billiard rooms, reading rooms and hostels with accommodation for four hundred men. Baron d'Erlanger was President of the Committee and Sir Arthur was the Honorary Treasurer.[6] The Baron served on the Board of the Forestal Company of which Sir Arthur was Chairman.

Back in business

Both Baron d'Erlanger and Sir Arthur Lawley were taken to the High Court on July 20 1920, accused of slandering and libelling Mr Patrick Campbell Olgivie, who they had said was not fit to be a director of the board of a company and had been guilty of dishonest conduct and of intriguing to injure the Forestal Company. Three days later Patrick Olgivie withdrew his action having discovered that his wife had conspired with a Mrs Handcock to bring the Company into disrepute by making false allegations of Forestal's pro-German sympathies during the Great War. Olgivie resigned as a director of Forestal's Land, Timber and Railways Company.[7]

Sir Arthur Lawley held directorships of several other companies too. These were the English, Scottish and Australian Bank, the Yorkshire Insurance Company, the World Auxiliary Insurance Corporation, Dalgety and Company, and the London and Northwestern Railway Company. In 1920, the London and North West Railway named a locomotive after him. For a man with a passion for railways no more fitting gesture could have been made. The 'Sir Arthur Lawley' was a 4-6-0 LNW Claughton 695 locomotive built in Rugby in 1920.[8]

Spain and Morocco

Towards the end of March 1919, Lady Lawley and her two daughters went on holiday to Algerciras in Spain. They were joined there by Geoffrey Dawson and Lionel Curtis. In a letter home to Langcliffe, Geoffrey Dawson wrote on March 31st, "This is a perfect place for a rest cure – a large sunny hotel with glorious gardens, running down to a deep blue sea and the Rock facing it across the bay. And here we lead a lotus life – a long ride one day up and down mountain paths and lunch high up in the cork woods – Lady Lawley and the two girls and Lionel Curtis and I – and this morning I've been shopping with them by the aid of a Spanish Phrase Book in the very picturesque little town – oranges and cakes for a picnic tea. It's so like Italy you wouldn't know the difference – little whitewashed cobbled streets and courtyards and laden donkeys. Tomorrow we go fox hunting."

On April 12th, Geoffrey wrote from Tangier in Morocco, "You can't imagine a more beautiful spot and the town itself is interesting beyond description with little narrow streets and Moorish houses and motley crowds of Arabs, Negroes and folk from the interior… I hope to start within a week for Fez and Marrakesh with the Lawleys."

On Good Friday, 1919, Geoffrey Dawson wrote, "Here I am again after another trip across the Straits and going on tomorrow to the French seat of Government at Rabat. I packed Lionel Curtis off to Paris (to the Versailles Peace Conference) and now I'm off on tour with the Lawleys."

Figure 244: A water colour painted in Morocco by Lady Lawley, 1919.

On April 26th, Geoffrey wrote, "We've been to Marrakesh, which is a joy reserved for very few, and what is more we've seen it under the best possible auspices, for my friend Walter Harris[L] was there and took us everywhere – to be received by the Grand Bashaw in his palace, to dine with some Moorish grandees, to see the ancient tombs of the kings, and to wander about the most amazing streets and bazaars. It's a glorious city, built of rose-red brick, about the time of the Norman Conquest, in a great plain surrounded by hills – groves of palms and oranges in and about it, and the great range of the Atlas with snow capped peaks lying 30 kilometres away….. And the bazaars and lanes were an endless joy – utterly unspoilt – straight out of the pages of the *Arabian Nights* – donkeys and camels and endless chatter of grave Moors and blacker men from the South all in their long striped robes and yellow slippers – baskets of oranges and pomegranates for eating and dyeing their leather…"[9] Lady Lawley painted several water colours in Southern Spain and Morocco.

On May 17th 1919, Geoffrey Dawson and the Honourable Margaret Cecilia Lawley announced their engagement. They were married on Saturday 14th June at St Margaret's Church, Westminster by the Reverend Lord Wenlock, uncle of the bride. The bride was given away by her father, Sir Arthur Lawley. The bridesmaids were Ursula Mary Lawley, Lorna Leatham and Cecily Blair. Lieutenant-Colonel Edward Grigg, M.C. of the Grenadier Guards was the best man. The Marriage Register was signed by Lord Milner and Aunt Kitty (Miss Perfect). Sir Arthur Lawley gave the bride diamond earrings and Lady Lawley gave her a diamond tiara and a diamond and sapphire brooch. Sir Arthur and Lady Lawley gave the bridegroom a motor car. From the groom's aunt, Kitty Perfect, the couple received a generous cheque.[10]

The honeymoon was spent at Chequers lent to Geoffrey and Cecilia by Lord and Lady Lee and then at Rest Harrow, Sandwich, lent to them by Lord and Lady Astor. In 1920, Cecilia gave birth to their first child, a son, Michael. There followed two daughters, Belinda and Elizabeth Jane.

An active retirement

Sir Arthur Lawley had close links with the Rhodes Foundation at Oxford. In the Oxford University Summer Meeting, during the first two weeks of August 1919, the theme was the Study of the British Commonwealth. The Inaugural Lecture in the Sheldonian Theatre was given by Lord Milner, Secretary of State for the Colonies. Later Sir Arthur Lawley gave a lecture on South Africa.[11] Sir Arthur was on the Committee of the Royal Colonial Institute and served as its president for some time.[12]

The British Legion

On January 30th 1920, there was a Meeting at the Mansion House in London to amalgamate the forty to fifty officers' benevolent societies into one organisation. The meeting was addressed by Earl Haig, Lord Beatty and Sir Hugh Trenchard. Earl Haig had invited Sir Arthur Lawley to become Chairman of the new organisation which was to be known as the Officers' Association. In due course this became the Officers' Benevolent Department of the British Legion. The purpose of the new organisation was to help officers readjust to post war life and in particular to assist wounded, disabled and traumatized officers. Sir Arthur threw himself whole-heartedly into the difficult task of organising a new and important piece of benevolent work and his eminent services in that capacity were remembered gratefully by all who were

---

[L] The Times correspondent in Tangiers

associated with him. When failing health caused Sir Arthur to resign from the Executive Committee, he became Vice President of the Officers' Benevolent Department of the British Legion. His work for the British Legion continued for the rest of his life.[13]

Public Speaking, Journeys South and Sad Farewells

Sir Arthur was a frequent speaker at school speech days. On June 25th 1921, he spoke at Shrewsbury School as the former Governor of Madras on "India as the Linch Pin of the Imperial Coach". He said that so long as England continued to be part of a great Empire, she must hold India.[14] At Dover Grammar School, the school magazine, "The Pharos", records Sir Arthur's visit to Speech Day in 1922. The Headmaster said, "Of course we were all delighted with Sir Arthur Lawley's speech and the presence of the member for Dover, Major J. J. Astor M.P., and Lady Violet Astor. Sir Arthur delivered a stirring address exhorting the boys to carry through life their lesson of comradeship, or good fellowship, a quality which helped to bind the Empire and also inspired such noble work as the defence of Flanders and the exploits of the Dover Patrol. At all times, and especially in a crisis of Imperial affairs, we needed comradeship 'to win through', and it was by such sacrifices as that involved that we had won victory and peace, and only by this means could we hope to solve the difficulties that lay before us."[15]

On June 22nd 1921, the Lawleys attended a League of Nations Dinner in honour of Dominion Prime Ministers and leaders of the Indian Empire at which General Smuts was one of the principal speakers. Sir Arthur and Lady Lawley knew Jan Christian Smuts well from their days in the Transvaal. On Friday 5th August 1921, the Union Castle liner R.M.S. Saxon set sail from Southampton for South and East Africa. Sir Arthur and Lady Lawley and their daughter, Ursula, were on board bound for Durban in Natal. Among the 74 First Class Passengers travelling with the Lawleys were Jan Christian Smuts and his cabinet colleagues from South Africa, returning from the Imperial Conference in London, and the Duke of Orleans. The ship called in at Madeira, but as it continued its voyage southwards on August 15th, a fire broke out in the coal bunkers. The Saxon proceeded to Freetown in Sierra Leone with Numbers 2 and 3 bunkers on fire. It was accompanied by the Waipara owned by the British India Steam Navigation Company. On August 16th, Captain Hoskins of the RMS Saxon cabled to the Arundel Castle to report that the fires were under control, that all on board were well, that there was damage to the structure and that coal from the bunkers would have to be discharged at Freetown. At Freetown the passengers transferred to the Kenilworth Castle which proceeded on Sunday 21st to Cape Town.[16] The Lawleys had an insatiable wanderlust. In February 1922, the same year that Howard Carter discovered the Tomb of Tutankhamun, they were in Egypt and stayed at the Winter Palace in Luxor.[17] In the late summer of 1923, they visited Western Canada.[18]

On 28th November 1924, Sir Arthur and Lady Lawley, their daughter, Ursula, and Brigadier General Ferdinand Stanley and his wife embarked on the RMS Almanzora to sail to Buenos Aires.[19] The gentlemen were travelling on behalf of the Forestal Company to visit the company's properties, estates and factories in Argentina.

The Company operated in the Chaco of Northern Argentina where the Rio Parana was the main artery of river transport. The company's lands lay between Reconquista to the south and Resistencia to the north. They produced timber and tannin from the quebracho forests and beef and leather from their herds of cattle. Sir Arthur and Lady Lawley, Ursula and the Stanleys departed from Buenos Aires on New Year's Eve and during the first three weeks of January they made a thorough inspection of the Company's factories, estancias, railways, ports and forests in the Chaco. They were accompanied by the local managing director, the chief engineer and one of the general managers. The company employed thousands of people. Around Villa Guillermina 9,000 people were dependent on the tannin factory and other company plants. Forestal had built schools, churches, hospitals, clubs, cinemas and stores in Villa Guillermina and Villa Ana. At Villa Ana, Sir Arthur laid the foundation stone for the new church. Further development was under weigh at Tartagal and Gallareta. The hospital at Villa Guillermina needed to be enlarged and a new hospital was to be built at Tartagal. Sir Arthur reported an improvement in housing since his last visit. The Lawleys and the Stanleys travelled extensively on the company's 550 kilometres of railways. Fifty more kilometres were under construction and further extensions were planned into the quebracho forests. One of the company ports on the River Parana was being destroyed by flood waters but the rail link to the port of Piraqua provided a viable alternative. The estancias at Aurora and Las Gamas had 50 thousand head of cattle and there were plans for improved stock and increased herd sizes. As an expert rider, Sir Arthur was in his element amongst the horses and gauchos on the company's estancias. The whole operation in Northern Argentina was enormous – more like a colony than a company.[20]

**Figure 245: Sir Arthur and Lady Lawley riding on the Forestal
Estates in Argentina.**

The Lawleys' and Stanleys' planned itinerary involved taking the train to Mendosa and thence travelling on towards the snows of the high Andes. Their rail journey took them to the entrance to the tunnel beneath the mountains. There they left the train and hired mules on which they crossed the famed Inca Bridge and the high Uspallata Pass (3180 metres) dominated by the impressive statue of the Christ of the Andes. They then descended to the Chilean side of the pass to take the train to the port of Valparaiso.[21] Here they embarked on a ship to sail to Arica and thence travelled by rail to Lake Titicaca. Their rail journey across the Peruvian Altiplano gave them the opportunity of seeing something of the Inca Empire before taking a ship from Callao, the port of Lima, to return via the Panama Canal to England. Sir Arthur and Lady Lawley, Ursula, General and Mrs Stanley arrived back in Liverpool on board the Oropesa on March 29th 1925 [22] Sir Arthur Lawley and General Stanley delivered a detailed report to the Forestal Land, Timber and Railways Company.

On Wednesday 13th May 1925, Lord Milner died. He had been a close friend of Sir Arthur and Lady Lawley. The funeral, on Saturday 16th May, was in Canterbury Cathedral and most of the members of Milner's Kindergarten were in attendance. The mourners included Sir Herbert Baker, Sir Otto and Lady Beit, Bob Brand, Lionel Curtis, Geoffrey Dawson, Earl Grey, Sir Edward Grigg, Philip Kerr, Sir Arthur Lawley, Lord Selborne and Sir John Hanbury-Williams, all of whom had worked with or been associated with Lord Milner in South Africa.

Sir Arthur Lawley frequently sought Milner's advice and conducted a correspondence with him for many years some evidence of which is recorded in the Milner Archive in Oxford. Lord Milner often dined with the Lawley family at their house at 9, Seymour Street. His death was a great loss.[23] Sir Arthur sent a telegram of condolence to his widow, Viscountess Milner. He wrote, "With the heartfelt sympathy of those who knew his worth and who know what real suffering means."[24] On the 11th January 1926, Violet Milner wrote in her diary, "It is so dreadful without him."

On November 3rd 1925, Lady Lawley's brother, Sir Bache Cunard, died. His estranged wife, Emerald, was a celebrated London hostess and socialite and their daughter, Nancy Cunard, was an icon of the 1920s, who founded "The Hours Press" in France, which published the works of several illustrious writers and poets including Robert Graves and Samuel Beckett. Later she espoused the causes of the American Negro, the Republic in the Spanish Civil War, and the Free French in the Second World War. Sir Arthur, Lady Lawley and their daughters attended the funeral.[25]

The Fairbridge Farm School

Sir Arthur Lawley had known the Fairbridge family from the early days in Rhodesia. Rhys Seymour Fairbridge was born in Port Elizabeth on 30th September 1861 and after leaving school he trained as a surveyor. On June 5th 1884, he married Rosalie Helen Ogilvie from Grahamstown in the Cape of Good Hope. Rhys and Rosalie's eldest son, Kingsley Olgivie Fairbridge was born on May 2nd 1885. In 1891, Rhys Fairbridge got a job with the British South Africa Company as a surveyor on the railway which was being built from Beira in Portuguese East Africa to Salisbury in Rhodesia. He joined the pioneer forces which put down the Matabele uprisings in 1893 and 1896. Meanwhile his wife and family stayed on in Grahamstown where Kingsley was educated at St Andrew's College. In 1896, the family moved to Umtali in Rhodesia. At the age of 13, Kingsley Fairbridge got a job as a bank clerk in Standard Bank of Africa at Umtali. Rhys Fairbridge often took his son on his surveying assignments in the foothills of the Inyangani and Vumba Mountains near Umtali. Kingsley would also go on expeditions, accompanied by his African friend Jack and his dog Vic, trekking across the high ridges and deep valleys of the Eastern Highlands. The tall grass and wide vistas of Africa made him dream of settling the empty plains with the poor from Britain's cities. In 1900, he tried to enlist for the Boer War but was turned down because he was too young. He then took up market gardening and became interested in agriculture.

Early in 1903, Kingsley went to visit his grandmother in England and saw the big cities with their slums, workhouses and orphanages.[26] The contrast with the open air life and abundant sunshine of the Rhodesian High Veldt could not have been more stark. Kingsley was deeply moved by what he saw. He began to formulate his idea of a "Vision Splendid". He said, "I saw great Colleges of Agriculture (not workhouses) springing up in every man hungry corner of the Empire. I saw children shedding the bondage of bitter circumstances and stretching their legs and minds amid the thousand interests of the farm. I saw waste turned into providence, the waste of un-needed humanity converted to the husbandry of un-peopled acres."

Kingsley Fairbridge planned to bring children from Britain's city slums out into the vast open spaces of Rhodesia and Australia where they would gain a sense of independence and self worth, and the training and skills necessary for their future in the sparsely populated rural areas of the British Empire. To realize his vision, he decided that he ought to try for a Rhodes' Scholarship, which eventually he won. He was given a place at Exeter College, Oxford. There, on the 19th October 1909, he addressed a meeting of 49 fellow undergraduates at the Colonial Club, on the subject of Child Emigration, and that night Oxford saw the foundation of the 'Child Emigration Society', which was later to send orphaned children to the Fairbridge Farm School. Despite recurring attacks of malaria, contracted in the Rhodesian bush, Kingsley worked tirelessly to achieve his dream.

Sir Arthur Lawley was an enthusiastic supporter of Kingsley Fairbridge's idea of providing a new and more promising life for orphaned children from the slums of Britain's cities. During his retirement, Sir Arthur devoted much time and energy to the Fairbridge Organisation in Britain, which supported the Fairbridge Farm School at Pinjarra in Western Australia. He was for many years the Chairman of the Child Emigration Society which sponsored orphan children to go to the Fairbridge Farm School. After the First World War, there were thousands and thousands of children who had lost their fathers in the trenches and whose mothers had died from the dreadful pandemic of Spanish influenza in 1919 and 1920. Annie Lawley had herself been an orphan. Her mother died when she was three and her father when she was six years old. Hence she was an ardent supporter of Kingsley Fairbridge. Sir Arthur used his considerable influence and large circle of business, political, aristocratic and royal contacts to support the Fairbridge Farm School. He tirelessly raised money for the Child Emigration Society and gave vital support to the Kingsley Fairbridge Foundation. Lord Milner was also a very good friend to the Child Emigration Society. He encouraged his colleagues on the Rhodes Trust to help the project with the result that the Trust granted considerable sums to support the Farm School. This was particularly the case when Kingsley Fairbridge was in dire and desperate need.[27] Sir Arthur's son-in-law, Geoffrey Dawson was an enthusiastic supporter too. His daughter and Sir Arthur's grand daughter, Belinda Dawson, serving as a W.R.E.N. in 1941, escorted a group of children to the Farm School in Western Australia.[28]

Sir Arthur continues the story,

"During the year 1910 a small but influential Committee was formed to carry into effect the aims of the Child Emigration Society.... Among Fairbridge's undergraduate friends, A. E. K. Slingsby, A. L. Johnston, and J. C. Stollery were enthusiastic helpers – all of them afterwards being killed in the Great War. By the end of the year they had collected some £2,000. This sum seems hardly adequate to the launching of so ambitious an enterprise, but nevertheless it was resolved that a start should be made. One can only wonder at the confidence and courage which Fairbridge was called on to display at this and at every stage of his life's work, and which never failed him. Fortunately, he had by his side from earliest undergraduate days a comrade worthy to share his ideals, his fiançée Ruby Ethel Whitmore, who hand in hand with him faced the privations and hardships of a Pioneer Existence. The fact that neither of them was richly endowed with this world's goods did not daunt them. It did not seem to occur to either of them that because their circumstances were straitened their wedding should be postponed, and in December 1911 they were married. [29]

"Simultaneously their passages were booked on board a crowded emigrant ship sailing in March 1912, which reached Albany on April 15th after five weeks of inevitable discomfort, seeing that their fellow-passengers were for the most part rough emigrants and that the crowd on board was great. After a week in Albany they pushed on to Perth, where they made many good friends who, from the first, have maintained their interest in the Fairbridge Farm School, as it came to be called. Meanwhile messages from England were frequent and insistent, urging immediate preparation for the arrival of the first batch of children, as it was found impossible to go on collecting subscriptions unless a start could be made. There was no time to lose. Fairbridge and his wife were strangers in this vast territory of Western Australia – a land of magnificent distances – ignorant of its conditions, new to its ways. The cash at their disposal was but scanty. Transport was often difficult to secure. It was, however, absolutely necessary to find some suitable cottage capable of accommodating the party and to find it at once. A small farm of 160 acres was found not far from Pinjarra which had been the Receiving Home for lads from a Home in Liverpool, and this was purchased in spite of its deficiencies and disadvantages on the principle of 'Any port in a storm'.

"Time pressed. Much had to be done to get this four roomed shanty fit for occupation before the boys arrived from England. The purchase of the property included a certain amount of livestock and an orchard where pruning had been sadly neglected. A gardener and his wife should have been there to run the house and farm; but their arrival was delayed and the only help forthcoming was temporary at the hands of two or three young men who looked in to lend a hand for a time. While everything was in disorder Fairbridge went down with a very sharp attack of malaria, from which he recovered to welcome the arrival of a little daughter on the scene. Thanks to the skill of the doctor and the kindly ministrations of the proprietress of the hotel at Pinjarra, all went well with mother and child, and soon Fairbridge himself threw off all traces of malaria. The orchard was pruned; a vegetable garden was laid out. A young Irishman came in to lend a hand and stayed for six months, rendering invaluable aid. As summer advanced the heat grew more intense, but nevertheless preparations had to be made to house the children whose advent was imminent. By January it had been found possible to run up some temporary shelters, half a dozen cotton tents and a

hessian roof which formed the dining-room. When these preparations were completed, Fairbridge went down to Fremantle to meet the first little party of orphans.

"These early days were never free from anxiety and worry. The newcomers rejected country fare such as fresh vegetables and fruit: they could not drink milk and they clamoured for meat and potatoes, which latter were not at first available. Another great trouble arose in that the Government refused to help in the matter of education. This meant that those twelve little boys aged from seven to twelve years had to be found some employment to fill in the long summer days. The elder boys soon learnt the simpler farm operations, also to help with the kitchen and laundry work. But it is not easy to get small children to do monotonous work with any regularity. The hard daily grind of keeping these little chaps to their work, encouraging them, infusing everything with cheerfulness and interest, all fell on Fairbridge's shoulders. It was of no use to tell the children to play when work was finished. They did not know how to play, and quarrelling was rife, but soon a new tone became evident, and a complete change in the bearing and the manners of all the boys. Throughout the summer Fairbridge was constantly down with malaria, and during an attack the boys would often carry his bed down to the orchard, and there he would lie in the shade of a great apricot tree reading to the boys and explaining what he read, oblivious of the fever which racked his limbs. With the end of summer came the completion of a new building into which a move was made, and the comfort of the inmates was vastly increased.

"In June 1913 the second party of 22 boys was due to arrive. In anticipation of their coming Fairbridge was luckily able to employ a builder to put up two sleeping sheds, open to the air, as dormitories for the party, while he himself, although not versed in carpentry, made from the roughest of material beds for the 22 boys as well as tables and forms for the dining-room. In a word he practically furnished the Home. Moreover, with help from Mr. Austin, he painted and oiled all the buildings inside and out, distempered the walls, and painted the roofs.

"Great difficulties were experienced in providing education for 30 odd children, but eventually these difficulties were overcome and the new boys settled down quickly and happily. All was going well when the outbreak of war threatened the undertaking with total collapse. The scheme had only been carried to its present state by constant labour and strenuous endeavour. At times the struggle had seemed desperate and the undertaking impossible of achievement. Remote though it was, war brought in its train conditions which formed a deadly menace to all that had been achieved hitherto. Of the few male members of the Staff, which never numbered more than two at any one time, all who could pass the medical test went away to the War. Ultimately three of them – Allen, Hartfield, and Alec Bond – gave up their lives for their country. Fairbridge's malaria was responsible for his rejection and he remained to run the Farm School. But for him the School must inevitably have broken up, and the experiment would have been written down as a failure.

"The members of the Oxford Committee were dispersed on war work of various descriptions and had little time to devote to Child Emigration. Subscriptions fell off, and early in the year the Oxford Committee telegraphed instructions to Fairbridge to close down. He, however, backed by the Perth Committee, undertook to carry on if £400 could be sent from England. A promise to that effect

*was forthcoming, and thanks for the devoted labour of Miss Dorothy Lane Poole,
who during the whole four years of the War carried on the work almost single
handed, the Committee were able to keep their promise, and so the work went on;
but if the struggle had been serious before it now became almost desperate.... At
one time closure seemed inevitable, but Fairbridge was able to make a bargain
with the State Authorities that, if they would make a weekly grant of 4s per head,
he would keep the School going. So the struggle went on. Economy in every
department was the order of the day; repairs were not done; renewals were not
made, and debts were increasing.*

Figure 246: Kingsley Fairbridge at Pinjarra Farm School.

*"During these difficult times Fairbridge had the offer of more than one attractive,
well-paid billet, but his devotion to his ideal and his loyalty to the School led him
to resist each one however advantageous it might appear. It was by his self-
surrender and sacrifice that the Farm School was enabled to survive those perilous
days; but Peace came at last, and with it fresh resolve and determination in the
mind of the Founder to carry his scheme to a successful issue. He was greatly
encouraged in this direction by the fact that of the 34 lads, brought out before*

1914, every one had made good and was qualified to go on to the land familiar with the rudiments of farming and the conditions of life in Australia. Still more was he encouraged by the staunch and loyal help-meet who, through all the seven years and more of stress and strain of the Old Farm bore, as only a brave and unselfish woman can, the whole brunt of domestic administration, often single-handed, but ever with courage undaunted and never-failing care for others, braving the hardships of a pioneer. There are but few who realize how greatly Mrs. Ruby Fairbridge contributed by her personal influence and tact to the successful launching of this remarkable enterprise!

"When the War came to an end, the finances of each European Power were in a deplorable state. The enormous losses in every theatre of war seemed to render hopeless any attempt to raise a substantial sum of money for the scheme that Fairbridge had in mind. Nevertheless, he made his plans to visit England, though before sailing he had much to do. He had to draw up a programme of meetings in England and Scotland. He had to secure definitely the grant of 5 shillings per head per week from the State Government of Western Australia for a School of 200 boys and girls. He had to make provision for the carrying on of the School in his absence. The coffers were depleted; the Staff were reduced to two. The boys were by now sufficiently advanced to go out into the world and command a wage of say 15 shillings to £1 a week. At the School they could not hope to receive more than 5 shillings a week. To ask them to remain was to ask them to give up a substantial sum, but every boy volunteered to stay and keep the School going, no matter what the monetary loss to each one might be. On arrival in England, Fairbridge received an invitation to speak before the Overseas Settlement Committee, at whose hands he received great encouragement. He spent eight months in England, and by the time that he again set sail for Western Australia he had got together a sum of £27,000. During that time the Central Office of the Child Emigration Society was transferred from Oxford to London.

"Experience had shown that there were many disadvantages attaching to the small farm which Fairbridge had bought, and it was resolved to sell it and start afresh on a more suitable site of 3,200 acres which was offered on very reasonable terms. It seemed ideal for the purpose, and at once Fairbridge set to work to build on his carefully worked out plans. A more difficult time in which to build could not have been found. Prices of material and labour went soaring upwards. No contractor would quote anything like a reasonable figure, and Fairbridge had to become his own buyer and clerk of the works. Delays were incessant, and for the moment it was necessary to keep the old farm going as a half-way house between London and the new Pinjarra. In 1921, boys and girls began to arrive from England and had to be housed in the old farm, and only moved into the new farm as cottage by cottage was built and furnished. For a time Fairbridge and some of his staff were in a temporary camp. Twice at this time he had to go across to Melbourne in an endeavour to obtain a grant from the Commonwealth Government similar to that provided by the State Government. In June 1922 he got word that his request was granted. The Government of Australia agreed to contribute £10,000 over five years to the scheme and with this in his pocket he hurried back to England hoping to secure a similar grant from the British Government. It was during this journey that his illness first began to manifest itself. His sufferings were acute; but in spite of intense physical pain he got through an immense amount of work, and his mission was entirely successful." [30]

On Wednesday 23rd November 1922, Sir Arthur Lawley presided at a luncheon of the Child Emigration Society at the Cannon Street Hotel at which the principal guests were the Duke of Devonshire and Mr Leo Amery, the First Lord of the Admiralty. A letter from the office of the Prince of Wales was read which said,

"The Prince of Wales was much interested to learn of the excellent work to which the members of the Child Emigration Society have put their hand, and trusts that you may be successful in your appeal for funds to aid you in the objects which your society has in view.

"The fact that the Government of Australia should be subsidizing the Farm School in Western Australia is in His Royal Highness's opinion, abundant proof of their satisfaction with the way it is being conducted."

Kingsley Fairbridge explained the nature of the work of the society that was being carried on at the School in Western Australia, and said that the Commonwealth and State Governments had offered them ten shillings per child per week for up to 100 children in the first year, and 200 children in the subsequent four years.

Sir Arthur Lawley, the Duke of Devonshire and Leo Amery all spoke in support of Kingsley Fairbridge. [31]

On Thursday 22nd March 1923, Sir Arthur Lawley addressed at a further meeting in Mayfair. He explained to a distinguished audience that the Child Emigration Society proposed to erect ten more cottages at the Fairbridge Farm School with the object of accommodating 120 additional boys and girls. Mr Ormsby Gore, Under Secretary of State for the Colonies, said he was quite sure that the Overseas Settlement Committee would continue its support. The Government felt that the children would be well cared for, well trained and given a real start in life with the prospect that they would become good citizens of the Empire.

On Thursday November 8th 1923, the Prince of Wales was the chief guest at a luncheon given at the Cannon Street Hotel by the Child Emigration Society. Sir Arthur Lawley presided. The Australian Prime Minister, Mr S.M. Bruce, the Duke of Marlborough, the Duke of Devonshire, Lord Milner and Mr J. J. Astor were also there. One hundred boys and girls who were about to sail to Australia were there too. They joined together to sing "God bless the Prince of Wales".

In his speech, the Prince of Wales said:

"I would like to say a word of congratulation to Mr. Fairbridge, the founder of the Society. I would like to congratulate him on what he has achieved in the last fourteen years. He is a South African. He was at Oxford, my old university, as a Rhodes Scholar. Both South Africa and his old university may well be proud of him; so would, if he were still living, Cecil Rhodes be proud of him for the idea that Mr. Fairbridge conceived at Oxford and has carried out in Australia is most certainly after Cecil Rhodes's heart. There are two points in connection with the Fairbridge Farm School, Western Australia. First of all the movement begins at the right end. It transplants not the adult but the child, and its transplants the child straight away from the worst to the best of surroundings.... My experience is that the younger the people who go out overseas are, the easier it is for them to shake down to the new life and to the new conditions. I do not think until you have actually...travelled in the Empire that you can realize how very different these lives and these conditions are from what they are in the old country.... From the worst to the best surroundings.... I have had an opportunity of going to Western

Australia myself, and I know that they are the best surroundings…. From the very day that the girls and boys step onto Australian soil at the age of from eight to ten they are trained on the farm itself. They are given a sensible education, both mental and physical, to fit them for the life they are going to lead later on. The great point is that when their education is finished they are not flung out to sink or swim. Closest possible touch is kept with them, and there is a wise system of after care exercised…. There is a letter from a boy who was brought up on the farm, a very striking proof of how well the system is working…. Another strong proof of the sound basis that it is on is found in the fact that the undertaking is very strongly backed by the Imperial Government and by both the Federal and State Governments of Australia…. I hope that in the years to come the Society will be able to extend its efforts to all our Dominions. All that I can now do is tell Mr Bruce as Prime Minister of Australia what we think of the Society over here in the Old World, and we think so highly of it that we mean to do everything we can to make it a permanent and ever growing success. That is the object of our meeting today. The Society wants to save more and more children. The Society wants £5,500, and surely the hundred boys and girls we have here today with us in the room who have been singing to us are a very eloquent appeal. £5,500 is not really such a very big sum when you come to think of the purpose it will serve. That sum will help our children. It will help the Empire, and it will help Australia."

With such strong support in England, Kingsley Fairbridge who had returned to Pinjarra in January 1923, at long last found himself comfortably bestowed in a well-built house of his own with his wife and four children, after years of discomfort in shared accommodation. Despite his sufferings, which increased day by day, Kingsley Fairbridge kept steadily before him the ideal which was the mainspring of his life.

"During his last years he saw the strengthening of the Society by the active and liberal co-operation of Dr. Barnardo's, from whom the Farm School received one hundred children in February 1924, doubling the school's numbers in a single night. Their advent necessitated the carrying out of an extensive building programme, which provided ample accommodation for 200 children as well as that of the Staff. In due course there would be 207 children at the school and forty substantial buildings, which were erected and furnished at a cost of over £23,000. In addition over £10,000 was spent on the development of the land. Of this total sum at least £30,000 was found by the Child Emigration Society in Great Britain. It was his remarkable achievement that before his tragic and untimely death, Kingsley Fairbridge should see the fulfilment of his heart's desire and a Farm School firmly established with its aim – the development of Character, Health, and Ability."

These were the three main planks of Kingsley Fairbridge's platform. He wanted to bring up the children as capable, clean-minded, Christian men and women and good Australian citizens. To help with this task he had a strong local Committee in Western Australia, including several of the leading citizens of Perth, whose assistance to and active co-operation with the London Committee were simply invaluable. At home he had the sympathy and generous support of the Overseas Settlement Department of the Dominions Office. The London Committee had but one resolve and that was to uphold through dark days and fair the ideals of the Farms School's founder, Kingsley Fairbridge." [32]

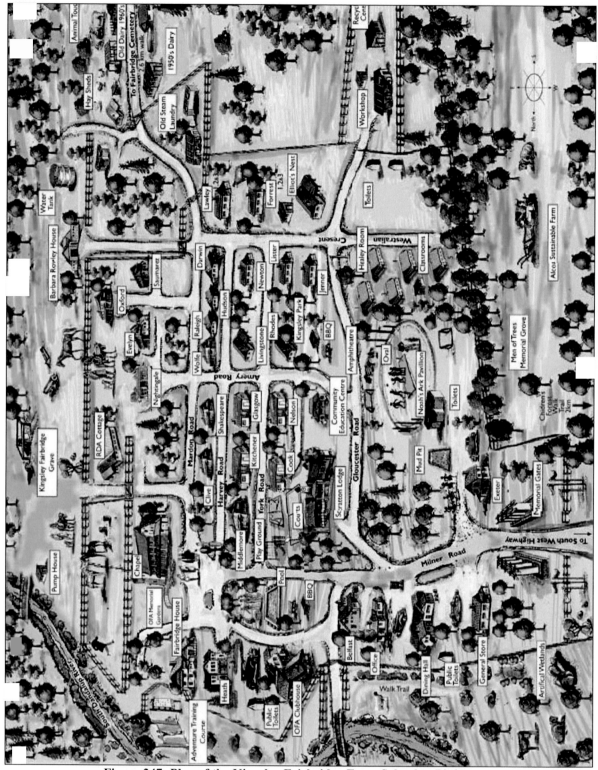

Figure 247: Plan of the Kingsley Fairbridge Farm School at Pinjarra.

Kingsley Fairbridge died on the 19th of July, 1924, in Perth, Western Australia, at the age of thirty-nine from a mixture of hard work, re-occurring bouts of malaria and what is thought today to have been cancer of the hip. He was sadly missed by Ruby, their four children, and their extended family – the children of Fairbridge.[33] Sir Arthur Lawley, who had lost his own son at the age of 22, now, as Chairman of the Child Emigration Society, devoted himself almost single-handedly to maintaining and developing the work in England.

On November 25th 1924, following the death of Kingsley Fairbridge, Sir Arthur Lawley presided at a luncheon given for the Child Emigration Society at the Canon Street Hotel. Prince Henry was the guest of honour and the Secretary of State for the Colonies, Leo Amery, a former Colonial Secretary, J. H. Thomas, and Mrs Ruby Fairbridge were also present. Sir Arthur, as Chairman of the Child Emigration Society, gave the main address. Prince Henry in his speech spoke in fulsome praise of the work of the Society. Both spoke in appreciation of the life and work of the late Kingsley Fairbridge and in support of his widow, Ruby Fairbridge. [34]

On Sunday 30th January 1927, Sir Arthur Lawley made a Radio Broadcast on London Call 2LO. This was followed by another broadcast on March 11th entitled "Keep it in the family." Both were an appeal for donations to the Child Emigration Society, which in association with the National Children's Home and Orphanage and Dr. Barnado's was becoming a significant charity for orphaned children.[35]

On Thursday May 19th 1927, the Duke and Duchess of York visited the Fairbridge Farm School at Pinjarra. They were on a tour of Australia and New Zealand and on May 9th had opened the new Australian Federal Parliament in Canberra. This was the same day that the First Federal Parliament had been opened in 1901. Speaking later at a Child Emigration Society lunch on March 28th 1928, the Duke spoke of their impressions of the Fairbridge Farm School. He said:

"I have been to Western Australia, and during my time there I was able to spend a most interesting and instructive day at the Fairbridge Farm. When the Duchess and I visited the school there were 90 boys and girls there, and never have I seen such a healthy and happy group of children. We watched them doing folk dances, and the boys carried out some exercises in physical training which they had practised for our visit. It was the only arranged part of the day, and after that we went over to the houses in which the children lived. Each house, which was the home of ten children, was looked after by a mother. We were taken round the farm by the farm superintendent, a man who understood exactly what was wanted and who was loved and respected by the children.... We were made to feel that this place was a real home to the children, that it was theirs and that they were really proud of it. I heard of one farmer who had been trained on the farm and when he got a holiday he went back to the school because he felt it was his home. Could you have a better advertisement for any school?"

On July 29th 1927, Sir Arthur and Lady Lawley embarked on the Walmer Castle to sail to Cape Town at the beginning of a six month tour of South Africa, the East Indies and Australia.[36] They returned home towards the end of January 1928. [37]

During their stay in Western Australia in September 1927,[38] Sir Arthur and Lady Lawley visited the Fairbridge Farm School at Pinjarra. Looking back later, they had the impression of a garden city. Row upon row of cottages seemed to mark the springing up of a country township. The capacity of each cottage was from 12 to 14 children, tended by a mother who looked after her flock. Each cottage was a home; there was no indication of an institution anywhere. They visited every cottage, and it was impossible not to feel the happy atmosphere which pervaded everywhere in that community. The physical development of the children was marvellous, and they had never seen a happier crowd. One of the Farm School's cottages was named the Lawley Cottage after Sir Arthur and Lady Lawley. The schooling and training given by the State school teachers struck the Sir Arthur as being sympathetic with the Fairbridge ideals. Thomas Sedgwick, who spent a whole day visiting the Farm

School in 1927, wrote in support of the venture, "The outstanding impression of my short visit was the happy and healthy appearance of the children and the absence of any institutional character." [39]

Figure 248: The Church, designed by Sir Herbert E. Baker at Kingsley Fairbridge Farm School, Pinjarra, Western Australia.

Sir Arthur and Lady Lawley took the train across the Nullabor Plain to Adelaide and then travelled on to Melbourne. During their visit to the new Federal Capital of Canberra, they were influential in gaining further support for the Farm School from the Federal Australian government and the Western Australian government. In December 1927, as a result of discussions with Sir Arthur Lawley, it was decided to increase the accommodation at the Farm School to take 300 children necessitating the expenditure of about £10,700 by the Federal Government. The zeal, energy and sympathy of the Perth Committee had helped enormously in achieving such results. The members of the Perth Committee completely agreed with the decision to increase the numbers at Pinjarra from 200 to 300. Mr Thomas Wall had promised £3000 for the building of a church and Sir Herbert Baker, an old friend of Sir Arthur, had agreed to be its architect.[40] In 1929, Sir Arthur Lawley resigned as Chairman of the Child Emigration Society because of ill health and Admiral Sir William Goodenough, a naval hero of the First World War, became the new Chairman. Sir Arthur and Lady Lawley's active support for the Fairbridge Schools continued for the rest of their lives.

In June 1931, one year before he died, Sir Arthur wrote a letter from Freiburg in Germany to his daughter Cecilia, which she read to the Annual Meeting of the Child Emigration Society. She said she had always taken the keenest interest in the

Fairbridge Farm School, both because of her father's association with the Society and because she was a child in Western Australia and retained a great love for the country. In his letter Sir Arthur said he was pleased to receive regular news of the Society and rejoiced to know that in spite of the general world depression they had been able to keep their heads above water due to the generosity of their friends and to the careful and harmonious working of the two committees in London and Perth. He hoped that this happy condition would long continue. [41]

On July 7th 1939, a party of boys and girls sailed for Australia on board the Strathnaver to go to the Kingsley Fairbridge Farm School. Before they left Annie Lawley, now Lady Wenlock, journeyed to London to meet them all at the Royal Empire Society. She wished them a safe journey and gave a present to each and every child. [42]

Figure 249: A special issue postage stamp commemorating Kingsley Fairbridge.

Although Kingsley Fairbridge died tragically young, his vision lived on and by 1939 over a thousand children had received their education at the Fairbridge Farm School. Fairbridge Farm schools were also established in other lands. Fairbridge's first project in Canada failed, even though the government of Newfoundland had agreed to give him the land he required. However, in 1924, his followers started working on a plan for a farm in British Columbia. Located at Duncan, BC, on Vancouver Island, the farm consisted of about 1,000 acres. It was situated about 40 miles north of Victoria, BC, the provincial capital. In 1935 the *Prince of Wales Fairbridge Farm School* was opened and in September of that year the first children arrived. The children came from Tyneside, Birmingham and London. The plan was to send children from 6 to 16 years of age. The farm school was designed for about 150 children. The children lived in cottages, each housing about 12 children. The children received a basic education and were trained in modern farming practices. The farm school continued to educate immigrant orphans until 1948 when it closed.

After the Second World War, in 1946, a Kingsley Fairbridge Memorial College was established in Bulawayo, Southern Rhodesia. The first party of eighteen Fairbridge boys sailed from Southampton on board the Caernarvon Castle on 18th November 1946. They disembarked at Cape Town, South Africa, on the 4th December to depart thence on the long train journey to Bulawayo. There they received their primary education at the Fairbridge School with secondary education being provided at Milton High School. William Milton was the Administrator of Mashonaland in Rhodesia at the time when Captain Arthur Lawley was the Administrator of Matabeleland.[43]

Sir Arthur Lawley introduced his Epilogue to Kingsley Fairbridge's autobiography with these words:

"The story which Kingsley Fairbridge has had to tell is one of conflict with the forces of nature from the very beginning to the end of his all too short life. Before his childhood days were over he was brought face to face with danger and difficulty, and emerged from each ordeal with fresh courage and nobility of soul. He was a Rhodes Scholar whose early years were spent in regions remote from civilization, an undergraduate cherishing a purpose which one day or another should contribute to the solution of a great Imperial Problem, and that is how to combine the work of Child Rescue with that of Emigration. He emerged to manhood an idealist who combined his idealism with marvellous fertility of resource.

"Every year tens of thousands of boys and girls seek admission to the labour market only to be told that there is no need of them, and they are flung back on to one or other of the great human scrap-heaps which lie at the gates of every one of our great cities – derelict little vessels on the Ocean of Life, children doomed to a blind alley existence and the squalor of the slums. His plan was simple enough. It was to take some at least of these little people before they were contaminated by their evil surroundings and to carry them off to a land of sunshine, there to be trained to become strong, sturdy, and efficient citizens able to play their part in developing the vast resources of Australia – a land where the prizes of life are open to all. He has told us how that scheme became all absorbing – something to live for, to work for, and, as he showed, to die for." [44]

After the Second World War, improved social conditions made child emigration less sustainable and in due course the movement drew to a close. There was considerable criticism of child emigration followed by Parliamentary Enquiries in Britain in 1998 and in Australia in 1999. While some of the criticisms were valid, the enquiries cast a shadow over the work of Kingsley Fairbridge, which was unfair and not deserved. The Fairbridge Farm School at Pinjarra was largely exonerated by these enquiries and was found innocent of the abuses witnessed in other establishments. Kingsley and Ruby Fairbridge were visionaries who sought not to victimize children but to rescue them and give them a bright new future.

The Parliamentary Enquiry in the United Kingdom was concerned mainly with the period after the Second World War and was triggered off by the fiftieth anniversary of the 1948 Children's Act of Clement Atlee's post-war Labour Government. We should not judge the past with the values of the present. Our society with its high divorce rates and materialistic consumerism should reflect carefully before casting aspersions on the children's charities of previous generations. Today Fairbridge continues its charitable work with young people – no longer in farm schools but in other endeavours. Indeed Fairbridge has contributed to the programme of activities for young people at Tyntesfield.

The Farm School at Pinjarra closed in 1981. In 1983 the land was purchased by ALCOA Australia Ltd., but 28 hectares were leased back to Fairbridge Incorporated. The Farm School has become a centre for Youth Activities, the Old Fairbridgian

Society, Musical and Recreational Events. In 1932 and 1933, a Clubhouse had been erected for Old Fairbridgians. Now Fairbridge Western Australia Incorporated plans to raise 6.25 million Australian dollars to preserve and enhance the Farm School at Pinjarra. Examining the plan of the site (figure 247) gives an idea of the present scope of the venture. Now there is also a Kingsley Fairbridge Child Development Unit at the Women's and Children's Hospital in Adelaide, South Australia. The present patron of Fairbridge is the Governor of Western Australia.[45]

Figure 250: George Abraham Gibbs, 1923.

Westminster Wedding

On July 20th 1927, Sir Arthur and Lady Lawley's eldest daughter, Ursula Mary, married George Abraham Gibbs. George was the eldest son of Antony and Janet Gibbs of Tyntesfield. He served with the North Somerset Yeomanry as a Captain in the Boer War. He was in the Imperial Yeomanry Bodyguard for Lord Roberts, the Commander in Chief in South Africa, during the campaign from Bloemfontein to Pretoria in May and June 1900.

Figure 251: Janet Merivale Gibbs with her son George Abraham painted by James Archer in 1875.

In November 1901, George married Victoria de Burgh Long, who was known as Via. In the winter of 1902 to 1903, they visited Egypt and travelled by rail to Khartoum in the Sudan. In the winter of 1904 to 1905, George and Via spent five months in India where they travelled extensively. They toured the Madras Presidency and visited the major towns and historical sites of the south. They twice went on holiday to Canada travelling by train from New York in 1911 and Quebec in 1912.

They journeyed across Canada through the Rocky Mountains to Vancouver.[46] In Alberta, Via shot a bison and the trophy still hangs in the billiard room at Tyntesfield.[47] Via bore her husband two sons, George Antony, who was born and died on the 5th September 1911, and Antony Eustace, who was born on the 24th September and died on the 29th November 1916. On the 17th September 1913, she had a daughter Doreen, who celebrated her 90th birthday at Tyntesfield in 2003. Tragically Victoria Gibbs died on 29th March 1920 in the Spanish flu pandemic after the First World War. She had been awarded a C.B.E. for her services to the Red Cross during that War.

As a Lieutenant-Colonel in the First World War, George Abraham commanded the Second Regiment of the North Somerset Yeomanry from 1914 to 1916. He was acting Brigadier-General, commanding his Regiment's Brigade at Ipswich from October 1916 until 1917. Between 1906 and 1927, he was Conservative Member of Parliament for Bristol West. In 1911 he became the Deputy Lieutenant for the County of Somerset. As a Freemason, he was Permanent Grand Master for the Province of Bristol from 1908 to 1931. From 1917 to 1919 he served as Parliamentary Secretary to his father-in-law, Walter H. Long, Secretary of State to the Colonies. He was a Conservative Whip in the House of Commons from 1917 to 1928, served as the Treasurer to the King's Household from 1921 to 1928, and became a Privy Councillor in 1923. It was during his service for the Royal Household, after many years as a widower that he met and fell in love with the Hon. Ursula Lawley, who was Maid of Honour to Queen Mary.[48] They became engaged to be married.

The Times Report of their wedding (minus the guest list) is as follows:

COLONEL GEORGE GIBBS, M.P., AND THE HON. URSULA LAWLEY

The King and Queen were present at St Margaret's, Westminster yesterday, at the marriage of Colonel the Right Honourable George Gibbs, M.P., Treasurer of his Majesty's Household, and the Hon. Ursula Mary Lawley, till recently Maid of Honour to the Queen, eldest daughter of the Hon. Sir Arthur Lawley, C.G.S.I., G.C.I.E., K.C.M.G. and the Right Hon. Lady Lawley of 9, Seymour Street. Their Majesties drove to the vestry entrance, where they were received by Canon Carnegie, and left the church by the great West door at the conclusion of the service with Sir Arthur and Lady Lawley. The Queen wore a dress of pearl grey silk romaine with deep grey silk fringes, with a coat of georgette trimmed with pleated ribbon medallions and a hat of folded silver tissue.

The Rev. Lord Algernon Wenlock (uncle of the bride) and the Rev. Stafford Crawley (brother-in-law of the bridegroom) officiated, and the bride was given away by her father. She wore a picture gown of rich gold brocade with long Venetian sleeves and a long full skirt with a court train of the same brocade draped with a rare old lace shawl, the gift of Mary Duchess of Hamilton. A veil of parchment-tinted silk tulle was arranged beneath a coronet of fine gold lace edged with orange-blossom, and she carried a sheaf of Madonna lilies. There were two pages – Master Michael Dawson and Master Paul Gore – who wore picture suits of gold tissue with shot green silk sashes and blue satin shoes; and six child bridesmaids – Miss Doreen and Miss Diana Gibbs (daughter and niece of the bridegroom), Miss Betty and Miss Carol Hay (cousins of the bride), Miss Belinda Dawson (niece of the bride), and Miss Ursula Gore (god-daughter of the bride). They wore dresses of shot green and gold silk taffeta, with full skirts in petals edged with gold net, and short sleeves of silk and net; they had wreaths of delphiniums, and each carried a sheaf of deep blue delphiniums to match the blue satin shoes.

Major Hubert Gibbs, brother of the bridegroom, was the best man, and a reception was afterwards held by the Hon. Lady Lawley at Admiralty House. The bride and groom left afterwards for a honeymoon abroad, the Hon. Mrs George Gibbs wearing a dress of flowered crepe-de-Chine, with a blue silk coat lined and faced with floral silk.[49]

Figure 252: Honiton Lace worn by Lady Lawley and her daughter Ursula Mary.

Ursula wore the veil of parchment-tinted silk tulle, which her grandmother, Mary Bache McEvers, wore at her wedding to Sir Edward Cunard in 1849. It was then worn by each of Mary Lady Cunard's daughters and grand daughters at their weddings. Annie Cunard wore the Honiton lace, given to her by Uncle Stephen, when she married Arthur Lawley. Uncle Stephen was the Honourable Reverend Stephen Willoughby Lawley (1823–1905). He graduated from Balliol College Oxford in 1841, and was the Rector of St Helen's Church, Escrick from 1848 to 1868. In 1868, he became a scholar of All Souls College Oxford and had connections with the Reverend Benjamin Jowett M.A., who was the Regius Professor of Greek in the University of Oxford, a Doctor in Theology of the University of Leyden and Master of Balliol College.[50] Under Jowett, Balliol played a prominent part in the education and training of officers for the Indian Civil Service. The Reverend Lord Algernon Lawley and Sir Arthur Lawley were Stephen Lawley's nephews. The tulle veil and the Honiton lace worn by Ursula are now kept at Tyntesfield.

In January 1928, George Abraham Gibbs retired and was raised to the peerage in recognition of his services. He became Baron Wraxall of Clyst St George. On the 16th May 1928, Ursula's first baby was born in the Wraxall's home at 22, Belgrave

Square, London. On Wednesday 26th June, the baby was christened George Richard Lawley Gibbs in memory of Richard, Sir Arthur and Lady Lawley's late son, and Ursula and Cecilia's late brother.[51] The christening took place at St Margaret's Westminster and Queen Mary was godmother. The other god parents were William Clive Bridgeman, the First Lord of the Admiralty, Colonel John Evelyn Gibbs and Mrs Geoffrey Dawson.[52] On Friday July 8th, the Duke and Duchess of York arrived at Tyntesfield to visit the family and see the new baby, who was to become the Second Lord Wraxall.[53] On the 3rd July 1929, a second son, Eustace Hubert Beilby Gibbs was born. He is now the Third Lord Wraxall.

Tragically on the 28th October 1931, George Abraham Gibbs, the First Lord Wraxall, died from an attack of pneumonia associated with cancer of the throat. He left his widow with two young boys to bring up and Tyntesfield and the family home at 81 Eaton Square in London's Belgravia to manage. Ursula rose to this challenge magnificently.[54]

A Passage to India

In the winter of 1928 to 1929, Sir Arthur and Lady Lawley's daughter, Cecilia, and her husband Geoffrey Dawson visited India. On October 30th 1925, Geoffrey's old friend, the Honourable Edward Wood, Lord Irwin, had been appointed Viceroy of India. On December 13th 1928, Geoffrey and Cecilia set sail for India from Toulon in the Orsova, a ship of the Orient Line.[55] They visited Ceylon where highlights were the Temple of the Tooth at Kandy and the Buddhist antiquities at Dambulla and Anuradhapura. Cecilia had first seen Ceylon with her mother in 1901, when Lady Lawley and her children spent a couple of days there en route to Australia. Geoffrey and Cecilia then went on to the Madras Presidency. "At Trichinopoly they were greeted everywhere with garlands, salaaming elephants and native bands".[56] They journeyed on to Madras where Mr A.Y.G. Campbell met them. He had been Sir Arthur Lawley's Private Secretary for over five years. They stayed at the Governor's Country Estate at Guindy. From Madras they journeyed on to Ooty where the train took them "above the clouds into blue hills with red foliage, monkeys chattering and amazing views of the plains." They toured round the town, drove around the Lake and up into the surrounding hills. The following day they explored Government House and its gardens, kennels and stables, and then went on to the beautiful churchyard of St Stephen's where Cecilia planted bulbs beside her brother, Richard's grave (See Appendix 3, Figure 261, page 354).

They were invited to Mysore by Sir Arthur Lawley's old friend, the Maharajah, and the Yuvaraja Mirza an Dervan who greeted them on their arrival on January 13th. The next day they were taken for a ride before breakfast by the Yuvaraja. Later they went to see the Race Course, the Fort and the Tombs of Tippo and Hyder Ali. That evening they visited the old Maharani and the Yuvaraja's children. At six they were received by His Highness in his Summer Palace and had half an hour's talk after which he illuminated the Palace especially for them. They drove up the hill to see it before dinner with the Yuvaraja. The following day they went for a misty morning canter with the Yuvaraja and then inspected all his horses and carriages – a very remarkable collection – before going on to visit the Zoo where tigers roam in a garden and climb trees. They were then shown the Technical Institute and the State Library. At 3.30 in the afternoon, they said farewell to the Yuvaraja and travelled on to Bhadravali, the Gereoppha Falls and the Mysore Jungle where they went hunting and their party shot a panther and a tiger. Returning to Madras, the Dawsons were once more the guests of the Governor and his wife, Lord and Lady Goschen, at Guindy. Thence they went on to Calcutta where a Garden Party was given in their honour. The Simon Commission was considering the future of India at this stage and Sir John Simon, another of Geoffrey's friends, was in Calcutta for discussions. They dined together at Government House and Geoffrey and Sir John Simon had long talks. Thence the Dawsons journeyed on to Benares, to Lucknow where Lord Irwin opened the Assembly, and to Agra to see the Taj Mahal. Their travels then took them to Delhi where they stayed for ten days as guests of the Viceroy. Geoffrey and Edward (Lord Irwin) had extensive and detailed discussions on political and other matters. On the 16th February, they left Delhi and travelled north-west to Lahore, Peshawar and the Khyber Pass visiting Malakand and Chaklara before retracing their steps back to Delhi where they arrived on February 27th. On March 3rd they left Delhi and visited the Amber Fort, Jaipur, Udaipur, Chittor, Indore, Dhar and Mandu on their way to Bombay to board the S.S. Rawalpindi on March 17th for their journey home. [57]

After serving his term as India's Viceroy, Lord Irwin became Lord Halifax and in due course Britain's Foreign Secretary under Neville Chamberlain, and then Britain's Ambassador to the United States during the Second World War.

Sir Arthur and Lady Lawley were fascinated to hear about the progress in India from their daughter and son-in-law. They were pleased that Dominion Status for India and more democratic representation in domestic affairs were being considered. Above all they were delighted to have news of old haunts and old friends from their years serving the Raj.

---

[1] The Times. Tuesday November 26th 1918. Page 3. Column A.

[2] The Pedigree of the Family Gibbs. Fourth Edition by Rachel Gibbs. 1981. Kingprint Limited. Richmond. Surrey.

[3] The Times. Monday December 9th 1918. Page 5. Column A.

[4] The Times. Saturday February 22nd 1919. Page 9. Column A,
The Times. Monday 24th February 1919. Page 8. Column C.

[5] Champions of Charity: War and the Rise of the Red Cross by John F. Hutchinson. Westview Press. (1997) ISBN: 0813333679

[6] The Times. Friday May 16th 1919. Page 11. Column E.
The Times. Thursday 29th May 1919. Page 8. Column A.

[7] The Times. Wednesday July 21st 1920. Page 4. Column E.
The Times. Friday July 23rd 1920. Page 22, Column E.

[8] HMRS Photo catalogue. HMRS 2002.

[9] Geoffrey Dawson and Our Times. Evelyn Wrench. Hutchinson. London. 1955. Pages 195 to 199.

[10] The Times. 15th June 1919

[11] Friday 4th July 1919. Page 4. Column A.

[12] The Times. Friday June 16th 1916. Page 5. Column B.

[13] Re Times Obituary for Lord Wenlock: letter from Major General Sir Frederick Maurice, President of the British Legion. Thursday 16th June 1932.
The Official History of the British Legion by Graham Wootton. MacDonald and Evans. London. 1956.
The Times. Friday January 30th 1919. Page 12. Column F.

[14] The Times. Monday June 27th 1921. Page 14. Column C.

[15] Pharos. Number 41. December 1922. Dover Grammar School.

[16] The Times. Tuesday 28th June 1921. Page 8. Column B.
The Times. Thursday 4th August 1921. Page 11. Column B.
The Times. Tuesday 16th August 1921. Page 8. Column F.
The Times. Wednesday 17th August 1921. Page 8. Column C.
The Times. Monday 22nd August 1921. Page 7. Column D.

[17] The Times. Tuesday January 31st 1922. Page 15. Column C.

[18] The Times. Friday November 9th 1923. Page 9. Column A.

[19] The Times. Saturday November 29th 1924. Page 15. Column A.
[20] The Times. Friday June 12th 1925. Page 23. Column A.
[21] Lord Wraxall's photo album of the South American visit.
[22] Lord Wraxall's photo album of the South American visit and Lady Lawley's water colour of an Inca woman near Lake Titicaca.
      The Times. Monday March 30th 1925. Page 17. Column B.
[23] The Times. Monday 18th May 1925. Page 17. Column D.
[24] The Milner Papers. Bodleian Library Oxford. Dep. 322. Fol. 337/40.
[25] The Times. Wednesday 4th November 1925. Page 16. Column E.
      The Times. Saturday 7th November 1925. Page 15. Column C.
[26] Australian Dictionary of Biography. Percival Serle. Angus and Robertson. 1949.
[27] The Times. 26th May 1925. Page 13. Column A.
[28] Geoffrey Dawson and Our Times. Evelyn Wrench. Hutchinson. London. 1955. Page 447.
[29] 1820 Settlers.com
[30] Epilogue by Sir Arthur Lawley to the Autobiography of Kingsley Fairbridge. Humphrey Milford. London. 1927
[31] The Times. Thursday November 23rd 1922. Page 9. Column D.
[32] Epilogue by Sir Arthur Lawley from Fairbridge Kingsley Olgivie. The Autobiography of Kingsley Fairbridge. Humphrey Milford. London. 1927
[33] World Wide Web Fairbridge.asn.au
      The Founding of Fairbridge. Kingsley Fairbridge's Vision Splendid. www. Kingsley's vision.htm Pinjarra.
      The Building of a Farm School. Ruby E . Fairbridge, Oxford University Press: London, 1937.
      Fairbridge Kingsley Olgivie. The Autobiography of Kingsley Fairbridge. With an Epilogue by Sir Arthur Lawley. Humphrey Milford. London. 1927
[34] The Times. 26th November 1924. Page 9. Column A.
[35] The Times. Saturday 29th January 1927. Page 22. Column A.
      The Times. Friday 11th March 1927. Page 7. Column C.
[36] The Times. Saturday 30th July 1927. Page 13. Column A.
[37] The Times. Monday 30th January 1928. Page 15. Column B.
[38] Lorraine Hayes. Lady Lawley Cottage, West Australian Red Cross
[39] Fairbridge Farm Schools. Department of Home and Teritories. 1916 to 1928. Canberra, Australia. "Fairbridge Kid". Fairbridge the Village and the man. John Lane. Freetrade Paperbacks 1990.
[40] The Times. Friday May 25th 1928. Page 9. Column G.
      The Geoffrey Dawson diaries. 1921 to 1925. The Bodleian Library. Oxford.
      The Milner Papers. The Bodleian Library. Oxford.
[41] The Times. Friday June 12th 1931. Page 9. Column F.
[42] The Times. Saturday July 8th 1939. Page 10. Column D.
[43] World Wide Web.fairbridge-worldwide.com/
[44] Fairbridge Kingsley Olgivie. The Autobiography of Kingsley Fairbridge. With an Epilogue by Sir Arthur Lawley. Humphrey Milford. London. 1927
[45] UK Parliamentary Select Committee on Health – Evidence submitted. 1998.
[46] Via Gibbs, A Memoir, by Madeline Alston. Pages 163 to 171. Constable. London. 1921.
[47] Doreen Bathurst Norman, Victoria Gibbs' daughter, in conversation.
[48] Pedigree of the Family Gibbs. Fourth Edition. Rachel Gibbs. 1981
[49] The Times, Friday July 22nd 1927.
[50] Lord Eustace Wraxall in conversation. November 4th 2004.
[51] Geoffrey Dawson's Diary for 1928. – Tuesday 15th February
[52] The Times. Wednesday 28th January 1928. Page 19. Column B.
[53] The Times. Saturday 7th July 1928. Page 8. Column E.
[54] The Times Obituary for Lord Wraxall, October 30th 1931.
[55] Geoffrey Dawson and Our Times. Evelyn Wrench. Hutchinson. London. 1955. Pages 242, and 266 to 273.
[56] Geoffrey Dawson's Diary for 1928.
[57] Geoffrey Dawson's Diary for 1929. March 17th.

Chapter 10
Journey's End

The Sixth and Last Lord Wenlock

In March 1927, Sir Arthur and Lady Lawley sailed to the United States for a spring vacation. Then only eight days after the wedding of George Abraham Gibbs and Ursula Lawley in July of that year, Sir Arthur and his wife set off on a six month cruise to South Africa, the Dutch East Indies and Australia. On Saturday 28th January 1928, shortly after returning home from their cruise, Sir Arthur and Lady Lawley were driven down to Tyntesfield by Ursula to see the magnificent Victorian Gothic house with its splendid park and gardens, which was now the country seat of Lord and Lady Wraxall.[1] On February 15th, the Lawleys went to see George Gibbs, now Lord Wraxall, take his seat in the House of Lords. On May 16th, Lady Lawley visited the Gibbs' Mansion at 22 Belgrave Square to see Ursula's newly born baby, Richard.

Sir Arthur suffered from ill health during the remaining years of his life. After returning from Australia in 1928, Sir Arthur's health gradually deteriorated. The strain of such a long voyage appeared to have taken its toll. As a heavy smoker, who smoked Turkish cigarettes, he may well have been afflicted with respiratory or heart problems.[2] He was obliged to resign from some of his directorships and to take life more easily.[3] Sir Arthur and Lady Lawley had often attended State Balls, Receptions and Dinners at Buckingham Palace, and Sir Arthur had been a frequent speaker at Rhodesian, Australian, South African, Indian, Colonial and Anglo-American dinners. Invitations now were not always accepted.

In June 1929, Sir Arthur went for a while into a nursing home. On July 3rd, his daughter Ursula gave birth to her second son, Eustace, in her new London home at 81 Eaton Square.[4] On August 7th, Sir Arthur and Lady Lawley were given the use of a cottage at Cliveden by Nancy Astor. Here Sir Arthur recuperated from his respiratory problems. His son-in-law, Geoffrey Dawson, was a close friend of the Astors and often lunched and played tennis with Nancy.[5] At Cliveden, Sir Arthur had the opportunity to meet with the former members of Milner's Kindergarten such as Basil Blackwood, Bob Brand, John Buchan, Lionel Curtis, Edward Grigg, Lionel Hitchens, Philip Kerr and Dougal Malcolm, who congregated at the Astor mansion.[6] In November, the Lawleys travelled to Zurich and then on to Freiburg in the Black Forest in Germany to seek expert medical care for Sir Arthur. On January 18th 1930, they returned to Woodside Place, but Sir Arthur's condition deteriorated and the doctor diagnosed pneumonia. During the months which followed he was most unwell, but he began to recover his strength in August. On October 1st 1930, the Lawleys once more left England for Freiburg to consult Dr Martin and give Sir Arthur the benefit of a "Kuur" at this German resort.[7] They rented out their house at Woodside Place in Hertfordshire for six months.[8] In January 1931, Sir Arthur and Lady Lawley rented the Villa Scarona at Alassio on the Italian Riviera for a few months to escape the English winter.[9] In April, George and Ursula Wraxall and Geoffrey and Cecilia Dawson and their children spent a three week holiday with them at their villa.[10] George's daughter, Doreen, arrived from Rome and joined the family. That summer, Sir Arthur Lawley went again for treatment to Freiburg accompanied by his wife. It was from Freiburg that Sir Arthur wrote to his daughter, Cecilia, about the Fairbridge Farm School in June 1931.[11]

Sir Arthur became Lord Wenlock on the death of his brother, Algernon, the Reverend Lord Wenlock at Monk Hopton on June 14th 1931. The Lawley family came from Monk Hopton near Bridgnorth in Shropshire.[12] The nearby Wenlock Edge gave its name to the peerage. Sadly Sir Arthur and Lady Lawley, who were in Germany, were unable to attend Algernon's funeral on June 17th and so they were represented by their two daughters, Ursula and Cecilia, and their husbands – Lord Wraxall and Geoffrey Dawson.[13]

Figure 253: Geoffrey Dawson by Frances Amicia De Biden Footner.

In September 1931, the Lawleys, now Lord and Lady Wenlock, returned to England and stayed for a few weeks with their daughter Cecilia Dawson and her husband at Langcliffe in North Yorkshire. After the death of Ursula's husband, George Wraxall, on October 28th, her father rallied and his health improved sufficiently for the family to spend the Christmas of 1931 at the Wenlock's country house – Woodside Place in Hertfordshire.[14] From here on March 12th 1932, Lord and Lady Wenlock left for Germany and travelled once more to Freiburg where Arthur sought further medical advice and treatment. On Saturday 11th June, Lord Wenlock collapsed, but later was able to speak to his daughters on the telephone – to Cecilia at her hotel nearby and to Ursula in England. Sadly on Tuesday 14th June 1932, exactly one year after his brother, the sixth and last Lord Wenlock died from pneumonia in Freiburg.[15] His wife Annie and daughter Cecilia were with him at the end.[16] They travelled to England where they were met by Geoffrey Dawson at Folkestone and by Ursula at the Dawson's home in Sussex Place near Regents Park in London.

In memory of
ARTHUR LAWLEY
SIXTH BARON WENLOCK G.C.S.I.,G.C.I.E.,K.C.M.G.
Born 12th November 1860. Died 14th June 1932
Capt.10th R.Hussars Admnstr of Matabeleland 1896-1900
Governor of Western Australia 1901-1902
Lt.Gov.of the Transvaal 1902-5. Gov. of Madras 1905-11
Commissioner of the British Red Cross Society 1915-19
RICHARD EDWARD LAWLEY
his only son
Born 9th May 1887 killed in a hunting accident
at Ootacamund India on the 4th September 1909

Figure 254: Memorial to Sir Arthur Lawley and his son Richard in St Helen's Church, Escrick.

The obituary in the Times said, "Sir Arthur Lawley (Lord Wenlock) had a strong sense of duty, great charm of manner and a power of sympathy which brought him hosts of friends at every stage and in every walk of life. To these advantages were added a sound judgement, a mind which at its best was extraordinarily quick and a great capacity for hard work in times of stress. He spent himself to the last ounce in every task that he undertook and in the end this took its toll.

"He was an extraordinarily good speaker and personally generous to a fault. He was a sincere, kind and loveable man. The Wenlock peerage passed to four brothers in succession of whom Sir Arthur was the last. He became the last Lord Wenlock in June 1931 and the peerage died with him."[17]

The funeral took place on Saturday 18th June 1932 at St Helen's church Escrick and was conducted by Dr William Carter, formerly Archbishop of Cape Town, and by the Reverend Charles Trollope, the Rector of Escrick. "It was a solemn and beautiful service on a bright and sunny afternoon." The funeral was attended by the family and a few friends.[18] There was an impressive Memorial Service at St Margaret's Westminster on Tuesday June 21st. On Wednesday October 2nd 1935, three Memorial

Tablets to the Fourth, Fifth, and Sixth Lords Wenlock were unveiled in St Helen's Church Escrick by the Archbishop of Canterbury.[19]

Lady Wenlock

Lady Wenlock travelled extensively in her latter years visiting South Africa, Northern and Southern Rhodesia, the Dutch East Indies and South America. In September 1939, she moved from her homes at 9, Seymour Street and Woodside Place near Hatfield in Hertfordshire to live at Tyntesfield with her daughter and two grandsons.[20] Woodside Place was let to tenants.[21]

In 1929, Sir Arthur Lawley had given a statue of Somaskanda to the Victoria and Albert Museum. It was cast in copper in about 1000 A.D. and came from from Tamil Nadu in India. As a staunch supporter of the Red Cross, Lady Wenlock gave two Indian Bronzes to the Lord Mayor's Red Cross Auction Sale in July 1940. They were a bronze of Ganesa (the Elephant God) and a larger bronze of Somaskandamurti – Siva with his consort Uma and their son Skanda. Later that year, she also gave a collection of old gold including a watch and nugget of gold to the Lord Mayor's Red Cross and St John's Fund.[22]

Figure 255: Siva with his consort Uma and their son Skanda (God of War) 11th Century. Donated by Lady Wenlock to the Lord Mayor of London's Red Cross Sale on July 17th 1940.

On 18th November 1939, Queen Mary visited the house at Tyntesfield. She wrote in her diary, after a visit to a Red Cross depot in Bristol – "then we went on to Tyntesfield to tea with Ursula Wraxall. Her mother, Lady Wenlock, was there and Mrs Hilary Glyn. Ugly house with some nice pictures and things, and a fine view from the terrace."[23] Mrs. Hilary Glyn was a relation of Geoffrey Carr-Glyn, who had been Arthur Lawley's aide in the Transvaal and the Madras Presidency. He had returned to England in 1908 and during the First World War served as Lieutenant Colonel commanding the North Somerset Yeomanry.[24] Queen Mary visited Tyntesfield again on August 14th 1941. In her diary she wrote, "At 2.45 with Constance (her lady in waiting) to Tyntesfield beyond Bristol to pay a visit to Ursula Wraxall and see the fine trees in the grounds. We found Lord and Lady Farnham there and Colonel Gibbs, and Ursula's Boys – Richard (my godson) and Eustace. There is a lovely view from the house. We stayed to tea and got back before 7.00 pm."[25]

Figure 256: "Lady Lawley, later Lady Wenlock," by Sir Oswald Birley, donated by the citizens of Madras in November 1911. A copy hangs in Government House, Ootacamund.

Lady Wenlock and her daughter and grandsons also paid visits to Queen Mary at Badminton House, the home of the Duke of Beaufort, where the Queen stayed during most of the Second World War.[26] The Duchess of Beaufort was Lady Victoria

Constance Mary Cambridge, Princess of Teck, before her marriage. She was Queen Mary's niece. The Duchess' sister, Lady Helena Frances Augusta Cambridge, Princess of Teck, was married to Colonel John Evelyn Gibbs, Lady Wraxall's brother-in-law. Thus there were links between the two families.

Figure 257: Eustace and Richard. Painted by Lydia Emmet in 1934.

On November 19th 1940, Lady Wenlock wrote a letter, sitting at the table by the window in the Oak Room at Tyntesfield, to her cousin Rosina Emmet Sherwood in America. She said, "Our R.A.F. has been out to look for the Germans' so called invasion. Our boys are doing absolutely astounding flights and the pilot who came back yesterday after a 1500 mile flight through terrific storms to Danzig said it was the best party he had ever been to, and it is that spirit which will help us win. I am a bit anxious today to hear of Molotov in Berlin; Russia has been silent all through. I wonder what plans those villains are hatching."[27]

Lady Wenlock died on the 28th April 1944. She was buried alongside her husband, Arthur Lawley, the sixth Baron Wenlock, in a grave at St Helen's Church, Escrick, the Wenlock family seat. Her son, Richard Lawley, is commemorated with a memorial beside his parents' grave and an inscription beneath that of his father on the memorial within the church. Lady Wenlock left her imprint on Tyntesfield.[28] She was the only grand parent that her grandsons, Richard and Eustace, ever really knew.

The Times' obituary of April 30th stated that "Lady Wenlock (or Lady Lawley as she then was) was an ideal Governor's wife. An admirable hostess, with great charm of looks and manner, she adapted herself easily to the various homes in which she was compelled to exercise her abundant hospitality. A hut on the veldt in the early days of Rhodesia seemed to present her with no greater difficulties than the splendid equipment of an Indian Government house. She was indeed a first rate organiser – a quality which she showed in another sphere when she was in charge during the 1914 - 1918 war of Queen Mary's Needlework Guild and was created G.B.E. in recognition of her work. She also remained an adventurous and indefatigable traveller and undertook several long journeys during her later years."[29]

Cecilia and Geoffrey

Lady Wenlock's youngest daughter, the Honourable Margaret Cecilia Dawson, died on May 3rd 1969.[30] Her husband, Geoffrey Dawson, who's Editorship of the Times, was later to become controversial for its support of Neville Chamberlain and the policy of appeasement, died on November 7th 1944. He like many others of his generation wished to do everything possible to avoid a Second World War. Once he saw that war was inevitable, his Editorship strongly supported the Wartime Governments of Chamberlain and Churchill. Geoffrey retired on September 30th 1941. He had the satisfaction of living to hear the news of his son Michael Dawson, an officer in the Grenadier Guards, entering Brussels with the first company to liberate that city in September 1944. Geoffrey Dawson was a family man, kind, dependable and supportive to his widowed sister-in-law and her sons.[31]

Lady Wraxall

Lady Wraxall, the Honourable Ursula Lawley, was Maid of Honour to Queen Mary from 1912 until her marriage in 1927. She followed her father's active engagement with the Red Cross and was Somerset President until 1971, running the central hospital supply service for the Western Region during the Second World War. She was also a Serving Sister of St John of Jerusalem. During this war, American Army Hospital (Number 74) was built on the Tyntesfield Estate in preparation for D-Day. For her services Lady Wraxall was awarded the Red Cross O.B.E. in 1945. In 1970, she did a Radio Broadcast for the B.B.C. on her experiences with the Red Cross during the First and Second World Wars.

Lady Wraxall was a close friend of Joan Grigg, who later became Lady Altrincham, and she visited her quite frequently at her home at Tormarton Court in Gloucestershire. Occasionally one of her sons, Richard or Eustace, would accompany her.[32] Joan's husband, Lord Altrincham, formerly Sir Edward Grigg, had been best man at the wedding of Ursula's sister, Cecilia to Geoffrey Dawson in 1919.[33]   Sir

Edward had succeeded Geoffrey Dawson as Secretary of the Rhodes Trust. Both ladies had served as VAD nurses during the First World War. Joan had also driven ambulances for the Red Cross. Both ladies had lived in Africa, Joan in Kenya where her husband was Governor from 1925 to 1931, and Ursula in Rhodesia and South Africa. Both were friends of Nancy Astor and had enjoyed Lady Astor's abundant hospitality at Cliveden, Hever Castle and St James Square. They shared a lasting interest in the work of the Red Cross.

Lady Wraxall, who as a little girl had been with her father to Rhodesia in the 1890s, witnessed the Lancaster House Conference in September 1979 whereby a settlement was negotiated for Rhodesia, which became the republic of Zimbabwe in April 1980. She lived to the ripe old age of 91, dying on the 16th October 1979.[34]

Figure 258: Lady Wraxall with her sons, Eustace and Richard, by John Hay.

Epilogue

Sir Arthur and Lady Lawley lived at a time when the British Empire was at its zenith. The Late Victorians and Edwardians regarded Empire as both an enterprise and a mission. The enterprise was based on industry, commerce and world wide trade. The dominions and colonies provided the raw materials and a captive market. The mother country manufactured the industrial products for domestic consumption and for export to the Empire and the World. As the greatest naval power in the world Britannia literally ruled the waves. The leading apostles of Empire were Joseph Chamberlain, Cecil Rhodes and Sir Alfred Milner (later Lord Milner). All three played a key part in the career of Sir Arthur Lawley.

Through today's eyes the whole imperial enterprise appears to be politically incorrect and racist. However the times have changed. Between 1896 and 1911, Africa was just emerging from its status as the unknown continent with the interior unexplored by the outside world. Livingstone, Stanley, Speke, Grant, Burton and Mungo Park had only recently pioneered routes into the heart of Africa. The Arab slave trade in the east and the European and American slave trade in the West had decimated the population. The fight against the slave trade and the evangelical mission to bring Christianity to the British Empire were both altruistic endeavours. The missionaries and colonial administrators established schools, colleges and medical services, which were for the welfare of the peoples of the Empire. The building of extensive railway networks, the development of agriculture, the encouragement of forestry, fisheries, mining and indigenous industries, the construction of new cities were all beneficial. If the manufactures of the mother country received imperial preference this was understandable in the given circumstances. The concept of the Pax Britannica based on good governance and the rule of law was fundamental to the imperial venture. The Royal Navy, the British Army and local police forces were the power behind the throne.

All this was shattered by the First World War. Although the Empire staggered on for a few more decades, British pre-eminence was ended and the Second World War would ensure that the United States emerged as the world's dominant super-power. It is ironical that America, founded from thirteen original colonies, should have taken up the struggle against colonialism. Indeed the History of the American Indians demonstrates clearly that the United States is by no means without blame in Colonial History.

The Lawleys, like so many others involved in the story of the British Empire, were people of their time. In the terms of this Zeitgeist, they were adventurous, brave, idealistic and dedicated. Their Christian faith and their kindness and generosity brought sincerity and a sense of service to their endeavours. Their views changed with the passage of time. India in particular worked its magic upon them and the earlier contacts with Mahatma Gandhi in South Africa seem to have mellowed the imperial bravado of the youthful Arthur Lawley.

In later life, Sir Arthur supported the English Speaking Union and the Pilgrims, an organisation fostering Anglo-American friendship. He was a firm believer in the role of the Anglo-Saxon peoples in furthering the spread of western civilisation. His enthusiastic promotion of the English language and his belief in the Anglo-American mission to civilise mankind were certainly controversial, but similar convictions are still evident today. He belonged to the Colonial Institute and presided or spoke at several of its meetings. He was in some senses a harbinger of the British

Commonwealth. He attended Australia Day luncheons, Rhodesian, Western Australian, South African, Madras and Calcutta annual dinners. At these functions he was frequently the guest speaker. Garden parties and theatre matinees to raise funds for the British Legion combined with Sir Arthur's tireless endeavours to support the Fairbridge Farm School in Western Australia. His enthusiasm for education was evident throughout his colonial service. His was a life long commitment to public service. Indeed he was a leading member of the Cavendish Association, which sought to inculcate a spirit of self sacrifice in building and strengthening the social fabric of the nation.[35] Above all, Sir Arthur Lawley was a peace maker promoting mutual understanding between the settlers and the native peoples after the Matabele uprising in Rhodesia, encouraging reconciliation between the British and the Afrikaaners after the Boer War in South Africa, and through the Red Cross and the Order of St John bringing medical aid, additional sustenance and contact with home to injured soldiers and prisoners of war. His work to promote the International Red Cross after the Great War was the beginning of what was to become a great multi-national endeavour.

His obituary in the Times written by his son-in-law, Geoffrey Dawson, described his character with the insight of a man who knew Sir Arthur well. It said,

> *"Starting without any special equipment for administration beyond the ordinary training of a young cavalry officer, he succeeded in the various responsible tasks that came his way through a strong sense of duty making the most of his natural gifts. He had great charm of manner and a power of sympathy which brought him hosts of friends at every stage and in every walk of life. To these initial advantages were added a sound judgement, a mind which at its best was extraordinarily quick, and a great capacity for hard work in times of stress. The nervous energy which made him so hard a worker, and incidentally so good a speaker, probably taxed him more than he realized during those anxious years in South Africa and in India, for he spent himself to the last ounce in everything that he undertook. He was personally generous to a fault, or at all events to the utmost limits of his means, as numberless unknown protégés could testify. But the sense of public duty was the dominating factor in what was at bottom a very sincere and most lovable character."*

The Lawley's daughters – Ursula and Cecilia – were exceedingly fond of their father and during his final years when he suffered from ill health were constantly there to offer their love and support. Ursula and Cecilia lived to see the end of the Empire which their father had so loyally served. Ursula when she married George Abraham in 1927 became a member of the Gibbs family. By a strange coincidence she saw the beginning of Rhodesia in the 1890s, and another member of the Gibbs family was to be there at the end. This was Sir Humphrey Vicary Gibbs, descended from Henry Hucks Gibbs, the First Baron Aldenham.[36] What follows is his story taken from the School Magazine of Peterhouse School in Zimbabwe, of which Sir Humphrey was a Founder and the Chairman of the Board of Governors.

Sir Humphrey Gibbs

> *"The Honourable Humphrey Vicary Gibbs was born on 22 November, 1902. He was the third son of the first Baron Hunsdon. His brothers, Lord Aldenham and Sir Geoffrey Gibbs, both became distinguished bankers in the City of London. He was educated at Eton and Trinity College, Cambridge. In 1928 he came out to Southern Rhodesia and bought a farm at Nyamandhlovu near Bulawayo. He very soon became active in farming administration and was largely instrumental in the early*

formation of the National Farmers Union.   He was also a pioneer of the Conservation movement.   In 1951 he was elected to Parliament though he never really became an enthusiastic politician.

"In 1959, he was appointed Governor of Southern Rhodesia and awarded the KCMG in 1960.   The Unilateral Declaration of Independence by the Southern Rhodesia Government in 1965 placed Sir Humphrey in a highly complex position. He was intensely loyal to Rhodesia, but at the same time he was equally loyal to his appointment as the Queen's representative.   Legality and honesty were not negotiable in this mind.   He therefore refused to accept the UDI and declared that by its action, the Government had established itself as an illegal regime.   At the same time he announced that he would remain in Government House as the representative of the Queen to whom he was bound by his oath of allegiance and as such was the only legal source of authority in the country.   This action led to four years of harassment and petty afflictions, including the withdrawal of his salary, the cutting off of the telephone, and the confiscation of the official motor cars.   Sir Humphrey and Lady Gibbs were virtually prisoners in Government House, they lived in a state of near siege.   They were however sustained during these years by many loyal friends, who ensured that they were not left wanting.   In 1965, Sir Humphrey was made a Knight Commander of the Victorian Order (KCVO), which is the personal gift of the Queen.   Lady Gibbs was appointed a Dame.   In 1969 the Smith Regime illegally proclaimed a Republic.

Figure 259: Sir Humphrey Gibbs.

"Sir Humphrey felt at last, that there was no further point in continuing to represent the Queen.   He left Government House and returned to his farm.   When Sir Humphrey and Dame Mollie went to London, in 1969, he was made a Privy Councillor and advanced to GCVO.   He was thus honoured by the Sovereign he had served so well.

When the Lancaster House Agreement came into force, Lord Soames (son-in-law of Sir Winston Churchill) was appointed as the last Colonial Governor to

Rhodesia. He made it one of his first duties to pay his respects to his predecessor. During the first ten years of Zimbabwean Independence, Sir Humphrey and his wife lived on at their farm. Sir Humphrey Gibbs died on 5 November, 1990 after a short illness".[37]

1. Geoffrey Dawson's Diary for 1928 – Saturday 28th January.
2. Eustace, Lord Wraxall in conversation. November 4th 2004
3. The Times. Wednesday May 29th 1929. Page 13. Column E.
   The Times. Saturday June 22nd 1929. Page 9. Column D.
   The Times. Thursday June 12th 1930. Page 8. Column D.
   The Times. Friday 26th September 1930. Page 18. Column G.
   The Times. Friday May 22nd 1931. Page 22. Column A.
4. Eustace, Lord Wraxall in conversation. November 4th 2004.
5. Very frequent references in the Geoffrey Dawson diaries. Bodleian Library. Oxford.
6. Nancy Astor, Portrait of a Pioneer. John Grigg. Sidgwick and Jackson. London. 1980. Page 108.
7. Geoffrey Dawson's Diaries for 1929 and 1930.
8. The Times. Wednesday 8th October 1930. Page 17. Column B.
   The Times Thursday September 25th 1930. Page 1. Column C.
9. The Times. Wednesday January 28th 1931. Page 15. Column A.
10. Geoffrey Dawson's Diary for April 1931.
11. The Times. Wednesday October 8th 1930. Page 17. Column B.
    The Times. Friday June 12th 1931. Page 9. Column F.
12. The Times. Saturday October 12th 1918. Page 9. Column B.
13. The Times. Thursday June 18th 1931. Page 17. Column D.
14. Geoffrey Dawson's Diary for 1931.
15. The Times. Wednesday June 15th 1932. Page 14. Column D.
16. Geoffrey Dawson's Diary for 1932.
17. Times Obituary for Lord Wenlock, Wednesday June 15th 1932
18. Geoffrey Dawson's Diary, June 18th 1932.
19. The Times. Thursday October 3rd 1935. Page 15. Column C.
20. "Who's Who?" 1933.
21. The Times. September 22nd 1939. Page 1. Column C.
22. The Times. Thursday July 18th 1940. Page 2. Column E.
    The Times. Saturday August 17th 1940. Page 7. Column E.
23. The Royal Archives Windsor. Letter of July 27th 2004
24. The Times. Friday June 18th 1915. Page 5. Column G.
25. Philippa Savoury, a girl from Clifton Girls School whose pupils boarded at Tyntesfield during the War. The Royal Archives Windsor. Letter of November 4th 2005.
26. Lord Wraxall in conversation. November 4th 2004.
27. Letter of November 19th 1940. Emmet Archive, Archives of American Art, Smithsonian, New York. Eustace Lord Wraxall in conversation December 18th 2006.
28. Times Obituary for Lady Wenlock, Monday 30th April 1944.
    "The Peerage.com." Daryl Lundy, Wellington, New Zealand. 2004.
    Tombs and Memorials in St Helen's Church, Escrick
29. Times Obituary for Lady Wenlock, Monday 30th April 1944.
30. Times Obituary of Mrs Geoffrey Dawson. May 5th 1969.
31. Eustace Lord Wraxall in conversation. September 20th 2005.
32. Eustace, Lord Wraxall in conversation. November 4th 2004
    Ray Llewellyn. Tyntesfield Estate Manager and Chauffeur. Conversation of April 25th 2005.
33. Geoffrey Dawson and Our Times. Evelyn Wrench. Hutchinson. London. 1955. Page 198
34. Geoffrey Dawson Diaries. 1921 to 1944. Bodleian Library. Oxford.
    Telegraph Obituary for Lady Wraxall, Ursula Mary Gibbs, 18th October 1979.
    The Pedigree of the Family Gibbs. Fourth Edition by Rachel Gibbs. 1981. Kingprint Limited. Richmond. Surrey.
35. The Times. London. Various announcements and articles between 1920 and 1932.
36. "The Peerage.com." Daryl Lundy, Wellington, New Zealand. 2004
37. Peterhouse Nostalgia Memories.html. On Sir Humphrey Gibbs. 1991

Appendices

Appendix 1: The Suakin Campaign in the Sudan

Winston Churchill in "The River War" describes the campaign:

General Charles Gordon writes from Khartoum in the Soudan, "I leave you the indelible disgrace of abandoning the garrisons in the Soudan". Sir Samuel Baker writes a long letter to The Times in passionate protest and entreaty.

But meanwhile other and still more stirring events were passing outside the world of paper and ink. The arrival of Gordon at Khartoum had seriously perplexed and alarmed Mohammed Ahmed and his Khalifas. They feared lest the General should be the herald of armies. As the weeks passed without reinforcements arriving, the Mahdi and Abdullah determined to put a brave face on the matter and blockade Khartoum itself. They were assisted in this enterprise by a revival of the patriotic impulse throughout the country and a consequent stimulus to the revolt. To discover the cause it is necessary to look to the Eastern Sudan, where the next tragedy, after the defeat of Hicks, is laid.

The Hadendoa tribe, infuriated by oppression and misgovernment, had joined the rebellion under the leadership of the celebrated Osman Digna. The Egyptian garrisons of Tokar and Sinkat were beleaguered and hard pressed. Her Majesty's Government disclaimed all responsibility. Yet, since these towns were not far from the coast, they did not prohibit an attempt on the part of the Egyptian Government to rescue the besieged soldiers. Accordingly an Egyptian force 3,500 strong marched from Suakin in February 1884 to relieve Tokar, under the command of General Baker, once the colonel of the 10th Hussars. Hard by the wells of Teb they were, on the 5th of February, attacked by about a thousand Arabs.

General Baker telegraphed an official despatch to Sir Evelyn Baring on 6th February, which said:

'On the square being only threatened by a small force of the enemy ... the Egyptian troops threw down their arms and ran, carrying away the black troops with them, and allowing themselves to be killed without the slightest resistance.'

The British and European officers in vain endeavoured to rally them. The single Sudanese battalion fired impartially on friend and foe. The General, with that unshaken courage and high military skill, which had already on the Danube gained him a continental reputation, collected some fifteen hundred men, mostly unarmed, and so returned to Suakin. Ninety-six officers and 2,250 men were killed. Krupp guns, machine guns, rifles, and a large supply of ammunition fell to the victorious Arabs. Success inflamed their ardour to the point of madness. The attack of the towns was pressed with redoubled vigour. The garrison of Sinkat, 800 strong, sallied out and attempted to fight their way to Suakin. The garrison of Tokar surrendered. Both were destroyed.

The garrisons they had refused to rescue the British Government now determined to avenge. In spite of their philanthropic professions, and in spite of the advice of General Gordon, who felt that his position at Khartoum would be still further compromised by operations on his only line of retreat[1], a considerable military expedition consisting of one cavalry and two infantry brigades was sent to Suakin.

The command was entrusted to General Graham. Troops were hurriedly concentrated. The 10th Hussars, returning from India, were stopped and mounted on the horses of the gendarmerie. With admirable celerity the force took the field. Within a month of the defeat at Teb they engaged the enemy almost on the very scene of the disaster. On the 4th of March they slew 3,000 Hadendoa and drove the rest in disorder from the ground. Four weeks later a second action was fought at Tamai. Again the success of the British troops was complete; again the slaughter of the Arabs was enormous. But neither victory was bloodless. El Teb cost 24 officers and 168 men; Tamai, 13 officers and 208 men. The effect of these operations was the dispersal of Osman Digna's gathering. That astute man, not for the first or last time, made a good retreat.

Ten thousand men had thus been killed in the space of three months in the Eastern Soudan. By the discipline of their armies the Government were triumphant. The tribes of the Red Sea shore cowered before them.[2]

Appendix 2: Lady Lawley Cottage Hospital

Lady Lawley Cottage provides respite care for children with special needs which are often the result of chronic complex medical conditions. These problems are often the result of physical or intellectual disabilities and require the specialised care the staff at Lady Lawley can provide.

Families can leave their children in a caring environment that is adapted for the needs of their child while they take a well deserved break. This time away from their responsibilities provides families with an opportunity to rest and focus on other relationships within the family. In the long term respite care helps families build their ability to cope with the extra pressures of caring for a special needs child.

Lady Lawley cares for babies through to children aged up to 12 years. The average period of respite care ranges from overnight to a week. While families are encouraged to plan respite breaks, the centre is equipped to care for children at short notice in emergency circumstances.

Figure 260: Children at Lady Lawley Cottage.

Children staying at Lady Lawley have access to specialised therapy and nursing services, and a special needs play group. When appropriate, children continue to attend school.

Lady Lawley Cottage also provides interim accommodation support for children who require residential options other than the family home. Throughout this period of time children receive intensive input into their development that will allow them the opportunity to become more independent.

Volunteers play an important role in the life of the children at Lady Lawley Cottage. Some of the duties volunteers assist with under the supervision of staff include playing with the children and helping with special activities. The volunteers enrich the experience of children staying at Lady Lawley by providing caring one on one attention. All Red Cross volunteers are encouraged to attend a free informative introductory workshop. Lady Lawley volunteers also receive orientation training and support to help them in their role.

Australian Red Cross, Perth, Western Australia.

Appendix 3: Richard Edward Lawley

Figure 261: Richard Edward Lawley's Grave, St Stephen's Church, Ootacamund.

Appendix 4: Sir Arthur Lawley's Speeches in India

At the close of the meeting of the Legislative Council held at Ootacamund, 1911

Before I dissolve this Council I should like to make a few observations. I regret to say that this is, so far as I can see, the last occasion upon which I shall have the honour of presiding over the deliberations of this Council. When this Council meets again it will meet under a new President, and I hope in new premises. Perhaps in passing it is not arrogant on my part to suggest that the promptitude which has been displayed in providing extended accommodation for the Council is only another proof of the sagacity and progressive spirit which are characteristic of Madras, and may also perhaps be taken as indicative of the readiness on the part of Government to accept the new order of things in the, spirit which prompted the introduction of the recent reforms in our Councils. I myself have taken a great interest in the design and actual construction of the new Council Chamber. I had hoped that it would have been possible for me to hold a session there myself, but I am afraid that that cannot be. I can only hope that the building will prove worthy of and well adapted and convenient for the purposes for which it has been built.

At such a moment as this one is tempted to indulge in a retrospect, but 1 do not propose to take the present occasion for anything like a review of what has passed during the past five years. They have been, thank God, years of prosperity and they have been also years in which activity in almost every field of administrative enterprise has been displayed. They have been years of change.

Redistribution, reorganization and readjustments have been going on in almost every department - changes not so rapid, perhaps, nor so thorough as some enthusiasts would desire, but yet I would venture to claim that the tally of work done is one of which on the whole the Government have no reason to be ashamed. The work both of Government and of Governor, I may say, has been multifarious. Of all the anxious public concerns with which I have been called upon to deal I propose just now to touch upon those in particular which appertain to the office of the President of this Council. Five years ago, it may be within the recollection of some gentlemen here present, when I took my seat for the first time in this Council, I declared it as my intention to endeavour so far as I could to conduct the affairs of this Council with the utmost impartiality and to give the fullest possible consideration to the views and the opinions of the non-official members. I sincerely hope that I have not altogether failed to carry my intention into effect. It has been inevitable of course that from time to time I should find myself opposed to the political opinions and feelings of some members of this Council, but I venture to hope that however widely I may have differed in my views from them on political matters, I have never allowed that difference to interfere with my treating their representations or their opinions or their arguments justly and fairly. Nay more I venture to hope and believe that my political intercourse with men of all shades of opinion in this Council has become invested with the attributes of personal friendship. At least that is how I have come to regard it, and I venture to hope that that feeling is not altogether one-sided.

There have been changes of course in the personnel of this assembly. Many have come and gone, some of them I doubt not to return once more but some whose faces we shall see never again. More than once in this Council we have been called upon to pass formal resolution expressing the regret which we felt at the loss of one or other of our comrades. In looking back, I am concerned to find that in one case no such formal resolution was passed. I allude to the case of Mr. Perraju, a man whose loss we all deplore, a man who consistently and strenuously supported what he believed to be for the public weal. The omission of such a formal resolution was altogether quite inadvertent, but I deplore it exceedingly myself because I am certain that there is not one member of this Council who would not have been glad to testify to the regret which was felt at the sudden and sad demise of our late comrade.

Quite apart too from any personal changes there have been others of which of course I need hardly say the greatest change has been that of the enlargement of the number of the members of this Council, and the extension of its functions. There is nothing which I could say regarding this change this afternoon which has not been said over and over again. We are still in an experimental stage, but yet I think I shall be deemed guilty of no undue optimism when I express the confident belief that these changes will go far to achieve the end for which they were introduced, and will result in associating the people of India ever more closely with the every-day work of administration. It was, you may remember foreshadowed by the author of this great scheme that it would add largely to the work and largely to the responsibilities of the heads of the local Governments, and I venture to say that when embarking on that vaticination he proved himself to be a prophet of accurate discernment, for experience shows that it has added very largely to the work both of my colleagues in the Executive Council and also of the members of the Secretariat. The demand upon their time and labour has been very great, but it has been met as I knew it would be and as I feel perfectly certain in the future it will always be with the utmost readiness and loyalty by the members of the Service. But I would press just this one fact on the non-official members of this Council, and that is that while it is in their power to add vastly to the labours of those whom I mentioned, yet to do so unnecessarily cannot fail to detract from the efficiency and the utility, and the businesslike capacity of this Council.

When the form of this great Reform scheme was first adumbrated I remember publicly stating, that I was confident that my Government would apply the principles embodied in that scheme with courage, with generosity and with sympathy. I venture to claim that my forecast has not proved in any way erroneous. Speaking at the same time of the spirit of non-officials in this assembly, I remember that I said that in the past the spirit had always been of help, of sympathy, and of co-operation, and now speaking here this afternoon, with even fuller experience of the attitude of the non-official members in this Council, I should like again to testify to my high appreciation of the way in which they have one and all shown themselves to be imbued with the single-hearted desire to help and not to hinder the progress of good Government. I do not wish it to be inferred from that remark that there has been no independence shown at all. On the contrary, I think that the actions of Government in almost every field have been subjected freely to analysis and criticism, but I am glad to say that we have shown ourselves able to turn a deaf ear to that voice of the syren which would lure us to the wholly fallacious theory, that the official and nonofficial view should always be in antagonism and their interests always in conflict. This is in my opinion a snare and a delusion, a net in the meshes of which I sincerely hope and believe that the non-official legislators of this Presidency will never allow themselves to be entangled.

For the consistent and loyal support which has been extended to me by all the members of this Council I beg to express my very sincere gratitude. Our debates in this Council have been multifarious; they have been often protracted and they have been often controversial, but I do honestly believe that the spirit and the tone of the debates in this Council have not only maintained, but have done much to enhance and to increase the dignity and the honour of this Council. For this end, I myself have striven to the best of my ability. There is one who will take my place here and will I know be no less jealous of the honour and prestige of this Council than I have been; and I am confident that he will receive to that end the loyal and consistent help and support of all the members, equal to that which I have received and for which today, I proffer you my most abundant thanks. It is my earnest hope and desire that the deliberations of this Council in future may tend to but one end, an end which I have often said I have dearly at heart, that is the betterment of the people of this Presidency.

With these few remarks, I feel called upon to bid you as a Council, good-bye, and thank you yet again for all the support which you have extended to me. And now it only remains for me to declare this Council dissolved, sine die.

Reply to the Ootacamund Municipality 'Farwell Address', 24th October 1911.

I feel deeply touched and honoured that you should have assembled here in such numbers this afternoon. I can honestly say I never anticipated so large a gathering, and I sincerely thank my many friends who have made it possible to be here this afternoon as a mark of good-will to Lady Lawley and myself.

You are good enough in your opening words to suggest that it is I who confer a favour by accepting a farewell address at your hands, whereas I feel under a great obligation to you for having met me here this afternoon to express in kind and courteous words your regret at our departure from this town. I thank you sincerely for what you have been good enough to say of our association with Ootacamund. For myself I rejoice to think that it has been one of the happiest possible descriptions. As Governor and as citizen my intercourse with all sorts and conditions of men here has been such that my memory of it will be through all the years a source of lively pleasure, and I can assure you with the utmost sincerity that while my wife and I contemplate with deep regret our imminent departure from the Presidency, it is with heartfelt sorrow that we bid good bye to Ootacamund and our many good friends here.

You remind me that five and a half years have passed since I stood here to receive a welcome at your hands. I can hardly believe that more than half a decade has fled since that exquisite spring morning when I had my first glimpse of Ootacamund. The recollection of your welcome still warms my heart, and the anticipations on which I then ventured as to the charms of Ootacamund and the pleasure which I hoped to experience in the midst of its beautiful surroundings have been amply realised. Then I stood amidst strange faces. Today I stand among friends, and I desire to take this opportunity of saying on behalf of my wife, my children and myself that we shall never forget the many kindnesses which we have received at all times. From our hearts we thank you sincerely.

I reflect with great pleasure on the fact that the happy co-operation of my Government with the municipality has not been infructuous. You have recited several directions in which progress has been achieved, and I am delighted to think that during my term of office many substantial improvements have been effected here, while others are in course of undertaking. Rome, we are assured, was not built in a day, and there is always much to be done. After all it is not so very long ago that Lord Macaulay, in a letter to a friend in London, wrote from this place: "You need not get your map to see where Ootacamund is, for it has not found its way into the maps. It is a new discovery."

Now Ootacamund resembles many other good things in that she is not exempt from criticism. And I am afraid that criticism is sometimes tempted in its desire for effect to dispense with the companionship of truth. I was reading the other day some essays on politics by a distinguished Canadian writer, and the opening words of one of his essays runs: "It requires about 33 years to remove a false impression from the public mind and about the same length of time to replace it by a correct one." Twice 33 is 66. Being of a sanguine temperament, I hope that it will be less than 66 years before the public mind will be disabused of the quite erroneous idea which has lately been assiduously promulgated in the Press and elsewhere and is to me quite incomprehensible that the sanitation and the drainage and the health of Ootacamund are in very parlous plight.

I am no expert on sanitary matters, but I have made it my business to obtain the opinions of those who are and who have carefully investigated the plans of the Ootacamund drainage scheme and the manner in which the designs have been carried out, and they are unanimous in assuring me that the scheme as a whole is admirably conceived and has been, so far, most efficiently carried out. Defects of detail of course there will be as there must be in every scheme of this nature, but these as they come into evidence are being corrected and I am confident that when complete you will have a most valuable asset conducing to the credit of those who introduced it and the great benefit of those whom it serves. Various works of sanitation have been completed; others are in progress, and others, here as in every other town in the world, are waiting to be taken in hand. Meanwhile, it is satisfactory to know that you can say and say with truth that public health is excellent.

Yes, it is good to know that progress and betterment are the burden of your song. And if in any degree I have contributed thereto I am indeed well content, for I do not hesitate to say that to me the name of Ootacamund is and always will be very dear. I love the place and all about it, its hills and valleys, its trees and flowers, its dark shadowy sholas and sunlit downs! I love them all. When in addition to the charm of these natural accessories I have had the privilege of your friendship and all that true friendship means you can well understand how sad a moment is the present one for me and mine. We bid you farewell and from the bottom of our hearts we hope that a full measure of happiness may attend you and all who dwell here.

At the Farwell Entertainment on the Island Ground, Madras, 28th October 1911.

There are certain scenes impressed on one's mind, certain pictures which hang in the store-house of one's memory, which remain bright vivid and clear, of which the outlines are never blurred even by Time's effacing fingers. Such a picture, such a scene is this! By what stage-craft it has been achieved I know not. But I do know that it could not have been accomplished without much forethought and care. Such an effect could not have been attained without infinite trouble! I can only wonder and express to the Committee, the Secretaries and Treasurer, and in particular, may I say to that Master of Art, Mr. Venkataswami Nayudu, my congratulations on the success which has crowned their resolve to do honour to my wife and myself. We can only thank you from the bottom of our hearts. I am indeed grateful that on the eve of our departure from Madras so many of its citizens should have thus made manifest to us their sympathy and good-will. And when I speak of Madras I would embrace the whole Presidency from all parts of which many of those whom I rejoice to claim as my friends have rallied round me tonight to bid me Godspeed on my way. Men of my own race officials and non-officials, though indeed there is no need to make any distinction between them, for I regard them as one fraternity of friends, one company of comrades banded together and standing together to uphold in this land the best traditions of the British race – from all of them whatever their profession or calling might be I have received invariable and uniform kindness and support.

Then as I look round I see on all sides men of other races and other creeds than my own – Indians who have been fellow workers with me in the task of administration, loyal and devoted fellow workers and staunch comrades! Sincerely do I thank them for their generous help. I see members of the land-owning aristocracy; I see colleagues of my own in the Legislative Council representing various communities and diverse interests; men engaged in public life; and many others who while not engaged in public affairs have yet generously admitted me to the privilege of their personal friendship; all gathered here to still further increase the debt of obligation under which I already lie for manifold kindnesses received at their hands.

The beautiful entertainment which you have organized, the generous donations which have been forthcoming in order that our portraits may hang on the walls of Government House, the presentation to my wife of this beautiful cup, for which she bids me offer you in her name her most heartfelt thanks – all these are tokens of your good-will towards us which believe me we prize more highly than any poor words of mine can express.

Finally there are the words which have just fallen from the lips of Sir S. Subramania Aiyar, a man whom we all, English and Indians alike, esteem and respect as a man of unblemished honour and lofty culture, a man of courage and spotless integrity. Speaking as he does with the authority with which his character, his high position and noble record of service invest him, his words which I am convinced came straight from his heart indeed cheer and gladden me more than I can say. To him and to each one of the committee, and to the Secretaries of the Committee who have striven to ensure that this charming entertainment should be as perfect in every detail as it has been – to all of you indeed, both Lady Lawley and I offer our heartfelt thanks. I know that it is in your capacity as our friends that you have proffered us this mark of your regard, and it comes to recompense me for the toil and anxiety, which I have undergone in the service of India and inspires me with the hope that I have not laboured altogether in vain. The remembrance of it will always be precious to us, and again we thank you most sincerely. We pray that God's blessing may rest on this land. My heart is too full to say more.[3]

Appendix 5: Sir Arthur Lawley's Speeches in Canada

Ottawa, August 27, 1912

MY LORDS AND GENTLEMEN:

On behalf of my fellow travellers I beg to express my best thanks to Sir Wilfrid Laurier[M] for the charming manner in which he proposed this toast, and to you gentlemen for the generous reception which it was accorded at your hands. I understand that the majority of those sitting around this table are Canadian-born men whose homes and lives and honour are fast bound to their native soil. Many of them take a distinguished and honourable part (none more so than the proposer of this toast) in the wise and sagacious, and, I may add, the unfettered control of the destinies of Canada; and I esteem their presence here today as a great compliment to ourselves, and an indication that our visit is not unwelcome. I suppose that there is hardly a soul in the room who is less qualified than myself to speak of Canadian affairs from personal knowledge. My acquaintance is that of a few hours only, and it would be impertinence if I were to hazard an expression of opinion, far less criticism, on Canadian conditions, whether physical, political, or economic. But this I can say, that there is not one of our party who does not rejoice to find himself in the Capital of Canada, not one who does not look forward eagerly to see for himself and to learn something of the illimitable resources of Canada – not through books and papers darkly but actually face to face. There is not one of us who does not share in your gratification in the prospects of an abundant harvest and your high hopes of greater prosperity in the years that are to come. I think we come in a season of happy omen.

Only at the beginning of last month it was my privilege as a member of the Colonial Institute to welcome Mr. Borden on his arrival and hear his first speech in the heart of London.[N] In simple yet stirring language he told us of the development of this country; of the great task undertaken by the two races working hand in hand – and carried by them in the face of great difficulties to a magnificent consummation. He foreshadowed the marvellous possibilities of the future with the inevitable accretion of wealth unmeasured. He aroused our sympathies by the portrayal of the growth of national sentiment and patriotism in the hearts of the Canadian people, above all by the message which the Canadian nation has sent to the Motherland by the mouth of her chosen ministers. That message has stirred the heart of every Englishman, however insular, however unemotional and self-centred he might be. I venture to hope and believe that Mr. Borden and his colleagues when they have all returned will not have reason to complain of the welcome which it was our desire in the Old Country to extend to them. It was no perfunctory recognition of the official position which they hold, however distinguished it may be, and was no mere formal outward act of ceremony. It was the handgrip of kinsmen and fellow citizens of Empire, of comrades in the ranks of a mighty host, bearing aloft the banner of peace, progress and civilization to the remotest confines of the greatest Empire upon earth.

I am no disciple of blatant Imperialism, but I am not one of those to whom the word "Empire" sends a shiver down the back. As our generous host in his

---

[M] Sir Wifrid Laurier was the first French Canadian Prime Minister (1896 – 1911). As leader of the Liberal Party, he lost the election of 1911.

[N] Robert Borden was the Conservative Prime Minister of Canada who won the election of 1911 *characteristically generous fashion has told you, it has been my privilege for the past sixteen years to serve my country in various capacities and various continents. In January last I left India, and after travelling leisurely through East Africa, Uganda, and South Africa, I found myself in London a few weeks ago, after over six years of absence. Today my foot is on Canadian soil, so that this is the fourth continent in which I find myself within a year. I hope that I shall not seem to you arrogant if I claim to have some slight inkling, some dim appreciation, of the full significance of the word "Empire". Do you remember how Lord Rosebery speaks of it as:*

> *"An Empire built not by Saints or Angels, but by the work of men's hands, cemented with men's honest blood, and in a world of tears; not without the taint and reproach incidental to all human work, but constructed on the whole with great and splendid purpose."*

That is not I think a bad definition. And the best that I can wish for Canada is that her sons should have an even wider conception of the mission of Empire and an ever closer participation in its work. Just at present there is, I know, a disposition to consider the question of closer organic union only from the standpoint of external defence. And indeed it is not surprising if this should be so. I look at Europe and I see one vast armed camp. I see the greatest military power on the continent, which is at the same time the second greatest naval power of the world, straining every nerve, making every possible sacrifice to increase her efficiency as a fighting machine. And when I reflect that all this effort is being made for no ostensible reason or visible purpose, I find it impossible in spite of what has been said this afternoon by other speakers, to escape the conviction that at any moment England may find herself embarked in a struggle of colossal magnitude in which her very existence as a nation may be at stake.

I will not insult your intelligence by asking whether you have ever considered what a paralyzing effect upon Canada any continental war must be, however brief its duration and whatever its issue.

I look at Asia, and along the rim of the Eastern world I see millions and millions of dark twinkling eyes watching, watching like molten masses within the crater of a vast volcano ready at any moment to pour forth in fire and frenzy and utter devastation. But with the manner of our kind, we heed it not. "The thing," we say, "is but a Yellow Phantom." It is so much more comfortable to prattle of the era of universal peace upon which we are about to enter. We flatter ourselves that mankind has shed his primitive instincts and thrown away his combative propensities as a snake sloughs its skin. We argue that in this twentieth century of civilization the day has gone by for the nations of Europe to submit questions of national honour to the arbitrament of the sword. But deep down in our own consciousness we know full well that the most potent factor for peace in the situation today is the British Navy. And paradoxical though it may seem, the more we augment its power as an engine of offence, the more do we increase its efficacy as an instrument for the maintenance of peace in the world. But I do not wish to dwell on questions of armaments and navies this afternoon. I would rather say a word as to the other "great and splendid purposes of Empire."

If time allowed I would like to take you by the hand and canter with you through the great self-governing Dominions to show you how, working out their own salvation with no interference from the Mother Country, they are moving along different lines of policy in such matters as customs, naturalization, and, which is of far greater import, the treatment of the various native races within their borders, as well as the immigration of Asiatics and Indians. But this would take me far too long. And yet there is one matter in which I have been personally associated and of which I would like to say a few words, and that is the Government of India.

It is sometimes said that the Government of India and the adjustment of the relations between the East and West do not come within the purview of Canadian interests, but in this I cannot agree. Today India is second in the matter of population and fifth in the matter of wealth amongst the nations of the world. And yet India is hardly a nation at all, but a great congeries of peoples of multitudinous races, creeds, and castes, differing widely in type, in language, in religion, and in degrees of civilization. We found India convulsed by incessant warfare, deluged by a ceaseless stream of anarchy, bloodshed, and crime; we have given her the benefits of universal peace. We found her people a prey to injustice, corruption and oppression; we have given them a pure judiciary, and justice between man and man. We have given them the ablest, most upright, the most devoted civil service that the world has ever seen. We have undertaken vast public works in the way of railways, and roads and systems of irrigation. By this latter we have saved millions of human lives, and today, thanks thereto and to a sagacious organization, we can fight famine as we could never fight it before. The land is dotted with hospitals and schools and all of what I may call the "plant" of higher civilization. In all ways we are seeking to restrain and push back the encroachment of ignorance and poverty, and disease, and sin, and to raise the people to a higher standard of life. During the past fifty years in spite of famine, plague, and cholera, and other ills to which oriental flesh is heir, the population has increased from 150 million to 320 million, and that is one fifth of the whole human race. It is a great work, and in only a less degree the same work is going on in Egypt, the Straits, East Africa, and other places. And the work must go on! We have put our hand to the plough and we cannot look back. If we were to withdraw from India tomorrow we should only fling her back into the welter of bloodshed and crime from which we rescued her long ago. It would be the betrayal of the noblest task which was ever committed to a people!

Apart too from any question of the abrogation of our moral duties to India, her loss would be a vital blow, for India is the strategic centre of the Indian and Pacific Oceans; and with her loss all the vast region over which we now hold sway, from the Mediterranean to New Zealand, and from Hong Kong to Cape Town, must inevitably fall away.

And with that what would be Australia's fate? Australasia as no doubt you know, has an area equal to that of Europe, with a population which does not exceed that of London. She is surrounded by Asiatic nations with a population which is three times that of the whole of Europe. It is inevitable that with our loss of India, Australia would pass under the tenure of another race and our great dynasty would crumble into ashes. But we cannot abandon our work in India and the East. It is the "white man's burden" and the day, thank God, has not yet dawned when we may dare to lay it down! For it is a noble work, not unworthy of the best traditions of our race, and one in which no member of the Empire need disdain to take a share. Until only the other day England was bearing this burden quite alone. But if I do not read the signs of the times amiss, there has come into Canada with the sense of nationhood, a sense also of national responsibility. Over the Atlantic has gone forth the message to the Motherland from her children overseas, claiming their right to share in the burden of the Empire. And what will the answer be? Is it not written in the book of the Seven Seas?

"Look I have made you a place and opened wide the doors,
That you may talk together, your Barons and Councillors,
Wards of the outer march, Lords of the lower seas.
Ay' talk to your grey mother that bore you on her knees.
Also we will make promise. So long as the Blood endures
I shall know that your good is mine, ye shall feel that my
strength is yours,
In the day of Armageddon, at the last great fight of all,
That our House stands together and the pillars do not fall."

Winnipeg, September 2nd 1912

MY LORDS AND GENTLEMEN:

I thank you sincerely for the kind wishes conveyed in the toast which has just been so cordially received, and I assure you that we reciprocate those wishes most warmly.

We do well, methinks, to be here!

It is good to feel one's pulse stirred by the romping vitality of the Golden West and the magnetism of exuberant confidence which seem to permeate all things, even to impregnate the very air which one breathes. And good it is to see the treasures of nature's storehouse in this land which you are wisely exploiting with no little advantage to yourselves. I rejoice to see something of this wonderful Canada of yours of which you may justly be proud. And I think we do well to be here under the auspices of Mr. Arthur Grenfell. [O] It is my privilege to count him amongst my oldest and best friends, and I may truly say of him that he is not only a stout hearted Englishman but also a good Canadian. You will say that in the light of British Citizenship the one is a corollary of the other. I do not demur. But do not let us stop there. Some philosopher has said that he is the best citizen who makes two blades of grass grow where only one grew before. Mr. Arthur Grenfell has done far more for the Dominion than this!

There are moments when the pride of race is strong in a man. And such a moment came to me last week when I stood in the power-house at the Soo [P] and looked round on all the vast enterprise which is growing there under his hand. He has harnessed the elements; he has laid hold of the inert masses which lie hidden in nature's womb that he may mould them to the purposes of man. With courage and imagination he is leading a band of men possessing high intellectual and scientific attainments in the pursuance of a work which will not only find employment for many a man, and thus lay the foundation of many a Canadian home, but will also

---

[O] Lieutenant Colonel Sir Arthur Grenfell married Lady Victoria Grey, the daughter of Albert Grey, the Fourth Earl Grey, Governor General of Canada (1904 – 1911). Lady Victoria died in 1907 at the age of 28, and he later married Hilda Margaret Wortley Lyttelton in 1909. Joyce Phipps married Sir Arthur and Lady Victoria Grenfell's eldest son - Lieutenant Colonel Reginald Pascoe Grenfell - in December 1929. She became the well known actress Joyce Grenfell.

[P] The Soo Locks and Hydro-Electric Power Station lie on the St Mary's River, near Sault Ste Marie, on the United States and Canadian border beween Lake Superior and Lake Huron. There is a drop of seven metres between the two lakes.

add greatly to the convenience, the progress and the wealth of the Canadian people. Thus he is proving himself a good Canadian; and I am sure I am only voicing the sentiments of all here when I express the fervent hope that his work may prosper abundantly and be carried to a triumphantly successful issue.

If I may strike a personal note I may say that I have been asked often why I have come to Canada. I have not formulated any precise answer yet; but my coming is no surprise to myself.

For some sixteen years I have been privileged to be a humble labourer in Australia, South Africa, and India, that the work of Empire might go on. That is work which seems to grip a man, and there have been times when I have wondered whether I was really more of an Englishman than an Australian or a South African, and it seems to me the most natural thing in the world that I should find myself in another integral part (and a very glorious part) of the Great Imperial Organization in which you and I are privileged to claim a Common Membership. I feel that this is not a strange land that I am in! That is no doubt due in great measure to the courtesy and consideration shown to us on all sides and the cordial and generous welcome which we have received. But at the same time I am all abroad in my endeavour to realize the vastness of all things about me – the scale on which nature has laid out her plans and carried out her designs; the scale on which man moves in his ideas and his works; the scale on which Canada is building herself up as a nation. Please do not think from this that I am about to embark on a dissertation on Canadian affairs. I refrain from any such impertinence!

But there are one or two matters of which I would like to speak which, if not of immediate concern to Canada, will, if I mistake not, be of no little interest to her before long.

Last May I found myself in London after many years absence with leisure to eat the bread of idleness and to take stock of my country and my countrymen.

I am startled at the changes on all sides. I am impressed with the restlessness of all classes. I am sensible that great social and industrial movements are astir. I am especially impressed by the wonderful evidence in all directions of the wealth of England – side by side, I know, with great poverty and widespread degradation of life – very awful but not I hope irremediable. If I dwell on the marvellous manifestation of wealth, on the amazing prosperity in trade and business of every kind – it is not in any boasting spirit, but because the enormous resources which England has at her command are an element of great strength to her in the Councils of the nations, and just now England has need to be strong. For when I look across the Straits of Dover, over that little silver streak which has meant so much to us as a nation – when I look at Europe, I see the marshalling of battalions – not in tens nor hundreds but in thousands – drilling marching and manoeuvring – I see a ceaseless and strenuous activity in every arsenal and dockyard – a prodigious expenditure of time and money and intellect on fleets and armaments. Is this a time, I ask myself, for us to lull ourselves to sleep with drowsy murmurs of a world-wide peace? Is this the moment for us to pretend that the throb of the war-drum and the thunder of the guns are but echoes of a dead past, and that the menace to our position as the leading naval power of the world is but a myth – a bogey to frighten children in the dark?

I can conceive of no more criminal folly, no greater dereliction of duty, than to lay such flattering unction to our souls. But if I discern the true temper of our people I need have no such fear. If I correctly gauge England's attitude of mind in the face of the momentous development in Europe it is this, that while she may accept as inevitable attempts to encroach on her commercial supremacy and the entry of rivals in the markets of the world, she is resolved to put beyond all doubt so far as it lies within the power of human agency to predispose such issues – the question of her supremacy at sea.

England's temper today is that no challenge of her naval supremacy shall find her unprepared to meet it, that no sacrifice is too great, that no expenditure is too onerous, to secure the maintenance of her superiority at sea. – In no spirit of militarism, nor for any aggressive purpose, nor for any ambitious schemes of self aggrandisement, but for the fulfilment of the noblest mission of our Race, and that is for the maintenance of the Peace of the World. For this insurance England is able and willing to pay the full premium; and if need be she will pay it in the future as she has paid it in the past ungrudgingly, uncomplainingly and alone. To my thinking there are compensations in the very incidence of the taxation. I deplore, as greatly as any man, the expenditure of millions yearly on the construction of battleships and other impedimenta of war which are in themselves economically unremunerative, but I believe that the material things of life are not all that God has revealed to man, and in the very sacrifice made I see a strengthening of the moral fibre of the nation. This, you may say, is a fantastic notion in which case I will point out that there is material satisfaction to be gained in contemplating the work which has been done in the past and is being done to-day by the Navy of Great Britain. Take Australia and New Zealand: in area they are equal to Europe, in population equal to London. These small communities have scattered themselves over a vast territory without any thought of molestation from without – free to build up their own institutions and inspire them with the spirit of extreme democracy. Felling their timber, winning their gold, shearing their sheep, sending their merchandise over every sea and into every port without any thought of menace or peril save those of wind and wave. In Northern Australia you have an enormous territory practically untouched and untraversed, a tropical region, which the white man has left alone, but one in which a brown or yellow race could live to the number of many millions and bring forth the fruits of the earth in abundance. But Australia has cried "Hands off", and no coloured race may dare to enter – not because of Australia's mandate but because behind Australia lie the ships of England's Navy. Round Australia are Asiatic nations numbering three times the population of Europe. Eliminate the Navy and how long think you would it be before Australia would have passed under the domination of an Eastern Race?

Only a decade ago our Navy enabled us to carry on a war in South Africa six thousand miles from our base in such fashion that the problem of transportation was comparatively easy of solution. Today, in South Africa, we see two races – who were recently at one another's throats – working hand in hand and working successfully under the sheltering arm of England to carry their country to a degree of material prosperity hitherto undreamed of in that continent. In North America the mere existence of the British Navy has enabled you to concentrate all your thoughts, all your energies, all your talents on your own material development without any fears of external attack. Without any interference in the enjoyment of

Canadian autonomy you have been free to build up your own institutions, to develop the resources with which you have been by nature lavishly endowed, to make your own commercial arrangements, and to dictate the terms on which members of other Races shall enter in and people this vast Dominion. Your growth as a nation has been rapid, vigorous and robust. But it has been hitherto a sheltered growth. Now has come the quickening of a national spirit – a sense of national self respect and desire to assume national responsibility, and heartily do I rejoice thereat not only that Canada may share in our naval policy but also in those questions of policy – many of them of great gravity – which are common to all the self-governing Dominions. I will touch on one only and that is the adjustment of the relations between East and West between the white and coloured Races, which is a question in world politics coming very rapidly to the front. You have laid down your own policy regarding Asiatic immigration and spoken with no uncertain voice. Australia has declared for an absolutely white Australia. In the Straits Settlements you find a heterogeneous population, including a large and rapidly growing number of Chinese all free to come and go as they please. In East Africa white settlers are coming in to find a great number of different indigenous tribes established in huge native locations, and in the coastal territories a mixed breed in which the Arab type is general, and on top of all this a practically unlimited flow of Indians all over the country right up to the border of the Congo. In South Africa again you have an enormous negro population in all degrees of civilization – some in some parts enjoying the franchise and rights of citizenship, some in other parts excluded therefrom entirely – in one region you find Indian labour eagerly sought for and encouraged, in another region resolutely forbidden and the colour bar insisted on with a vindictiveness almost amounting to persecution. Then there is India herself keenly alive to the ignominy with which Indians (though accredited in England and India with full rights of citizenship) are subjected in the self-governing Dominions – full of bitter resentment and indignant protest against the humiliation to which they are submitted merely because they are Indians.

Hasn't the time come for some co-ordination of policy, for the statesmen in the various Dominions and dependencies and colonies, who have had to tackle the problem on the spot, to come together and devise some logical and uniform line of action, which shall not be in conflict with local sentiment and yet not add unnecessarily to the difficulties of the Government of India? For India is the linch pin of the Imperial coach. Remove it and our Eastern Empire would founder and lie helpless and derelict at the mercy of our foes. If you doubt it take the map! It needs no military expert to point out to you that India is the strategic centre of the Indian and Pacific Oceans, and that if England is to remain an Empire at all she must hold India with her latest breath. But it is not for strategical reasons alone that we must remain in India.

There is to my thinking no task to which a man can put his hand more noble than that of administration, and of all the pages on which are inscribed the records of our history none are brighter than those whereon is writ the story of British Rule in India. It has been made recently the subject of hostile criticism but these are days of disparagement when our every act is subjected to intense scrutiny under the strongest microscope. But put down the microscope and stand back from the canvas and you will see a picture good to look on.

Travel through India and as you move northward you will find the country scarred with ruins - vast cities standing broken and shattered and rent in pieces; shreds of palaces and temples; wrecks of ancient dynasties, which have been brought to their knees by powers mightier than they and humbled to the dust. There they stand and have stood, some a hundred, some a thousand years, milestones on the down road which the centuries have passed, all telling the same story of the storm track of war, with all its hideous accessories of bloodshed and devastation; of rapine and lust and crime. To-day from the snow-clad ranges of the Himalayas to the sweltering reaches of the Coromandel Coast the land is wrapt in universal Peace. The pages of Indian history in the past are one dreary record of corruption, dishonesty and intrigue of oppression and injustice; the tyranny of the strong against the weak. Today between all races and sects and creeds the scales are held evenly and equally for all, and slowly British standards of truth and justice and honour are coming to prevail. By roads and railways and irrigation; by hospitals and schools; and by all the impedimenta of a Christian civilization we are fighting the ogres of famine and plague, of ignorance and sin, so that in fifty years the population has increased from 150 to 320 millions of people – one fifth of the whole human race – and for them slowly but surely the standard of life is being raised.

For India's sake the work must go on. We cannot abandon India and leave her defenceless against herself to fall back into the slough of despondency from which long ago we helped her to emerge. No less is this the case in Egypt and our other Eastern dependencies. The cause of humanity calls us forward and we cannot go back without humiliation and disgrace. Such an eventuality is unthinkable.

I spoke just now of the quickening of the Canadian national spirit which has found expression in your claim to share with the Motherland not only in her naval policy but also in the guidance and control of those events which lead up to decisions of peace or war. Soon I hope it will be yours to claim a fuller participation in such work of empire as that of which I have tried to give some faint outline to-night. It may mean some demand on your labour, some renunciation of material advantage, some subordination of self, whether of the state or of the individual, but the cause is not an ignoble one, the goal is worth the winning! And the reward? Shall we not find it in the thought that we have played some little part in bringing the humbler denizens of Empire, the downcast and degraded, the hapless, helpless victims of barbarism and injustice and wrong, to the conception of a higher civilization? Shall we not find it in the thought that we have done some little thing to weld more closely the bonds of British citizenship, and thus strengthen the bulwarks of our Empire? [4]

---

[1] Sir Evelyn Baring to Earl Granville, Cairo, 23rd February.

[2] Winston Churchill. The River War. Prion. London. 1997.

[3] Lawley, Sir Arthur, Speeches delivered by His Excellency the Honourable Sir Arthur Lawley while Governor of Madras, 1906-11. Madras Government Press. India Office. 1912.

[4] Canada and the Empire: Speeches delivered by Sir Arthur Lawley. A.M. Grenfell, Montreal, 1912. Montreal Herald. Notes: "Ottawa, August 27, 1912, Winnipeg, September 2, 1912." National Library of Canada. FC243

Bibliography

1. The Memoirs of the Tenth Royal Hussars (Prince of Wales Own), historical and social. Lieutenant Colonel Robert Spencer Liddell. Longmans. 1891.
2. Thomas Addis Emmet: "The Emmet Family: With Some Incidents Relating to Irish History." (New York, privately printed in 1898).
3. "Rhodes, the Race for Africa" by Anthony Thomas. BBC Books. London. 1996.
4. "Handbook to the Federation of Rhodesia and Nyasaland". Edited by W.V. Brelsford. Salisbury, Southern Rhodesia. 1960.
5. The Real Rhodesia. Ethel Tawse Jollie M.L.A. Rhodesiana Reprints. Volume 19. Bulawayo. Rhodesia. 1973.
6. Joseph Chamberlain, Entrepreneur in Politics by Peter Marsh. Yale University Press. 1994.
7. "Rhodes" by J.G. Lockhart and the Hon. C.M. Woodhouse. Hodder and Stoughton. London 1963.
8. "Heroes of Discovery in South Africa." N. Bell. Walter Scott, Ltd. London. 1899.
9. Rhodes. A Life by J.G. McDonald. Rhodesiana Reprints, Volume 16. Bulawayo, Rhodesia. 1974.
10. Arthur Conan Doyle. The Great Boer War: A Two Years' Record, 1899-1901. London, Smith, Elder & Co., 1901.
11. Queen Mary. James Pope-Hennessy. George Allen and Unwin. London. 1959.
12. "Jan Christian Smuts" by his son J.C. Smuts. Cassell and Co. Ltd. Cape Town. 1952.
13. Milner, Apostle of Empire. John Marlowe. Hamish Hamilton. London. 1976.
14. The Life of Mahatma Gandhi by Louis Fischer. Jonathan Cape. London 1951.
15. "Raj. The Making and Unmaking of British India". Lawrence James. Little, Brown and Co. 1997.
16. "The Ruling Caste. Imperial Lives in the Victorian Raj." David Gilmour. John Murray. London. 2005.
17. Notes on the administration of His Excellency the Honourable Sir Arthur Lawley, Governor of Madras, 1906-11. Madras Government Press.
18. Speeches delivered by His Excellency the Honourable Sir Arthur Lawley while Governor of Madras, 1906-11. Madras Government Press. India Office. 1912.
19. Lady Lawley and Penny F.E. (Fanny Emily) Southern India, Painted by Lady Lawley. A&C Black. London. 1914.
20. The Students of Asia. G. Sherwood Eddy. The Religious Tract Society. London. 1916.
21. A Message from Mesopotamia. Sir Arthur Lawley. Hodder and Stoughton. London. 1917.
22. Geoffrey Dawson and Our Times. Evelyn Wrench. Hutchinson. London. 1955.
23. The Autobiography of Kingsley Fairbridge. Kingsley Olgivie Fairbridge. With an Epilogue by Sir Arthur Lawley. Humphrey Milford. London. 1927
24. The Building of a Farm School. Ruby E. Fairbridge, Oxford University Press: London, 1937.

Index

Illustrations